NINTH EDITION

Teaching Children
Science

A Discovery Approach

Donald A. DeRosa
Boston University

Joseph Abruscato
Late, University of Vermont

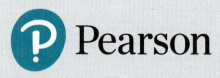

330 Hudson Street, NY NY 10013

Director and Publisher: Kevin M. Davis
Portfolio Manager: Drew Bennett
Managing Content Producer: Megan Moffo
Content Producer: Yagnesh Jani
Portfolio Management Assistant: Maria Feliberty
Development Editor: Jill Ross
Executive Product Marketing Manager: Christopher Barry
Executive Field Marketing Manager: Krista Clark
Procurement Specialist: Deidra Smith
Cover Design: Studio Montage
Cover Art: gettyimages.com
Editorial Production and Composition Services: SPI Global
Editorial Project Manager: Heather Winter, SPi Global
Printer/Binder: LSC Communications
Cover Printer: Phoenix Color

Credits and acknowledgments borrowed from other sources and reproduced, with permission, in this textbook appear on the appropriate page within text.

Library of Congress Cataloging-in-Publication Data is on file with the Library of Congress.

Printed in the United States of America
1 18

Pearson

www.pearsonhighered.com

ISBN-10: 0-13-474287-7
ISBN-13: 978-0-13-474287-8

Brief Contents

Contents

3 Planning Units and Lessons   41

How can I plan and manage inquiry-based, discovery-focused units and lessons?

4 Creating Environments for Discovery   70

*How can I effectively create an inviting science discovery space, encourage
science talk, and foster cooperative learning in my science classroom?*

5 Assessment of Understanding and Inquiry   88

A good teacher asks, "How am I doing?" A great teacher asks, "How are my students doing?"

6 Integrating Science and Engineering   111

How can I integrate inquiry-based science and engineering with other subjects in a child's school day?

PART TWO   The Earth/Space Sciences   129

7   Earth and Space Science   136

Preface

About the Authors

Don DeRosa, Ed.D., is a clinical associate professor at Boston University School of Education, where he teaches science teaching methods to elementary and secondary education pre-service teachers.

Joseph Abruscato was a nationally prominent educator and author of professional books in the field of science teaching. He retired from The University of Vermont in 2006 with the rank of Professor Emeritus after a distinguished career that began there in 1969. Joe received his B.A. and M.A. degrees from Trenton State College in science education, physics and chemistry and his Ph.D. in science education and curriculum development from The Ohio State University. At The University of Vermont, Joe was the chief architect of enhancing the Elementary Teacher Preparation Program with articulated campus-based pedagogy and public school practica.

About this Book

Teaching Children Science was written with the K—5 pre-service elementary teacher in mind. The authors understand that teaching science may be out of the comfort zone for many readers. A primary goal of the text is to help aspiring elementary teachers understand their roles not as science experts, but as lead learners of science who can inspire and guide their young students to experience science through the joys and challenges of inquiry and discovery. It emphasizes methods and strategies for teaching the subject that invite students to learn science through doing science. Practices are grounded in theory that reflects research about how students learn science and scientific ways of thinking. Effective science teaching requires a familiarity with science practices and content as well as strategies and methods. Chapter 1, *Inquiry: The Path; Discovery: The Destination*, begins with some insights about what it means to do science and the nature of science. Chapters 7–12 are devoted specifically to providing fundamental content knowledge in the Earth/space, life, and physical sciences for the elementary school teacher.

New to This Edition

● Expanded coverage of (and alignment to) NGSS Standards

As the Next Generation Science Standards become more embedded in the national curricula, evidence and resources that inform effective three-dimensional teaching and learning continue to emerge. This text addresses each science practice and incorporates resources to support three-dimensional instructional strategies.

- NGSS curriculum bundles are addressed in Chapter 3, and evidence statements are used to support three-dimensional assessment in Chapter 5.
- Strategies for culturally responsive teaching based on NGSS Appendix D, "All Standards, All Students," are included in Chapter 3. You will also find references of NGSS to Common Core State Standards in Chapter 2.

- Sample lessons and activities throughout the text model the integration of science practices, disciplinary core ideas, and crosscutting concepts.
- The content in Chapters 7–12 and the ideas for putting content into action in Appendices A, B, and C are organized around NGSS Disciplinary Core Ideas.

Updated videos that reinforce key ideas

Chapters 1–6 have been updated to include short video excerpts of experienced teachers in science classrooms as well as their personal reflections on their practices. Each video includes prompts that invite pre-service teachers to critique the videos that highlight key concepts addressed in the text.

Revised chapter on planning now focuses on the 5E learning cycle

The 5E learning cycle, developed by the Biological Science Curriculum Studies in the late 1980s, continues to be the basis for concept development in lesson planning strategies reflected throughout the text. More examples of hook questions for engagement are provided as well as a lesson plan template with explicit guidelines for developing lessons that incorporate criteria for the "Engage, Explore, and Explain" phases of the 5E instructional strategy in Chapter 3.

Reorganized and condensed chapters provide a more streamlined learning experience

- The text has been reduced from 18 to 12 chapters and organized into two parts rather than four. Part 1 addresses science teaching theory and practice, while Part 2 provides a refresher of science content knowledge in the areas of Earth/space sciences, life sciences, and physical sciences.
- Previous edition chapters on using technology and adapting the curricula have been eliminated, and the information presented in these chapters has been integrated throughout the book. For example, in Chapter 3, Sheltered Instruction Observation Protocol (SIOP) has been coupled with elements of the 5E instructional strategy to illustrate accommodations for English language learners. In Appendix A, students are directed to access and analyze data on the latest earthquake activity across the globe provided by the United States Geological Survey to explore the dynamics of plate tectonics.
- Previous edition Chapters 12, 15, and 18 have moved to Appendices A, B, and C. These sections include suggested ideas and activities for implementing content in Chapters 7–12. Ideas for each content area—Earth/space sciences, life sciences, and physical sciences—are organized as follows:
  - **Unit Plan Ideas and Questions:** These are organized by the Disciplinary Core Idea Arrangements of the NGSS and include a unit title, question, and brief unit overview.
  - **Make the Case—An Individual or Group Challenge:** This section challenges the reader to reflect on the use of phenomena in three-dimensional teaching and identify potential phenomena for disciplinary core ideas.
  - **Classroom Enrichment Ideas:** This section makes suggestions for discovery centers, bulletin boards, and field trips that could enrich each content area. Suggestions for articulation with disciplinary core ideas are listed in parenthesis for each enrichment idea.
  - **Examples of Topics and Phenomena:** Suggested phenomena are given for selected topics in each discipline along with motivating questions, activities, and science content that support the topic for teachers.

- **Discovery Activities:** These are activities that you may find helpful to support teaching the content area. Each activity includes objectives, science processes, materials, a motivation (engagement), directions, discussion questions, and science content for the teacher.

Real Teaching vignettes provide insight and reflection on practices

Included in each content chapter (7, 9, 11 and 12), these vignettes describe real lessons taught or observed by the author. The narratives include brief reflections about the teaching moves and decisions made by the teacher during the class. Bracketed references to instructional strategies addressed in the text are also included. The examples are meant to illustrate actual teaching "episodes," with the hope that readers will learn from these small victories and failures! See *Real Teaching: Air Pressure* in Chapter 11.

Key Content Updates by Chapter

- Chapter 1, previously Chapters 1–2, provides updates with more depth on key topics such as how children learn science, the nature of science, and an introduction to the NGSS as essential resources for science educators.

- Chapter 2 addresses each of the science practices in much more depth than the prior edition as well as the role of inquiry and discovery in science learning with sample activities that illustrate inquiry skills.

- Chapter 3 addresses planning learning experiences for children based on relevance, rigor, and coherence utilizing resources such as the NGSS bundles and Understanding by Design to guide unit planning. Elements of the 5E instructional strategy are used as frameworks for organizing science lessons that emphasize scientific ways of knowing. A sample lesson is included that illustrates lesson design using NGSS resources. Universal Design for Learning and Response to Intervention are included for consideration in lesson planning. Lesson plan templates, new to this edition, provide scaffolds for pre-service teachers to develop lesson plans that inspire scientific explanations and solutions to problems.

- Chapter 4, *Creating Environments for Discovery*, addresses more nuanced strategies for creating dynamic science learning experiences, ranging from the physical work space and discovery stations to an in-depth discussion about fostering accountable science talk through effective questioning, talk-tools, and science circles.

- Chapter 5 focuses on assessing across three dimensions with examples based on NGSS assessment tasks and evidence statements. Both formative and summative assessment strategies are addressed, including traditional and reform-based assessments such as science notebooks, student interviews, and portfolios. As in the previous edition, examples of analytical and holistic rubrics are provided.

- Chapter 6 addresses integration of science and engineering with other disciplines. New to this edition are discussions about STEAM in the context of integration.

- Chapters 7, 9, 11 and 12 provide a refresher of science content knowledge and have been updated and aligned with disciplinary core ideas. Sections referred to as *Real Teaching* have also been included in content chapters. *Real Teaching* consists of selected reflections by the author on his experiences teaching concepts in the discipline to elementary children. References to teaching strategies introduced in Chapters 1–6 are bracketed to illustrate how the strategy may be implemented in practice.

Instructor Resources

The following supplements to the textbook are available for download under the "Educator" tab at www.pearsonhighered.com. Enter the author, title, or ISBN, then select this textbook. Click on the "Resources" tab to view and download the supplements detailed below.

- **Instructor's Resource Manual with Test Bank**

  The Instructor's Manual/Test Bank (0-13-474292-3) provides activity ideas for class sessions as well as multiple-choice quizzes.

- **PowerPoint™ Presentations**

  Ideal for lecture presentations or student handouts, PowerPoint™ Presentations (0-13-474284-2) for each chapter include key concept summaries.

Enhanced Pearson eText

The Enhanced Pearson eText provides a rich, interactive learning environment designed to improve student mastery of content with the following multimedia features:

- **Video Examples:** Embedded throughout the eText, these video clips illustrate key concepts and strategies. The videos in Chapters 1–6 have been updated to illustrate instructional strategies in practice by experienced teachers as well as their personal reflections on the use and effectiveness of those strategies.

- **Chapter Quizzes:** Located at the end of each chapter, these multiple-choice questions give students the opportunity to check their understanding of the learning outcomes introduced at the beginning of the chapter.

- **Internet Resources:** Included in the *Resources for Discovery Learning* section at the end of Chapters 1–6, these links provide students with an opportunity to extend their learning beyond the text.

Acknowledgments

Many people have shaped this book's content, directly and indirectly. Most of all, I would like to acknowledge Joseph Abruscato, who passed away in 2009. Joseph was a gifted educator whose contributions to the field of science education have undoubtedly informed and inspired generations of teachers and students. He is responsible for the quality and success of this text and several other publications of which he is the author. It is with humility that I assume responsibility for carrying on the legacy of his wonderful work.

I would like to thank those who have reviewed this edition of *Teaching Children Science* for sharing their expertise and valuable insights: Audrey Cohan, Ed.D., Molloy College; Sarah J. Carrier, NC State University; Todd F. Hoover, Bloomsburg University of Pennsylvania; Joe Sciulli, University of North Carolina at Pembroke; John D. Tiller, Tennessee State University.

Finally, I would like to thank Drew Bennett, Jill Ross, Heather Winter, and Yagnesh Jani for their patience, guidance, and attention to the details of this book.

D. D.

one

Strategies and Techniques

The roar of waves crashing on a beach; the careful maneuvering of a brightly colored ladybug, making its way through branches and leaves, touching, smelling, and tasting all in its path; and the first dark, belching breaths of a volcano coming to life after being dormant—all are parts of the natural world in which we live.

Wanting to make sense of that world is a powerful drive that leads us humans to inquire, to discover, and, ultimately, to understand. To empower children to be able to inquire, discover, and understand—not just now but throughout their lives—is the greatest challenge we teachers face. To teach children science is to meet that challenge head on.

Now I might be wrong, but my guess is that you are not very confident about teaching children science. You may fear that science will be difficult for children to understand and that it will provoke questions that will be hard for you to answer. You may also think that science time will be a period of utter chaos and confusion, as liquids bubble out of beakers and chemicals flash, pop, and bang.

It is my hope that most of you have had wonderful experiences in science and that you will share the thrill of discovery with your students. On the other hand, perhaps your encounters with science have emphasized the memorization of facts, formulas, and vocabulary that made science boring and tedious. If so, I deeply regret that you did not experience science. I hope that you will come to know science as a journey of adventure and discovery that you can share with your students.

Now, the phrase *doing science* may elicit a range of images. As you will find out, there is no single way to do science. You may even think that doing science is beyond the ability of your elementary students and that they need to learn vocabulary and theories before they can practice science. I hear this sentiment often. But it does not make sense. Imagine if children learning to play soccer or play the violin were given books to study the rules, history, and techniques of soccer or music. Think of what it would be like if practices consisted of lectures, reviews, and videos of "real" soccer games or violin recitals. How many of those children do you think would want to play soccer or the violin? What are the chances that any of them would pursue a career in soccer or music? On the other hand, if we give 5-year-olds a ball and put them on a soccer field (it may not be pretty) or let a child run a bow across the violin strings (it won't sound great), then they are much more likely to be inspired to learn the rules, strategies, theory, and techniques associated with soccer and music as they grow toward being accomplished athletes or musicians. Introducing young children to science is no different. Science is an *active* way of knowing that engages the body and brain. Your job is to engage the students in science practices while they grow in their knowledge of science concepts. They won't look or act like pros for a long time, but the first step on the journey is the opportunity to get on the field.

My goal with this book is to help you along the path to becoming enthusiastic teachers who have the knowledge and confidence to put their students on the playing field of science. But first you must experience the joy of science. If you enjoy teaching science, then your students will be inspired to learn science, and have fun along the way.

Part One of this text will help prepare you to meet that challenge. To be sure, there is much to know! How do children learn, and what can you do to enhance their learning? How can you help them learn the science practices and inquiry process skills to make sense of the world using accurate scientific knowledge? What should you teach (as well as what not to teach) and what is the best way to teach it for your students? What are the national trends that guide the science content and practices children are expected to learn? How can you plan meaningful lessons and manage an inquiry-based classroom? How can you make good use of the valuable resources of the Internet? How can you integrate science with other subject areas? And how can you respect diversity and ensure equity so that *all* your students have the best opportunities to succeed? Throughout all of this, you need to know how and when to assess children's progress and respond in meaningful ways that advance their knowledge.

The chapters in Part One (Chapters 1–6) address these questions. In completing them, you will build a foundation of general knowledge about teaching children science. You can add the **specific pedagogical content knowledge** and skills related to the Earth/space, life, and physical sciences, through the chapters in Part two. Lesson ideas have been moved to the Appendix. They include starter ideas to engage students, activities in each discipline that inspire inquiry, demonstrations, in-class learning centers, field trips, and bulletin board material. I encourage you to use this book in a manner that fits your needs. Some students prefer to go directly to the content in Part Two and refer back to the theory in Part One as needed. Other students opt to familiarize themselves with the theory first and then put it in practice. You may opt to go directly to the activities in the appendix.

Yes, it's a lot to learn!

The truth is, becoming an okay teacher isn't too difficult. But becoming a truly excellent teacher takes focus and determination. That's what you and I will be working toward throughout this text!

Inquiry: The Path; Discovery: The Destination

It is not just teaching science,
it is using science to teach thinking.

Vasilyev Alexandr/Shutterstock

Learning Objectives

After completing the activities in this chapter, you should be able to:

1.1 Develop a working definition of science.

1.2 Describe how research about learning science informs science teaching.

1.3 Describe the purpose and three dimensions of the Next Generation Science Standards.

▶ **GETTING STARTED**

In order to teach science, it is important that we reflect on how we understand science and what scientists do. This chapter will start us thinking about science and look to the Next Generation Science Standards as a resource that informs and guides the content of our science teaching. We will also consider research about how students learn science that informs our teaching.

Science: What Is It, Really?

Before we begin to think about teaching science, let's pause to think about what science means. We all probably have some notion, based on our prior experiences and knowledge, of what scientists do. Perhaps some of you know scientists or are scientists yourselves. Maybe you have read about people making scientific discoveries, or perhaps you have a vision of science provided by the media. In any case, suppose you were asked by non-scientist friends, "What is science? What do you teach when you teach 'science'?"

Settling on a precise definition of science is not so easy, even among the science community. Here are some ways organizations and scientists have described science.

"Science is more than a body of knowledge. It is a way of thinking; a way of skeptically interrogating the universe with a fine understanding of human fallibility.[1]—Carl Sagan

Some key themes can be identified in these definitions:

- Science is a process—it is a pursuit, practical activity, application
- Science is a way of knowing—understanding/explaining the natural world
- Science is systematic—use of methods to the process of seeking explanations and making sense of the world
- Science is knowledge—the principles, laws, and theories that explain the natural world

Note that science is active. It is an endeavor that seeks knowledge—knowledge pursued in a systematized way. Unfortunately, science is often associated solely with its outcomes or a body of knowledge. This is tantamount to skipping a movie and watching only the final scene. The ending does not make sense if you do not know the plot. When science is presented as only facts and answers, it ceases being science. Anyone with access to the Internet can find information. Science involves the process of generating explanations based on evidence and logic. Scientists rarely have answers. If they did, they would not need to practice science. Similar to Jean Piaget's quote, "Intelligence is what you use when you don't know what to do," I like to think of science as knowing what to do when you do not have an answer. Science is a systematic search with a variety of strategies that results in a dynamic body of scientific knowledge. Most important to remember is that science is a way of knowing that uses *evidence* supported by logical reasoning to help us make sense of the world.

As an elementary school science teacher, you will teach practices, values, and attitudes associated with seeking scientific explanations as well as core ideas and principles that support current scientific explanations of natural phenomena (see Table 1.1).

What Is Scientific Thinking? A Look at Some Masters

Great thinkers such as Einstein, Galileo, and da Vinci had the ability to create detailed mental models. We all create mental models to some extent. When we can "see" or "picture" a situation in our minds, we can often understand and explain it better. Expressions such as "I see what you mean" and "It is like . . . " suggest this tendency to create mental models. Great thinkers have the extraordinary ability

Table 1.1 Examples of science as a body of knowledge, as a process, and values

Body of Knowledge	
• Energy can change form.	• For every action, there is an equal and opposite reaction.
• Matter can change form.	• Like poles of magnets repel each other.
• The total amount of matter and energy in the universe never changes.	• Unlike poles of magnets attract each other.

Inquiry Process Skills		
• Descriptive modeling	• Explanatory modeling	• Experimental modeling
Questioning	Questioning	Questioning
Observing	Hypothesizing	Predicting
Enumerating	Inferring	Identifying variables
Classifying	Interpreting data	Controlling variables
Measuring	Communicating	Controlling experiments
Comparing		Communicating
Communicating		

Values and Attitudes Associated with Scientific Inquiry	
• Skepticism	• Cooperation
• Criticism	• Persistence
Ability to criticize	• Freedom to think originally
Acceptance of criticism	

to create and keep complex mental models of a system in their mind and imagine what would happen when variables in the models interact in novel ways. For example, Einstein could imagine what would happen when someone rode a beam of light, and da Vinci could imagine the miracle of flight. As educators, we need to teach our students the cognitive skills necessary to create mental models and to create a culture of thinking in which these cognitive skills become habits of mind. Habits of mind take years to develop; they cannot be covered in a lesson or two. The habits of good, scientific thinking must become a conscious part of the culture of learning; children need to be made aware of their thinking strategies when they are thinking scientifically.

Doing Science and the Next Generation Science Standards

One of the principles specific to science teaching and learning suggested by the National Academies of Science is not only teaching what scientists know, but how they know.[2]

You may recall reading about the scientific method in textbooks. It usually read something like the following: Ask a question, form a hypothesis, make a prediction, test the prediction, analyze results, make a conclusion. While these components may be associated with science practice, there is much more to doing science. Solving problems and seeking explanations is a messy business, often fraught with uncertainty. Doing science means taking wrong turns, encountering road blocks, doubling back, and trying alternate paths that inform the next turn. It requires imagination and creativity to think about explanations and solutions in novel ways. By acknowledging uncertainty and purposefully designing instruction through which students encounter uncertainties that challenge their understanding, we can foster the development of cognitive tools that will help students seek explanations and solve problems.[3] When we teach students science, we teach them to use observation, reasoning, creativity, and imagination to think in ways that are new for them and lead them to personal discoveries and deeper understandings. In the words of Freeman Dyson,[4] "All of science is uncertain and subject to revision. The glory of science is to imagine more than we can prove."[5]

Scientists use a variety of practices when they do science. Practices include the use of both skills and knowledge. Eight science practices have been identified in the Next Generation Science Standards (NGSS).[6, 7] These standards were developed by teams of scientists and educators to identify what students in grades K through 12 should know and be able to do upon completion of each grade with respect to science and engineering. The NGSS will be introduced in more detail in Chapter 2 and referenced throughout the text. The eight practices are as follows:[8]

1. Asking questions (for science) and defining problems (for engineering)
2. Developing and using models
3. Planning and carrying out investigations
4. Analyzing and interpreting data
5. Using mathematics and computational thinking
6. Constructing explanations (for science) and designing solutions (for engineering)
7. Engaging in argument from evidence
8. Obtaining, evaluating, and communicating information

Practicing science and learning core scientific concepts go hand in hand. Scientists and science learners both seek to make sense of the world as they encounter new information and discover relationships. Therefore, the NGSS also identify core ideas and cross-cutting concepts be taught along with the science practices. Disciplinary core ideas are scientific principles and concepts that support explanations in science and problem solving in engineering. Disciplinary core ideas are grouped in four domains: the physical sciences; the life sciences; the Earth and space sciences; and engineering, technology, and applications of science.

Crosscutting concepts are the big ideas common across the domains of science and engineering: Patterns; Cause and effect; Scale, proportion, and quantity; Systems and system models; Energy and matter; Structure and function; Stability and change. The crosscutting concepts help students organize ideas and make connections across disciplines.[9]

The integration of these science practices, disciplinary core ideas, and crosscutting concepts in science teaching is known as three-dimensional instruction when they are used together by students to make sense of phenomena.

As with content standards in general, the NGSS do not dictate or instruct about how to teach. They address what students should know and be able to do in a content area by the end of a particular grade. It is important to note that the authors of the NGSS recognize that science and engineering cannot and should not be taught in isolation. This is particularly the case in elementary school, which puts an emphasis on language arts and math. Therefore, the NGSS include connections to the Common Core State Standards (CCSS), which is an educational initiative that details what K–12 students should know in English language arts and mathematics at the end of each grade. No doubt you are or soon will be familiar with the CCSS through methods courses you take in math and language arts. We will consider articulation of the CCSS with science education throughout this text.

There are many excellent resources available on the NGSS website to support the understanding and implementation of the standards. The resources continue to grow on a regular basis as the science education community becomes more familiar with the standards. In fact, the resources can be a bit overwhelming at first glance. It will take some time for you to become familiar with them. This may be a good time to visit the NGSS site and get to know the standards. Go to http://www.nextgenscience.org/. Scroll down and view the introductory video. Several of the resources will be embedded as they apply throughout this text.

How Children Learn Science

"Be very, very careful what you put into that head, because you will never, ever get it out."

—Cardinal Wolsey (1475?–1530)

Research in the past decade has forced us to rethink traditional views of how children learn science. This is not to suggest that theories put forth by people like Jean Piaget and Jerome Bruner are not important. Piaget's cognitive theories described stages of development with increasingly complex schemas. Bruner recognized the import and power of the individual's own discovery and progressive construction of knowledge through a spiraling curriculum that reinforced and advanced prior learning in a deliberate manner. While Piaget was concerned with cognitive development, Bruner was concerned with teaching and learning. He suggested that children should not be limited by predetermined developmental stages, but that any subject can be taught effectively in an intellectually honest way if taught appropriately for the developmental level.[10] There is variation among children in their capacity to think and understand at higher levels of thinking. We know that we can help children develop capacities to think and learn by providing stimulating and thoughtful learning experiences. Carl Wieman, Nobel Prize winner in physics and director of the Carl Wiemen Science Education Initiative at the University of British Columbia, sums up how people learn in the following statement: "Much of educational and cognitive research can be reduced to this basic principle: People learn by creating their own understanding. Effective teaching facilitates that creation by engaging students in thinking deeply about the subject at an appropriate level and then monitoring that thinking and guiding it to be more expert like."[11]

In 2005 the National Academies of Science published *How Students Learn: History, Mathematics, and Science in the Classroom*.[12] The publication was the result of work by committees created to study developments in the science of learning. The following three principles that emerged from the study inform how we should think about learning science:[13]

- Students come to the classroom with preconceptions about how the world works. If their initial understanding is not engaged, they may fail to grasp the new concepts and information, or they may learn them for purposes of a test but revert to their preconceptions outside the classroom.

- To develop competence in an area of inquiry, students must (a) have a deep foundation of factual knowledge, (b) understand facts and ideas in the context of a conceptual framework, and (c) organize knowledge in ways that facilitate retrieval and application.

- A "metacognitive" approach to instruction can help students learn to take control of their own learning by defining learning goals and monitoring their progress in achieving them.

Let's unpack each of these principles.

1. Students come to the classroom with preconceptions about how the world works. Each student brings unique understandings based on a host of variables influenced by family, culture, race, ethnicity, socioeconomics, religion, gender, and geography. If their initial understanding is not engaged, they may fail to grasp the new concepts and information, or they may learn them for purposes of a test but revert to their preconceptions outside the classroom.

Enhanced eText Video Example 1.1

Watch this video of a teacher as he explains his understanding of prior knowledge. In what ways does prior knowledge inform his approach to teaching?

Children come to us with a wealth of ideas about how the world works. Their understanding is based on the evidence and the contexts in which they experience the world. Knowledge of student preconceptions provides a starting point for teaching. Campbell et al. suggest that student preconceptions act as stepping stones for children to make sense of the world.[14] Discourse and activities wherein students' preconceptions are challenged compel them to address their preconceptions and either modify or replace them.

Suppose, for example, that Juan enters class believing Earth is flat, which makes sense to Juan because all the evidence from his experience suggests a flat Earth. When Juan is told that Earth is round (in fact, the Earth is spherical), he is reluctant to let go of his flat-Earth notion. In order to reconcile his prior belief that Earth is flat with the new information, he creates a mental model of a pancake-shaped Earth that fits both with his prior understanding of a flat Earth and with the new information that Earth is round.[15] Cognitive psychologists use the term *assimilation,* a term also used by Jean Piaget to describe how we combine new experiences with existing ideas that may support or deepen but do not change our fundamental understanding.

Suppose, however, that Juan observes ships sailing over the horizon that do not fall off the edge of Earth. When challenged to explain this phenomenon, he cannot reconcile it with his current mental model of a flat Earth. He is faced with the choice of either having to reject the evidence or accommodate his mental model to one of a spherical Earth. When new evidence cannot be reconciled with prior understanding, mental models are forced to change, resulting in a new rather than simply revised schema. Replacement of an extant schema with a new one is accommodation, also described by Jean Piaget. Assimilation and accommodation are not mutually exclusive. They often complement each other in the learning process.

2. To develop competence in an area of inquiry, students must (a) have a deep foundation of factual knowledge, (b) understand facts and ideas in the context of a conceptual framework, and (c) organize knowledge in ways that facilitate retrieval and application.[16]

This principle speaks to a tension between facts and big ideas. Science education has been characterized by memorization of facts. Generally, rote memorization is one of the least efficient learning strategies. One of my undergraduate students recently wrote in a reflection that "it was almost like a chore to have to memorize all of the new ideas" she was learning in her science classes. I wrote back that, "It is unfortunate that you had to memorize ideas, rather than those ideas being memorable because they were meaningful." It is difficult to make sense of facts apart from a meaningful context. Principle 2 suggests that in order to be an effective inquirer, one must both know the facts and understand the concepts that connect the facts. For example, memorizing parts of the digestive system alone does not result in deep understanding or retention. But questioning the changes that take place as an apple passes through our digestive system creates a context that makes the structures and functions of the digestive system meaningful and logical. As science teachers, we can assist students in making connections of facts to concepts that help them make sense of the world.

3. A "metacognitive" approach to instruction can help students learn to take control of their own learning by defining learning goals and monitoring their progress in achieving them.[17]

Metacognition is a term that will not be familiar to our students, but one that we need to think about and allow to inform our teaching. Metacognition in the context of teaching and learning is self-monitoring of one's learning. Simply stated, it is a self-awareness of the strategies that help us learn. For example, suppose a student is learning about characteristics and relationships among producers and consumers in a food web. She finds that organizing photos of plants and animals in categories of producers and primary, secondary, and tertiary consumers helps her learn the relationships among trophic levels. Another student finds that if he creates a story linking the organisms in a food web's trophic levels, then it makes sense to him. In both cases, students are aware of strategies that help them learn. Research suggests that experts in any discipline are able to ask themselves, "Do I understand this?" and "How can I check my understanding?"[18]

We can foster student metacognition in the science classroom by creating opportunities for students to think about strategies that help them learn. Have students keep a science notebook in which they can write about what they learned and how they learned it as well as what confuses them. When students experience difficulty learning science, ask what they do when they do not understand, whether their strategy is working, and what they could do differently.

Good teaching of any discipline will consider these three basic principles. For those of us teaching science, we add another principle: Doing Science. Perhaps you are familiar with the saying that people learn by doing. Wieman noted that new graduate students in his physics lab are often clueless about how to proceed when faced with a research project, despite having been very successful undergraduate students. However, after working with knowledgeable researchers for a few years in the lab, the graduate students turn into experts. He suggests that this is because the students are "engaged in exactly the same cognitive processes required for developing expert competence."[19] Now, your elementary students are not learning at the same level as graduate physics students, and we do not expect them to be experts by the end of elementary school. But they, too, will learn how to inquire and construct knowledge if they are engaged in learning science principles and concepts while actively involved in the practices of science. Of course, they cannot do so without guidance provided by you, the teacher.

The Nature of Science

In order to understand and teach science, we need to consider values and beliefs associated with science. These are collectively referred to as the nature of science. Underlying the nature of science is the notion that science is a human endeavor.

Science is a very social process. Science advances through peer reviews that evaluate and critically assess claims based on evidence and reason. Explanations are based on varying degrees of certainty. In some cases, such as climate change and evolution, the evidence is extremely strong and certainty very high. Unfortunately, without an understanding of the nature of science and scientific inquiry, it is possible to be deceived or manipulated by a slim margin of uncertainty.

Of all the climate experts—individuals with the resources, knowledge, and experience to make informed analysis—97% support the consensus that humans are responsible for climate change.[20] Yet there continues to be significant doubt, largely among non-scientists, concerning the impact of humans on climate change. With the increasing role science, technology, and engineering play in personal and global well-being, it imperative that all citizens hold a functional understanding of the nature of the science and demonstrate a working knowledge of scientific literacy. The Next Generation Science Standards identifies the following basic understandings that all high school graduates should have about the nature of science for which the foundations need to be established in elementary school.[21]

- Scientific Investigations Use a Variety of Methods
- Scientific Knowledge Is Based on Empirical Evidence
- Scientific Knowledge Is Open to Revision in Light of New Evidence
- Scientific Models, Laws, Mechanisms, and Theories Explain Natural Phenomena
- Science Is a Way of Knowing
- Scientific Knowledge Assumes an Order and Consistency in Natural Systems
- Science Is a Human Endeavor
- Science Addresses Questions About the Natural and Material World

The nature of science is not a separate NGSS dimension. The understandings of the nature of science are embedded in lessons and modeled by teachers. The nature of science is also reflected through lessons about the history of science. One of the most famous examples is spontaneous generation, the belief that life can emerge from nonliving matter. This idea was fueled by observations of rotting meat in which maggots seemed to spontaneously appear. As early as 1668 an Italian scientist named Francesco Redi thought otherwise, suggesting that maggots came from eggs laid by flies in the meat. He tested his hypothesis by boiling meat in several flasks, sealing some and leaving others open. Sure enough, maggots only grew in the open flasks exposed to air. However, most people were not convinced, suggesting the data only proved that spontaneous generation required air. It was not until 1859 when Louis Pasteur boiled meat in a flask in such a manner that air could enter the flask but not microorganisms that the refutation of spontaneous generation was accepted by the scientific community. While this example may seem remote, new evidence about health and medicine is constantly changing our lifestyles. Each day we are faced with reports about dieting, exercise, and drugs that claim to improve our lives. Should children be vaccinated? How much sunblock is necessary? Will cell phones cause cancer?

Science as a Set of Values

Although there are many values you can emphasize as you help children experience science processes and learn core ideas and crosscutting concepts, there are six that you will find particularly useful:

1. Truth
2. Freedom
3. Skepticism
4. Order
5. Originality
6. Communication

Because science seeks to make sense out of our natural world, it has as its most basic value the search for the truest, most accurate explanations based on evidence. A scientist seeks to discover not what should be but what is. The high value placed on truth applies not only to the discovery of facts, concepts, and principles but also to the recording and reporting of such knowledge.

The search for explanations relies on another important value: freedom. Real science can only occur when a scientist is able to operate in an environment that provides him or her with the freedom to follow paths wherever they lead. Fortunately, free societies rarely limit the work of scientists. Freedom to follow pathways also means the freedom to risk thinking independently and creatively. As educators, we must provide opportunities for students to think while taking care to think with, not for, students. Let me state that again: We must think *with*, not *for*, students. Thinking with students means modeling and guiding scientific thinking. Some of the best opportunities occur when we do not know the answer to a student's question, which will inevitably be the case no matter how much we prepare. This can be a time to panic and brush the student's question aside for fear of looking ignorant, or it can be a teaching and learning opportunity by which we model good thinking as lead learners. We can foster the development of foundational thinking strategies so that children take advantage of the freedom to think afforded them in our open society. A successful free society depends on the ability of its citizens to make informed decisions.

Skepticism—the unwillingness to accept many things at face value—moves scientists to ask difficult questions about the natural world, society, and even each other. Scientists value skepticism, and skepticism sometimes causes nonscientists to doubt the results of scientific enterprise. We will teach our students to be informed skeptics and teach them to argue scientifically so that their skepticism fosters constructive discussion that leads to deeper understanding.

There is, then, an underlying order to the processes and content of science. As suggested, science is a systematic process. There are many ways to study phenomena. The marine biologist observes dolphin behavior, while the botanist tests the effects of soil samples on plant growth, and the molecular biologist seeks ways to manipulate genes. All are collecting data in different ways. But all have a deliberate and organized plan for collecting and organizing data. It is this systematization and order that allow scientists to discover patterns in the natural world. Children need to develop this ability to organize information, which is why you will be helping them learn how to organize and keep track of their observations and discoveries.

For all its order, however, science also values originality. Although some may view science as a linear activity—one in which people plod along, acquiring more and more detailed explanations of phenomena—in reality, science is fueled by original ideas and creative thinking. It is this kind of thinking that leads to discoveries. Children have wonderful imaginations that can be assets for their science learning. As teachers, we can nurture and foster their imagination and creativity while learning science.

Children love to talk with each other; so do scientists. The talk of scientists includes reports, articles, speeches, and lectures, as well as casual conversations. The ability to communicate results and ideas is vital if knowledge is to grow. Without extensive communication, progress would be greatly limited. Students will learn how to argue scientifically and use claims, evidence, and reasoning to support their arguments and to critique those of others.

As a teacher, you will need to help children understand that science is more than a collection of facts and a group of processes. Science is a human activity that has as its framework a set of values that are important in day-to-day life.

Developing a Science Learner Identity   Our goal as teachers is not to inspire all students to become scientists or engineers. Neither is it our goal to inspire students to become journalists, lawyers, plumbers, or carpenters. It is our goal to inspire students to believe in themselves as individuals with the ability to learn in any of these disciplines.

Developing Positive Affect   For many teachers, a lesson about a caterpillar becoming a butterfly will only be about a caterpillar and a butterfly. But the same lesson in the hands of a master teacher—a great teacher, an extraordinary teacher, a truly gifted teacher—will be an experience in which the children are thunderstruck with the realization that one living thing has become a completely different living thing right before their eyes.

The day of that lesson will be one on which those children's lives will be changed forever. They will leave school filled with a sense of wonder that was sparked by the thrill of discovering brand-new knowledge that is as extraordinary as anything they will see on television. They will want to know more—curious about what may lie around the corner. They will also leave with new attitudes, values, and a confidence in their ability to learn that will shape who they are and who they will become.

This change in attitudes and values signals the development of positive affect. The science experiences you deliver to children will do much to create positive affect about science, school, and the wonders of the natural world. Most of all, we want our students to believe in themselves as successful learners of science, to "think about themselves as science learners and develop an identity as someone who knows about, uses, and sometimes contributes to science."[22]

Developing Psychomotor Skills

You might not think of your classroom as a place where children learn to coordinate what their minds will do with what their bodies perform—but it is. Children need to develop gross motor abilities as well as fine motor skills, and well-planned science experiences can help them do so.

Gross motor skills can be developed through inquiry-based activities such as assembling and using simple machines, hoeing and raking a class vegetable garden, and carefully shaping sand on a table to make various landforms. Examples of experiences that develop fine motor skills include cutting out leaf shapes with scissors, drawing charts and graphs, and sorting seeds on the basis of physical characteristics. So, in addition to gaining knowledge and understanding and developing positive affect, science time can be a time to improve a child's physical skills.

Developing Responsible and Informed Citizens

When your children look at you during science time, they aren't thinking about issues such as raising taxes to pay for a park's underground sprinkler system or what impact the new factory under construction in town may have on worldwide CO_2 emissions and global warming trends. However, at some time in their lives, they will be called upon to make decisions that will significantly impact them as individuals, members of a local community, and part of a global community—decisions that no generation before them has had to face. And to be responsible citizens, they will need to address such issues with wisdom—wisdom and the ability to make informed decisions based on a foundation of knowledge and evidence.

With your guidance, children will learn that real inquiry requires gathering evidence before reaching a conclusion. Learning to gather knowledge systematically and to reach carefully thought-out conclusions will be skills they apply as they confront personal and societal issues in the future. If we do our job, then today's children will be prepared to make positive contributions to the civic decision-making processes that will lead to a better life for us all.

To create citizens who understand the implications of developments in science and technology is an enormous task. But the task for you, as a teacher, is more specific and reachable: teaching children to become scientifically literate. There is debate about what it means to be scientifically literate. Scientific literacy is less about *what* one knows as it is about *how* one knows. A scientifically literate person seeks to understand the reasoning behind claims. They do not have to agree with the claims, but they should be able to discern whether the claims were made based on evidence, how the evidence was collected, and who collected the evidence. Even the most experienced scientists have to rely on evidence and data analyzed by others to make informed decisions. All citizens should be familiar with questions to ask that support evidence and analysis: What is the question/problem? Who is collecting the data? What is driving them to collect the data? How did they collect the data? Was the data critiqued by other respected experts in the field? Being scientifically literate means knowing enough about the practices and core ideas of science to ask these types of questions and make informed decisions based on the answers. Scientific literacy is not just for scientists. It informs our big and small judgments spanning decisions about our health, government, and even the pair of shoes we buy. Does that belly band really take inches off your waist? Will krill oil improve liver, heart, and brain function? You can get both for the low price of $19.99! Scientific literacy helps us to make informed decisions by asking, "What's the evidence?" "How did

Enhanced eText Video Example 1.2

Listen to noted astrophysicist Neil deGrasse Tyson speak about scientific literacy. How do his comments reflect the importance of scientific literacy for the non-scientist? [https://www.youtube.com/watch?v=PGNxgm3tdG0]

you get the evidence?" "How did you analyze the evidence?" "What does the evidence mean?" "What did other, non-biased experts in the scientific community have to say about it?" As an elementary teacher, you will start your students on the path to scientific literacy.

Equity Issues: Your Science Teaching Will Help Resolve Them

The scientist is a brain. He spends his days indoors, sitting in a laboratory, pouring things from one test tube into another. . . . He can only eat, breathe, and sleep science. . . . He has no social life, no other intellectual interests, no hobbies or relaxations. . . . He is always reading a book. He brings home creepy things.[23] Although students made these observations almost 50 years ago, their attitudes reflect, to a large degree, the views of society today. The students' choice of pronoun does not seem to reflect the purposeful use of *he* for *she* but rather the strength of the stereotype of the scientist as a white male.

Such stereotypes may discourage young females, minorities, and students with disabilities from considering science or science-related careers and foster the notion that they are not expected to succeed in science. Hopefully, you will be a classroom leader who is able to create an environment that helps to overcome these stereotypes.

The science classroom can also provide you with a wonderful opportunity to assist children from cultural minorities and for whom English is not their first language. When children are encouraged to explore phenomena that are real to them, to learn and use inquiry skills, and ultimately to make their own discoveries, the power of these experiences will do much to integrate all children into the task at hand.

Just think of how fortunate you are to teach children science, a subject whose natural allure for children will draw them into learning experiences irrespective of gender, language, and cultural barriers. By having a classroom that respects racial, gender, socioeconomic, and linguistic diversities, you can make a real difference in the lives of children. That's right! You can and will make a difference.

Your Attitude Makes a Difference

If, as a teacher, you emphasize only the facts of science, children will learn that science is an accumulation of factual knowledge. However, if you emphasize the process of science, children will learn that science is a way of seeking explanations. A well-rounded student understands science as both a process and a body of knowledge. Children will enter your classes with their own perceptions of science formed through experiences outside of school, at home, and through the media. As their teacher, you will have a significant impact on their understanding and attitude about what science is and how science is done. It is not only what you teach but also your attitude toward science that will impact students.

Consider Ms. Jones, a third-grade teacher, on bus duty early one spring morning, greeting and directing the children as they clamor off the buses. Ashley, a curious third-grader, can hardly contain her excitement as she runs up to Ms. Jones with a plastic container teeming with wriggling worms she and her mother found while planting a garden. Ashley grabs a handful of worms to show Ms. Jones and asks excitedly, "Can we keep them in the classroom?"

Ms. Jones smiles and shares in Ashley's excitement. "Wonderful idea Ashley," she exclaims. "Let's build a home for them. What do you think the worms will need in their home to stay healthy?" Ashley pauses and wonders, "Well, I found them in the garden. They probably need dirt." Ms. Jones, replies, "Great idea, Ashley. I wonder if any dirt is okay to use, and how much dirt should we get?" "Hmmn," says Ashley. "I don't know. What do worms eat?" "Great question," responds Ms. Jones. "Maybe we can share your discovery with the class, and present the question about a suitable home (habitat) for the worms and see if they have ideas about how to find out what the worms need."

Soon the class is planning an investigation by visiting gardens, searching for worms, testing the properties of the soil, and measuring the depth at which worms are found.

Connecting Technology and Engineering in Your Teaching

What do these terms have in common: video games, solar panels, prescription drugs, fuel cells, autonomous cars, CAT scans, X-ray treatment for cancer, and ramen noodles (noodlelike material that can be reconstituted through the addition of tap water)? The answer, of course, is technology. They all are products or procedures that apply science to the solution of human needs and desires—real or imagined.

Today, one of the most immediate challenges concerns climate change and the rising costs and finite supply of fossil fuels, which have created a need to seek alternative methods to generate energy. Green buildings that take advantage of wind, solar, geothermal, and even human energy are emerging at an increasingly rapid pace. These technologies integrate Earth science, energy transfer and conversion, simple machines, and biology in meaningful and relevant contexts. In your role as an elementary school teacher, you will have a tremendous opportunity to lay the foundation of energy literacy for generations of young people who may become engineers, architects, and designers who make pivotal decisions about lifestyle changes that will affect our planet and its inhabitants for years to come.

Enhanced eText Video Example 1.3

Watch third-graders designing, constructing, and testing a waterwheel. Note their engagement and creativity as they integrate science, technology, and engineering. Describe the science and engineering practices the children exhibit.

Changes in technology are occurring more rapidly than perhaps at any other time in history. The computers and smartphones we are using today will likely be outdated within the year. Drones, self-driving cars, and virtual reality are already realities, posed to play increasingly significant roles in our society. Biomedical engineers continually create new devices to speed recovery, treat emergencies, and restore movement, sight, and hearing. Technology, science, and engineering are integrally connected. Engineering is the application of science to serve human needs through design and development processes that lead to new technologies. Science, engineering, and technology are mutually beneficial. Needs and desires inspire engineers to apply scientific principles in creative ways. The technology that results often helps scientists investigate more deeply explanations of natural phenomena.

How might teaching about technological design be translated into your own real-world classroom?

Some building projects that are easily integrated into technology/engineering design projects are as follows:

1. A bridge out of newspaper and tape that supports two bricks and has a clearance of 12 inches
2. A machine for removing and sorting garbage and trash from lunch trays
3. A solar oven to cook s'mores
4. An automatic fish feeder for the aquarium during vacations

The point is that new and emerging technology impacts virtually every minute of a child's day. In order for children to lead lives in which technology is used intelligently, with minimal negative side effects, they need to understand how technology, engineering, and science are related, how new products and procedures are designed, what science is applied, what resources are needed, and what deleterious consequences may occur, such as allergic reactions, environmental pollution, and safety hazards. Students need to fully understand the larger impact of science, engineering, and new technologies within the context of how they affect their communities—and themselves.

REALITY Check

The NGSS provide many resources to guide your teaching. To become familiar with the three dimensions of the NGSS (science practices, disciplinary core ideas, and crosscutting concepts) imagine you are preparing a unit about forces and interactions for your third-grade students. Go to the NGSS website. Navigate through the site to find a standard 3-PS2-1. Identify the performance expectation that your students should be able to demonstrate by the end of third grade along with the science practices, disciplinary core ideas, and crosscutting concepts associated with the standard that will inform your unit. How does the standard relate to the nature of science and the Common Core State Standards?

● Yes, You Can Do It! Science for All Children, Every Day, in Every Way

This text is full of resources that will help you create wonderful classroom experiences for children—experiences in which they explore, inquire, and discover. In Part One of this text (which includes this and the next five chapters), you will learn basic science-teaching methods that will help you create that wonderful classroom! And beyond Part One, you will find three very specific parts of the text that deal with teaching the Earth/space sciences, the life sciences, and the physical sciences. In the Appendix, you will find unit and lesson "starter ideas," activities and demonstrations as you prepare to teach children science.

I am confident that you will be successful if you are motivated to use your talent to its fullest and the available resources to the maximum. If you do, each day in your classroom will be a day when every child has the opportunity to explore, inquire, and discover. So get started on your journey to discover how children actually learn science.

Summary

1.1 Develop a working definition of science.

Science is both a body of knowledge about the natural world and a systematic way of gathering knowledge. Scientific thinking can be thought of as a progression of inquiry consisting of descriptive, explanatory, and verification models. Scientific ways of knowing do not consist of one sequential set of tasks. On the contrary, seeking explanations based on evidence uses many approaches ranging in degrees from experimental to field based, all of which represent systematic, well-thought-out approaches.

Self-Check 1.1
Click to gauge your understanding of the concepts in this chapter.

1.2 Describe how research about learning science informs science teaching.

The following principles are from *How Students Learn: History, Mathematics, and Science in the Classroom* (Bransford & Donovan, 2005):

- Students come to the classroom with preconceptions about how the world works. If their initial understanding is not engaged, they may fail to grasp the new concepts and information, or they may learn them for purposes of a test but revert to their preconceptions outside the classroom. Building on and challenging students' prior knowledge will allow students to adapt and modify their understanding and make learning both relevant and meaningful.

- To develop competence in an area of inquiry, students must (a) have a deep foundation of factual knowledge, (b) understand facts and ideas in the context of a conceptual framework, and (c) organize knowledge in ways that facilitate retrieval and application. As science teachers, we can assist students in making connections of facts to concepts that help students make sense of the world. Teaching both facts and the concepts in a meaningful context will help students make sense of new knowledge and organize it in a way that supports retention.

- A "metacognitive" approach to instruction can help students learn to take control of their own learning by defining learning goals and monitoring their progress in achieving them.

- Metacognition is a term that will not be familiar to our students, but one that we need to think about and inform our teaching. Metacognition in the context of teaching and learning is self-monitoring of one's learning. It could be rehearsing a phone number to remember it, or asking probing questions about a new idea to figure out what it means and how it fits with preexisting ideas. I often think of good detectives, who ask probing questions that follow up previous responses, as an example of challenging ideas and monitoring one's learning to get to the bottom of a case. Scientific argumentation is similar and a strategy you can promote in the science classroom.

- Learning science requires students to be participants in doing science.

  Doing science means dealing with the uncertainty of not knowing the answer and using a variety of thoughtful systematic strategies to seek an explanation. It requires imagination and creativity, looking at events and phenomena and thinking about explanations and solutions in novel ways. When we teach students science, we guide them to use observation, reasoning, creativity, and imagination to think in ways that are new for them and lead them to personal discoveries and deeper understanding so they can make sense of the world.

Self-Check 1.2

Click to gauge your understanding of the concepts in this chapter.

1.3 Describe the purpose and three dimensions of the Next Generation Science Standards.

The Next Generation Science Standards were developed by teams of scientists and educators to identify what students in each grade should know and be able to do with respect to science and engineering. They consist of three dimensions: science practices, disciplinary core ideas, and crosscutting concepts. Three dimensional instruction means using each dimension together, not in isolation, to help students make sense of phenomena or figure out solutions.

Self-Check 1.3

Click to gauge your understanding of the concepts in this chapter.

GOING FURTHER
On Your Own or in a Cooperative Learning Group

1. Think about your experience in science classes. What did you enjoy? What didn't you enjoy? More importantly, how were you engaged and inspired to learn science? If you were not engaged, what disengaged you? How would you want students to describe the science learning experiences that you lead?

2. If possible, interview an elementary school teacher to find out how she or he answers such questions as these: What does science mean to you? What do your students thin k science is? What advice can you provide about how children learn science?

3. Ask friends, family, colleagues what they think science is and what the nature of science means to them. Ask them their ideas about how children should learn science.

4. Talk with your colleagues about how gender, race, ethnicity, and culture, your own and those of your students, could inform your science teaching.

5. A criticism of science education has been that we teach students *about* science rather than having them *do* science. Interview a scientist and a non-scientist about what it means to *do* science. Write an article or produce a brief video about what you discover.

6. Do you consider yourself scientifically literate? Why or why not?

RESOURCES FOR DISCOVERY LEARNING

Internet Resources

- **Next Generation Science Standards:** www.nextgenscience.org

- **Common Core State Standards:** www.corestandards.org/

- **National Science Teachers Association:** www.nsta.org

- **Phenomena** https://www.nextgenscience.org/resources/phenomena

- **Skeptical Science:** https://www.skepticalscience.com/

Print Resources

Akerson, Valarie, & Donnelly, Lisa A. (2010). Teaching nature of science to K-2 students: What understandings can they attain? *International Journal of Science Education, 32*: 1, 97–124.

Jesky-Smith, Romaine. (2002). Me, teach science. *Science and Children, 39*(6): 26–30.

Kelly, Catherine A. (2000). Reaching the standards. *Science and Children, 37*(4): 30–32.

Koenig, Maureen. (2001). Debating real-world issues. *Science Scope, 24*(5): 18–24.

Manz, E. (2015). Resistance and the development of scientific practice: Designing the mangle into science instruction. *Cognition and Instruction, 33*(2): 89–124.

McDonald, C. V. (2009). The influence of explicit nature of science and argumentation instruction on preservice primary teachers' views of nature of science. *Journal of Research in Science Teaching, 47*(9): 1137–1164. Retrieved March 15, 2017.

McDuffie Jr., Thomas E. (2001). Scientists—geeks and nerds. *Science and Children, 38*(8): 16–19.

Sagan, C. (1996). *The demon-haunted world: Science as a candle in the dark.* New York, NY: Ballantine Books.

Science, evolution, and creationism. (2008). Washington, DC: National Academies Press.

Shamos, M. H. (1995). *The myth of scientific literacy.* New Brunswick, NJ: Rutgers University Press.

Timmerman, Barbara. (2002). Keeping science current. *Science Scope, 25*(6): 12–15.

Understanding the scientific enterprise: The nature of science in the Next Generation Science Standards. (2017, February 8). Retrieved March 15, 2017, from http://www.nextgenscience.org/

Wieman shares teaching, learning insights at Univ. of Pittsburgh event. (2014, February 6). *States*

News Service. Retrieved March 15, 2017, from http://www.highbeam.com/doc/1G1-358549998.html?refid=easy_hf

Wieman, Carl. (2008). Science education in the 21ˢᵗ century using the tools of science to teach science. Forum for the Future of Higher Education, Aspen Colorado, 2007. Cambridge, MA: Educause.

Notes

1. Carl Sagan's last interview with Charlie Rose: Science as a candle in the dark. (December 17, 2011). www.singularityweblog.com/carl-sagans-last-interview-science-as-a-candle-in-the-dark/

2. Donovan, M. S., & Bransford, J. D. (2005). *How students learn: History, mathematics, and science in the classroom*. Washington, DC: National Academic Press, p. 398.

3. Manz, E. (2015). Resistance and the development of scientific practice: Designing the mangle into science instruction. *Cognition and Instruction, 33*(2): 89–124.

4. Freeman John Dyson is an English-born American theoretical physicist and mathematician, known for his work in quantum electrodynamics, solid-state physics, astronomy, and nuclear engineering.

5. *Science on the rampage, Freeman Dyson.* **(2012, April 5). The New York Review of Books.**

6. Next Generation Science Standards (NGSS) is a registered trademark of Achieve. Neither Achieve nor the lead states and partners that developed the Next Generation Science Standards was involved in the production of, and does not endorse, this product.

7. Ibid

8. NGSS Lead States. (2013). *Next Generation Science Standards: For states, by states*. Washington, DC: The National Academies Press.

9. *A framework for K-12 science education: Practices, crosscutting concepts, and core ideas.* (2012). Washington, DC: The National Academies Press, 2012.

10. Bruner, J. S. (1960). *The process of education*. Cambridge, MA: Harvard University Press.

11. Wieman, Carl. (2008). Science education in the 21ˢᵗ century using the tools of science to teach science. Forum for the Future of Higher Education, Aspen Colorado, 2007. Cambridge, MA: Educause.

12. Donovan & Bransford.

13. Ibid., p. 4.

14. Campbell, T., Schwarz, C., & Windschitl, M. (2016). What we call misconceptions may be necessary stepping-stones toward making sense of the world. *Science and Children, 53*(7). doi:10.2505/4/sc16_053_07_28

15. Vosniadou, S., & Brewer, W. F. (1989). A cross-cultural investigation of children's conceptions about the earth, the sun, and the moon: Greek and American data. In H. Mandl, E. DeCorte, N. Bennett, & H. F. Friedrich (Eds.), *Learning and instruction: European research in an international context* (vol. 2.2, pp. 605–629). Oxford, UK: Pergamon.

16. Donovan & Bransford, p. 6.

17. Ibid, p. 10.

18. Wieman, p. 63.

19. Ibid.

20. Cook, J., Oreskes, N., Doran, P. T., Anderegg, W. R., Verheggen, B., Maibach, E. W., . . . Rice, K. (2016). Consensus on consensus: A synthesis of consensus estimates on human-caused global warming. *Environmental Research Letters, 11*(4), 048002. doi:10.1088/1748-9326/11/4/048002; Cook, J., Nuccitelli, D., Green, S. A., Richardson, M., Winkler, B., Painting, R., . . . Skuce, A. (2013). Quantifying the consensus on anthropogenic global warming in the scientific literature. *Environmental Research Letters, 8*: 024024.

21. Understanding the scientific enterprise: The nature of science in the Next Generation Science Standards. (2013, April). Appendix H.

22. Fraser, J., & Ward, P. (2009). ISE professionals' knowledge and attitudes regarding science identity for learners in informal environments: Results of a national survey. ILI Report 091104. Edgewater, MD: Institute for Learning Innovation.

23. Mead, M., & Metraux, R. (1957). Image of the scientist among high school students. *Science, 126*(3270): 384–390.

CHAPTER 2

Science Practices and Inquiry Process Skills

How can I help children use science and engineering practices to make discoveries?

BIGANDT.COM/Shutterstock

Learning Objectives

After completing the activities in this chapter, you should be able to:

2.1 Create a vision for discovery learning in your classroom.

2.2 Describe science practices and inquiry skills as they relate to learning science and engineering.

▶ GETTING STARTED

Her lips are starting to swell and crack under the broiling desert sun. Hot dry air has been relentlessly attacking since daybreak. She stops for a moment, lifts the bandana covering her mouth and nose, and shakes out her stringy hair. Incredibly, with that headshake, something catches her attention. To her left, a tiny, gray fossil bone fragment sticks out from the soil. The last gust of wind must have revealed it. Now she doesn't feel the sun or the heat or the dust at all! Her full attention is focused on the fragment.

A series of images flashes through her mind as she compares what she can tell about this fragment to what she already knows. Her mental pictures are of dinosaur skeletons, and none has the anatomical structure into which this tiny bone would fit. It is a toe bone, for sure—but one she has never seen before. Her heart starts to race at the thought of this.

From her grimy tool pack, she carefully pulls several tiny dental picks and small brushes and gently works away the material around the bone. With each gentle poke and sweep of the brush, she grasps more clearly what has just been revealed to her eyes alone: A brand-new dinosaur has stuck its toe into her world and ours. Her careful observation has led to an extraordinary discovery.

She will draw the fossil, photograph it, plot its location, and then ever so slowly search the surrounding area for mor e fragments. Eventually, she will pull from the reluctant Earth a creature that so far has only been imagined. A wonderful discovery has been made—and she made it!

A Vision For Learning Science and Engineering through Discovery

Discovery learning has its foundation in constructivist learning theory, which is based on the premise that learning builds upon past experiences and new interactions with ideas and phenomena through exploration and manipulation.[1] In his book *The Act of Discovery*, Jerome Bruner advocates for a discovery learning.[2] When we discover, we find or gain knowledge, usually for the first time, using our own mind. In doing so, we as learners have invested in the acquisition of knowledge, and the knowledge takes on relevance and meaning. Bruner states that "the most uniquely personal of all that he (humankind)[3] knows is that which he has discovered for himself."[4]

In terms of learning, discovery for students is *making sense of the world* based on accurate scientific concepts and principles. This is a key point. While discoveries by your students will likely not be new to the scientific community, they will be new to your students. The idea behind *discovery* as it is used in this text is that students will actually engage in the practice of doing science rather than learning about science secondhand, resulting in a deeper understanding of scientific practices and content. Keep in mind that learning is an iterative process. Deeper understanding is built slowly over time. Resist the temptation to teach everything there is to know about a topic in one lesson. Knowing what *not to* teach is as important as knowing what *to* teach. Students' understandings will progress throughout their formal and informal education as lifelong learners. You, as the elementary science teacher, have a unique opportunity to establish a foundation upon which your young students will learn to think like scientists and engineers. Therefore, the practices and skills introduced in this chapter are among the most important you can initiate among your students to start them on a path of critical, evidence-based thinking that is the foundation of scientific and engineering ways of knowing.

When we teach with the focus on discovery, we prepare children to make personal discoveries with our guidance. We equip them with their very own "tool packs." And with any luck at all, they will use those tools in a variety of contexts throughout their lives. It is possible that a few children may find brand-new dinosaurs, but more importantly, all of them will use the tools of scientific inquiry to unearth evidence and develop the concepts, principles, attitudes, and values that will help them lead full and productive lives.

Discovery suggests that we need to respect and value learners and their role in constructing knowledge. As teachers, we cannot learn for our students; each child ultimately needs to forge his or her own understanding. Problem-based learning, project-based learning, expeditionary learning, and case-based learning are some of the many expressions of learning that are discovery based.

How Do I Teach So Discovery Learning Happens?

In the words of Louis Pasteur, "Chance favors the prepared mind." The same sentiment is shared by Jerome Bruner when he states, "Discovery, like surprise, favors the well-prepared mind."[5] By teaching science, you are preparing young people's minds to make discoveries. Discovery learning happens when a child uncovers new information, makes new connections, and gleans new insight that deepens his or her understanding. It is an individual and personal experience. Children need to discover new knowledge that is meaningful and offers a better explanation than their prior understanding. Otherwise, common misconceptions can persist into adulthood. A classic example is the reason for the seasons. Most people are taught the reason for the seasons at some time in their schooling. Yet, when asked to explain the reason for the seasons, their explanation falls short or is incorrect.

To teach for discovery learning, you must, wherever possible, provide hands-on, mind-stretching experiences that will enable children to use their knowledge and skills to make discoveries. Your challenge is to provide physical and intellectual contexts that inspire new discoveries connected to past and to future learning.

Your role as teacher goes beyond providing students with the opportunity to discover; you must also teach them how to discover. Your charge is to craft interactive learning experiences that guide students to develop the intellectual and physical tools necessary to seek explanations.

Discovery Is a Time of Enthusiasm, Excitement, and Energy!

Many of the preservice elementary teachers in my classes worry about the apparent lack of structure associated with a classroom of third-graders actively engaged in "doing" science. Discovery learning is filled with excitement. Not unlike a three-ring circus, there can be a lot of activity during discovery. Some students will be talking to each other, others will become animated; they will argue, wonder, and test ideas. This is good. If they are wondering and arguing about the science and/or engineering challenges you provide, congratulations, you are doing our job well. The science classroom should be dynamic and filled with energy. But there will be quiet, reflective times as well. The discovery process has a rhythm of learning alternating among periods of high activity, individual reflection, peer discussion, and explanation. Okay, it's true: Some science classrooms do become a bit chaotic, which can be unnerving. This is often a concern, especially for new teachers who are just developing their classroom-management strategies. It happens from time to time when teachers make the naive assumption that if they just provide a super-rich context of science "stuff," then good things will automatically happen. Well, sometimes they do, but they usually don't.

A science teacher must carefully plan student encounters with new ideas and orchestrate learning experiences that appear spontaneous to the casual observer but are nevertheless well planned and executed. There is nothing accidental about good teaching. Teaching discovery does not happen by simply providing an engaging activity and hoping children will learn something of value. Avoid the temptation to let the activity drive the learning. Watching the product of baking soda and vinegar

Enhanced eText Video Example 2.1

Watch children involved in inquiry learning. What is the teacher doing? What are the students doing? Describe the evidence that makes this an inquiry-based learning experience.

bubble out of a volcano may be engaging, but it can also be misleading with respect to the true mechanism of volcanic reactions. Select activities carefully and use them as experiences to develop the targeted learning objectives.

The term *inquiry* has been used extensively in science education, particularly in science education reforms of the recent past. As a result, the term *inquiry* has been interpreted in several different ways. Therefore, the Next Generation Science Standards associate science practices with science inquiry to better specify what is meant by inquiry. In this chapter, we take a closer look at inquiry and the science practices.

What Is Inquiry?

I will explain inquiry as clearly as I can, beginning with this straightforward definition: Inquiry is the careful and systematic method of asking questions and seeking explanations.

As suggested in Chapter 1, systematic does not suggest a single method or approach. The idea of a single scientific method is inaccurate and an oversimplification. Distance yourself from this idea. It is better to think of science and engineering methods as carefully planned investigations to collect valid and informative evidence to explain phenomena, answer questions, solve problems, or design solutions. Evidence consists of measurable data and can be either qualitative, quantitative, or both. Evidence is used to support or fail to support proposed explanations.

When students are actively involved in the processes of inquiry, they learn to inquire and employ science practices, concepts, and skills to seek explanations and make better sense of their worlds.

Learning Content Through Inquiry and Learning to Inquire

Learning content *through* inquiry means that the students construct knowledge through the processes of asking questions, seeking evidence, formulating explanations based on evidence, and justifying their explanations. Learning *to inquire* means students become aware of and consciously apply the processes associated with inquiry as part of their thinking strategies. Learning through inquiry and learning to inquire are complementary and often taught simultaneously.

Enhanced eText Video Example 2.2

Watch this video of students exploring properties of sound energy. How does the teacher guide inquiry?

The use of inquiry to learn science practices and core concepts varies on a continuum of teacher and student participation in the inquiry process. Inquiry is considered more guided to the degree that the teacher makes decisions about the inquiry processes for students and more open if students make decisions about inquiry on their own. The student who asks a question or makes a claim, seeks evidence, and formulates and justifies an evidence-based explanation on his or her own is participating in open-ended inquiry.

The NGSS Science and Engineering Practices

This section addresses the NGSS science and engineering practices. Later in this chapter we will address inquiry skills. Practices are distinguished from skills in that practices are accompanied by knowledge and understanding about how skills can be used to make sense of the world. Skills could be thought of as techniques that one could practice without knowledge of their application or purpose. Most of the practices in science and engineering are similar enough to be addressed together. We will consider them separately when necessary.

Asking Questions and Defining Problems   Knowing the best questions to ask is the first step in seeking an explanation. Science usually begins by asking questions about phenomena—for example, "Why does my dog walk in circles before it lays down?" or "How do turtles find their way back to their birthplace?" Engineers usually begin with a problem that needs to be solved—for example, "Plastics don't decompose easily and pose a danger to marine life. How can we make plastics more environmentally friendly?"

What kinds of questions should you encourage in your elementary students? Good science and engineering questions can be answered using evidence collected from direct observations or secondary data (data collected by someone else and accessed by the user). Questions such as "How do people catch colds?" or "How do hurricanes form?" can be investigated based on data collected by students or data shared by others. Questions based on values or opinion generally are not good scientific questions—for example, "Is football a better sport than hockey?"

In a later chapter, we will address strategies for questioning students. Here the focus is on the types of questions that we want to encourage students to ask. Children's questions frequently fit into one of the following categories:

- **Information-seeking questions:** Often students seek information to better understand a system. They need more facts: "Do frogs have teeth?" "What does a snake eat?" These are convergent questions, and the information can be acquired through direct observation or from a secondary source. Information-seeking questions provide opportunities for students to develop basic observational and descriptive skills. Don't dismiss these questions. If students ask whether frogs have teeth, make a claim based on their prior knowledge, and seek confirmation by looking in a frog's mouth, they are practicing scientific ways of thinking!

- **Wonderment questions:** Students may ask, "I wonder what will happen if . . . ?" These questions suggest a proposed relationship between two variables. Such a question is a precursor to an investigation. For example, a student might say, "I wonder what would happen if I used two batteries instead of one in the circuit." The student might predict that the light will get brighter. If she tests her prediction by adding a second battery to the circuit, records the data, and uses the data to confirm or falsify her prediction, she is doing science.

- **"How does it work?" questions:** How something works can lead to rich scientific reasoning. *How* questions seek explanations. Such questions include science-centered questions such as "How do penguins survive the cold?" and engineering-oriented questions such as "How does a solar panel work?" These higher-order questions may be phrased in more than one manner, sometimes beginning with *what* or *why*: "What causes the seasons?" "Why do cats have whiskers?" These types of questions present real opportunities for inquiry—if the teacher takes advantage of the question. Instead of telling students the answer (transmissional teaching), guide students to employ science practices and use inquiry skills to seek their own explanations. Encourage them to observe more closely, ask questions based on observations, look for evidence, generate ideas, test ideas, and share results. For example, observe cats, note how they use their whiskers and the structure of whiskers. Generate specific questions about whiskers, test ideas by observing other animals with or without whiskers, and share ideas with classmates, teachers, and if possible, experts.

- **How-to-solve-a-problem questions:** How to solve a problem is at the heart of engineering. It often leads to modification of an existing system or the creation of a new one. Students might ask how to make an automatic feeder for the class gerbil or how to make a birdfeeder that is squirrel-proof. Your job is to guide the design process so that students become aware of the iterative design, build, test, analyze, and redesign processes of engineering.

There are many other ways to categorize questions: convergent and divergent; descriptive, relational, and causal. I find the categories described above easy to identify and work with at the elementary level.

Developing and Using Models

Scientific models are representations of systems or phenomena that can help explain and make predictions regarding phenomena.[6] They can be diagrams, three-dimensional models, computer simulations, mathematical representations, or analogies. Models can be mental representations as well. Most important is to recognize that models are more than descriptions or miniatures of a larger object, such as a model house or model car. Art projects, while important in their own right, are not scientific models if they are not useful for explaining or predicting. Models have explanatory power that moves beyond description or definition of a concept.

The big idea for the use of models in science education is that students should develop models to represent their understanding and revise their models through an iterative process based on new evidence. For example, at the beginning of a unit on electricity, fourth-graders were asked to diagram their model of the inside of a flashlight and to use the model to explain how the flashlight (a simple circuit) works. An example of a student diagram is provided in Figure 2.1.

As units progress and students acquire more evidence about circuits, their understanding is reflected in revised models that not only support explanation and prediction, but also provide important formative assessment.

Modeling in particular invites students to observe, create, and analyze representations of phenomena. Modeling affords particularly rich language demand opportunities for all students, but can be especially supportive for English language learners (ELL). Diagrams, illustrations, three-dimensional models, and virtual representations are largely language independent and allow students to express their sense-making with minimal reliance on language. Students may not know the term for a lever or how to describe the relationships in a food web, but they can point to these ideas in a diagram or picture to express their thoughts and understanding. Furthermore, the desire to share descriptions and ideas motivates students to develop language skills. Using a model to clarify an explanation of simple circuits in a flashlight can support and enrich students' language use for explanations and predictions of simple circuits.

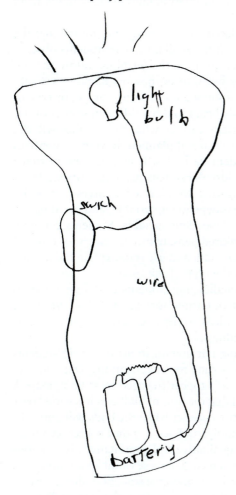

Figure 2.1 Observation is the most basic of all inquiry process skills.

Planning and Carrying Out Investigations   Planning and carrying out investigations may seem like a tall order for elementary school students. I know graduate students who struggle with such challenges. As elementary teachers, you are called to set the foundation for children to plan and execute scientifically sound investigations. It takes time, just as developing other knowledge and skills. The important help you must provide is to start them on the journey of developing science and engineering knowledge and skills. In elementary school, the NGSS suggest that K–2 students build on prior knowledge from and progress to simple investigations based on fair tests, which provide data to support explanations or design solutions. In grades 3 through 5, students carry out investigations with controlled variables and provide evidence to support explanations or design solutions.[7] This is a good time to distinguish between data and evidence to clarify the progression from K–2 to 3–5 students. Data and evidence are often used interchangeably, but they are distinct. Data are factual pieces of information that often consist of raw measurements. Data may or may not be relevant for an explanation. Data become evidence when they are used to justify an explanation. For instance, increased average global temperatures and increased levels of atmospheric CO_2 are data. Together they can provide evidence of global warming caused by increasing levels of CO_2. Does this still seem overwhelming? It need not be.

Enhanced eText Video Example 2.3

Watch how termites respond to ink lines on paper.

I use termites as a phenomenon to introduce students to the idea of planning and carrying out investigations. Termites will follow fresh lines made with ink from certain pens.

The ink contains a chemical closely related to a tracking pheromone that the termites use. The chemical is present in some but not all inks. The students observe the termite behavior and immediately question how the termites follow the ink trail. With very little or no prompting, they begin to propose explanations. Common explanations suggest that the termites follow color, texture, shape, or type of ink. Third- and fourth-graders spontaneously begin to draw different shapes or use different colors with different pens in an attempt to see what the termites will do. They are collecting data. Most of these forays are ill planned, having no controls or identification of independent or dependent variables. It is at this point that I stop the class (not an easy feat, given the children's excitement) to identify students' questions, ideas, claims, and evidence. Together we plan a fair investigation by controlling variables, manipulating just the independent variable, and deciding the type of data we will collect to measure the dependent variable. Students can now carry out the investigation using different-colored pens, textures, shapes, or types of ink in a systematic manner. They collect more data and use it to explain the termite behavior—that is, termites are attracted to the type of ink used.

Engineering design emerges easily by challenging students to design a way to use their discovery to create a way to control termite infestations. You would be surprised with the creative and innovative ideas students generate—for example, use the ink to lure termites away from buildings.

A final note about planning and carrying out investigations is to help students recognize that the natural world is often the setting for investigations. Did you ever wonder when the leaves on the old oak tree will appear (referred to as budburst)? A look at the past data in your region will reveal that the time of budburst has varied over the years.[8] You might challenge your students to predict when the buds will burst. To find out, have students adopt a tree in the schoolyard. Each day they collect data (e.g., temperature, rainfall, day length [9] and make qualitative and quantitative observations of the buds: color, size, shape. Have them keep a record of these variables accompanied by occasional drawings or photographs of the buds. Soon the students will realize that they need a definition of budburst. How will they know it when they see it? They do some online searches and find out that the scientific community identifies budburst at the time when new leaves are visible through openings in the swollen bud. Finally, the day arrives and they confirm budburst by having three independent classes observe the buds. Next they look for patterns in their data that might explain the signs leading to budburst. Students use the data as evidence to make claims, and then share their evidence and reasoning with classmates.

Analyzing and Interpreting Data   At the elementary level, students begin to arrange their data to display patterns. You can scaffold the presentation of data by creating tables, graphs, diagrams, or similar ways to display data. Be creative. Square-foot floor tiles work wonderfully for making large bar graphs. When I plan a discovery unit that investigates plant growth, I have students arrange their data such that it displays a pattern that they can recognize. Note how the data are organized in Table 2.1 to help the children see patterns.

Using Mathematics and Computational Thinking   There is no getting around it: Mathematics is an elegant language for representing relationships in a concise and predictable manner. However, math has been known to turn people away from science and engineering. The math you teach to your elementary children need not be intimidating. Applications of math in science and engineering can be as simple as counting the number of acorns on the ground in a given area to study resources in an ecosystem. Technology provides easy methods for collecting data such as temperature or speed to generate data sets that young children can analyze. Simple bar graphs, scatter plots, and line graphs make relationships and trends easily recognizable. I challenge students to make pizza box solar ovens that heat up quickly and cool down slowly. Measuring temperature over time and graphing the data provide rate measurements. The slopes of the graphs clearly represent trends about the efficacy of their designs and provide feedback for redesign. Your responsibility is to think creatively about how you can integrate math and computational thinking into your science and engineering instruction.

Table 2.1 Comparison of plant growth

Day	Plant growth in inches with 4 hrs. of light per day	Plant growth in inches with 8 hrs. of light per day
1	0	0
4	2	4
8	3	6
12	4	7
16	5	10
20	7	14

REALITY Check

Make line graphs and bar graphs for the data in Table 2.1. Discuss the pros and cons of each with your colleagues. Integrate technology by using a program such as Microsoft Excel to make the graphs.

Constructing Explanations (Science) and Designing Solutions (Engineering)

When all is said and done, constructing explanations based on evidence is at the core of science education. If students ask good scientific questions, plan and carry out investigations, collect and analyze data, then the culmination of their efforts should be explanations based on evidence. While they may not have a complete explanation or fully accurate understanding of the targeted concepts, they will have extended their knowledge and understanding.

When teaching students to construct explanations or design solutions, it is important that the learners express their own explanation or solution in order to effect conceptual change. Only after learners have expressed their discoveries should teachers challenge and guide their explanations. Communicating understanding is consistent with reflection that inspires ownership of learning through discovery. This approach will be addressed in more depth in Chapters 3 and 4.

Constructing an explanation means identifying the salient parts of a system, the properties and relationships among the parts, and how they all come together to make the system work. At first glance this may seem too advanced for elementary school children. For example, suppose a unit began with the essential question, "How are seeds formed?" To investigate, students grow and observe Fast Plants® over a period of about 35 days. At the end of that period, they have encountered the parts of the plant as it grows and differentiates, examined and described distinctive properties of the flower parts (stamen, anther, pistil), seen the flowers bloom, gathered pollen with bee abdomens, transferred the pollen to the pistils and noted the relationships among bees and plant parts, and observed the pistils swell and produce seeds. During this time the students will have kept notebooks and responded to guided questions and prompts. Having gathered data, they use the data as evidence to propose explanations. Lastly, students engage in discourse to discuss and critique explanations. The science circle is an example of a strategy to engage children in discourse. You will learn more about the science circle in Chapter 4.

Designing Solutions

For engineering, the goal is to design and create solutions to problems. Making a bridge out of a limited amount of paper and masking tape that is 1 foot tall, spans 1 foot, and supports a stack of books (about 6 pounds) is a popular lesson. Sometimes I provide a budget for students and have them pay for tape and paper, thereby modeling economic limitations. As with all engineering endeavors, this turns out to be an iterative process during which the children plan, build, test, and redesign. Of course, there is a synergy between science and engineering that leads to great complementarity in the classroom. Building bridges leads to considerations of energy and forces.[10] Reading, writing, and communicating science explanations and design solutions creates a need for students to use language in context or to meaningfully employ "language for use."[11]

Engaging in Argument from Evidence

Talking about an idea forces one to think about it. Being challenged to defend an idea makes one think about it deeply and sometimes passionately. Good arguments are rich learning experiences. Sometimes I find it unfortunate that we use the term *argument* to refer to specific science discourse. Colloquially, *argue* has a negative and combative connotation. *Argument* in the context of science is not a shouting match; it is a team effort to strengthen and improve an explanation through challenges from peers working to explain the same phenomenon. It is noble to revise or reject an explanation in light of good evidence. An argument in science is not lost if our understanding deepens.

Teaching children to make claims, gather data, use data as evidence to support claims, and explain their reasoning will engage and guide them in constructing arguments from evidence.[12] Doing so immerses students in discourse that requires them not only to use written and verbal language that clearly communicates their thinking, but also to read and listen to other children's claims, evaluate them, and challenge each other's arguments, thereby providing them with multiple ways of expressing ideas.

For example, I ask students to make a claim about whether a can of Diet Coke and a can of regular Coke will sink or float. Testing reveals that the Diet Coke floats and the regular Coke sinks. The challenge is to explain why. During investigation, students gather data and use evidence to make claims. They then justify and defend their explanations to their peers.

Developing explanations and designing solutions inspires language development by increasing the demand for clarity and precision. Both native speakers and ELL students will be challenged to communicate new thoughts and ideas about science and engineering using terms and ideas that are new to them, providing opportunities for scaffolding and support to nurture language development. Language demand is familiar to anyone who has traveled as a foreign speaker in a country. Necessity to communicate clearly and accurately creates a need to find the proper words and phrases to express our thoughts.

Obtaining, Evaluating, and Communicating Information
Reading, writing, and verbally communicating ideas are not unique to science and engineering. One might argue that they are more appropriately addressed in language arts classes. Well, this may be true to some extent, but reading, writing, and talking about *science and engineering* are different than reading, writing, and talking about a novel, comic book, or newspaper. As suggested, science and engineering use precise language. Reading science and engineering requires attention to the specific meanings of words. Often terms are unfamiliar or understood differently outside science and engineering.

Obtaining information provides another point of reference for language learning. Students obtain information about science and engineering in a variety of ways through direct observation, textbooks, science stories in trade books, Internet websites, and popular articles about science. Science notebooks provide students with an opportunity to write about their observations. Technology allows for students to share their observations through video, audio, and various social media.

Young children need to be involved in describing their observations, investigations, results, and conclusions, beginning with their first science and engineering experiences.

To make a point for the importance of clarity when communicating ideas in science and engineering, a common activity is to make a jelly sandwich. (In the past, we typically made a peanut butter and jelly sandwich, but the prevalence of peanut allergies should give you pause before using peanut butter.) Be sure to precisely follow the directions given by the students. If you follow their instructions literally, they will soon realize that the outcomes are not what they intend. Another activity is to pair the students and provide one student with an illustration of different-colored shapes. Give the other student cutouts of the colored shapes. Have the students sit back-to-back. The student with the illustration must communicate the arrangement of shapes verbally, without either student looking at the other's shapes. Do this on a regular basis but change the shapes and patterns to coincide with the concepts you are teaching (i.e., wires, batteries, and bulbs for circuits).

Inquiry Skills

Recall that science is about the process of seeking explanations based on evidence. There are certain skills, frequently called *inquiry skills*, that children can develop to become better investigators.

● Inquiry Process Skills Used to Create Descriptive Models

We begin with the inquiry skills commonly associated with descriptive models:

- Observing
- Using space/time relationships
- Using numbers
- Questioning
- Classifying
- Measuring
- Communicating

Observing   I find that while teachers often ask students to make observations, rarely do we teach children how to observe. Observing means using the senses to obtain information, or data, about objects and events. Merely looking is not the same as observing. When we look at things, we are passive and wait for something to happen; when we observe, we are active participants. Casual observations spark almost every inquiry we make about our environment. Organized observations form the basis for more structured investigations. Acquiring the ability to make careful observations creates a foundation for making inferences or hypotheses that can be tested by further investigations and observations.

Sherlock Holmes continues to be a popular character in contemporary media, known for his powers of observation and clever inferences. Arthur Conan Doyle based the Holmes character on a real person, Joseph Bell, who was a Scottish surgeon during the late 19th and early 20th centuries. Are such powers of observation innate, or can they be learned? I think we all have potential to be like Sherlock Holmes. In fact, we routinely make observations, but we may not be aware of how we do so.

For example, imagine that you are assembling a jigsaw puzzle. You have a vision of the big picture given to you on the box, but you don't know how the 1,000 pieces in a pile fit together to make that picture. The first step is to identify the pieces by their properties: color, shape, and size. You might find the border pieces first because they help to define the boundaries of the puzzle. Next you look for possible relationships among the pieces. How do they fit together based on shape and color? While you do this, you continue to find new properties. Some relationships are easier to identify than others. Eventually the picture begins to fill in, and you see the final picture. The picture emerges from the unique pieces, their properties, and relationships. Peter Bergethon identifies five key questions that enable inquirers to be active observers. The parallel between these fundamental questions for observation and the puzzle example are listed in Table 2.2.[13] These

Table 2.2 Generalization of the fundamental questions for observation

Puzzle Terms	Questions for Observation
What are the pieces of the puzzle?	What are the parts of the system?
What are the properties of the pieces?	What are the properties of the parts?
What are the boundaries of the puzzle?	What is the context or background space of the system?
How do the pieces relate to each other?	What are the relationships (connections) among the parts?
What picture emerges when the pieces are put together?	What are the emergent properties (characteristics) of the system?

REALITY Check

Sample Activity: Developing Observation Strategies

To build habits of mind associated with descriptive modeling, begin each class with "Do Now" activity (a brief activity at the beginning of class that sets the tone for the class). Project pictures of familiar scenes for 1 minute and then take the pictures away. Ask students to describe what they observed. Review the descriptions in terms of the fundamental questions for observation. Project the picture again for students to see how accurately they observed. After a few classes, students expect to find a picture and immediately make their observations. As the weeks progress, exchange the familiar pictures with unfamiliar pictures and dynamic systems (microscopic images, pond life, ecosystems, molecules), and ask students to develop descriptions based on their observations. Doing so consistently over a period of time develops habits of mind associated with observation strategies for creating descriptive models as a first step to inquiry.

In addition to observing a static picture, have children use the fundamental questions for observation to describe an event or phenomenon. You might start by asking children to observe how a fish swims or a bird flies. Let the children watch real fish and birds. Show them a video of the same in slow motion. Ask them to make observations based on the fundamental questions to describe how the bird flies or the fish swims.

questions can guide our observations. It is a way to help us systematize the way we observe. The next time you are stuck on a problem, step back and ask yourself these five questions to see if you recognize any connections that may help you understand the situation better and make some connections and inferences of your own.

Using Space/Time Relationships   All objects occupy a place in space. The inquiry skill using space/time relationships involves the ability to discern and describe directions, spatial arrangements, motion and speed, symmetry, and rate of change.

Sample Activity   Many schools have square-foot tiles on the floor. Use the tiles to make a grid with an x and y axis. Roll a ball along the grid and show students how to describe the direction, speed, and even rate of change based on the path of the ball along the grid.

Using Numbers   We need numbers to manipulate measurements, order objects, and classify objects. The amount of time spent on the activities devoted to using numbers is not relegated to the school's mathematics program. Using numbers is of course central for using mathematics and computational thinking.

PRACTICAL applications

Using Inquiry Process Skills to Create a Descriptive Model of a Butterfly

Table 2.3 illustrates how the fundamental questions for observation may be used to generate a simple descriptive model of a butterfly. Note how the descriptive model facilitates other inquiry process skills, such as enumeration (number of legs) and ordination (wings attached to the middle of the butterfly). Construction of a descriptive model inevitably leads to more system-specific questions: "Why do some butterflies have brightly colored wings while others have very plainly colored wings?" "How do butterflies eat?" and so on. Children can measure the length of the butterfly or the height and width of the wings. Children may use space/time relationships, noting that the butterflies move among similar types of flowers and are most active at certain times of day. Finally, children need to communicate their models, which can be achieved through a variety of modalities such as writing, drawing, verbalizing, or simulating. Note the dependency of a good descriptive model on the implementation of inquiry process skills.

Table 2.3   Description of a butterfly—based on the fundamental questions of inquiry

Parts	Properties	Background space	Relationships	Emergent properties
• Legs	• 5 (visible), black	• (while not apparent in the photo, the system takes place at a certain temperature, humidity, and light intensity.)	• Legs and wings attached to the middle of butterfly	• Colorful
• Antennae	• 2 Thin black		• Butterfly stands on leaf	
• Head	• Round, black			
• Wings	• Black with 14 white, 15 yellow, and 6 blue spots			
• Abdomen	• Black, white dots			

Sample Activity   Encourage children to include quantitative observations in their descriptions. Growing plants can serve many learning outcomes. Look for opportunities to include numbers to support quantitative data collection: the number of days to germination, sprouting, blossoming, and seed production. Measure the number of plants, leaves, blossoms, fruits; height of stems, length and width of leaves. These numbers can be used to generate tables, charts, and graphs that will aid in pattern recognition and analysis. Nurture quantitative observations throughout your lessons to set the foundation for using mathematical and computational skills.

Classifying

Classifying is the process scientists use to impose order on collections of objects or events. Classification schemes are used in science and other disciplines to identify objects or events and to show similarities, differences, patterns, and interrelationships.

Sample Activity   Obtain a collection of plastic dinosaurs. Pictures will suffice if plastic representations are not readily handy. Tell students you would like arrange the dinosaurs for a display for family night, but that you cannot decide how to group them. Assign student groups to develop a grouping system (claim) and to explain their rationale for the groupings (reasoning based on evidence).

Measuring

Measuring is of course an extension of using numbers. Skill in measuring requires the ability to use measuring instruments properly to collect precise and accurate data. The process involves judgment about which instrument to use and how to approximate measurements to ensure that the actual measurements make sense and are not blindly accepted. Children can learn to measure length, area, volume, mass, temperature, force, and speed as they develop this process skill.

Sample Activity   Have children estimate the linear dimensions of classroom objects using centimeters, decimeters, or meters, and then use metersticks to measure the objects. Measure daily weather properties: temperature, rainfall, cloud cover, relative humidity, etc. Join students around the world using simple measurement protocols that provide scientists with valuable information. See the link at the end of the chapter to Global Learning Observations to Benefit the Environment (GLOBE) for vetted protocol data collection and sharing.

Communicating   Clear, precise communication is essential to all human endeavors and fundamental to all scientific work, which makes communicating skills valuable. Scientists communicate orally, with written words, and through the use of diagrams, maps, graphs, mathematical equations, and other visual demonstrations.

Sample Activity   Have each student make a map to a location of their choice in the schoolyard. You can set boundaries for safety. Have the children exchange maps and see whether they can find the location specified. Facilitate oral communication and language demand by simulating a launch to an international space station. Students must role-play specific responsibilities in mission control.

Inquiry Process Skills Used to Create Explanations

Explanations often begin with preliminary ideas based on observations generated using the following process skills:

- Inferring
- Hypothesizing and predicting

Inferring   *Inferring* is using logic to make assumptions from data collected. The ability to distinguish between an observation and an inference is fundamental to clear thinking. An observation is based on an experience that is obtained through the senses. An inference is an assumption based on an observation. Consider the observation that butterflies are often found on flowering plants. One might infer that butterflies use the flowers as a source of food.

Sample Activity   Take children on a mini fieldtrip to a tree on school property and have them prepare a list of observations about the ground at the base of the tree, the tree bark, and the leaves. Ask children to make inferences from their observations about the animals that may live in or near the tree (e.g., birds, insects, squirrels).

Hypothesizing and Predicting   *Hypotheses* are often confused with *predictions*. A *hypothesis* is a proposed relationship put forth to explain a phenomenon. One might hypothesize that butterflies prefer yellow flowers. The *prediction* is the basis for an experiment. A prediction based on our hypothesis would be that if butterflies are presented with yellow flowers and white flowers, then the butterflies will land on the yellow flowers.

Sample Activity   Ask your students what causes bread to mold. They might propose warm, moist air causes bread to mold. This is their hypothesis. Ask them to make a prediction to test their hypothesis (i.e., bread kept moist and warm will grow mold faster than bread that is kept dry and cool). They can design an experiment to test their prediction using baggies, bread, water, and specific temperatures. See the sample activity in the next section.

Inquiry Process Skills Used to Create an Experimental Model

Experiments test predictions. A good experiment should test one variable and keep all other conditions the same. Students often understand this in terms of a fair test. An unfair test results in confusion about what variable caused the results. (A word of caution: It is not necessary to do experiments in order to *do science*. I frequently hear preservice teachers describe science as experimentation. Experimentation is one method for testing predictions, but not all predictions can be tested by experimentation.)

Good experiments employ the following inquiry process skills:

- Predicting
- Identifying variables
  - Independent
  - Dependent
  - Controlled
- Designing experimental controls

Predicting   A *prediction* is a specific forecast of a future observation or event. Predictions are based on observations, measurements, and inferences about relationships between observed variables. A prediction that is not based on evidence is only a guess. Accurate predictions result from careful observations and precise measurements.

Sample Activity   Have children construct a questionnaire about breakfast cereal preference and gather data from all the classrooms in the school except one. Have students analyze their data and make a prediction about the outcome of the survey of the children in the last room before polling those children.

Identifying Variables   *Variables* are factors that can make a difference in an investigation. Experimental design consists of one independent variable, one dependent variable, and several controlled variables:

- **Independent variable:** The independent variable is the variable being tested. It is the variable that the experimenter manipulates or changes. For example, if one were to follow through with an experiment to test the hypothesis that butterflies prefer yellow flowers, the independent variable is the color of the flowers.
- **Dependent variable:** The dependent variable is the change that is measured. It changes in response to the independent variable. In our example, the dependent variable would be the numbers of butterflies that are attracted to yellow or white flowers.
- **Controlled variables:** For an experiment to be informative, it must measure the effects of just one variable. Therefore, the only variables that change are the independent and dependent variables. All the other factors that could change must be kept the same or controlled. Referring to the sample experiment, the same butterflies and types of flowers should be used under the same conditions, such as location, lighting, time of day, and temperature.

Sample Activity   Ask children whether bread will last longer (not become moldy) if it is kept at 4°C rather than at room temperature. Design an experiment by leaving one piece of bread in a plastic bag on a counter and one piece of bread in a plastic bag in a refrigerator at 4°C. Record the room temperature. Count the number of days until each piece of bread becomes moldy. The independent variable is temperature. The dependent variable is the time for the bread to become moldy. The controlled variables are bread from the same loaf, same size of bread pieces, same size and type of plastic bag, and the same handling procedures.

Interpreting Data   The process of interpreting data involves finding patterns and trends based on the data collected in an investigation. We are constantly interpreting data when we read weather maps, watch the news on television, and look at photographs in newspapers and magazines. Data, used to justify an explanation, becomes evidence. It helps if students have had previous experience in observing, classifying, and measuring before the process of interpreting data is addressed.

Sample Activity   Ask students to interpret the data in the graph shown of the distance from the starting point a bicyclist travels over a time period of 15 seconds.

- How far away from the starting point was the bike after 5 seconds? 10 seconds? 15 seconds?
- How fast was the bike traveling expressed as meters per second during the first 10 seconds?
- Infer what took place after 10 seconds.

Defining Operationally   When students define operationally, they define terms in the context of their own experiences. That is, they assign meaning through an experience and then associate a term with the meaning.

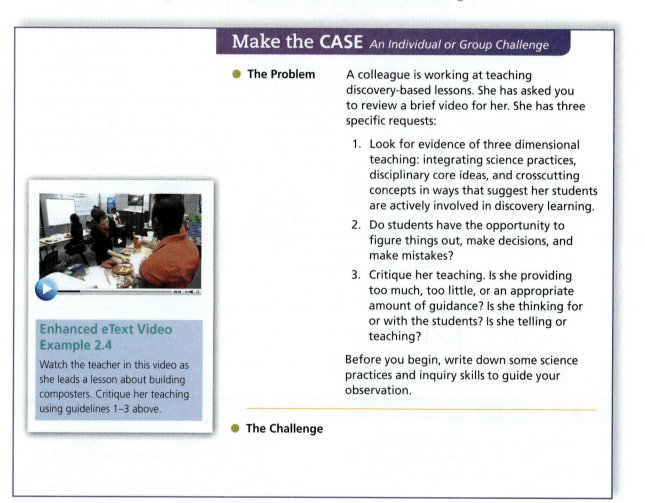

Make the CASE *An Individual or Group Challenge*

● **The Problem**   A colleague is working at teaching discovery-based lessons. She has asked you to review a brief video for her. She has three specific requests:

1. Look for evidence of three dimensional teaching: integrating science practices, disciplinary core ideas, and crosscutting concepts in ways that suggest her students are actively involved in discovery learning.

2. Do students have the opportunity to figure things out, make decisions, and make mistakes?

3. Critique her teaching. Is she providing too much, too little, or an appropriate amount of guidance? Is she thinking for or with the students? Is she telling or teaching?

Before you begin, write down some science practices and inquiry skills to guide your observation.

Enhanced eText Video Example 2.4

Watch the teacher in this video as she leads a lesson about building composters. Critique her teaching using guidelines 1–3 above.

● **The Challenge**

Summary

2.1 Create a vision for discovery learning in your classroom.

Keep in mind that students learn and teachers teach. When students discover, they make sense of the world. Their discoveries may not be new to the scientific community, but they are new and genuine discoveries for the students. Teachers are the knowledgeable others who create and guide the experiences for discovery to happen. Discovery teaching and learning are highly coordinated activities during which the teacher orchestrates experiences that facilitate discovery. Of course, there is no guarantee that students will discover what the teacher intends they learn. Therefore, discovery is not left to chance. Rather, teachers prepare learning experiences with purpose and intent that lead to a path of deeper understanding and sense-making through discovery.

Self-Check 2.1

Click to gauge your understanding of the concepts in this chapter.

2.2 Describe science practices and inquiry skills as they relate to learning science and engineering.

Science is a way of knowing based on evidence gained through inquiry. Young children need to start doing science just as young musicians need to start playing their instruments. Science practices and skills are the fabric of your science curriculum that will lead to a lifetime of discoveries for your students. Students who discover will make sense of their experiences to create explanations and design solutions. Left to their own devices, children's discovery is hit or miss. Under the guidance of an educator who is knowledgeable in both content and science practices, students will make discoveries that deepen their understanding of the natural world.

Knowing how to do science requires developing a set of skills that facilitate data collection and analysis. The skills support practices but differ from practices. Practices are accompanied by knowledge and understanding about how skills can be used to make sense of the world. Certain skills are conducive to creating descriptions, explanations, or experiments, but they all work together to help us generate knowledge and understanding.

Self-Check 2.2

Click to gauge your understanding of the concepts in this chapter.

On Your Own or in a Cooperative Group

1. The next time you are with young children, *observe* how they make sense of the world. What are their strategies for figuring out and seeking explanations?

2. Interview a child in your class. Present the child with a discrepant event: something with an unexpected outcome. Ask the child how he or she makes sense of the event, how he or she would figure it out. For example, draw an arrow on a piece of paper. Place the paper behind a drinking glass. Fill the glass with water and watch the arrow change directions.

3. Practice observing. Try being an active observer. Choose a place you want to observe more closely. For example, the next time you are in a restaurant, at a concert, in an art museum, at a sporting event, or even in your classroom, start by asking yourself the fundamental questions of observation. See what you notice that you did not notice before.

4. Some resistance to including the inquiry process skills comes from teachers who have not had much personal experience with science in college. To what extent did your college-level experience include opportunities to utilize the inquiry process skills?

REALITY check

Application Exercise:
Observation of Inquiry Process Skills

Use the chart provided to identify the use of inquiry process skills by students.

Enhanced eText Video Example 2.5

Watch the video of students investigating the responses of earthworms to stimuli.

Inquiry process skills	Frequency	Comments
Observing		
Using space/time relationships		
Using numbers		
Questioning		
Classifying		
Measuring		
Communicating		
Predicting		
Identifying variables		
Independent		
Dependent		
Controlled		
Designing experimental controls		
Inferring		

RESOURCES FOR DISCOVERY LEARNING

Internet Resources

- **Science and Engineering Practices in the NGSS:**
  http://www.nextgenscience.org/sites/default/files/Appendix%20F%20%20Science%20and%20Engineering%20Practices%20in%20the%20NGSS%20-%20FINAL%20060513.pdf

- **Discovery Education:**
  http://www.discoveryeducation.com/

- **Bozeman Science and the Next Generation Science Standards:**
  http://www.bozemanscience.com/next-generation-science-standards/

- **Christa McAuliffe Center for Integrated Science Learning:**
  http://christa.org/

- **Project BudBurst:**
  www.budburst.org/phenocam

- **Discovery Learning - Learn NC:**
  http://www.learnnc.org/lp/pages/5352

- **National Science Teachers Association:**
  http://www.nsta.org/

- **Engineering is Elementary:**
  http://www.eie.org/

Print Resources

Abrams, E., Southerland, S. A., & Silva, P. C. (2008). *Inquiry in the classroom: Realities and opportunities*. Charlotte, NC: IAP.

Ash, D., & Kluger-Bell, B. (2000). Identifying inquiry in the K-5 classroom. In *FOUNDATIONS Thoughts, Views, and Strategies for the K–5 Classroom* (vol. 2). Arlington, VA: Division of Elementary, Secondary, and Informal Education Directorate for Education and Human Resources National Science Foundation.

Bruner, J. S. (1961). The act of discovery. *Harvard Educational Review*.

Bruner, J. S. (2009). *The process of education*. Cambridge, MA: Harvard University Press.

Colburn, A. (2000). An inquiry primer. *Science Scope, 23*(6): 42–44.

Grandy, R., & Duschl, R. A. (2007). Reconsidering the character and role of inquiry in school science: Analysis of a conference. *Science & Education, 16*(2): 141–166.

Hanuscin, D. L., et al. (2008). Learning to observe and infer. *Science and Children, 45*(6): 56–57.

Koschmann, M., & Shepardson, D. (2002). A pond investigation. *Science and Children, 39*(8): 20–23.

McWilliams, S. (2003). Journey into the five senses. *Science and Children, 40*(5): 38–43.

Morrison, J. A. (2008). Individual inquiry investigations in an elementary science methods course. *Journal of Science Teacher Education, 19*(2): 117–134.

Pine, J., et al. (2008). Students' learning of inquiry in 'inquiry' curricula. *Phi Delta Kappan, 88*(4): 308–313.

Thompson, R., et al. (2007). Investigating minerals: Promoting integrated inquiry. *Science Activities, 44*(2): 56–60.

Thompson, S. L. (2007). Inquiry in the life sciences: The plant-in-a-jar as a catalyst for learning. *Science Activities, 43*(4): 27–33.

Waffler, E. (2001). Inspired inquiry. *Science and Children, 38*(4): 28–31.

Wilcox, J., Kruse, J., & Clough, M. (2015). Teaching science through inquiry: Seven common myths about this time-honored approach. *The Science Teacher, 82*(6): 62–67.

Wittrock, Cathy A., & Barrow, Lloyd H. (2000). Blow-by-blow inquiry. *Science and Children, 37*(5): 34–38.

Notes

1. Davey K. Discovery learning (Bruner). In *Learning theories*. Retrieved February 2, 2017, from https://www.learning-theories.com/discovery-learning-bruner.html
2. Bruner, J. S. (1961). The act of discovery. *Harvard Educational Review*.
3. Parenthetical text is author's addition.
4. Ibid., p. 1.
5. Ibid.
6. Schwarz, C., & Passmore, C. (2012). Preparing for NGSS: Developing and using models (webinar). Retrieved from http://bit.ly/1qw7FXV; http://bit.ly/1OBmYV7
7. NGSS@NSTA STEM starts here, http://ngss.nsta.org/Practices.aspx?id=3
8. Visit Project BudBurst, www.budburst.org/phenocam
9. You can add other variables as well such as barometric pressure and relative humidity.
10. For more information on engineering for elementary children, go to Boston Museum of Science's Engineering is Elementary site, http://www.eie.org/
11. Lee, O., Quinn, H., & Valdes, G. (2013). Science and language for English language learners in relation to Next Generation Science Standards and with implications for Common Core State Standards for English language arts and mathematics. *Educational Researcher, 42*(4): 223–233. doi:10.3102/0013189x13480524
12. McNeill, K. L., & Martin, D. M. (2011). Claims, evidence, and reasoning. *Science and Children, 48*(8): 52–56.
13. Bergethon, P. (1999). *Learning the language of patterns*. Holliston, MA: Symmetry Learning Systems.

CHAPTER 3

Planning Units and Lessons

How can I plan and manage inquiry-based, discovery-focused units and lessons?

Debbi Gerdt/Shutterstock

Learning Objectives

After completing the activities in this chapter, you should be able to:

3.1 Distinguish among curriculum, unit, and lesson planning.

3.2 Use NGSS bundles and Understanding by Design → to guide unit planning.

3.3 Design inquiry-based science lessons based on the 5E Learning Cycle and Sheltered Instruction Observation Protocol.

▶ **GETTING STARTED**

Children are beginning to gather in the schoolyard. Family and parents of the youngest children give a final hug and wave good-bye, pausing just out of sight, only to peek back around the corner for one last look at their children as they begin the first day of school. Friendly teachers greet the younger children, who make their way tentatively into the schoolyard.

The older children run without hesitation onto the playground, greeting classmates and immediately starting a spirited game of tag.

Suddenly, I am standing alone in the classroom, the walls are bare, and my plan book is empty. A wave of panic slowly begins to creep over me. In an instant, the children are somehow sitting at their desks. Twenty-four little faces look up at me with great expectations. I have nothing to offer them.

Several teachers have had similar dreams just before the start of a new school year. Although this chapter may not prevent such dreams, it will help you plan thoughtful and effective science/engineering lessons in advance so waking will be much more pleasant.

Curriculum Planning, Unit Planning, And Lesson Planning: How Are They Different?

Sometimes the terms *curriculum*, *unit*, and *lesson* are used interchangeably, but they differ—primarily in scope. Curricula are made up of a sequence of units and lessons that address a primary subject. Curricula usually include a broad view of topics to be studied and an approximate window of time in which to address the topics with the students. Units address subtopics within a curriculum, such as a unit on life cycles or the forces that shape Earth. In this chapter you will read about "bundles" suggested by the Next Generation Science Standards (NGSS). Bundles help organize instruction for units that make up a curriculum. Lessons address topics within a unit and target specific learning outcomes. Describing the four stages of the butterfly life cycle or discovering that collisions transfer energy to change the motion of objects (NGSS PS3.C) are examples of lesson topics. As you read on, you will gain a deeper understanding of each term.

● The Scope of the Science Curriculum

Imagine a magnificent sailing ship gliding across the ocean. How does each component of this scene fit into the areas of knowledge we call *science, engineering and technology*? The people on the ship, as well as the plethora of organisms in the ocean, are understood through the life sciences. The ocean, wind, and waves are indicative of the Earth/space sciences, while the energy of the wind, sun, and waves are understood through the physical sciences. Engineering, technology, and the applications of science are responsible for the ship and its systems that enable humans to harness the vast stores of energy in nature to move the ship with purpose and direction.

The scope of the curriculum refers to the range and depth of content, while the sequence of the curriculum refers to the order in which the content is addressed. The scope of science, engineering, and technology illustrated in the brief example of the ship on the ocean reminds us that science, technology, and engineering are closely integrated. Together, the elements in the ship example represent integration of the natural and human-made world along with the scope and breadth of content associated with science, engineering, and technology.

The Sequence of the Science Curriculum

Your state, district, or school will likely determine the subject matter you will teach and the broad goals and learning outcomes, commonly referred to as the curriculum. How the curriculum is realized and taught in the classroom will be determined by you, the teacher, who will determine the sequence of content. Should children learn about the food webs and then ecosystems before they learn about sunlight and plants, or should the sequence be reversed? Frequently there are several effective sequences one could use. In fact, the more we learn about science and engineering education, the more we realize that science/engineering education is best taught as an integrated whole, especially at the elementary level. Therefore, crosscutting concepts have been identified that are common across science and engineering disciplines and practices. Rather than a sequence of disconnected one-off topics, you should envision the curriculum as a logical progression of learning experiences that build upon and reinforce core ideas, science and engineering practices, and crosscutting concepts.

As a teacher, especially a new teacher, you will not be developing curriculum as much as compiling curriculum. Assuredly, someone has already taught the content you want to teach. In this age of information technology, you can and should look to curricula, lessons, and strategies shared by our colleagues. Expect to modify and adapt the lessons to fit your teaching style and the needs of your class. One of my students described the process as, "Practicing lesson larceny!"

Enhanced eText Video Example 3.1

Listen to this teacher share her perspectives. What are her thoughts on curriculum development?

Science Standards: How They Inform Scope And Sequence

The NGSS provide resources to guide scope and sequence by organizing standards for each grade in bundles. Bundles identify logical progressions of conceptual development organized around performance expectations to guide instruction. Bundles use key questions that serve as anchors for the scope and sequence of unit progression. For example, a bundle question for third-graders is, "How does the climate affect organisms?"[1] The bundle identifies connections among the disciplinary core ideas, science/engineering practices, and crosscutting concepts as well as the performance expectations that the unit supports. (For examples of bundles, visit Next Generation Science Standards website.)

The NGSS support cohesiveness across grades as well as with a grade level. Table 3.1 illustrates the disciplinary core ideas (DCI) organized by grade level. Each row represents a different DCI. The overlap among core ideas across grade levels supports learning progressions that revisit concepts at increasingly deeper levels as students grow in experience and maturity.

Table 3.1 Disciplinary Core Ideas Organized by Grade Level

DCI	Kindergarten	First	Second	Third	Fourth	Fifth
K-PS2 Motion and Stability: Forces and Interactions	√			√		√
K-PS3 Energy	√				√	√
K-ESS3 Earth and Human Activity	√			√	√	√
K-ESS2 Earth's Systems	√		√	√	√	√
K-LS1 From Molecules to Organisms: Structures and Processes	√	√		√	√	√
K-2-ETS1 Engineering Design	√	√	√	√	√	√
1-PS4 Waves and Their Applications in Technologies for Information Transfer		√			√	
1-LS3 Heredity: Inheritance and Variation of Traits		√		√		
1-ESS1 Earth's Place in the Universe		√	√		√	√
2-PS1 Matter and Its Interactions			√			√
2-LS2 Ecosystems: Interactions, Energy, and Dynamics			√	√		√
2-LS4 Biological Evolution: Unity and Diversity			√	√		

Guidelines For Planning Your Curriculum

Below are six general recommendations to guide you in the development of effective science and engineering learning experiences for your students. Each will be developed and integrated throughout the text.

1. Make lessons *relevant* and *meaningful* for your students. Have you ever had a child ask, "Why do we need to learn this?" Maybe you asked the same question of your teachers. It is a good question. Educators and learning theorists understand the power of relevance for teaching and learning. Piaget recognized that children modify existing prior knowledge to make sense of new information through assimilation and accommodation.[2] Attention to prior knowledge is one of the guiding principles supported by research on how people learn science, encouraging us to "start where the students are" when developing learning experiences.[3] We also know that the human brain attends more to meaningful stimuli.[4] Quite simply, while planning your lessons you need to understand how your students are making sense of the core ideas that you are trying to teach.

   As a general rule, organize learning experiences from the child outward. That is, select experiences that relate first to the child and then to the science content. When learning about sound, play music in class that is relevant to the students. Bring instruments to class with which your children are familiar. Use these as starting points to explore high and low pitches and investigate how pitch is related to frequency. Use science to seek explanations and technology/engineering to solve problems through applications of science. When deciding to expose children to a concept that can be considered concretely or abstractly, use the concrete approach first.

Your classroom is likely to represent a rich diversity of students. Do not assume you know their experiences, even if you grew up in the same neighborhood and attended the same school. The term diversity can apply to a broad range of backgrounds and experiences. In Appendix D for NGSS entitled "All Standards, All Students," the NGSS use the terms dominant and non-dominant in reference to student diversity. Dominant groups refer to those with social prestige and institutionalized privilege. Non-dominant groups refer to students representing groups who have been traditionally underserved by the educational system.[5] The NGSS go on to identify student diversity with the following categories:[6]

- economically disadvantaged students,
- students from major racial and ethnic groups,
- students with disabilities, and
- students with limited English proficiency.

Student diversity also includes gender, students in alternative education programs, and gifted and talented students.

Teaching is ultimately one-on-one. It is about building relationships and trust with each student. Being a student can be risky business at any age. As students, we need to deal with a degree of ignorance about new knowledge consisting of concepts, skills, terminology, and ways of knowing that are novel. Think about what it is like to be in a science classroom where the words and concepts are unfamiliar and strange. Now consider that the language and culture are also new or different from that which you are familiar. Learning takes courage.

You are probably familiar with the phrase *culturally responsive teaching*. It recognizes the importance of including students' **cultural** references in all aspects of learning (Ladson-Billings,1994). A culturally responsive classroom respects the beliefs, norms, and customs of its community as well as broadens cultural perspectives beyond the immediate community. The authors of NGSS state, "Effective teachers ask questions that elicit students' funds of knowledge related to science topics. They also use cultural artifacts and community resources in ways that are academically meaningful and culturally relevant."[7, 8]

Central to culturally responsive teaching is knowing your students and what is relevant and meaningful for then in the context of their culture, experiences, and ways of knowing.[9] Students and their communities have understandings based in culture as well as resources that teachers can use to enhance science learning. You may know these resources as "Funds of Knowledge." It is likely that you have encountered strategies to tap funds of knowledge in support of culturally responsive teaching in other courses or field experiences. Perhaps we can add to those strategies in the context of science.

The "brown bag" activity is one such strategy. It works well with upper elementary, but you might also try it with younger children. Ask students to bring an item to class that represents something they wonder about in science and/or engineering. It is helpful to provide an example about yourself. For instance, a bird feather might mean you wonder about how birds fly, or a movie ticket from Star Wars means you wonder if there is life on other planets. We don't encourage children to bring in live animals, like a pet turtle or snake, although a photo would be acceptable. Pair the students and ask them to exchange items without revealing the meaning of items to their partner. Of course, students will be tempted to blurt out the meaning of their items, but encourage them not to do so, making it a game for the other person to figure out what the items mean. Have the students write down what they think each item from their partner represents. After they have written their ideas, let them share them with their partner, who in turn will let them know whether they inferred correctly the meaning of the items. The point is for the students to get to know each other better in the context of discourse about science and engineering. Finally, ask each student to introduce their partner to the class along with the items, their initial inferences, and the true meaning they have for their partner. You will find that you can learn a lot about your students and the potential funds of knowledge they and their communities afford to the class.

Student interviews also provide opportunities to learn more about your students. Interviews can be centered around content, permitting you to better understand what your students know and how they think about a concept, while helping to understand the experiences and reasoning students use to make sense of phenomena. For example, prior to a unit about ecosystems, pre-service teachers interviewed the third grade students in their class. They gave the children a set of pictures representing biotic and abiotic components of an ecosystem. They asked the students to organize the pictures in any way that made sense to them. The pre-service teachers engaged the students in conversation about the relationships suggested and their reasoning. These conversations can reveal not only the students' understandings, but also the cultural lenses and experiences that serve as backdrops for how they make sense of the world.

The NGSS Appendix D, "All Standards, All Students," urges connections of school science to home and community. Strategies for fostering connections among school and community include the following:[10]

- Invite adult family members (and when possible, extended family members such as siblings) to participate in field trips.
- Hold science nights that feature science/engineering activities/movies/discussions and dinner.
- Partner with middle and high school science teachers to provide information and discussion sessions about relevant issues related to science in the community: water quality air, quality, safety.

One program that I have found effective for getting to know the community and better understand the funds of knowledge within the community is through a program called Dad's Read. Dad's Read was started several years ago in at an elementary school in Boston, MA consisting largely of non-dominant communities. The program was originally conceived for fathers or father figures to have a casual, fun reading time with their pre-K-2 children. It has expanded to include mothers, siblings, and extended family members as well. The evening consists of dinner and time to read from a selection of children's books all relating to a theme. Families read together, respond to prompts that encourage writing, illustration, and discussion. We also integrate a science/engineering activity. For example, students read stories about seeds and plant growth. Some complementary science activities include germinating seeds in a plastic bag, transferring and planting the seeds, talking with a beekeeper and examining dried bees to look for special structures to collect nectar and pollen. The evenings are a time for building community through sharing and discovery. The informal dinner, reading, and science activities provide windows into the culture and funds of knowledge in the community. Dad's Read is an example of home and community connections advocated by the NGSS through which parents and families become partners in science learning.[11]

2. Make lessons rigorous. Don't confuse rigor with degree of difficulty, detail, or tedium. Rigorous lessons challenge students to think in new and more accurate ways about how to make sense of big ideas about the natural or designed world. Rigorous learning experiences tap children's curiosity in ways that encourage them to make new discoveries. Rigorous lessons are cognitively demanding. They inspire and support students to progress beyond the boundaries of their current understanding. Cognitively demanding tasks challenge students to make connections and understand relationships among concepts that lead to analysis and explanation.[12] They provide opportunities for students to engage in scientific reasoning about science content or practices.[13]

   Rigor and cognitive demand bring student learning to the zone of proximal development described by Lev Vygostsky—the conceptual construction zone that straddles what learners can understand on their own and the deeper knowledge they begin to grasp only with guidance and coaching from a knowledgeable other.[14] Strive to put students in the zone.

3. Make lessons coherent by creating lessons that follow a logical progression. Today's lesson should make sense in the context of yesterday's lesson so that ideas and understandings reinforce and build upon each other. An initial lesson may introduce the idea that light is reflected off objects and enters our eyes (NGSS PS4.B). But your fourth-grade student may not grasp the idea well enough to make a connection that moonlight is actually sunlight. In fact, she may not make that connection until the fifth grade. But the foundational understanding you provide will enable her to understand deeply enough to transfer her understanding of light and reach that "aha" moment years later. Thus, coherence refers to logical progressions not only within a series of lessons, but also across grades. (Refer to the NGSS bundles and Table 3-1 to inform coherence of conceptual development.)

4. Assess, assess, assess! Stay in touch with your students' learning: Get feedback and give feedback. In other words, embed formative assessments throughout the lesson. This means providing students consistently with opportunities to express their understanding. Listen to what they say, watch what they do, read what they write, analyze what they draw. It also means providing targeted feedback along the way by talking, demonstrating, writing, and illustrating. Chapter 5 is entirely devoted to assessment.

5. Reflection and practice are key elements of learning. Thinking and reasoning about an idea or concept deepens understanding and sense-making. Children can be bombarded with new ideas each day. There is a lot going on in the school day: language arts, math, science, art, and music, not to mention all the extracurriculars and social interactions with both friends and family. It is no wonder children may forget what they did in science class the day before. Children are amazing learners, but too much information too fast can lead to cognitive overload. Providing students with opportunities to reflect on ideas and experiences leads to meaningful connections that boost retention. It helps students recognize successful personal learning strategies (refer to metacognition in Chapter 1). Reflection is nurtured when students have opportunities to express their ideas through discourse, writing, and illustrating.

6. You may have heard the joke about the person who asked how to get to symphony hall. The response being, "Practice, practice, practice." Students need to *practice* and *reason* with ideas in similar but different contexts. It is may be expedient to "cover" a topic and move on, but the learning will not be as effective or efficient without practice. For example, students learning that

forces acting on a particular object have both strength and direction (NGSS PS2.A) will need to grapple with the notion from several different perspectives over time. They might consider the forces involved when a ball rolls down a ramp and when a ball is kicked on the soccer field. Each time they recognize strength and direction of forces they will deepen and strengthen their understanding. One practice is good, but several opportunities to practice over time are even better. This can be done by revisiting a previously taught idea in other units or integrating them across disciplines. Remind students to think about forces in other contexts: When they study the water cycle consider forces that created the Grand Canyon, and read the story about Stellaluna (a baby fruit bat) and consider the forces when she is hanging by her feet.

Unit Planning

What Makes a Good Unit Plan?   When full-time teachers lack a sense of the "big picture," their students have, in effect, a substitute teacher every day of the school year. Each school day that children have learning experiences that are not part of any larger context is a day that relates neither to the past nor to the future. It is like taking a trip with no destination. A good unit plan is like a good travel plan. It clearly states your destination, how you want to get there, landmarks along the way, and when you will arrive. It provides an overview or big picture of the trip, like a trip itinerary.

Grant Wiggins and Jay McTighe developed a strategy known as Understanding by Design™ that is useful for informing and guiding unit planning.[15] The framework emphasizes the need to clarify the desired outcomes of a unit, evidence that the students are learning the desired outcomes, and finally the activities and events that will define the learning plan. Planning for the unit is similar to lesson planning. They differ in the degree of detail. The unit provides a big picture strategy, while the lesson plan will address a particular teaching session. Wiggins and McTighe describe three stages of unit development: desired outcomes, assessment evidence, and learning plan.[16]

Desired Outcomes   Desired outcomes consist of four components: established goals, understandings, essential questions, and targeted knowledge and skills.

Established goals identify goals that are meaningful and transferable for students. The goals should identify something the students can do with the knowledge learned in the unit. Performance expectations suggested in the bundles of the NGSS can inform outcomes. For example, one suggested NGSS bundle focuses on the theme of light for grade 1. The following performance expectations from that bundle can serve as outcomes for a unit:[17]

> 1-PS4-2: Make observations to construct an evidence-based account that objects in darkness can be seen only when illuminated.
>
> 1-ESS1-1: Use observations of the sun, moon, and stars to describe patterns that can be predicted.
>
> 1-ESS1-2: Make observations at different times of year to relate the amount of daylight to the time of year.

Understandings address the specific ideas that students will learn in order to attain the goal. The disciplinary core ideas associated with each performance expectation in NGSS bundles inform understandings. For example, during the course of the unit students will need to construct the following understandings:[18]

> PS4.B: Electromagnetic Radiation—Objects can be seen if light is available to illuminate them or if they give off their own light.
>
> ESS1.A: The Universe and Its Stars—Patterns of the motion of the sun, moon, and stars in the sky can be observed, described, and predicted.
>
> ESS1.B: Earth and the Solar System—Seasonal patterns of sunrise and sunset can be observed, described, and predicted.

Wiggins and McTighe also suggest that anticipated misunderstandings be identified. In this case, a common misunderstanding about light is that all objects, such as the moon, give off their own light as opposed to reflecting light.

Essential questions inspire curiosity and more questions. They do not have a singular answer, but are open to a variety of possible explanations. Again, the NGSS frame each thematic bundle with a big question. For example, "Can patterns of the sun, moon, and stars be used to make predictions of future observations?"[19] This question could be reframed to be more open by asking, "What kind of predictions can be made from patterns of sun, moon, and stars and how can we make them?"

Knowledge and skills describe what students will know and be able to do as a result of successful completion of the unit.

Continuing with our example, knowledge might be described as students *will know* that light can vary in intensity or brightness; light can be absorbed or reflected; celestial bodies, such as planets and stars, move in patterns that tend to repeat and are predictable; the Earth travels in an elliptical orbit around the sun; the sunrise and sunset grow closer and further apart regularly with the seasons.

Skills may be articulated as students *will be able to* differentiate between objects that reflect and generate light; observe and record patterns of the sun, moon, and stars; describe relationships among patterns of the sun and sunrise/sunset; predict seasonal changes based on patterns of sunrise/sunset; and describe relationships of the phases of the moon with the shapes of the moon.

Assessment Evidence   Assessment evidence refers to the observable and measurable tasks that your students will do that demonstrate learning. Assessment evidences should be authentic, meaning they relate to real-world phenomena or problems. Performance expectations can be used to inform tasks. Recall one of the performance objectives identified earlier: 1-ESS1-1: Use observations of the sun, moon, and stars to describe patterns that can be predicted. Assessment evidence related to 1-ESS1-1 could be, "Students will make nightly illustrations of the moon as it changes shape, keeping track of the date and number of days it takes for the moon to return to its starting shape." Similarly, assessment evidence related to 1-ESS1-2 might be, "Students will use length of day data to recognize patterns that lead to predictions of seasonal transitions." Assessment can also include other evidence that is not task based such as writing open responses to questions such as, "What events can you predict by looking at patterns of the moon (or sun)? How would you make those predictions?" A quiz about the properties of light could also provide evidence of student learning.

Learning Plan   Having created a vision of the unit by considering the desired outcomes and assessment evidence, you will have a clear vision of the learning goals and how you will know your students arrive at the destination. The learning plan identifies activities that will guide students on the journey. Note that a learning plan is not the same as a lesson plan. Lesson plans will be developed later to support the learning plan activities and put them in a meaningful context.

The principles of how students learn science—prior knowledge, doing science, metacognition—inform learning plans. For our example, consider activities that require students share their prior knowledge about light and the patterns of celestial bodies. Choose activities that are relevant and involve students in acts of doing science. Consider how students will reflect on and articulate their learning (metacognition), and how the activities can be accessible to all learners in your class. Ensure the activities are rigorous and coherent.

For example, components of the learning plan may be as follows:

- Use K-W (What do you **k**now and what do you **w**onder about?) to assess and identify students' prior knowledge.
- Model the sun, moon, and Earth orbits using student simulations on the school playground.

Enhanced eText Video Example 3.2

Listen to teacher Ashley Welch speak on unit planning. How does her unit plan reflect the idea of coherence?

- Create a moon phases or seasons book with illustrations and photographs each accompanied by a brief description or poem.
- Read aloud nonfictional and fictional literature about the influence of the patterns of the sun, Earth, and moon as used and interpreted by different cultures and historical periods.

Unit plans can take a variety of forms. Most importantly, unit plans provide a relevant, coherent, and rigorous vision of the content students will learn, strategies for assessing student learning progress, and a framework of strategies that will guide the learning experiences that you will create through lesson plans for your students.

Having developed a unit plan, you are now prepared to create the detailed lesson plans that will guide the direct experiences of the students. They are analogous to the detailed daily itinerary of your journey.

What Makes a Good Lesson Plan?

Plans are of little importance, but planning is essential.
—Winston Churchill

If you were to lock three teachers in a room and ask them (under pain of losing their parking spaces) to reach a consensus about the best format for a lesson plan, you would probably end up with three different approaches. The fact is, there are many approaches to lesson planning and it is difficult to know in advance which one will work best for you.

Developing a Good Lesson Plan: Six Essential Elements

The lesson plan outline discussed here includes major elements to be considered in your lesson planning. Your department or district will likely have variations that you should incorporate as well. Hopefully this discussion will help you develop effective and engaging lessons.

Although developing lesson plans can be daunting at first, the payoffs are well worth the effort. Good lesson plans result in focused, dynamic learning experiences wherein children are thoughtful and engaged. Well-thought-out lesson plans also facilitate good classroom management, which maximizes student time on learning and minimizes disorder and discipline issues. Be that as it may, you need a starting point for lesson planning. The following six key elements—enhanced with additional components suggested by veteran teachers, school administrators, and others—will serve you well. Creating a targeted learning experience is similar to writing a play with a thought-provoking engagement to set the plot, development of the plot, and a culminating scene that ties the story together. As you plan, keep in mind that plans are just that: plans. In sports, the actual game often turns out much different than the game plan. In the classroom, the actual class may not unfold exactly as you intended. However, the plan provides a framework to guide the learning experience. Without it, the class will surely flounder. As Winston Churchill said, "Plans are of little importance, but planning is essential." As I share each element, I will simultaneously provide examples of each as I build a lesson for third-graders about chemical reactions. Let's walk through a sample lesson plan together.

Element 1: Content to Be Taught: Identify What You Want Students to Learn
Although identifying the content to be taught may be an obvious first step in lesson planning, it is often taken for granted. Be very clear about what you intend to teach. If you are unclear about what you want the children to learn at the start, then your lesson will become increasingly more difficult to plan. Like any good journey, you need to know your destination to plan your route. The content to be taught answers the question, "What do I want my students to learn from this lesson?" It is the ideal answer that you like to hear when a parent asks their child, "What did you learn in science today?" Identifying the desired results of your lesson is the foundation

on which you will build the lesson procedures, objectives, and assessments. Whenever possible, strive to ensure that the content moves beyond facts to address relationships and connections among core ideas and practices.

Lessons are developed based on a unit plan. For this example, let's suppose you are teaching a unit on the structure and properties of matter. The unit plan identified two NGSS disciplinary core ideas: PS1.A "Measurements of a variety of properties can be used to identify materials" and PSB1.A, "When two or more different substances are mixed, a new substance with different properties may be formed."[20]

Next, consider what students will do in the lesson to develop an understanding of these core ideas. Some suggestions are provided by the performance expectations listed in the NGSS. Standard 5-PS1-3 suggests that students who demonstrate an understanding of the structure and properties of matter can make observations and measurements to identify materials based on their properties.[21] Simple chemical reactions involving baking soda and starch with vinegar and iodine will address this performance. The content to be taught can be summarized as follows:

Students will learn that

- Controls are tests that provide known results to compare with experimental results.
- Claims are based on evidence.
- Multiple trials are used to collect data.
- Chemical reactions result in new substances.
- Chemical reactions can be used to identify baking soda and starch.
- Starch will react with iodine to turn black and baking soda will react with vinegar (acetic acid) to form a gas.

Element 2: Identify Students' Prior Knowledge

All children have ideas about the world based on their prior knowledge and experiences.[22] Sometimes these ideas are accurate and complete, but more often they have inaccuracies and/or are incomplete. I make the distinction between preconceptions, which are incomplete, and misconceptions, which are inaccurate. (If they were complete and accurate, we would not need to teach them!). Either way, it is incumbent upon us to consider what we can reasonably learn about how our students make sense of a concept.

It is not enough to discern whether students know vocabulary associated with a concept. What one says may not reveal what he or she understands.[23] There are several ways to investigate how students make sense of a topic. For example, prior to a unit on circuits, ask children to draw a diagram of their perception for the inner workings of a flashlight. Have them label the diagram and describe how the components of the flashlight work together. Paige Keely has written many probes consisting of a multiple-choice or true-false question followed by a request for the student to create a rule or guide for making the choice (cf. probes Chapter 6).[24] Student interviews can shed light on how students make sense of phenomena and relationships. For example, ask students to organize pictures of animals, plants, water, and soil according to how they understand relationships among the elements. Ask them why they organized the pictures the way they did. Their answers will provide insights about how they make sense of relationships in ecosystems.

Preconceptions and misconceptions can present teachable moments for students. Our inclination as teachers is to offer students explanations prior to helping them construct new knowledge or simply tell them the answer. Knowledge given based on authority of teachers is less powerful than knowledge constructed by students based on evidence. Studies of misconceptions by Schneps and Sadler, who investigated enduring misconceptions such as the reason for the seasons and reflections in a mirror, suggest that misconceptions endure.[25] Even well-educated adults default to the common belief that the reason for the seasons is a function of the distance of the Earth from the sun, or that we see more of our image as we move away from a mirror. While it is easy to tell students the correct answer, it is rarely sticks unless the answer makes sense. Ultimately, it is the individual who must realize his or her mental model no longer suffices and the explanation needs to be modified (assimilation) or replaced (accommodation). Campbell et al. (2016) suggest using students' misconceptions to support student sense-making through discourse and science practices that lead students to modify and advance their understanding.[26]

You might also look to the preconception/misconception literature for insights into common misconceptions held by students about certain topics. Identifying preconceptions will become easier with experience and the longer you work with the children in your class.

For the example investigation, we will keep in mind that students often confuse chemical changes with physical changes. A chemical change results in a new substance and is irreversible. A physical change is a change in state and is reversible.

Element 3: Performance Objectives
Performance objectives provide a clear statement of the behaviors that the children will exhibit to demonstrate their learning. Performance objectives consist of three components: a *condition* for learning, an *observable performance* to indicate learning, and *criteria* to rate the level of performance.[27] A sample performance objective for a lesson about frequencies may read as follows:

[Condition] Given a guitar, [Observable Performance] students will explain in writing why two strings of the same length and tension produce different pitched sounds. [Criteria] The response will satisfy the level of proficient based on an accompanying rubric.

A performance objective for our example might read, "Given two white powders, students will distinguish each powder based on evidence produced by chemical reactions of the powders and explain their reasoning sufficiently to score 3 on the rubric provided." (We will address the rubric later.)

Element 4: Concept Development
The 5E learning cycle, developed by the Biological Science Curriculum Studies in the late 1980s, is an instructional strategy that provides a useful framework for creating inquiry-based learning experiences.[28] Based on previous learning cycles developed by Atkins and Karplus for the Science Curriculum Improvement Study (SCIS) initiated during the late 1950s, Roger Bybee and associates developed the 5E instructional model, which has been widely adopted and used for science education.[29] The following concept development elements are based on the 5E instructional strategy.

Engagement   I often hear statements that science should be fun. While I agree, I fear that fun is sometimes confused with entertaining. While science can be both, the joy of science you inspire will hopefully be the joy of discovery and sense-making. Who doesn't like to watch an egg-drop challenge, a butterfly emerge from its chrysalis, or a can crush?! Well, maybe some people, but the real fun comes from the satisfaction of designing, engineering, and testing the capsule to hold and protect the egg; wondering how a caterpillar can morph into a butterfly; and trying to explain what made the can implode can be compelling, fun, and rewarding. A good science learning experience begins with an attention-getting, thought-provoking engagement. Engagement has four criteria:

- Pique curiosity
- Probe for prior understanding
- Establish a hook question/focus
- Prepare the students for investigation

Recall that effective learning occurs when context is meaningful. In a good movie or novel, the writer engages the attention of the audience quickly. The NGSS encourage teachers to use phenomena to engage and motivate students to seek explanations or solve problems. [30]

As an elementary school teacher, you will find that the window of opportunity to capture and hold the children's attention usually closes rapidly. I find that beginning teachers tend to make the engagement more complex than it needs to be. Be creative yet simple. Pique curiosity using a mystery picture, riddle, brief movie clip, or mystery item. Search for fun facts about a topic and use the facts to create true-false questions. Choosing true or false forces students to think about a topic and invest an opinion. For example, suppose you wanted to begin a lesson about fossils (NGSS 3-LS4-1). The following true-false questions might start students wondering about fossils:

- Fossils can be from things other than animals, such as footprints or animal poop.
- Scientists usually find fossils of whole animals rather than bones.
- Scientists have found fossils of feathered dinosaurs.

Hook questions are also designed to capture students' interest. They should connect with students. McTighe and Wiggins recommend good hook questions to interest students around a new topic, to spark curiosity, questions, or debate, framed in kid language.[31] For example, "If a basketball and baseball collide at the same speed, what will happen?" This might pique curiosity about the effects of balanced and unbalanced forces on the motion of an object (3-PS2-1).

Demonstrating a discrepant event is one way to engage children. Discrepant events are counterintuitive experiences that pique curiosity and a desire to seek an explanation. They grab attention and interest because the outcome is usually the opposite of what is expected. An example of a discrepant event is given in Figure 3.2.

Figure 3.1 A science unit may have many components, but each component has a specific purpose

Component	Purpose
• Rationale	• Helps you think through the reasons for doing a unit on a particular topic
• Performance objectives	• Help you focus on the intended outcomes of the unit
• Content to be taught*	• Clearly identifies and specifies the content children are intended to learn in the unit
• Content outline (for teachers)	• Helps you review the content that will provide the foundation for the learning experience
• Daily lesson plans*	• Help you think through learning activities and their relationship to engagement, exploration, and concept explanation
• Materials list	• Helps you make certain that you have all the materials needed for science activities that occur in daily lessons
• Audiovisual materials and list	• Help you make certain that you have such tools as computer hardware and software, videotapes, and other required equipment
• Accommodations	• Identifies accommodations and modifications necessary to provide the least restrictive and most accessible learning experience for the children in your class
• Assessment strategies	• Help you consider informal and formal ways to assess the extent to which children have achieved cognitive, psychomotor, and affective growth during the unit

*Considered in greater detail later in this chapter

I decided to use the following engagement for the example lesson: Prior to class, prepare two unlabeled containers: one filled with baking soda and the other with cornstarch. Announce a plan to make cookies as part of a lesson about chemical reactions, but that you've forgotten which container contains baking soda and which container has cornstarch. The challenge is to determine which of the powders is baking soda and which is cornstarch. To probe for prior knowledge, ask for suggestions. The teacher's role is to listen, value student input, and keep the conversation going. (Suggestions for leading discussions will be addressed in Chapter 4.) Do not offer any explanations at this point. Record ideas and questions and make mental notes of possible misconceptions.

Prepare the students to investigate by asking, "How can we distinguish between two powders that look identical?" Suggest that substances that look identical can be distinguished by how they react with chemicals. Of course, you should not reveal how each powder reacts. State the hook question clearly: "How can chemical reactions be used to identify cornstarch and baking soda?" Remember to keep the question simple. If students struggle to understand the question, they are unlikely to discover an explanation.

Enhanced eText Video Example 3.3

Watch this video showing exploration in action. What is the teacher's role during exploration? What characterizes what students are doing during the exploration?

Exploration   Exploration provides an opportunity for children to encounter and reflect on new content. Whatever strategy one chooses for the exploration, it should enable the children to be active participants in the learning experience, such as describing changes, manipulating variables, or designing solutions. Exploration is the concept development stage during which a variety of teaching methods can be employed. Children should be collecting and/or using evidence during the exploration. The teacher's role is to orchestrate an encounter with the new information and guide and scaffold students to use evidence either firsthand or secondhand. Firsthand evidence is evidence collected by the students. Secondhand evidence is evidence collected by another source and used by the students. For example, secondhand weather data from other parts of the world collected via the Internet can be compared with the local firsthand data weather data collected by children.

For the sample lesson, we will organize students in collaborative groups of three and use the following prompt questions as a guide to plan the investigation together:

- We have iodine, vinegar, and the unknown powders. What else do we need to identify how vinegar and iodine react with these powders? [ans. Samples we know to be baking soda and cornstarch as controls.]
- How will we make this a fair investigation? [ans. Keep all variables constant, except the reagent.]
- Should we test the powders more than once? If so, how many times? [ans. Multiple trials are preferred. Each group will represent one trial.]

Provide the students with instructions (Figure 3.3) and a means to collect and organize data that facilitates analysis by suggesting patterns (Figure 3.4A).

Explanation   The explanation follows the natural flow of the inquiry lesson. It is tempting to simply tell the children the answer. But it is best to provide an opportunity for the children to communicate their explanation first, so they can make logical connections on their own. Begin the explanation by inviting students

Figure 3.2   Discrepant Event: The Ping-Pong Ball and the Funnel

Present the children with a Ping-Pong ball and funnel. Put the Ping-Pong ball in the funnel with the stem pointing down. Ask the children to predict what will happen to the Ping-Pong ball when someone blows through the stem into the funnel. Most often children will predict that the ball will be pushed out of the funnel. In fact, the ball will remain in the funnel, no matter how hard you blow.

Explanation: Air exiting the stem into the funnel must travel faster to get around the ball. The fast-moving air around the bottom of the ball creates an area of lower pressure relative to the slower air movement above the ball, resulting in a higher pressure area above the ball, which pushes the ball down and keeps it in the funnel. This is an example of the Bernoulli effect.

Figure 3.3   Instructions for the Mystery Powder Experiment: Cornstarch Control

Part A: Cornstarch Control

1. **Use the electronic balance to measure 2.0 g (grams) of cornstarch on a piece of aluminum foil.**

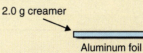

2. **Add 5 drops of solution 1 (iodine) to the creamer.**

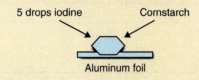

3. **Record your observations in the powder data sheet.**

Part B: Baking Soda Control

4. **Use the electronic balance to measure 2.0 g (grams) of baking soda on a piece of aluminum foil.**

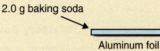

5. **Add 5 drops of vinegar to the baking soda.**

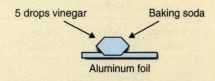

6. **Record your observations in the powder data sheet.**

NOW TEST THE SAMPLE USING THE PROCEDURES IN PARTS A & B TO DETERMINE THE IDENTITY OF THE SAMPLE.

to respond to the hook or essential question. Let them tell you what they learned from the exploration. Their explanations may be expressed in writing, through diagrams, illustrations, orally, kinesthetically, by story-telling, multimedia use, or with a simulation. Reinforce correct answers and challenge inaccuracies through questioning and concept attainment methods. It is at this point, *after* students have had an opportunity to express their discoveries and new understandings, that the teacher can provide her explanation. Direct teaching after the students have expressed their own explanations is meaningful because they will have a genuine investment in the question and consequently will be more eager and receptive to the explanation.

For the mystery powder investigation, restate the hook question: "How can chemical reactions be used to identify cornstarch and baking soda?" Ask the students to enter the results from their investigations on a class data table. See Figure 3.4B. Note how the hook question grounds the lesson by providing coherence, consistency, and purpose.

After the data are posted, ask each child to write the identities of the two mystery powders and explain in writing his or her reasoning, based on the evidence collected. Ask students whether the reactions were chemical or physical and

Figure 3.4A   Individual Student Data Collection Table

Powder	Observations	
	5 drops of iodine	*5 drops of vinegar*
Cornstarch		
Baking soda		
Mystery powder 1		
Mystery powder 2		

Figure 3.4B   Class Data Table

Mystery Powder Data Sheet

Teams	Class Observations							
	5 drops of iodine				*5 drops of vinegar*			
	Cornstarch	Baking Soda	Mystery Powder 1	Mystery Powder 2	Cornstarch	Baking Soda	Mystery Powder 1	Mystery Powder 2
1								
2								
3								

Figure 3.5   Sample Data Table with Reactions

Teams	Sample Data Table							
	5 drops of iodine				5 drops of vinegar			
	Cornstarch	Baking Soda	Mystery Powder 1	Mystery Powder 2	Cornstarch	Baking Soda	Mystery Powder 1	Mystery Powder 2
1	Black	Brown	Brown	Black	No change	Bubbles	Bubbles	No change

to explain their reasoning. Either read their responses or have the students report them. Note their responses, reinforce correct responses, and challenge incorrect responses. Finally, summarize the elements of an appropriate response. You can include the following elements, based on the sample data table in Figure 3.5.

- Powder 2 is cornstarch because it turned black when mixed with iodine and displayed no evidence of a reaction when mixed with vinegar. It reacted the same as the control samples of cornstarch.
- Powder 1 is baking soda because it formed a gas when mixed with vinegar and turned light brown when mixed with iodine. It reacted the same as the control samples of baking soda.
- Substances that are the same have the same chemical properties.
- The reactions appeared to be chemical reactions because new substances appear to be formed and cannot be reversed.

Element 5: Evaluation (Assessment)   "Did the children learn what you thought you taught?" Assessment is an opportunity to rejoice in the fruits of your labor. After all, you worked hard to design and execute a learning experience for the children in your class that is thought provoking and productive. Don't let the fact that evaluation is listed as the fifth element misguide you. Evaluation is ongoing throughout the lesson. It is both formal and informal. Suffice it to say that you will, whether you want to or not, be constantly receiving feedback from your students. Listening to, planning for, and acting on feedback is at the center of assessment. There are several strategies for assessments that probe children's understandings and abilities at a variety of levels: nominal, descriptive, and explanatory. Chapter 5 will address assessment strategies in more depth.

In our example, we ask students to analyze the results of a similar set of data. Note that the assessment addresses the same concepts in a slightly different context to assess the ability to transfer knowledge. It goes something like this:

Your friend in a school across town is working on a similar mystery powder investigation that includes chalk as a mystery powder. She asks you to help her solve the mystery based on the evidence she collected. Reactions of the mystery powder with the test chemical are given in Figure 3.6. Write your response (claim) to your friend and explain your reasoning.

Figure 3.6   Reactions of the Mystery Powders

Powder	Observations		
	5 drops of iodine	*5 drops of vinegar*	*5 drops of phenolphthalein*
Cornstarch	*Turns black*	*No change*	*No change*
Baking soda	*Turns brown*	*Bubbles*	*No change*
Chalk	*Turns brown*	*No change*	*Slight pink*
Mystery powder	*Turns brown*	*No change*	*Slight pink*

You can use a rubric to assess and grade the response (Figure 3.7).

Element 6: Accommodations   Accommodations referred to in this section are meant to be understood in the more general sense as methods to provide all children with the least restrictive environment for learning experiences.

Accommodations should benefit all children. Equity means all children are provided with the resources they need to be successful. Universal Design for Learning (UDL) is one teaching strategy that addresses equity in learning for all children. It is based on the following:

- Multiple means of representation to give learners various ways of acquiring information and knowledge
- Multiple means of expression to provide learners alternatives for demonstrating what they know
- Multiple means of engagement to tap into learners' interests, challenge them appropriately, and motivate them to learn

Science presents intense language demand for all students and particularly for students who are English Language Learners. You may be familiar with the

Figure 3.7   Rubric for the Mystery Powder Assessment

3 points	2 points	1 point
Claims that the mystery powder is chalk.	Claims that the mystery powder is cornstarch or baking soda.	No claim is made.
Clearly states evidence that the mystery powder and chalk turned brown with iodine, turned slight pink with phenolphthalein, and exhibited no change with vinegar.	States evidence, some of which is either inaccurate or incomplete.	No evidence or incorrect evidence is provided.
Provides reasoning that suggests the mystery powder is chalk because it exhibited the same chemical reactions with iodine and phenolphthalein as did chalk. Substances that have the same chemical properties are probably the same.	Reasoning does not include evidence presented and/or no suggestion that the same substances have the same properties.	No reasoning is attempted or reasoning is incorrect.

Sheltered Instruction Observation Protocol (SIOP), a model for instruction that helps English language learners develop language proficiency as they build content knowledge. Vanashri Nargund-Joshi and Nazan Bautista suggest a synergy between the SIOP and 5E instructional frameworks that are informative for science education. They suggest that science content and language learning can happen simultaneously.[32] SIOP blended with the 5E strategy can provide a workable template for integrating inquiry-based science, culturally responsive pedagogies, and language literacy for English language learners.

SIOP consists of eight components: Preparation, Building Background, Comprehensible Input, Strategies, Practice/Application, Lesson Delivery, and Review/Assessment. The following lesson describes how the integration the 5E instructional strategy and SIOP may be used together in a lesson to support English Language Learners. For each component of the 5E Instructional Strategy, an overview of a connection to SIOP is provided followed by an example of the SIOP and 5E integration.

Third Grade: Weather NGSS 3-ESS2-1

SIOP: Lesson Preparation

Overview

During lesson preparation content and language objectives are identified. The objectives are orally reviewed with the students. Teachers provide supportive supplementary materials to address multiple modes of interaction. Building background entails connecting new concepts with students' personal experiences and prior knowledge.

Example

Content objective: Students will describe different types of clouds
Language objectives:

- Students will verbally describe the different types of clouds
- Students will turn and talk with peers and share examples of clouds
- Students will watch a cartoon about naming clouds
- Students will read a book about naming clouds

Key vocabulary

clear, cloudy, cumulus, stratus, cirrus (nimbostratus and other cloud types using altitude prefixes *alto* and *cirro* can be used at the teacher's discretion.)

Engage

SIOP: Building Background

Overview

In addition to eliciting prior knowledge and making connections with students' backgrounds, the engagement is explicit with respect to vocabulary.

Engagement: Clearly state the objectives and post them in the classroom. Ask students to write three words that describe clouds. Permit them to write in their L1 language. Turn and talk to share descriptions of the clouds. Post the student cloud descriptions around the room. Take time to review the descriptions in a class discussion. Summarize the meanings of terms in English and create a word wall with new vocabulary.

Essential Question: How can we describe clouds?

Explore

SIOP: Comprehensible Input, Strategies, and Interaction

Overview

Ideas must be presented so students can understand. Talk tools such as restatement and paraphrase (chapter 4) are useful. Body language may be exaggerated for emphasis. Scaffolding strategies using demonstrations, realia, pictures, simulations, and role-plays support comprehension. Other strategies include methods that promote reflection and sharing. Ask questions that challenge students to make connections or think critically. Although students may have difficulty articulating their ideas, they can still think deeply and critically, which will create language demand that inspires language growth. Interactions with the learning community, peers and teachers, that demand expression of ideas contributes to the development of language and science talk. Create opportunities that demand discourse beyond naming to include claims, evidence, and reasoning.

Example

Read aloud the book *Clouds* by Anne Rockwell. Stop and discuss after each cloud type is encountered. Ask students to draw a picture of the cloud and to write descriptive words below. For example, cumulus clouds might be described as puffy. Use prompts that help students connect to their prior knowledge. For example, "Cumulus clouds look like . . . " Post the pictures with cloud names and descriptions on a word wall.

   After the story is read, use the cloud identification key provided by GLOBE to practice cloud identification to practice cloud identification.[33]

Explain

SIOP: Interactions, Review

Overview

Students express their understanding first, followed by the teacher feedback on correct or incorrect responses.

Example

Clouds identification is ripe for discussion because clouds often fall into more than one possible category. It is not uncommon for children to make different claims about the name of the same cloud, requiring them to defend their claim using new vocabulary to make their point. As students identify clouds in the exploration above, engage them in discussion with each other. Encourage them to turn and talk in small group to vote on a type of cloud. Permit ELL's of similar levels to work together. If low proficiency, let them express their ideas first in their native language and work together to write or verbally express their consensus in English. Your role as teacher during the explanation remains the same, with an emphasis on restating and summarizing to clarify and reinforce the content and language objectives.

Elaboration

SIOP: Practice/Application

Overview

All students benefit from practice and applications of new concepts, vocabulary, and ideas.

Example

Use the GlOBE[34] cloud observation protocols to make daily observations of cloud types. The protocol requires students to work in teams of four to identify clouds in each cardinal direction (north, south, east, west) and reach consensus on the types of clouds (as well as percent cloud coverage). This exercise also demands the use of language to reach consensus.

Evaluate

SIOP: Assessment

Overview

Evaluation and assessment should be ongoing throughout the lesson with frequent checks for progress and comprehension. Ensure multiple means of expression consistent with UDL.

Example

Include prompts during the lesson. Periodically check to see that students are using terms correctly and articulating understandings. For example: Prompt – Can you tell me why you think that is a cumulus cloud?

● Sample Lesson Plan Templates

Following is a lesson plan template that reflects the elements listed in this chapter's discussion.

Lesson Plan Template

Prerequisite Knowledge	Specifies relevant prior/knowledge and skills that students are expected to have in order to successfully complete the lesson
NEW CONTENT TO BE LEARNED (CTBT)	• States in detail the specific new content to be taught in this lesson • Explicitly names the system • Identifies system elements, properties of elements, and relationships among the elements • States key terms and definitions • States science practices
ANTICIPATED Pre/ Mis-conceptions	Common grade level misconceptions associated with the CTBT
RATIONALE	• Provides a justification for why the content taught is meaningful for students to learn • Quotes at least one core concept from Mass Science and Technology/Engineering Standards Draft (Dec. 2013) and/or The Next Generation Science Standards

GOALS	• Provide a general statement of the desired learning outcomes based on the content to be taught
	• Should begin with, "Students will understand . . . "
HOOK (anchor) QUESTION(S)	• Thought-provoking and intellectually engaging
	• Requires explanation and justification; cannot be effectively answered by recall alone
	• Raises additional questions and inspires further investigation
PERFORMANCE OBJECTIVES (PO)	• Statement of the observable behavior that you expect each student to do that demonstrates understanding of the content to be taught
	• Each PO must include a condition, performance, and measurable criterion
	• Open response questions must have an associated rubric that is included in the appendices
MATERIALS/ PROVISIONS	State the types and quantities of materials you will need for the lesson

OPENING/ENGAGEMENT Time: (typically about 5–10 min)
• Piques student interest
• Establishes the essential question(s)
• Provides an opportunity for students to express their knowledge of the topic

Procedures

TRANSITION
Provides purpose and meaning for doing the exploration (follows from essential question(s))

EXPLORATION Time: (usually takes majority of the lesson. The exploration could be 20 minutes or extend over several weeks of data collection)
• Actively involves students in the process of encountering essential elements, properties, and relationships identified in the content to be taught
• Provides an opportunity for students to be active participants in acquiring data/evidence
• Requires students to record data/evidence in a manner that reveals trends and patterns that support CTBT
• Indicates at least two or more modes of encounter with new content (i.e., direct manipulation of variables, simulation, video, graphics)

Procedures

TRANSITION
Provides purpose and meaning for doing the explanation (follows from essential question(s))

EXPLANATION Time: (varies depending on the depth and extent of exploration. Usually about 10–15 min. of a 60-min class)

- Begins with a restatement of the essential question(s)
- Provides a method for students (collectively or individually) to make claims and state evidence for claims in response to the EQ (gallery walk, report outs, take a stand, etc.)
- Includes a class discussion of claims and evidence that challenges misunderstanding and reinforces accurate understanding (science circle)
- Includes an explanation by the teacher that summarizes and deepens student understanding of content to be taught

Procedures

EXIT TICKET (5 min.)

A brief formative assessment that informs student understanding of the CTBT (probe, prompt and rubric, thought stem, etc.)

● Aids to Planning

Using Textbooks as Resources Your science classroom will be filled with imperfect resources: computers with Internet access that may lock up just as your children reach the best part of your research assignment, stacks of outdated science videotapes and no VCR (remember those?!), and bookshelves of textbooks that seem far too dull for your active children. You can spend a great deal of time wishing that you had better resources, but doing so will make no difference at all.

Over the years, science textbooks have been enlarged accordingly to accommodate growing knowledge in the field, "making it challenging for teachers to explore any topic in depth or to decide how to prioritize what should be taught— 'coverage' has marginalized exploration and discovery."[35] The vision of science/ engineering education inspired by the NGSS relies less on reading textbooks and answering end-of-chapter questions and more on students reading multiple sources from relevant magazines, journals, and web resources.[36]

Although modern textbooks have definite weaknesses, they also contain some resources that you, a discovery-oriented teacher, can make good use of—if you are creative. They contain science content written at particular grade levels and provide many hands-on science activities. In addition, they usually come with a teacher's guide that includes enrichment ideas.

The activities in a textbook series, of course, reflect a particular scope and sequence of science content. If you have the freedom and the desire to create your own science curriculum, the textbook can still be quite useful. By omitting some of the structure present in the textbook's directions to the children, you can modify the activities so that they place more emphasis on science practices and discovery learning.

Textbooks are typically divided into a number of units, or groups of chapters. If you look over the units and the teacher's guide that accompanies a textbook, you will find many helpful teaching ideas. You will also find that many of the suggestions can be applied to learning units that you devise on your own. Many teacher's guides for textbooks provide bulletin board ideas, suggestions for fieldtrips, lists of audiovisual materials, lists of children's books, and other helpful information that you can use to enrich your learning units.

Textbooks can provide you and your children a general structure for science content and experiences. Keep in mind, however, that the extent to which textbooks lead to discovery learning will, in the final analysis, depend on you.

Science Kits   You are likely to teach at a school that uses any one of several prepared science curriculum kits consisting of a series of modules comprised of equipment and materials with supportive student worksheets and teacher's guides. Science kits often provide background for teachers, inquiry-based activities, assessments, Internet resources, and ideas for integration across disciplines.

Integration of the kits into your science class requires proper professional development and support from people who have used the kits in their classroom. It takes an initial investment of time and energy to become familiar with a kit's layout and approach. Kits, like textbooks, are not designed (or should not be designed) to be teacher-proof. Rather, they provide a framework that a good teacher will modify to fit his or her teaching style and students' needs.

- **Keep It Simple.** If it is your first time using a kit, begin with one module, preferably one on a topic with which you feel comfortable and that you enjoy. Once you get a feel for the teaching progression and layout of the module, other modules will be easier to implement.

- **Familiarize Yourself with the Kit.** Spend some time unpacking the kit and reading through the manual to be sure the materials are sufficient and the progression of inquiry makes sense. Jones identifies material management and time management among the common challenges that teachers using kits encounter.[37] Therefore, familiarize yourself with the activities on your own prior to using them in class. Often kits go unused because some of the consumable materials are missing; therefore, check and restock the kits after each use. Most consumables can be located and replenished easily (i.e., cotton balls, rice, tongue depressors). Most science kits have web resources that include comprehensive teacher guides and videos that inform preparation, content knowledge, and instruction.

- **Use the Kit as a Guide.** Teaching science inquiry can be challenging if you are not comfortable with the science content or with the student-centered and sometimes chaotic dynamic of discovery learning. Science kits can be a welcome guide to keep you anchored the first time you teach a unit. Research suggests that science kits, by providing focus and structure, help teachers overcome the initial apprehension of teaching inquiry.[38]

- **Modify the Kit to Fit Your Needs.** You don't have to do everything in the kit. Use the elements of the kit that suit your purpose without compromising the integrity and intellectual honesty of the lesson. As you become more familiar with the kit and its options, you will find yourself adapting it to fit your needs.

- **Do It! Use the Science Kit QuickCheck.** Science kits can provide a foundation for rich learning experiences. Good kits can introduce you to new teaching strategies as well as provide the basis for dynamic learning experiences for your students. Use the Kit QuickCheck (Figure 3.8) to assess science kits.

Figure 3.8 Kit QuickCheck

Science Kit QuickCheck

1. **Content**

   _____ What science topics does the kit address?

   _____ Is the content appropriate for the grade level?

   _____ Does the content address the NSES or the local standards?

   _____ Is the content accurate and up to date?

   _____ Is there a content background for teachers?

   _____ Is it clear and informative?

2. **Process**

   _____ Does the recommended teaching strategy include engagement and exploration activities?

   _____ Do the activities connect meaningfully with the science content?

   _____ Do the activities support inquiry?

   _____ Is there evidence that students will use science process skills to create descriptive, explanatory, or experimental models?

   _____ Are both formative and summative assessment strategies included?

   _____ Are the student guides clear?

   _____ Does the kit reflect principles of universal design for learning (see Chapter 9), providing multiple means of engagement, representation, and expression?

   _____ Are there enrichment activities?

   _____ Are there suggestions for interdisciplinary connections (e.g., to math and language arts)?

   _____ Is safety addressed? Are Material Data Safety Sheets provided as needed?

3. **Materials**

   _____ Are the materials and equipment complete?

   _____ Is the equipment in good working order?

   _____ Are consumables inexpensive and easy to replenish?

REALITY check

Go to the NGSS example bundle for fourth-graders. (It is good practice for you to navigate the NGSS website on your own to find the bundle.) Use the bundle to plan a unit using the Understanding by Design™ framework. Use the six elements of lesson planning to develop one lesson for the unit.

Summary

3.1 Distinguish among curriculum, unit, and lesson planning

Remember Relevance, Rigor, Coherence, Assess, Reflect, and Practice. The success of an inquiry-based, discovery-focused classroom depends on your abilities to plan learning experiences for your students. The science curriculum for children typically consists of a number of learning units. Unit plans are long-term plans for science experiences that focus on particular topics. Daily lesson plans are single components of unit plans. This chapter suggests six elements in the lesson planning process and offers an example of each in the context of a complete lesson plan. Of course, there are other lesson plan formats, but this will serve as a framework from which to begin the planning process. Hopefully, you will use this framework to create your own approach to planning lessons.

Self-Check 3.1
Click to gauge your understanding of the concepts in this chapter.

3.2 Use NGSS bundles and Understanding by Design → to guide unit planning

A good unit plan is like a good travel plan. It clearly states your destination, how you want to get there, landmarks along the way, and when you will arrive.

Organizing a unit can be daunting without a framework. NGSS bundles are useful resources for planning science units. Wiggins and McTighe developed a strategy known as Understanding by Design → that provides such a framework to help you organize the unit. Time spent creating your vision for the unit by planning the desired outcomes, assessment evidence, and learning plan (not to be confused with a lesson plan) is time well spent contributing to coherence and efficiency for lesson planning and teaching.

Self-Check 3.2
Click to gauge your understanding of the concepts in this chapter.

3.3 Design inquiry-based science lessons based on six elements

You will be responsible for planning and executing science learning experiences. Most teachers do not create learning experiences from scratch; rather we compile lessons based on a variety of resources and customize them for our students. This chapter suggested six elements in a lesson plan and utilized the 5E instructional strategy. As your own teaching evolves, you will develop your own style of lesson planning that retains the intent of these essential elements. Language demands of science learning can help ELL students develop language proficiency when Sheltered Instruction Observation Protocol (SIOP) is used with the 5E Learning Cycle to assist all students, but especially ELL's to meet the language demands of science.

Self-Check 3.3
Click to gauge your understanding of the concepts in this chapter.

Resources

Science texts, whether hard copy or online, may be used less frequently but still have some value as resources for planning and sequencing. Science kits are frequently used in elementary schools to provide a one-stop resource for science teaching. Every science teaching resource must be customized for the unique learning environment of teacher and students.

On Your Own or in a Cooperative Learning Group

1. Follow the example given in this chapter and design your own science lesson for the grade and topic of your choice. Use the six elements in concert with the NGSS to develop your lesson.

2. Choose a presentation medium (PowerPoint, Prezi, etc.) and prepare a persuasive argument intended for an audience of school committee members and parents to provide students with engaging opportunities to experience how science and engineering are actually done.

3. Choose a curriculum topic and outline a unit using the Understanding by Design™ framework. Use the NGSS to inform your outline.

4. Role-play a job interview between a school principal and a teaching candidate for either a self-contained classroom or a departmentalized school. During the interview, the "principal" should ask about the following:

   a. The teacher's awareness of the NGSS
   b. The science content and experiences appropriate for children at a given grade
   c. The planning style the prospective teacher would use

DISCOVERY LEARNING

Internet Resources

- **BSCS 5E Instructional Model:**
  https://bscs.org/bscs-5e-instructional-model

- **Exemplars: Standards-Based Assessment and Instruction:**
  http://www.exemplars.com/education-materials/science-k-8

- **The Inquiry Project:**
  https://inquiryproject.terc.edu/index.html

- **Discovery Education:**
  http://www.discoveryeducation.com/

- **RTI Action Network: A Program of the National Center for Learning Disabilities:**
  http://www.rtinetwork.org/learn/what/whatisrti

- **WGBH Educational Resources:**
  http://www.wgbh.org/learn/resources.cfm

- **NOVA Education:**
  http://www.pbs.org/wgbh/nova/education/

- **Phenomena for NGSS:**
  https://www.ngssphenomena.com/

Print Resources

Ansberry, K. R., & Morgan, E. (2005). *Picture perfect science lessons: Using children's books to guide inquiry.* Arlington, VA: NSTA Press.

Avraamidou, L., et al. (2005). Giving priority to evidence in science teaching: A first-year elementary teacher's specialized practices and knowledge. *Journal of Research in Science Teaching, 42*(9): 965–986.

Campbell, T., Schwarz, C., & Windschitl, M. (2016). What we call misconceptions may be necessary stepping-stones toward making sense of the world. *The Science Teacher, 83*(3). doi:10.2505/4/tst16_083_03_69

Dorsey, C., Eberle, F., Farrin, L., Keeley, P., & Tugel, J. (2008). *Uncovering student ideas in science. Another 25 formative assessment probes.* Arlington, VA: NSTA Press.

Jones, M. T., et al. (2007). Implementing inquiry kit curriculum: Obstacles, adaptations, and practical knowledge development in two middle school science teachers. *Science*. DOI 10.1002/sce.20197

Molledo, M. (2001). The resourceful teacher. *Science Scope, 24*(6): 46–48.

Mooney, N. J., & Mausbach, A. T. (2008). *Align the design: A blueprint for school improvement*. Alexandria, VA: Association for Supervision and Curriculum Development.

Morrison, J. A., et al. (2008). Using science trade books to support inquiry in the elementary classroom. *Childhood Education, 84*(4): 204–208.

National Research Council. (2005). *How students learn: Science in the classroom*. In M. S. Donovan & J. D. Bransford (Eds.), Committee on *How People Learn*, A Targeted Report for Teachers. Division of Behavioral and Social Sciences and Education. Washington, DC: National Academies Press.

Reeve, Stephen L. (2002). Beyond the textbook. *Science Scope, 25*(6): 4–6.

Sutton, K. K. (2000). Curriculum compacting. *Science Scope, 24*(4): 22–27.

Wiggins, G. P., & McTighe, J. (2008). *Understanding by design*. Alexandria, VA: Association for Supervision and Curriculum Development.

Notes

1. NGSS Bundle Examples (2016) Retrieved from http://nextgenscience.org/sites/default/files/3rd%20 Grade%20Thematic%20Summary%20and%20Flowchart.pdf
2. McLeod, S. A. (2015). Jean Piaget. Retrieved from www.simplypsychology.org/piaget.html
3. Donovan, M. S., & Bransford, J. D. (2005). *How students learn: History, mathematics, and science in the classroom*. Washington, DC: National Academic Press.
4. Zull, J. E. (2002). *The art of changing the brain enriching teaching by exploring the biology of learning*. Sterling, VA: Stylus Pub.
5. NGSS Lead States. 2013. *Next Generation Science Standards: For States, by States*. Washington D.C.: National Academies Press
6. Ibid. Appendix D, p. 2
7. Ibid. p. 7
8. Wlodkowski, R. J., & Ginsberg, M. B. (1995). A Framework for Culturally Responsive Teaching. *Educational Leadership,53*(1), 17-21.
9. Strachan, Samantha. "The Science Standards and Students of Color." *The Science Teacher* 084.04 (2017): n. pag. Web.
10. NGSS Appendix D (2013) https://www.nextgenscience.org/sites/default/files/Appendix%20D%20 Diversity%20and%20Equity%20-%204.9.13.pdf
11. NGSS Lead States. 2013. Appendix D, p. 9
12. Smith, M. S., & Stein, M. K. (1998). Selecting and creating mathematical tasks: From research to practice. *Mathematics Teaching in the Middle School, 3*: 344–350.
13. Tekkumru-Kisa, M., et al. (2015). A framework for analyzing cognitive demand and content-practices integration: Task analysis guide in science. *Journal of Research in Science Teaching, 52*(5): 659–685.
14. Vygotskij, L. S. (1978). Interaction between learning and development. In *Mind in society:The development of higher psychological processes* (pp. 79–91). Cambridge, MA:Harvard University Press.
15. Wiggins, G. P., & McTighe, J. (2008). *Understanding by design*. Alexandria, VA: Association for Supervision and Curriculum Development.
16. Ibid.
17. http://www.nextgenscience.org/sites/default/files/1st%20Grade%20Thematic%20Summary%20 and%20Flowchart.pdf
18. http://www.nextgenscience.org/sites/default/files/1st%20Grade%20Thematic%20Model%20 Bundle%201.pdf
19. Ibid.
20. Achieve, Inc. on behalf of the 26 states and partners that collaborated on the NGSS. Next Generation Science Standards (Topic Arrangements for the Next Generation Science Standards p. 28). Copyright 2013.
21. Ibid.
22. Vygotskij.

23. Duckworth, E. R. (1987). Having wonderful ideas. In *"The having of wonderful ideas" & otheres says on teaching & learning*. New York, NY: Teachers College Press.

24. Dorsey, C., Eberle, F., Farrin, L., Keeley, P., & Tugel, J. (2008). *Uncovering student ideas in science. Another 25 formative assessment probes*. Arlington, VA: NSTA Press.

25. Crouse, L., Schneps, M. H, & Sadler, P. M. (2003). *A private universe; Minds of our own*. Cambridge, MA: Harvard-Smithsonian Center for Astrophysics.

26. Campbell, T., Schwarz, C., & Windschitl, M. (2016). What we call misconceptions may be necessary stepping-stones toward making sense of the world. *The Science Teacher, 83*(03). doi:10.2505/4/ tst16_083_03_69

27. Robert F. Mager. (1997). *Preparing instructional objectives: A critical tool in the development of effective instruction*. Atlanta, GA: The Center for Effective Performance.

28. Engagement, Exploration, and Explanation based on the 5E Instructional Model in Bybee, R., Taylor, J. A., Gardner, A., Van Scotter, P., Carlson, J., Westbrook, A., & Landes, N. (2006). *The BSCS 5E instructional model: Origins and effectiveness*. Colorado Springs, CO: BSCS.

29. Atkin, J. M., & Karplus, R. (1962). Discovery or invention? *The Science Teacher, 29*(5), 45–51.

30. Using Phenomena in NGSS-Designed Lessons and Units (2016) https://www.nextgenscience.org/sites/ default/files/Using%20Phenomena%20in%20NGSS.pdf

31. McTigh & Wiggins Essential questions Copyright © 2013 by ASCD

32. Nargund-Joshi, Vanashri, and Nazan Bautista. "Which Comes First—Language or Content?" *The Science Teacher* 083.04 (2016): n. pag. Web.

33. Cloud Identification Key https://zebrazapps.com/embed/#/e7ac1eeb4717444183a36606035ecfd7

34. Global Learning Observations to Benefit the Environment (GLOBE) globe.gov

35. Wilson, S. M., Schweingruber, H. A., & Nielsen, N. (2015). *Science teachers' learning: Enhancing opportunities, creating supportive contexts*. Washington, DC: The National Academies Press, p. 30.

36. Ibid.

37. Jones, M.T., et al. (2007). Implementing inquiry kit curriculum: Obstacles, adaptations, and practical knowledge development in two middle school science teachers. *Science Education, 91*(3): 492–513.

38. Ibid, p. 509.

CHAPTER 4

Creating Environments for Discovery

How can I effectively create an inviting science discovery space, encourage science talk, and foster cooperative learning in my science classroom?

Rawpixel.com/Shutterstock

Learning Objectives

After completing the activities in this chapter, you should be able to:

4.1 Explain how an effective classroom layout piques curiosity, invites inquiry, and inspires students to discover.

4.2 Describe how to lead discussions using effective science talk.

4.3 Explain how to plan for a cooperative learning group in which all members are interdependent.

▶ **GETTING STARTED**

My greatest challenge as a teacher is to refrain from telling my students far more than they want to know. This problem seems to be a highly contagious ailment that can be transmitted from professor to student. I have reached this conclusion because I find that teachers in grades K through 8 tell their students too much— usually more than the children really want to be told or need to know. A favorite story of mine concerns a first-grade child who asked a teacher to explain nuclear fusion. The teacher replied, "Why don't you ask your mother? She is a nuclear physicist." The child replied, "I don't want to know *that* much about it."

Perhaps it is just human nature to tell people more than they really want to know. In my case, it happens when I get excited about the content I am sharing; I want everyone to get the information quickly. When I work in science classrooms, I try to restrain from talking so much because I know that I will enjoy watching children discover something special on their own, and I know that will happen only if I talk less. That smile or screech of excitement from a child who makes a discovery is powerful medicine that stops my wagging tongue. A colleague of mine reminded me that if I find myself talking more than my students, there is something wrong.

How can we do more real science with children? Perhaps the first step is to talk less and to use more creative strategies that help children learn on their own—with our guidance, to be sure, but not with so much guidance that the smiles and screeches are lost.

I'm not going to provide an elaborate treatise on maintaining appropriate classroom behavior. The fact is, I have seen more teachers produce discipline problems than I have seen children cause them. If you are able to maintain appropriate behavior when you teach social studies, reading, math, or any other subject, you will be able to do so when you teach science. If you have problems with classroom control, science activities will neither solve your problems nor make them worse. Even so, you can take some steps that will help things go more smoothly for everyone. Appropriate classroom behavior is not hard to achieve; it just requires creating an atmosphere of discovery that students *want* to experience.

Creating a Dynamic and Inviting Science Workspace

When I walk into some classrooms, I can sense the atmosphere of excitement around science. You may have been in one of these classrooms. The walls are lined with colorful posters and student work chronicling class investigations. Discovery stations are nestled in the corners of the room, looking somewhat cluttered with wires, lightbulbs, stringed instruments, and terrariums. Students are intent yet smiling as they try to figure out how to light bulbs with one battery and wire, design a stringed instrument with the lowest pitch, and explain how millipedes walk. A chart of daily temperature, precipitation, and wind readings borders pictures of plants from the school garden and records of their growth. Posted on the bulletin board is the question of the week: "Why do I get a shock when I touch a doorknob on a cold, dry day?" It sure looks like science is happening in this classroom.

Discovery Stations

My father used to say that he was going to the workbench to tinker. Sometimes the best learning occurs when we tinker with ideas. Discovery stations are well-prepared in-class learning centers that offer children many opportunities to make their own discoveries. To be well prepared, such a center must provide a wide range of materials that encourage hands-on, discovery-based learning, ranging from print and audiovisual resources to art supplies and games. In addition, the learning center must be located where children have ready access to it yet can also be somewhat removed from the larger classroom setting while doing independent activities. Provide challenge questions at the discovery station: "Try to get the box [provide a small box with a mass of about 10 grams] from the floor to the desktop using the least amount of effort. Use a spring scale to measure effort." (You could also use an elastic band and measure the amount of stretch as a function of effort.) Provide an array of ramps, pulleys, small carts, and other assorted materials. Also provide an organizer for collecting data.

Adding Some Life to the Classroom

Set up an aquarium. Better yet, have your students set up an aquarium. Find out what types of critters they want and what the critters need in order to live (habitat). Take a fieldtrip to an aquarium. Write aquarists and ask them questions. Once the aquarium is established, use it as a source of learning. Set up a data center where students alternate taking responsibility for collecting daily temperature readings. Record the time of day and positions of critters. (Create an x-, y-, z-axis by putting rulers on the horizontal bases and vertical corners of the aquarium for the students to record where the fish, crabs, and snails tend to congregate.) Add strips of pH paper to record simple pH readings. Children may not understand what pH is, but at least they will learn some of the properties of pH and encounter the idea of pH, which will prepare them for deeper understanding of pH at a later date. Keep feeding charts that document when, how much, and by whom food was given. Be creative. Think of other ways for students to record quantitative and qualitative data. Graph the data and post it in the room. Add to graphs weekly, giving each student the task of graphing a week's data. Before you know it, you will have several months' worth of data that suggest trends and patterns. Try the same approach with an outdoor garden.

Adding aquariums is not the only way to add life to a room. Try terrariums. **Bottle Biology** provides wonderful ideas for student-generated, inexpensive habitats. Include insects (yes, the hissing cockroach is a favorite), frogs, lizards, and even snakes. Perhaps try mammals such as mice, hamsters, or gerbils. Of course, these animals bring responsibilities, which can also provide many learning opportunities for your children. Before acquiring any of these animals, take time to learn how to care for them responsibly. Be sensitive to allergies, especially to animals, that students in your class may have.

Don't forget plants! Include several representatives of different phyla if you can: mosses, flowering plants (monocots, dicots), ferns, and so on.

Remember to Consider Other Senses

Consider all the senses. Don't forget the use of sound in your classroom. There is little doubt that there will be noise in your classroom, but look for opportunities to fill the room with sounds that inspire . . . sounds of the ocean, a jungle, a woodland, animal noises, among others that inspire curiosity and questions. The Internet is a great source for finding bird calls and other sounds of nature. Make your own recordings. I have yet to be in an area—urban, suburban, or rural—where the morning is not rich with bird calls. Ask students to use their listening skills to identify the locations and sources of sounds. They will be different at the seashore than in a mountain meadow. Challenge students to make their own mystery recordings and bring them to class.

Distributing Materials

The expression herding cats comes to mind when I think of 20 children trying to acquire a magnet from a tote tray containing 10 of them.

In order to distribute materials effectively, you need to devise techniques that are appropriate for the setting. In some settings, for example, two or three children can distribute materials to all the groups. Another technique is to have one child from each group come forward to acquire needed materials. Regardless of the procedure you employ, try to avoid having all the children get what they need simultaneously. Another hint with regard to provisioning materials: If you want the students' attention, do not distribute the manipulatives first. It is difficult to compete with a beaker full of termites or goop in the middle of a table full of third-graders and expect them to pay attention to you. It will work better if you show and demonstrate the items first and then distribute them to the students. Also, collect items or make them visible but not touchable during discussion time.

Providing Work Areas

"Stop bugging me." "It's my turn." "Gimme that, or I'm gonna . . . "

These are rather common classroom requests (threats) among children involved in science activities. One way to diminish this type of problem is to give your learning groups adequate work space. This may be difficult if you have a small room, but you should try anyway. Movable bookcases, room dividers, and similar objects should be pressed into service to give groups of children semiprivate work areas. Because science activities provide ample opportunities for social interaction among group members, there is little need for groups to interact with one another during exploration.

The most important element of a science workspace is a flat surface. If you have the opportunity to select furniture for your classroom, choose tables and chairs rather than conventional desks. The typical classroom desk for children is designed for writing, not for doing science activities. If your classroom has desks with slanted tops, you will need to acquire tables, build your own tables, or use the floor as the place for science activities. Some teachers find that the inflexibility presented by traditional desks can be overcome by placing tables along the periphery of the room. Students can then carry out their science activities on the tables and use their desks during other instructional activities. And remember that outdoors can be a wonderful classroom.

Providing Clear Directions

"I didn't know what I was supposed to do with the ice cubes, so I put them down her back."

Children (and adults) seem to get into trouble when they don't understand what they are supposed to be doing. So it should come as no surprise that problems arise in the classroom when children don't understand what your expectations are. If you learn to announce your expectations clearly and simply, you will find that misbehaviors decrease.

If the science activity the children are going to do requires procedures or materials they are unfamiliar with, you will need to model the use of the materials or procedures (except, of course, when the objective of the activity is the discovery of how to use them). Children who do not know how to read a meterstick will use it as a baseball bat or sword rather than as a device for making linear measurements. By taking a few minutes to teach children how to use materials and equipment properly, you can make the process of discovery more pleasant—for you and for them.

● Creating Routines

Elementary school is full of transitions. Students move from one activity and subject to another several times throughout the course of a day. (This is something we do not ask of most professionals but somehow deem appropriate for our children!) Routines are helpful for signaling these transitions. One routine I like to use is the observation challenge.

Observation Challenge   Although mentioned in Chapter 2, it bears repeating that good observation skills are essential for good science. As mentioned previously, there is a difference between observing and looking. But such skills are not acquired during one lesson. Like any other good skill, practice is required. You can provide your students with practice throughout the year by presenting regular observation challenges. I usually do these at the beginning of science class. You can also use them in the morning, when children arrive, or after recess, as they are getting settled. Begin with a familiar scenario, either live or simulated through media, and either static or active. Ask students to describe the scene using an observation strategy such as systems analysis: identifying the elements [pieces], the properties of the elements, the context or background space, and the connections among the elements. As the year progresses and students' skills improve, provide less familiar subjects for observation. You can use a caterpillar if you are beginning a unit on life cycles or a rotting log during a unit on diversity. Or take the children to a rock outcropping in the schoolyard to introduce a module on weathering and erosion. Develop a routine with students so their observation skills become honed and a habit of mind. Occasionally I use examples of change blindness based on research by Ronald Resnick to exercise students' observation skills.[1] Two almost identical pictures flash rapidly. The observer needs to find the differences between the pictures. The technique is not unlike that used by Clyde Tombaugh to discover Pluto (now considered a dwarf planet). He used a blind comparator that rapidly changed the photographs of identical regions of space taken at different times. A difference in the positions or brightness of bodies in space might indicate a planet. This is what Tombaugh noticed when he discovered Pluto. See if your students can spot the differences between the flashing pictures.

Another common routine is the "Do Now." The "Do Now" is a brief activity usually at the beginning of class that the students can do independently. Usually the "Do Now" initiates student thinking about the topic for the day or reviews ideas from recent lessons. For example, as students enter the room there might be a black baseball cap and a white baseball cap on a table in the front of the room with the instructions, "Choose the hat that you think would keep you coolest on a hot sunny day. Imagine you had to defend your choice to a friend. Write the reasons for your choice ." This might precede an investigation of reflection and absorption.

"Do Nows" should become a regular routine so that students begin the "Do Now" as soon as they enter class without the need for instruction from the teacher. This not only initiates student work, but also gives you time to greet students and attend to last minute details as students settle into class.

Demonstrations "Do it again!" This exclamation should bring joy to your heart after you do a science demonstration for children. These three little words send a clear message that you have made contact with a child's mind. Regular demonstrations can establish an atmosphere of expectation. You can use demonstrations to reinforce important ideas, introduce new challenges, or address a particular misunderstanding that has emerged during the unit. If you are lucky, students will begin to make suggestions for demonstrations or offer their own.

Presenting a Good Science Demonstration In recent years, I have observed fewer and fewer demonstrations in elementary science classrooms. It seems that a long-overdue emphasis on having children do activities has taken an important job away from the teacher: showing children phenomena they cannot efficiently, effectively, or safely investigate for themselves. Because it has enormous potential for focusing attention on a given phenomenon, the science demonstration can be an important tool for promoting inquiry in children. A demonstration can raise many questions for children, which can then be addressed in greater detail via individual science activities.

Of course, demonstrations in the classroom can be misused. They should never replace children's involvement in science activities, and they should not be used solely to reproduce phenomena that children have already read about. Instead, demonstrations should be used to intensify children's curiosity about a unit to be studied, to clarify the confusion that may result from attaining contrary results by children who have carried out identical science activities, and to tie together various types of learning at the end of a unit. Be sure to consider safety precautions and maintain a safety zone for students if using hot liquids or potentially hazardous materials.

Make the demonstration interactive. Although you may be manipulating equipment and materials, actively involve the children in the thought process of the demonstration. Ask them to make predictions, to seek explanations, and to make suggestions about how you might proceed with the demonstration. Let the students do the thinking and you the execution of their ideas. Interactive demonstrations provide a great opportunity for you to model thinking.

Do It! Use the Demonstration QuickCheck The chapters in the Appendix of this text include elementary school demonstrations for the life, physical, and Earth/space sciences. Bear in mind that you can transform virtually any science activity into a demonstration. Be sure students can participate visually by arranging students around the demonstration so they can see or use of a document camera or similar device. You can attach your phone or tablet to a projector if no document camera is available. Live video is particularly helpful for making small items visible to the whole class such as intervals on a thermometer or hairs (setae) on a bee's body.

A number of considerations must be made to present an effective demonstration. Use the Demonstration QuickCheck in Figure 4.1 to assess the effectiveness of the science demonstrations that you or others do. Check off (✓) each item that applies.

Figure 4.1 Use this checklist to evaluate a science demonstration for children that you observe or lead

Demonstration QuickCheck

_____ 1. The teacher began the demonstration promptly; the children didn't have to wait an excessive amount of time while the teacher got prepared.

_____ 2. The demonstration was essentially simple and straightforward, not elaborate and complex.

_____ 3. All the children in the class could observe the demonstration.

_____ 4. It seemed as if the teacher had pretested the demonstration; there was no evidence that this was the first time it had been tried—for example, missing equipment, confusion in the sequence of steps.

_____ 5. The teacher was able to create a bit of drama by presenting purposely puzzling situations or outcomes that were unexpected to the children.

_____ 6. The demonstration did not endanger the health or safety of the children.

_____ 7. The demonstration seemed to fit the topic under study.

_____ 8. The demonstration was appropriately introduced, carried out, and concluded.

_____ 9. The children had an opportunity to ask questions, make statements, and give reactions.

_____10. The demonstration provided a significant learning experience for the children.

Encouraging Science Talk

The scientist is not a person who gives the right answers, he's one who asks the right questions.

—Claude Levi-Strauss[2]

● Questioning Strategies

Every now and then, I visit a classroom that makes me feel like I've entered a time machine and have been transported back to the days of the Spanish Inquisition. At those times, I feel like I'm an observer in an interrogation room—not a classroom. Questions, questions, and more questions!

Asking children a reasonable number of purposeful questions can be a helpful strategy. But too often, I hear rapid-fire questions that simply require recall and not much actual thought. In fact, sometimes children don't even have a chance to think about the possible answers before the next question is put forth. In Chapter 2 we addressed the types of questions children ask. Now we consider the questions teachers ask.

Improving the Questions You Ask   Educational researchers have long been concerned about the quantity and quality of teacher questions. As a teacher, you have found or will soon find that it takes self-discipline to ask questions that actually stimulate thought and move children along the road to inquiry-based, discovery-focused learning.

Fortunately, you can take some practical steps to ensure that the time you spend probing what children actually know will be well spent. To begin, gather data about what you presently do in terms of questioning. You can do this by videorecording or audiorecording lessons or parts of lessons you teach to children or to peers. Then classify the types of questions you ask. One system for classifying questions has as its foundation the six cognitive levels—knowledge, comprehension, application, analysis, synthesis, and evaluation.

After carefully studying these six cognitive levels, Orlich and others proposed three simple categories for classifying questions: convergent, divergent, and evaluative.[3] *Convergent questions* get children to think in ways that focus on basic knowledge or comprehension. They usually have discrete answers. For example, "How many legs does an insect have?" and "How is a mineral different than a rock?" are convergent questions. *Divergent questions* get children to think about a number of alternative answers. For example, "What are some ways you could use less energy?" and "What are some ways animals change their behavior to survive in the winter?" are divergent questions. *Evaluative questions* get students to offer a judgment based on some criteria. For example, "What type of design do you think would be safest for your playground?" and "What type of simple machine would you choose for lifting a heavy box onto the auditorium stage?" are evaluative questions.

Enhanced eText Video Example 4.1

Watch and listen as teacher Nicole Bay employs questioning strategies to teach about sound. How does she use questions to guide student thinking and discovery?

Sometimes we spend so much time preparing questions that we forget to listen to answers. This is most apparent when I watch new teachers lead a science class for the first time. A child will express a wonderful insight in response to a question. But because it is not the answer the teacher sought, the teacher barely acknowledges the student's response and moves on to the next question. Before reading further, watch Video Example 4.1 and listen as a teacher employs questioning strategies to teach about sound.

Do It! Use the Questioning QuickCheck To create an inquiry-based, discovery-focused classroom, a balance must be reached among the types of questions you ask. Using the Questioning QuickCheck in Figure 4.2 will help you start that process.

Wait-Time/Think-Time Strategies

Have you ever heard of *wait-time*, or *think-time?* Unfortunately, teachers' questioning behavior tends to follow a certain pattern known as the Initiate-Response-Evaluate (IRE) model of questioning: We ask a question, receive a response from a child, and then *immediately* evaluate the response and move on to the next question. IRE is more effective for inspiring recall than higher order thinking. When IRE is used, the generally too-short gap between our question and the child's answer is known as wait-time, or think-time. Experts tell us that the wait-time is usually between 0.7 and 1.4 seconds long, if that.[4] It is too brief for the children to actually think deeply about one question before hearing its answer or yet another question. Increasing wait-time can increase students' number and length of responses.[5]

Figure 4.2 Use this form to count types of questions used during a live or recorded teaching episode

Questioning QuickCheck

Date of episode _____   Start time _____   End time _____

Observe

1. *Convergent questions* get children to think in ways that focus on basic knowledge or comprehension.
   Tally of questions asked:

2. *Divergent questions* get children to think about a number of alternative answers.
   Tally of questions asked:

3. *Evaluative questions* get students to offer a judgment based on some criteria.
   Tally of questions asked:

Evaluate

1. How long did you observe, listen to, or watch the teaching episode? _____

2. How many of each type of question were asked?
   Convergent _____
   Divergent _____
   Evaluative _____

3. What was the total number of questions asked? _____

Allowing More Time   Allowing a very short wait-time/think-time turns your classroom into a gameshow of sorts, in which you are trying to determine how quickly the students think rather than how deeply they think. By increasing wait-time/think-time, you can produce some very positive results. In particular, by allowing more time between questions, you can change a traditional classroom into a richer environment for inquiry-based, discovery-focused learning.

Researchers Tobin and Capie, in building on the previous work of Mary Bud Rowe, found that increasing wait-time beyond 3 seconds improved the quality and frequency of responses by students.[6]

Think-Pair-Share   Make a real attempt to slow the pace of questioning in your classroom. Use a think-pair-share strategy. This is particularly helpful for evaluation-type questions that require deep thinking. Instruct students not to answer immediately. Rather, give them about 5 minutes to write their ideas individually. After individual reflection, pair students and have them share their responses with each other. Let students modify their original answers or reach a consensus response with their partner. Then you can ask students to share their answers with you and the rest of the class. Turn and Talk is a variation strategy without the initial individual reflection.

Do It! Use the Wait-Time/Think-Time QuickCheck   The Wait-Time/Think-Time QuickCheck in Figure 4.3 lists a variety of strategies you can use in the classroom to improve your own wait-time/think-time. Check off (✓) the strategies as you try them and make note of which ones seem especially effective by using an asterisk (*).

Figure 4.3 Use the strategies in this checklist to slow the pace of questioning

Wait-Time/Think-Time QuickCheck

1. *To improve wait-time/think-time:*

_____ Prompt the children to think about the answer before answering.

_____ Mentally count off five seconds after you ask a question.

_____ As you wait, look around the room to observe any signs of confusion about the question.

_____ If the child's answer is appropriate, praise him or her and then count off another five seconds mentally before asking another question.

2. *If the children don't respond:*

_____ Ask the children if they would like you to ask the question in a different way.

_____ Repeat the question with some modifications.

_____ If possible, represent the question graphically on a chalkboard, whiteboard, or transparency.

_____ Try to ask a simpler form of the question.

_____ Ask if anyone in the class can rephrase the question for you.

_____ Ask if part of the question is too difficult, and modify it accordingly.

_____ Use the think-pair-share technique. After the children have reflected individually, ask them to share their ideas with their neighbor and then report to the class.

3. *If the children do respond appropriately:*

_____ Liberally praise the responding child or children.

_____ Ask the child to elaborate on his or her answer.

4. *If the children offer a partial response:*

_____ Focus on the adequacy of the answer and capitalize on it (for instance, by asking "Can anyone add to Jamie's answer?")

_____ Ask the child to elaborate on his or her answer.

5. *If no one is answering a question:*

_____ Use a think-pair-share strategy to inspire thoughtful responses.

● Fostering Active Listening Strategies for Your Students

"For the third time, you draw the food chain arrows so the arrowheads point to the living things that receive the energy. Why do I keep seeing people draw the arrows from the killer whale to the seal? Was anyone listening when we talked about the food chain?"

It's very frustrating to realize that your students are not listening to you, their classmates, or even visiting speakers as intently as you might wish. To help them improve this skill during science time, focus on the idea of *active listening*, which is the conscious effort to focus one's attention on what people are saying as they are saying it. This is an important life skill that children need to master—and *you* may need a little work on it yourself! (I am relatively easily distracted, since I find everything around me quite interesting, so I need to work on active listening, also!)

Increasing Active Listening   You can take some practical steps to increase active listening among students in your classroom:

1. **Restructure the physical setting to minimize distractions.** A classroom in which children are involved in hands-on activities will not be as quiet as a library. As you speak, there will be the bubbling sounds of the fish tank, the background noise of shifting chairs and desks, and so on. The first step in providing an environment in which active listening can occur is to compensate for background noise. Do this by having the children speak louder when asking or answering questions, by moving classroom furniture so that everyone can see the speaker, and by having the children look directly at and speak directly to the group or person they are addressing. While it may seem formal, asking students to stand when they answer provides a physical attention cue for both speaker and listeners and also conveys a sentiment of import and respect for student contributions.

2. **Have children listen for key science words.** One way to keep students' attention on the speaker is to listen for words such as *up*, *down*, *under*, and *above* that signal what is to follow. You will need to teach the children to use such terms as *observe*, *classify*, *graph*, *measure*, and *predict* and then reinforce the use of these words through your praise. On a regular basis after a child has spoken or you have spoken, ask a question such as "Did you hear any key words when Emilio told us about last night's storm?" By teaching the children to listen for key words and what follows them, you and they will hear more of what is actually being said.

3. **Have children create questions for the speaker.** Challenge them to become such good listeners that you and they will be able to ask the speaker a question that uses some of his or her own words and ideas. For example, if Nadine is reporting the results of her group's work on rock classification to the full class, ask the class at the end of the report if they have any questions for Nadine or her group. By doing this, you will help the children realize that they should be so attentive to the speaker that they can later ask good questions about what was said.

4. **Practice summarizing what the speaker has said.** When children speak or ask questions, encourage them to listen so attentively that they can restate in summary form what was said. Model this by occasionally restating or rephrasing a child's question in a shorter form and then checking with him or her to see if you have captured the point or question.

Do It! Use the Active Listening QuickCheck   You can apply these four guidelines to a real classroom setting by using the Active Listening QuickCheck in Figure 4.4. It provides some very specific steps you can take to increase active listening. Check off (✓) each strategy as you try it.

● Science Talk and the Science Circle

You know that the unit on sound is going well if students are arguing with each other about whether one could hear a guitar on the moon and you find it difficult to get a word in the discussion. This suggests that the students are engaged and thinking about the science they are learning. There are several benefits of science talk. Talking about science helps reveal student prior knowledge or misconceptions. It also challenges students to reflect about their reasoning, articulate it coherently, and listen to the thoughts of other students. Talking about ideas, sharing

Enhanced eText Video Example 4.2

Prior to reading this section, listen to and watch Ashley Welch and her students discuss what science talk means and how to facilitate it.

Figure 4.4 Use this checklist to apply specific strategies for improving the quality of listening in the science classroom

Active Listening QuickCheck

_____ 1. Move the classroom furniture as needed so everyone can see the speaker.

_____ 2. Remind the children to look directly at and speak directly to the speaker.

_____ 3. Encourage children who are asking or answering questions to speak loudly enough for everyone to hear.

_____ 4. Remind the children to listen for signal words that the speaker uses, such as *up, down, under,* and *above.*

_____ 5. Remind the children to listen for key science words that the speaker uses, such as *observe, classify, measure,* and *predict.*

_____ 6. Challenge the children to come up with questions for the speaker that use some of his or her own words and ideas.

_____ 7. Model how to summarize what a speaker has said by restating or rephrasing what the children say.

_____ 8. Have the children practice summarizing or restating what the speaker has said.

discoveries, asking questions, and arguing scientifically (as opposed to yelling at one another) in a class or small group setting inspires students to clarify thoughts, question ideas, and develop new explanations.

Stimulating discussion is not easy. It requires planning thoughtful and engaging learning experiences that provide opportunities and resources to investigate and deepen understanding. Here are four talk moves suggested by Chapin, O'Connor, and Anderson that you can apply to your science talk with students:[7]

1. **Recap:** Summarize what was just said to clarify ambiguous or incomplete ideas.

2. **Redirect:** Ask questions to redirect or clarify children's thinking.

3. **Revoice:** If a student says something that is not clear to you or you think is not clear to other students, rephrase it and ask whether that is what he or she meant.

4. **Restate:** Ask another student to restate what another student just said and then check with the student who uttered it originally to see if it is an accurate restatement.

Encourage students to express their ideas by valuing what they say. Prompt them to elaborate on a statement: "So it looks like the bridge is about to collapse. What do you observe that suggests the bridge is about to collapse?" Ask whether they agree with another student's statement or reasoning: "Do you agree that the deck of the bridge is showing signs of both compression and tension?" Or ask students to comment on differing views: "Latoya seems to think that compression is the only sign of force on the bridge, but Tyrone seems to be suggesting something different. What do you think, Jonathan?" See Table 4.1.

Table 4.1 Summary of Talk Tools[8]

Goals	Talk Tools	Prompts
Help individual students to **share their reasoning** so that it **can be heard** and **understood**.	• *Wait time* • *Stop and jot (1–2 minutes)* • *Turn and talk (1–2 minutes)* (also known as Think-Pair-Share, Consider & Commit, etc.) • *Then . . . ask the question again.* • *Revoicing*	• *Can you say more about that?* • *Could you say that again?* • *Could you give us an example?* • *So let me see if I understand what you're saying. Are you saying . . . ?*
Help students to **orient to others** and **listen** to what others say.	Rephrasing/Repeating	**Can anyone rephrase or repeat that?**
Help students to work on **deepening their own reasoning**.	Press for Reasoning	**Why do you think that?** • *What's your evidence?* • *Can you explain your reasoning to us?* • *How did you figure that out?* • *What led you to that?*
Help students to **work with the reasoning of other students**.	Rephrasing/Repeating	**Can anyone rephrase or repeat that?** **What do other people think about that?** • *Who agrees or disagrees and why?* • *Who wants to add on to that?* • *Does anyone have a different view?* • *What do you think about that?*

Enhanced eText Video Example 4.3

Watch the video of teacher–student discourse during a science circle. Use the talk tools summary to identify the talk moves the teacher uses during the discussion.

Using the Science Circle to Promote Accountable Science Talk   Using a science circle is one method for stimulating science discussion. It creates a physical atmosphere where students are expected to talk about science. Central to science talk is accountable talk. Accountable talk is talk based on evidence and reasoning from evidence.

Arranging students in a circle facilitates talk among students rather than a series of individual conversations with the teacher.[9] I find science circles most helpful for engaging students in talk about the evidence that led to their discoveries, but science circles can also be used to introduce new topics and to probe for students' prior knowledge and preconceptions about a subject. You might begin the discussion with a provocative question. For example, after students have grown plants from seeds, you might ask where the mass that makes up the plant comes from, stating, "Where does the seed get all the matter to become a giant tree? Where does all the stuff come from?" Although they may have been growing plants from seeds for the past month, and even studied the basic concept of photosynthesis, few may realize that most of the mass of plants comes from carbon in the air. When discussing results, it is important for students to have their notebooks and data handy to facilitate reasoning from evidence.

Use these suggestions to guide discussion and encourage student–student interactions. Keep in mind that you are a facilitator, not unlike an expert interviewer, who identifies clear goals for the interview, listens carefully to responses, and responds to input by using talk moves that inspire the interviewees to reveal more about their understanding.

Encouraging Collaboration

Enhanced eText Video Example 4.4

Watch kindergarten teacher Sheri Geitner invite and guide children to work together in collaborative, cooperative groups.

Scientists usually do not work in isolation. Scientists work together and depend on one another. In fact, the scientific process relies on sharing and challenging ideas. Therefore, young scientists need to be exposed to cooperative learning. But just because students are sitting at the same table or working on the same problem in a group does not mean it is productive work. One promising approach to improving the quality of group work is the use of *cooperative learning groups*, which consist of children who are, in fact, working *together* on a project. That is to say, they are supportive of one another and accountable for both their individual learning and the learning of every other person in their group.

Creating and Using Cooperative Learning Groups   Cooperative learning groups have very special characteristics that distinguish them from traditional classroom learning groups.

In fact, these characteristics of cooperative learning groups emerge from three fundamental elements, or strategies, of cooperative learning. If you can incorporate these strategies into your work with children before, during, and even after group work, you will increase the chances for successful group work. Here is a brief discussion of each:

- **Teach for positive interdependence.** Help all members of each group understand that their success depends on the extent to which they agree on goals, objectives, and the roles each member is expected to carry out. They also need to agree in advance on an acceptable way to share available resources and information.
- **Teach for individual accountability.** Help all members of each group understand that they are accountable not only for their own learning and behavior but also for helping other group members learn and work productively.
- **Teach interpersonal and small group skills.** If you expect children to work together and display appropriate group process skills, you will have to take the time to teach them those skills. Before group work, discuss group process skills such as sharing leadership, praising good work done by others, and active listening. Also, teach children how to analyze how well the group process works and how to improve it.

Do It! Use the Cooperative Learning QuickCheck   The Cooperative Learning QuickCheck in Figure 4.5 is a tool that you can use as you guide group work in your own classroom or as you observe another teacher's groups at work. Simply observe a group or a number of groups at work for a period of time, and use the points in the QuickCheck to help you determine the true nature of the group work that's occurring. You should check off (✓) each cooperative learning behavior that you observe. Think about whether you are observing a cooperative or a traditional learning group. Then use the results of your observation for guidance when you create and oversee future cooperative group work during science time.

Figure 4.5 Use this checklist to determine the level of cooperative learning among students working together

Cooperative Learning QuickCheck

1. Does the group display *positive interdependence?*

   _____ Group members agree on general goals.

   _____ Group members agree on specific objectives.

   _____ Group members agree on roles for each group member.

   _____ Group members are sharing resources.

   _____ Group members each have a role that is integral to the completion of the task.

2. Does the group display *individual accountability?*

   _____ Group members try to keep the group on task.

   _____ Group members help one another complete tasks.

   _____ Group members try to keep their resource materials organized.

3. Does the group demonstrate *interpersonal and group process skills?*

   _____ Leadership is being shared among group members.

   _____ Group members praise each other.

   _____ Group members actively listen to one another.

   _____ Group members say and do things that keep the group moving ahead.

Summary

4.1 Explain how an effective classroom layout piques curiosity, invites inquiry, and inspires students to discover

Artists' colonies are often situated in picturesque settings. Writers immerse themselves in a particular setting. The space in which we work can be inspiring. The same holds true for where we learn. Create a physical setting in your classroom that invites science discovery and learning. Discovery stations provide a place for students to play with ideas. They provide some guidance but allow students to discover through tinkering. The scaffolding you provide serves as a gentle guide that encourages science practices and seeking explanations. Add life to your room with aquariums, terrariums, and habitats for a variety of plants and animals. Make them part of an ongoing learning experience for children. Do so responsibly and attend to the needs of children with respect to allergies.

Don't forget the ears. Use sounds and music to set the tone in your classroom—not only to identify animals and places but also properties of sound such as pitch and amplitude. In short, try to make a welcoming and inviting atmosphere for discovery and learning. It may make coming to work more pleasant for you, too!

Establish routines such as "Do Nows" that signal when it is time for science. Use observation exercises to build good observation skills over time that will eventually become habits of mind among your students. Use demonstrations to reinforce, introduce, or address misconceptions.

Self-Check 4.1

Click to gauge your understanding of the concepts in this chapter.

4.2 Describe how to lead discussions using effective science talk

Humans tend to talk a lot. Most of the time, we think before we talk. (We know the consequences of not doing so.) Science talk is accountable talk. It requires that students think about what they say and base their talk on reason and evidence. As a teacher, you can facilitate science talk using talk moves and science circles to generate thoughtful talk among your children.

Self-Check 4.2

Click to gauge your understanding of the concepts in this chapter.

4.3 Explain how to plan for a cooperative learning group in which all members are interdependent

Classroom teachers can use a variety of strategies to teach children science in an effective and creative way. Cooperative learning groups can be used as an important part of any learning environment that encourages discovery learning. Creating cooperative teams requires planning so that students are compelled to work together to achieve an outcome. Don't expect cooperative learning to happen just because you planned it. It may take several small steps to get students to the point where they can collaborate effectively.

Self-Check 4.3

Click to gauge your understanding of the concepts in this chapter.

On Your Own or in a Cooperative Learning Group

1. Reflect on the science activities you experienced in elementary school.

   a. Specifically, what activities do you remember? Why do you think you remember them?

   b. If you remember activities, were they carried out by individual children or by groups? What do you think motivated the teacher's decision in this respect?

   c. While the activities were underway, were there any specific problems with workspace, classroom behavior, or the availability of science materials? If so, what?

   d. Would you say that your teacher(s) encouraged discovery learning?

2. How could you use some of the ideas in this chapter to create an ideal unit for children at the grade level you are most interested in? Be specific and focus on the following:

- The physical setup of the room
- The use of cooperative learning groups
- The use of teacher demonstrations and hands-on student activities

3. Take turns leading a discussion with your peers about a topic of your choice. Practice using the talk moves addressed in this chapter. Try to use each talk move at least once. In addition, you might assign one person to record the frequency with which you used each talk move.

4. Create an interactive demonstration and share it with your peers.

5. Create a routine among your students by regularly practicing observation skills. Use the images in Figure 4.6 to get you started.

Figure 4.6   Practicing observation skills

Chipmunk Eating Corn

Morning Glory

Weathered Rocks in Streambed

Photographs by Susan Rivera Russo Photography LLC

RESOURCES FOR DISCOVERY LEARNING

- **Education.com:**
  https://www.education.com/

- **Institute for Learning:**
  http://ifl.lrdc.pitt.edu/ifl/index.php/home

- **National Science Teachers Association:**
  http://www.nsta.org/

- **Change Blindness:**
  http://cogsci.uci.edu/~ddhoff/cb.html

- **Pets in the Classroom:**
  http://www.petsintheclassroom.org/

Internet Resources

- **The Need for Attention to See Change:**
  http://www2.psych.ubc.ca/~rensink/flicker/index.html

- **Questioning Techniques for the Classroom: Wait-Time:**
  https://questioninganddiscussionforteaching.wordpress.com/wait-time/

- **TeacherVision 2015,** *Your Secret Weapon: Wait Time*, **Teaching Methods and Strategies, TeacherVision:**
  https://www.teachervision.com/teaching-methods/new-teacher/48446.html

Print Resources

Bigelow, M. (2013). Arranging a science classroom [Web log post]. Retrieved April 17, 2017, from http://nstacommunities.org/blog/2013/03/22/arranging-a-science-classroom/

Black, R. (2005). Why demonstrations matter: Teacher-centered demonstration still has a place in the constructivist classroom. *Science and Children* (September): 52–55.

Ebert II, E. S., Ebert, C., & Bentley, M. L. (2011, November 18). Questioning strategies in the classroom. Retrieved April 17, 2017, from https://www.education.com/reference/article/questioning-strategies-classroom/

Ebrahim, A. (2012). The effect of cooperative learning strategies on elementary students' science achievement and social skills in Kuwait. *International Journal of Science and Mathematics Education*, 10(2): 293–314. doi:10.1007/s10763-011-9293-0

Freedman, M. (2000). Using effective demonstrations in the classroom. *Science and Children*, 38(1): 52–55.

Ingram, J., & Elliott, V. (2014). Turn taking and "wait time" in classroom interactions. *Journal of Pragmatics*, 62: 1–12. doi:10.1016/j.pragma.2013.12.002

Irwin, Leslie, et al. (2003). Science centers for all. *Science and Children*, 40(5): 35–37.

Michaels, S., & O'Connor, C. (2012). *Talk science primer* (Rep.). Cambridge, MA: TERC.

NSTA Position Statement. (2008). Responsible use of live animals and dissection in the science classroom. Arlington, VA: NSTA Press

Notes

1. Rensink, Ronald A. (2004). Visual sensing without seeing. *Psychological Science, 15*: 27–32.

2. **Claude Lévi-Strauss** is widely regarded as the father of modern anthropology.

3. Donald Orlich, et al. (1994). *Teaching strategies: A guide to better instruction.* Lexington, MA: D. C. Heath, pp. 186–193.

4. Stahl, R. J. (1994). Using "think-time" and "wait-time" skillfully in the classroom. *ERIC Digest.* Retrieved April 22, 2017, from http://files.eric.ed.gov/fulltext/ED370885.pdf

5. TeacherVision. (2015). *Your secret weapon: Wait time, teaching methods and strategies.* Retrieved April 22, 2017, from https://www.teachervision.com/teaching-methods/new-teacher/48446.html

6. Tobin, Kenneth G., & Capie, William. (n.d.). *Wait-time and learning in science.* Burlington, NC: Carolina Biological Supply, p. 2.

7. Chapin, S., Connor, M., & Anderson, N. (2009). *Classroom discussions: Using math talk to help students learn, grades K–6.* Sausalito, CA: Math Solutions.

8. Adapted from Michaels, S., & O'Connor, C. (2012). *Talk science primer.* Cambridge, MA: TERC.

9. Winokur, J., Worth, K., & Heller-Winokur, M. (2009). Connecting science and literacy through talk. In *Science and children.* Arlington, VA: National Science Teachers Association.

Assessment of Understanding and Inquiry

A good teacher asks, "How am I doing?" A great teacher asks, "How are my students doing?"

wavebreakmedia/Shutterstock

Learning Objectives

After completing the activities in this chapter, you should be able to:

5.1 Describe scenarios in which assessment strategies could be used for formative or summative assessment.

5.2 Describe and identify three-dimensional assessment.

5.3 Explain how rubrics and scoring guides are used and describe their effectiveness as assessment tools.

▶ **GETTING STARTED**

"What d'ja git?"
"She gave me a C!"

Would overhearing this exchange between two students—after you've taught a unit that took 3 weeks to plan and far too many afternoons shopping at discount stores for inexpensive activity materials—get your attention? And would it sting just a bit?

It would and should for three reasons. First of all, it would tell you that the end-of-unit test probably didn't assess whether your children actually learned some science. Second, it would tell you that your children have the extraordinary idea that the teacher *gives* a grade. Notice the phrasing "She gave." Does that imply, even slightly, that the student's grade was *earned*? Thirdly, and perhaps most important, it suggests that you, the teacher, should critically review your formative assessment strategies to learn how you could make adjustments as the unit was unfolding that better support student success.

In this chapter, you will learn about a range of assessment techniques that will help you discover whether your children are actually learning the target core ideas and practices in real time (formative assessment) and whether they reached the target level of content mastery (summative assessment) at the end of the unit. Carefully studying these materials will help you create a classroom in which you are well informed about how students are *learning* and how you are *teaching* as well as what they learned and what you taught.

Know What to Assess

Before planning a trip know the destination, otherwise you will never know if you got to where you wanted to go. While this may be self-evident, it is all too tempting to ignore this simple principle when taking students on a journey of learning. It is tempting, especially when teaching relevant, active science, to begin with an activity because it is dynamic and engaging. The problem is that unless the activity serves a predetermined desired learning outcome, learning will be hit or miss. As emphasized in Chapter 3, the first crucial step in lesson planning is to identify the content to be taught. It bears repeating that we cannot design how we will teach and what we will assess until we know what we intend to teach. This is the fundamental principle espoused by Wiggins and McTighe in Understanding by Design™. This chapter makes the assumption that the content to be taught has been identified. On the other hand, it is sometimes the case, particularly with responsive teaching, that our lessons and the content taught vary from our intended desired outcomes. Should this be the case and you are aware that your lessons taught more, less, or different content, you will need to reevaluate your assessment strategies to fairly assess students on the content you taught.

Distinguishing Formative and Summative Approaches to Assessment

I do not recall where or when I heard the statement, "A good teacher asks, 'How am I doing?' A great teacher asks, 'How are my students doing?'" But a truly outstanding teacher should ask both questions. Formative and summative assessments are two approaches that help us focus on these two very important aspects.

Formative assessment is used to assist teaching and learning. "Such assessment is designed to provide diagnostic feedback to teachers and students during the course of instruction. Teachers need assessment information about their individual students to guide the instructional process."[1] Formative assessment serves as a check on the execution of your plan, answering the questions "Are the children doing what you intended them to do, and learning what you want them to learn?" and "Is there evidence that children are developing the science practices, core ideas, and crosscutting concepts targeted for learning?" If the children are on track to learning, then you can continue as planned. If feedback from your formative assessment indicates that the children are not on track, then it is not too late for you to revise and adjust the lesson accordingly. Formative assessment keeps you from being surprised when plans falter and provides you with time to adjust and redirect the lesson. In this respect, formative assessment addresses how you are doing as well as how your students are doing.

Research suggests that feedback based on formative assessment can be one of the most powerful influences on student learning.[2] Feedback, to be most effective, needs to be shared with students as well as teachers. Personal feedback such as "Well done" or "You can do better" while potentially motivating, is ineffective according to research.[3] Feedback should address three key questions for students: "Where am I going?" "How am I going?" and "Where to next?" [4]

Summative assessment answers the questions "What did the students learn?" and "Did they learn what I intended to teach?" Summative assessments are usually used for purposes of placement, grading, accountability, and informing parents and future teachers about student performance.

Enhanced eText Video Example 5.1

Listen to a veteran teacher describe assessment. How does she use assessment to understand students' prior knowledge?

Teachers often ask me for a list of formative and summative assessment tools. Unfortunately, it is not that easy. Although some assessment tools are usually associated with one of the two approaches, often the methodologies overlap. Whether an assessment is formative or summative depends on how you choose to use the data.

I will resist the urge to classify any assessment methodology as strictly formative or summative. Throughout this chapter, we will consider several assessment methodologies and evaluate the strengths and weaknesses of each. It will be up to you choose the appropriate assessment strategies for your purposes.

Assessment and the NGSS

The advent of the NGSS impacts the way we think about the outcomes of science education. The NGSS challenge science educators to look at assessment in context of the three dimensions of science practices, core ideas, and crosscutting concepts. This is a more in-depth consideration of assessment than more traditional standards-based science assessments, which tend to measure particular content or facts students know at a specific grade level. This implies that assessments need to be multidimensional. Therefore, "Students will need multiple-and varied-assessment opportunities to demonstrate their competence on the performance expectations for a given grade level."[5] Because the three dimensions overlap, assessments will often address more than one practice, core idea, or crosscutting concept.

I begin by offering you a summary of assessment strategies that use multiple assessment tasks to assess three dimensions of the NGSS. Use this example to inform the more specific assessment strategies that follow in the chapter. The example blends the disciplinary core idea, *PS4.A: Wave Properties*, with the crosscutting concept *patterns*, and two science practices: *developing and using models* and *constructing explanations*.

Lesson summary: Fourth-graders came to the lesson understanding that vibrations are associated with sound. The unit began by seeking patterns in waves on a beach (via videos). They described the patterns of the waves and made initial models of waves as a class (simulating the human wave used at sporting events) and using water tanks (small plastic aquariums) to identify components including amplitude, wavelength, and frequency. They made diagrams of waves and physical models of waves using jump ropes. They were challenged to use their models of waves to explain how waves make an object move.

Assessment tasks were based on the lesson and informed by the Evidence Statements provided for PS4.A by NGSS.

Assessment Task	Core Idea	Science Practice	Assessment Purpose	Crosscutting Concept
1. Develop a model to make sense of wave behavior.	PS4.A: Wave Properties Waves, which are regular patterns of motion, can be made in water by disturbing the surface.	Developing and using models	Formative	Patterns
2. Describe the relationships among components of your wave model.	PS4.A: Wave Properties Waves of the same type can differ in amplitude (height of the wave) and wavelength (spacing between wave peaks).	Analyzing and interpreting data	Formative	Patterns
3. Explain how waves make an object move.	PS.A: When waves move across the surface of deep water, the water goes up and down in place; there is no net motion in the direction of the wave except when the water meets a beach.	Constructing explanations	Formative	Energy and matter
4. Explain how waves make an object move.	PS.A: When waves move across the surface of deep water, the water goes up and down in place; there is no net motion in the direction of the wave except when the water meets a beach.	Constructing explanations	Summative	Energy and matter

At first glance assessment tasks 3 and 4 may look like a typo. They are not. They illustrate how the same assessment task can be used as formative or summative assessment. The difference is more apparent when you consider how the tasks are presented. They differ in the degree of scaffolding each provides. Task 3 was presented with guiding questions for students that prompted them to measure the horizontal and vertical movement of a cork in waves. Task 4 did not provide students with any guided questions to construct explanations. It assessed what students learned with respect to wave properties and motion.

Developing Assessment Strategies

● Prompt and Rubric

A *prompt* is a question or group of questions that includes a statement about a task to be done along with directions on how to do it. A *scoring rubric* (pronounced "roo-brick") is used to describe the criteria that should be used when assessing a child's performance. Let's look at examples of prompts and scoring rubrics in the classroom.

▶ EXAMPLE of a Prompt and Rubric

TOPIC: Sound (for grades 1–3)

CONTENT TO BE ASSESSED: Sounds are caused by vibrations.

PERFORMANCE OBJECTIVE: Given a drum, a pencil, and rice, students will hit the drum with the pencil and explain orally that sound is produced by vibrations.

PROMPT: "This little drum is made by stretching plastic wrap over a jar. I'd like you to tap the drum with the eraser, look at the plastic, and tell me what you see and what you hear. Then sprinkle some rice grains on the plastic and look at it as you tap it again."

QUESTIONS:

1. What do you observe when you hit the drum with an eraser?

2. What do you think causes sound?

RUBRIC:

3	2	1
Student's description of what was observed includes *the plastic moves up and down, the vibration causes sound*	Student's description includes a response with one correct observation.	No response is given or incorrect responses are given.

You could use this prompt and rubric as a formative assessment if it were administered during the lesson or as a summative assessment after the lesson.

● Performance Assessment

Inquiry is a central component of science education. It involves developing descriptive models, explanatory models, and experimental models using science practices such as asking questions, modeling, planning investigations, carrying out investigations, analyzing and interpreting data, and engaging in argument from evidence.[6]

Because inquiry is a process, assessing students' ability to do inquiry frequently takes place over an extended time. This suggests the need to observe and document students' practices while they are actually engaged in processes of doing science. Performance assessment strategies are well suited for assessing students' abilities to inquire. They require children to perform a task that reflects their understanding

REALITY check

Write a prompt and scoring rubric for the following content and performance objective:

Content: Plants convert energy from the Sun into food. Animals such as mice and rabbits eat the plants to get their food. Animals such as snakes and hawks eat mice and rabbits. When living things die, they are broken down by organisms such as bacteria and fungi and returned to the soil, where they can be used again by plants. When elements of the food chain are removed, the organisms that depend on them have to find other food sources or die.

Performance objective: Given a food web diagram, students will explain what will occur if the mice are removed from the food web. The students will score at least satisfactory on the rubric that you will create.

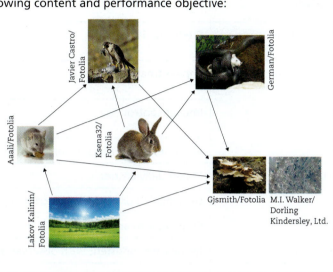

and ability to do science through applications of concepts and skills. Note that a collection of data from several assessment instruments over time will provide you with a good idea of what students can do with respect to inquiry.

As their name implies, *performance assessments* are based on observations of students as they demonstrate a specific task or problem-solving skill. Performance assessments are usually evaluated using a rubric or scoring guide. The evaluator collects data about the student's procedures and conclusions through direct observation of behavior, written records such as notes, worksheets, lab reports, or products such as posters, role-plays, and recordings.

▶ Example of a Performance Assessment

TOPIC: Light and plants (for young learners)

ENGAGEMENT: What will happen if Mrs. Cortez's plants are kept in the closet without light?

EXPLORATION: I will give each group two plants. You have one week to find out what will happen to the plants if they are kept in a closet without light. Use the following questions to guide your investigation:

1. Make a prediction that you can test.
2. Describe how you will test your prediction.
3. Carry out your test.
4. Make observations of your plants each day and record your observations in your science notebook, using words and drawings.
5. At the end of your test, state your results.

EXPLANATION: Students will describe whether their evidence supports their prediction or does not support their prediction.

Enhanced eText Video Example 5.2

Listen to how a teacher integrates a performance assessment as part of a comprehensive assessment plan about composting. Toward the end of the video, she describes a performance assessment. Write a performance objective for the assessment task described by the teacher in the video.

SCORING GUIDE:

Criteria	Performance	Potential score	Student score
Prediction	Prediction is testable	3	
Test of prediction	Implies treatment	2	
	Implies control	2	
	Identifies observables (color, height . . .)	2	
Daily observations	Makes daily entries	2	
	Uses labeled drawings to describe observables	2	
	Observations are accurate	2	
Results	Results are consistent with observations	3	
Explanation	Students relate that the presence of light is necessary for Mrs. Riley's plants to live	3	
Total possible score		21	

● Portfolios

Enhanced eText Video Example 5.3

Listen to teacher Kathy Boone share how she uses portfolios and children's self-assessment as assessment tools. In what ways could science portfolios be informative for students, teachers, and parents?

A *portfolio* is an organized collection of a student's work representing the best that he or she can do. Although each piece placed in a portfolio can be assessed with respect to the degree to which the student achieved specific unit objectives, the portfolio as a whole will illustrate the child's progress.

You may be wondering what specific examples of a child's science work should go in a science portfolio. Here are some products that could be included:

- Written observations and science reports
- Drawings, charts, and graphs that are the products of hands-on, discovery-focused activities
- Thank-you letters to resource people who have visited the classroom (e.g., beekeepers, veterinarians, health care providers)
- Reaction pieces, such as prepared written responses to science software, videos, discovery experiences, fieldtrips, and websites
- Media products, such as student-produced science work in audio, video, or digital form

● Anecdotal Records

Name: Jimmy Green   Age: 8
Grade: 2   Date: May 5
This week Jimmy's group, the Science Stars, which was responsible for taking care of the aquarium, found a dead guppy. Jimmy volunteered to bury it in the school lawn. He told the group, "Even though it's dead, it'll help the grass grow."

A teacher's brief notes about a child's behavior can reveal a great deal about what the child has or has not learned. The notes, called *anecdotal records*, can help you assess how well individual children are doing. They can be particularly helpful when you wish to reflect upon and assess how well individual children are mastering inquiry process skills or developing desirable attitudes and values.

Affective Development Checklists

"Boy, do I hate science!"

If you heard one of your students say this, what would you conclude about his or her affective development? Your only basis for assessing changes in *affect* is your observation of the affect-laden behaviors students exhibit. Their comments, smiles, frowns, in-class behavior, and out-of-class behavior reveal a great deal about whether they are developing favorable attitudes toward science and your teaching.

Science Conferences with Children

The words we speak tell a great deal about what we know and how we feel. The quickest and possibly most reliable way to find out if children in a discovery-focused classroom are learning is to give them an opportunity to talk to you. If you learn to listen carefully and gently probe around the edges of a child's talk, you will discover whether he or she has grasped the real meaning of a food web, has had anything to do with creating the group's drawings showing the movement of the continents, or is becoming increasingly curious about the natural world. Conferences with children can provide a window into their minds and reveal children's thought processes about how they make sense of concepts.

Science Notebooks

Have you ever watched a child fish around in his or her desk to locate a yogurt-stained sheet of paper that contains yesterday's science notes? Some teachers have found that a notebook devoted only to science can be a great asset for children as well as a useful tool for assessing how well individual students are doing. I have noticed an increase in the use of science notebooks in elementary school science classes during the past few years. While it may seem like semantics, science notebooks can be distinguished from science laboratory notebooks in that science notebooks allow for more reflection and less structure than laboratory notebooks typically do (Figure 5.1). In this respect, they can serve the third principle of how children learn: metacognition.[7] Children are encouraged to include not only formal investigative elements, such as procedures, data, and results, but also their questions, predictions, reflections, and feelings about science and how they learn science. Most importantly, notebooks provide a place for students to record new concepts they have learned or want to learn. Here are some suggestions for implementing the use of science notebooks:

1. At the start of the year, ask each child to obtain a notebook he or she will devote exclusively to science.
2. Encourage the children to design covers for their science notebooks. The ways students choose to represent science on their notebook covers will shed insight on students' perceptions of science.

Figure 5.1   Example of a Science Notebook Entry

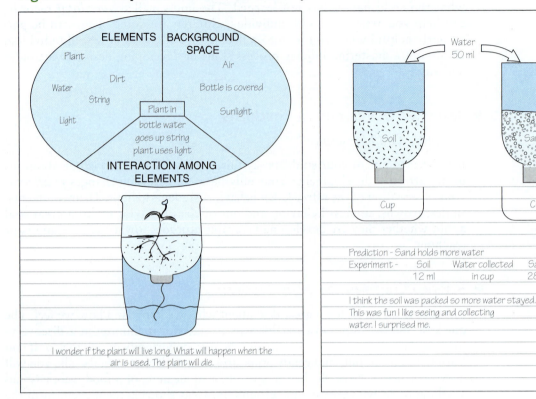

Enhanced eText Video Example 5.4

What does it look like when kindergarteners are doing science? Watch as they write what they notice about rolling balls. What do *you notice* about the teachers' coaching and the students' responses? How do the students use notebooks as part of their science practice?

3. Provide encouragement and time for children to write in their notebooks each day. Offer guiding questions, such as "What did you do?" "What did you learn?" "How do you feel about what you have learned?" "What confused you the most?" and "What surprised you the most?"

4. Schedule time at the end of each teaching unit for children to discuss some of the things they have written.

5. Consider using the science notebooks during parent–teacher conferences. Also consider putting the notebooks on display for parents' night or back-to-school night.

Analyzing Notebook Entries: A Systems Approach   Notebook entries can give us insight into student understanding. If students are able to name the parts of a system, they express at least a nominal level of understanding. If they can express an understanding of the functions or properties of the parts of a system, then they approach functional literacy. If students are able to explain how the parts of a system function together to make it work, they are closer to thinking at a conceptual level of scientific literacy.[8]

For example, fourth-graders were asked to draw a circuit (the system) in their notebooks.

Note that the example of one student's diagram in Figure 5.2 reveals a misconception about the function of wires. Wires do not cause electricity. Nor does the student seem to understand how the wires, lightbulb, and battery function together to light

Figure 5.2 Example of Student's Circuit Diagram

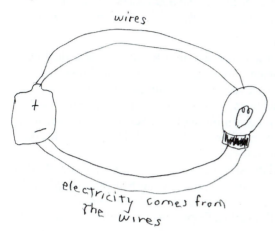

the bulb. Did you notice that the connection of the wires to the lightbulb is incorrect? Placing a wire on the glass globe of the bulb will not conduct electricity. While we must be careful not to draw conclusions without further examination of the student's work and perhaps having a conversation with the student, the notebook entry suggests that the student has a nominal understanding but not a functional or conceptual understanding of circuits.

● Science Probes

Probes are similar to prompts and rubrics, but they are designed more specifically to uncover whether a student understands a particular rule of interaction targeted in the lesson. A *probe* includes a simple question that seeks a two-part answer. The first part usually involves lower-order thinking skills such as identification or naming. The second part of the probe requires students to demonstrate higher-order thinking by stating rules of relationship between or among elements. The following example is adapted from one of the many designed by Paige Keeley, Francis Eberle, and Lynn Farrin.[9]

Example

Is it a physical change or a chemical change?
The list below involves situations that cause changes in materials. Put a *P* next to the situations in which the materials in italics undergo a physical change and a *C* next to the situations in which the materials in italics undergo a chemical change.

_____Ice cream melts in the Sun

_____Wood is cut to make sawdust

_____A car rusts

_____Wood is burned in a fire

_____Water evaporates from a pan

_____ An egg is fried

Explain your thinking. Describe in writing a "rule" to decide if something undergoes a physical or chemical change.

● Children's Self-Assessment

As teachers, we may forget that children naturally reflect on how well they do in each activity that is a part of their science experience. And so it should seem logical to capitalize on self-reflection when you incorporate assessment into your classroom.

There are many ways to stimulate children's self-assessment. For example, before the children begin to write in their science notebooks, you might say, "So far this month, you have worked on two projects. One was building a flashlight, and the other was using a flashlight and mirrors to study how light behaves. What did you learn in each project?" The children's responses will represent their efforts to assess what they have done. Their responses could hold important information for you as a teacher.

● Concept Mapping

A family is seated around the dinner table. The dad passes a bowl of mashed potatoes to his son and asks, "So, what did you learn in science today?" The child responds, "Nuthin."

How can this be? That child spent the entire day in a lovely, pastel-walled classroom overflowing with books and science materials, was taught by knowledgeable and motivated teachers, had access to a variety of resources (including computers with Internet access), took an around-the-schoolyard nature fieldtrip with his class, and also attended a special all-school assembly with Dr. Science, who performed demonstrations that flashed, popped, and banged. Yet the child answered his dad's question with "Nuthin." What went wrong?

The answer is simple: The child doesn't really know what he learned. By that, I mean that the child has had no opportunity to make what he learned *explicit*. He probably learned many things today, but he has not brought them to the forefront of his consciousness and tied them all together. Consequently, both the child and his dad finish their meal thinking that the day was as bland as those mashed potatoes.

One way to help a child assess self-learning is to have him or her make a concept map after an inquiry-based experience. You can even use a concept map as a personal unit-planning device. Even so, I am presenting it here as an assessment tool, so you can see what children have learned in a concrete way. They will literally draw you a picture!

A *concept map* is a diagram that represents knowledge by identifying basic concepts and topics and showing how these items are related. Such a map is created using these two symbols:

1. **Node**—A shape (typically a circle or an oval) that contains a word or phrase to represent the item of content knowledge.

2. **Link**—A line with an arrowhead at one or both ends that's used to connect the nodes and to show the relationship between them. A single arrowhead indicates that one node leads to or is part of another. A double arrowhead indicates that nodes are reciprocal or mutually supportive of each other.

Figure 5.3 This concept map represents what one child learned in a schoolyard fieldtrip to observe types of living things

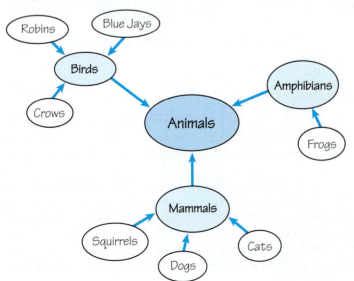

Figure 5.3 shows the concept map a child drew after going on a schoolyard fieldtrip to observe types of living things in the environment. Starting with "Animals" in the center of the page, the child branched out to classes of animals, such as "Mammals" and "Birds," and then became even more specific by noting types of animals within each class, such as "Dogs" and "Squirrels" under "Mammals." Note that all of the arrows point the same way: back to "Animals."

By studying a child's concept map, you can assess what he or she may have learned during an experience and how he or she has tied specific pieces of knowledge together. The child will benefit from creating the map because he or she will make what might have been abstract or general more concrete and specific. As a result, the child will have a much fuller knowledge of what was learned—and it won't seem like "Nuthin"!

● Creative Assessments

Think creatively about ways you can gain access to student thinking and understanding. If you have the means, give students a camera to make a picture book about the different types of living things found in a log. Ask them to prepare and video a news report about local weather phenomena to share with other classes. Give them an explanation and ask them to critique or refute it. In all these cases, identify the criteria you are looking for that represent understanding.

Evaluating Traditional Assessment Strategies

Traditional assessment strategies became traditional because of an ongoing perceived value. But as the science education community acknowledges science practices and abilities to seek explanations based on evidence, the limitations of traditional strategies become more apparent. Like any other strategy, used properly, traditional assessment strategies contribute to our overall assessment of young learners. Read about the pros and cons of some assessment strategies with which you are no doubt familiar.

● End-of-Chapter Assignment

" . . . and then do numbers 1 through 5 on the last page."

Does this bring back a few classroom memories? Giving children an end-of-chapter assignment is a common way for teachers to discover whether the children remember what they have read. When you make such an assignment, you believe that children will read the chapter first and then answer the questions. Perhaps in elementary and middle school, you read your science chapters before you did your assignment. If so, I congratulate you! If you didn't, this is a good opportunity to consider what a traditional end-of-chapter assignment does and doesn't accomplish.

What Does It Accomplish? An end-of-chapter assignment tells the children that you are serious about the content you are teaching. It forces them to look at and, if you are fortunate, read text material, if only to find answers to the questions they have been assigned. This type of assignment provides you with one small indicator of how serious a child is about his or her schooling. If assigned for homework, the actual appearance of a textbook also tells parents that the child is doing something in science class. Finally, assignments that are *not* done provide you with a reason for talking with a child and the child's parents about his or her effort.

What Doesn't It Accomplish? End-of-chapter assignments do not tell you much about what children know, and they don't tell you if they like science. Completed assignments seldom reveal any understanding of information beyond the recall level. End-of-chapter questions will probably not pique children's interest to the point that they will want to learn more about the topic.

Using End-of-Chapter Assignments Effectively Before making an assignment, talk with children about the purpose of the assignment and the reading they have done. Use statements such as "You know this first chapter on living things told us about the differences between living and nonliving things. But it is not always easy to know if something is living or nonliving. The questions at the end will help you find out if you remember and understand some of the big ideas." After this introduction, give children a few minutes of class time to begin the assignment. Doing so will increase the probability that children will complete the assignment and possibly make the experience somewhat more meaningful to them.

Quizzes

Do you still live in fear of the "pop" quiz? Does your heart flutter a bit just hearing the term *quiz?* Quizzes are a part of the classroom assessment process from elementary school through graduate school, and their effect on students seems to remain rather constant. A quiz takes little time and is usually used as a quick assessment of whether students remember or understand factual information or concepts.

What Do They Accomplish?   Quizzes tell teachers whether children can think fast and have a sufficient command of writing to get their responses on paper before time is up. They are easy to grade and provide a snapshot of the students' recall of information. They also serve to keep children "on their toes," but they should not divert teachers from science experiences that should be taking place in the classroom.

What Don't They Accomplish?   Quizzes usually do not tell teachers much about in-depth understanding. Children's lack of success on quizzes may not reveal a deficit in knowledge or understanding but rather a deficit in being able to express themselves quickly.

Using Quizzes More Effectively   Quizzes should be used in moderation. Keep them short and focused. If you wish to find out whether children are learning, giving a quiz now and then that is focused on the important ideas of a science unit can provide some information about student progress. Doing so can also help you discover whether you need to modify your teaching or help a particular child before a unit is completed.

End-of-Unit Tests

Given the large numbers of children in most classrooms, most teacher-developed tests are composed of short-answer questions and some multiple-choice items. At the end of the test, there may be a few essay questions. In inquiry-based classrooms, teachers who use tests are likely to include some questions dealing with how science activities were conducted and what was learned from them.

What Do They Accomplish?   Test results tell children, parents, and you how well the children answered the questions that were asked. Test results give children a way to assess their own progress and a way to compare themselves to others. They give you a neat and tidy way to get information to use for grading. They also tell you which children in the class are good test takers. That information is important if you want to teach children skills that will be useful in later life.

If you create a test with questions that discover children's reasoning more than children's recall abilities, you may get more useful information. The test results can reveal whether children understood concepts, were able to apply what was learned, and were able to analyze the science phenomena studied. If, however, the test consists solely of recall questions, only the children's memory will be assessed.

What Don't They Accomplish?   Tests tell you only what children know and understand about the particular questions you asked. Very few tests assess how well children can express their thoughts. Questions that elicit this information are challenging to create, require many minutes for children to complete, and demand that the teacher spend a considerable amount of time outside class carefully reading each response, reflecting on the work, offering informative feedback, and assigning grades. Remember, you want to find out what students know and understand as well as what they do not know and understand.

Tests probably do little to motivate children to think about science as an interesting subject area or to increase their career awareness. Nor does success on science tests indicate that children like science, are interested in science, will engage in free reading about science topics, will watch televised science programs, or even will become interested observers of the natural world.

Using Tests More Effectively   As you prepare a test, try to cross-reference each item to one of the cognitive, affective, or psychomotor objectives of the teaching unit. By doing this, you can measure student progress over all of the unit's objectives. To help you assess student achievement on the objectives of the unit and the quality of the questions you have asked, after the test, prepare a chart on which you will record the number of children who answer each question correctly.

Research Reports

Research report are easily conflated with literature reviews. A true research report is the outcome of a research investigation. It uses the information to support an explanation in science or solve a problem in engineering. It also includes the use of data either generated firsthand (primary data) or from another source (secondary data). Choosing a topic, reading about it and writing about what is learned is a literature review. However, research reports at the elementary level are often used synonymously with literature reviews of a topic. The following refers to research reports in this respect.

What Do They Accomplish?   Research reports provide students with information and ideas that can round out what they have learned through hands-on activities, demonstrations, and class discussions. They can lead children to think about topics and questions that were not considered during class. They can also help improve a child's grade for a marking period by making up for low quiz or test grades.

What Don't They Accomplish?   When used in the traditional manner, research reports do little to extend and enrich the basic knowledge, skills, and attitudes emphasized in a discovery-focused classroom. They do not present children with an opportunity to touch science materials or to move through the full learning cycle. In the best circumstances, research reports tell you whether children can look up information in reference books and summarize what they have learned.

Using Research Reports More Effectively   In order for research reports to be meaningful, they should engage children in a quest that resolves some issue or problem for which they need to seek an explanation or find a solution. Therefore, if the children are engaged in inquiry-based science experiences related to the life cycle of insects, you might say, "I would like you to do work in the learning center that will help you answer the question 'Why don't we ever see baby butterflies?'" This type of assignment captures the same curiosity that you are hoping to capitalize on with hands-on discovery science. Children should be going to the computer or library to learn how to use media and books as *tools* that are as essential to the pursuit of science as microscopes and metersticks.

Activity Writeups

How will you know that children are learning, fitting new learning into previous knowledge, and constructing new meanings? You can discover this by observing them, by listening to them, and by reading what they have written in their activity writeups. Activity writeups are brief descriptions in children's own words of what they did and what they discovered.

What Do They Accomplish?
Having children synthesize and share what they have learned in activity writeups tells them that you believe thinking, talking, and writing about what they have experienced is important. Listening to a child's observations of water droplets forming on an ice-filled glass or reading their written observations gives you valuable information about the learning that is occurring in your classroom.

What Don't They Accomplish?
A variety of problems can arise when you use activity writeups. The most obvious one is that a child may have completed an activity successfully but may not be a good writer. Under these circumstances, a poor report may tell you more about his or her language arts abilities than science abilities. If you rely only on activity writeups, children with language difficulties will be unable to express what they have learned.

By necessity, an activity writeup is a very brief sketch of the work the child has done. While it will tell you a good deal about the results of a child's investigation, it will tell you little about all the experiences he or she may have had as the activity was carried out.

Using Activity Writeups Effectively
When you look at or listen to a child's activity writeup, you need to be able to assess whether the efforts reflect the child's or the group's work on the activity. To help you make this assessment, take some time to explain to the children the importance of clearly identifying all the group members involved in preparing the report.

Another component of assessing the quality of a writeup is determining whether an incomplete report shows a lack of effort on the child's part or a limitation in his or her ability to use language. The only way to make this distinction is to ask the child clarifying questions.

Standardized Tests

If you walk down a school hallway and notice that it is strangely quiet, that the children are seated quietly at their desks, and that the public address system is not blaring messages, chances are the children are taking a standardized test. For some reason, standardized tests create a time of palpable quiet and anxiety.

In addition to the usual battery of conceptual and attitudinal inventories, most school districts have children take achievement tests in a variety of subjects. If you teach in a school that requires a standardized science achievement test, you may find that *you* are more concerned about the results than the children are. Especially if your evaluation depends on students' performance on standardized tests . . . but that is a topic for another discussion.

What Do They Accomplish?

A standardized achievement test in science compares how much the children in your class know compared to children nationwide or districtwide, as reflected in norms. The children in your class doing well may make you feel very successful. If they do poorly, you may feel obliged to rethink what and how you are teaching. The results provide teachers, administrators, and members of the community with an opportunity to compare the success of their children to that of other children. Standardizations are good for providing a comparison, not unlike blood pressure is compared to a standard range based on a population.

What Don't They Accomplish?

Standardized tests are typically limited to assessing children's knowledge of science concepts and principles. It is much more difficult and rare for standardized tests to assess children's achievement with respect to practicing science and understanding the nature of the scientific endeavor. Creativity, innovation, and sense-making strategies are among some of the important attributes that standardized tests tend not to address.[10] Such measures are not easily assessed using high-throughput machine scoring resources.

Using Standardized Achievement Tests More Effectively

First, help children understand that the results of a standardized test will not measure all that they have learned. If, for example, your class has completed a unit on the use and waste of water in your school, explain to the children that they should not expect to see questions about it on the test. Point out that some of the science units they have studied have given them a lot of information that will not be measured. Emphasize that they should not feel bad if many of the things they have learned are not on the test.

Also, take some class time before the test to teach basic standardized test-taking strategies. The children likely will take many standardized tests while they are students and when they pursue employment. Investing time and energy to improve test-taking skills may annoy you because of your own feelings about testing, but it may help children become more successful test takers. Finally, take a leadership role in your school or district that enables you to contribute to the formation of standardized tests that measure science practices, disciplinary core ideas, and crosscutting concepts.

Creating Rubrics and Scoring Guides

Most of the assessment strategies presented to this point are fine for collecting data about student performance. Frankly, collecting student work is relatively easy compared to analyzing student outcomes and making judgments about a student's performance. For each assessment strategy, you will need a tool to analyze the outcomes. Most often you will use an answer key or a rubric.

Answer keys are helpful when clearly defined answers are required. The students either name the parts of a flower or they don't. Rubrics, on the other hand, provide a guide for you to evaluate less structured and more open-ended responses typical of students seeking to provide explanations. They are often helpful when assessing procedural rather than factual content. There are two basic forms of rubric: analytical and holistic. Analytical rubrics specify performances and values for each criterion. They provide a numerical value. Holistic rubrics provide a general assessment based on several criteria at once. They provide categorical values (e.g., excellent, satisfactory, needs improvement).

The analytical rubric used earlier in the performance assessment example about Mrs. Cortez's plants is included below. In addition, I provide examples of an analytical continuum rubric and holistic rubric for the same example so that you can compare the different rubrics. Note that rubrics all include criteria, performances for criteria, and a rating scale. They differ by degrees of specificity.

Analytical List: Lists desired performance and score for each criterion.

Criteria	Performance	Potential score	Student score
Prediction	Prediction is testable	3	
Test of prediction	Implies treatment	2	
	Implies control	2	
	Identifies observables (color, height, etc.)	2	
Daily observations	Makes daily entries	2	
	Uses labeled drawings to describe observables	2	
	Observations are accurate	2	
Results	Results are consistent with observations	3	
Explanation	Students relate that the presence of light is necessary for Mrs. Cortez's plants to live	3	
Total possible score		21	

Analytical Continuum: Specifics of each criteria are scored collectively rather than individually.

Criteria	Meets criteria, 3 pts/criterion	Satisfactory, 2 pts/criterion	Needs improvement, 1 pt/criterion
Prediction	Clearly stated, testable	Stated but not clearly testable	Difficult to discern prediction
Test of prediction	Demonstrates experimental model: Clearly implies treatment Experimental control Variable control Identifies observables (color, height, etc.)	Implies treatment Suggests an awareness of controls but does not clearly discern variables or observables	Does not suggest an awareness of an experimental model

Criteria	Meets criteria, 3 pts/criterion	Satisfactory, 2 pts/criterion	Needs improvement, 1 pt/criterion
Daily observations	Evidence of descriptive modeling, addresses elements, rules of interaction, and background space Makes comprehensive daily entries Uses drawings to describe observables Observations are accurate	Makes daily observations Observations are generally accurate Intermittently supported by text or labeled drawings Moderate evidence of descriptive modeling	Sporadic entries Little or no evidence of descriptive modeling
Results	Results are consistent with observations	Results exhibit some inconsistencies with observations	Results are inconsistent with observations
Explanation	Explanatory model based on descriptive model Students relate that the presence of light is necessary for Mrs. Riley's plants to live	Explanatory model partially based on descriptive modeling Students relate light to plant growth in general without expressing cause and effect related to Mrs. Riley's plants	Explanatory model is unrelated to descriptive model Students demonstrate no awareness of the relationship of light to plant growth
Total possible score	15		

Holistic Rubric: Does not list specific levels of performance for each criterion. It provides a general assessment based on overall criteria.

Meets criteria
• Makes a clear and testable prediction • Designs a solid experiment with appropriate controls and variables • Records accurate and informative daily observations • Results are consistent with observations • Explanation is consistent with observations
Satisfactory
• Prediction is stated but not testable • Observations are fairly consistent and descriptive • Results are mostly consistent • Explanation relates light to plant growth

Needs improvement

- Prediction is difficult to discern
- Experimental design has most of the controls and variables
- Demonstrates little awareness of experimental design
- Exhibits minimal descriptive modeling
- Results are largely inconsistent with observations
- Does not articulate a connection between plant growth and light

REALITY check

Parent Conferences and Assessments

It is your first parent conference night. You are well prepared; you have displayed student work for the parents, and you have been sure to include a sample from each child in your class. You have portfolios for each student as well as their grades on all the assignments to date. Although you look forward to meeting the parents of your students, you are also a bit anxious. It will be easy to report to the parents of the students who are doing well, but what do you say to the parents of the children who seem to be struggling? You are particularly concerned about explaining Amanda's performance in science to her parents. You search for a way to describe her performance in a manner that will be informative and constructive. While reviewing Amanda's portfolio, you realize that she has done well on matching and fill-in-the-blank sections of probes and that she is often but not always able to link ideas on concept maps and diagrams, but she does not perform well on performance assessments that require her to generate explanations. Based on the following guide, what can you tell Amanda's parents about the level of understanding exhibited by Amanda?

Level of understanding	Assessment strategies	Comments
Nominal	Matching Fill-in-the-blank Vocabulary quiz	Demonstrates ability to identify and associate elements and concepts Answers often memorized No indication of deep understanding
Descriptive	Concept map Diagram Essay Poster Lab report Activity writeup	Demonstrates ability to express rules of interaction/connections among elements
Explanatory	Performance assessment Lab practical Model Simulation	Demonstrates ability to propose an explanation or demonstrate ability based on the rules of interaction among the elements of the system

Sample response: Amanda does well identifying scientific terms and recognizing most of the main concepts. Her concept maps and diagrams demonstrate that she is able to recognize the fundamental relationships and main connections among most of the science concepts. She is off to a good start. The next step for Amanda is to use her ability to create good descriptive models and recognize important connections to generate responses to open-ended questions more independently. I will continue to help her make the transition to this higher level of mastery by providing her with opportunities to use her concept maps, which she does quite well, as a guide to generate answers to open-ended questions. You can support her in this at home by suggesting that she make a concept map when she is working on a response to an open-ended question and help her use the concept map by pointing out connections that lead to an explanation. We should see her progress in her responses to open-response questions on standardized testing this spring.

Summary

5.1 Describe scenarios in which assessment strategies could be used for formative or summative assessment

Assessment addresses three fundamental questions:

- How are we, as teachers, doing?
- How are our students, as learners, doing?
- Did our students learn what we intended to teach?

Formative assessment addresses the first two questions. It lets us know if the learning community, consisting of the teacher and class, is on the path to discovery. If not, formative assessment helps us adjust teaching strategies based on data collected from the students. Summative assessment addresses the third question. It provides evidence that demonstrates whether the children learned what we intended to teach.

Self-Check 5.1
Click to gauge your understanding of the concepts in this chapter.

5.2 Describe and identify three-dimensional assessment

How do you create a meaningful assessment system that will tell whether your students understand the science practices, disciplinary core ideas, and crosscutting concepts that you aim to teach? Three-dimensional assessment is the phrase used to describe assessment that is multiple and varied to capture the progress of students toward and their achievement of performance expectations. The NGSS provides many resources to assist your development of three-dimensional assessment. In particular, the NGSS Evidence Statements can provide some structure to guide development.

Use as your foundation the major approaches to assessment discussed in this chapter. Then consider your curriculum—specific units you teach or observe being taught. With that material in mind, try to answer the question, "What is the ideal way to assess whether children are understanding, making sense, and seeking explanations successfully across all dimensions?" Certainly, the answer must lie in your clever integration of assessment strategies plus your familiarity with what you teach.

Self-Check 5.2
Click to gauge your understanding of the concepts in this chapter.

5.3 Explain how rubrics and scoring guides are used and describe their effectiveness as assessment tools

Choosing the proper assessment instrument to collect informative data is helpful only if you have a way to interpret the data. Multiple-choice and true-false assessments are relatively straightforward to interpret and use to assign a level of achievement. Science notebooks, problem-based challenges, and explanations require rubrics that serve as guides to assess understanding and achievement. Rubrics can be analytical or holistic. Together, assessment strategies and rubrics can help you identify not only whether students are progressing in their understanding but also their strengths and weaknesses with respect to the depth of understanding they demonstrate.

Assessments let you know the impact of the many hours spent planning and agonizing to get a lesson or unit just right. Good assessment begins with the identification of clear and concise content to be taught and an awareness of the student behaviors and outcomes that you will measure to indicate learning. Remember that there is no one-size-fits-all assessment strategy. Use a variety of traditional and performance assessments because your students will have a variety of achievement levels, aptitudes, and attitudes. If you are able to assess students' performances well and use the information to inform your teaching, your students will become better students, and you, of course, will become an even better teacher. Use the guide in Figure 5.4 to help plan your assessment.

Self-Check 5.3
Click to gauge your understanding of the concepts in this chapter.

Figure 5.4 Use the guide to help you plan your assessment

Know what you intend to teach
  • Look to the content to be taught for guidance

Decide which of your assessments will be formative or summative
  • On the path to learning (formative)
  • Mastery of content (summative)

Know which student performances indicate learning
  • Look to your performance objectives for guidance
  • Be sure that the criteria are measurable

Choose assessment strategies that meet your needs

Develop a rubric that you can use to analyze student outcomes

GOING FURTHER

On Your Own or in a Cooperative Learning Group

1. Select a science topic you might teach to children at a grade level of your choice. For that topic, suggest a specific subject for an age-appropriate, inquiry-based project. Then briefly describe how you would apply the strategies suggested in this chapter to determine whether the children were successful in completing the project.

2. Imagine that you and some other teachers have decided to give a back-to-school night presentation that will provide the rationale for using science portfolios in place of traditional assessment techniques. Prepare a PowerPoint presentation that you could use as part of the presentation.

RESOURCES FOR DISCOVERY LEARNING

- **NGSS Evidence Statements:**
  https://www.nextgenscience.org/evidence-statements

- **Next Generation Science Assessment:**
  https://concord.org/projects/ngss-assessments

- **Authentic Assessment Toolbox:**
  http://jfmueller.faculty.noctrl.edu/toolbox/

Internet Resources

- **Science Notebooks in K12 Classrooms:**
  STEM Notebooks
  https://www.wastatelaser.org/science-notebooks/

- **The Science Spot:**
  http://sciencespot.net/Pages/ISNinfo.html

Print Resources

Coray, Gail. (2000). Rubrics made simple. *Science Scope*, 23(6): 38–49.

Craven, John A., & Hogan, Tracy. (2001). Assessing student participation in the classroom. *Science Scope*, 25(1): 36–40.

Eberle, F., et al. (2008). Formative assessment probes. *Science and Children*, 45(5): 50–54.

Guskey, Thomas R. (2003). How classroom assessments improve learning. *Educational Leadership*, 60(5): 6–11.

Herman, J. (2013). *Formative assessment for Next Generation Science Standards: A proposed model*. Paper presented at the Invitational Research Symposium on Science Assessment, Washington, DC. Sep 24-25, 2013: K-12 Center at ETS.

Jabot, M., et al. (2007). Mental models of elementary and middle school students in analyzing simple battery and bulb circuits. *School Science and Mathematics*, 107(1): 371–381.

Keeley, P. (2015). Formative assessment probes: Constructing Cl-Ev-R explanations to formative assessment probes. *Science and Children*, 53(03). doi:10.2505/4/sc15_053_03_26

Neill, Monty. (2003). The dangers of testing. *Educational Leadership*, 60(5): 43–45.

Otero, V. K., et al. (2008). Preservice elementary teachers' views of their students' prior knowledge of science. *Journal of Research in Science Teaching*, 45(4): 497–523.

Pelligrino, J. W. (2002-2003). Knowing what students know. *Issues in Science and Technology*, 19(2): 48–52.

Pellegrino, J. W. (2014). *Developing assessments for the next generation science standards*. Washington, DC: The National Academies Press.

Siegel, M. A., Wissehr, C., & Halverson, K. (2008). Sounds like success: A framework for equitable assessment. How to revise written assessments for English language learners. *The Science Teacher*, 75(3): 43–46.

Sunda, Ruth. (2003). Thinking about thinking—What makes a good question? *Learning & Leading with Technology*, 30(5): 10–15.

Waters, M., et al. (2008). Science rocks! A performance assessment for earth science. *Science Activities*, 45(1): 23–28.

Wiggins, G., & McTighe, J. (2012). Understanding by Design Framework. White paper. ASCD: Alexandria, VA.

Notes

1. *A Framework for K–12 Science Education: Practices, Crosscutting Concepts, and Core Ideas.* (2012). Washington, DC: National Academies Press, p. 261.
2. References Herman, J. (2013). *Formative assessment for Next Generation Science Standards: A proposed model.* Paper presented at the Invitational Research Symposium on Science Assessment, Washington, DC. Sep 24-25, 2013: K-12 Center at ETS
3. Ibid.
4. Sadler, D. R. (1989). Formative assessment and the design of instructional systems. *Instructional Science, 18*: 119–144.
5. Pellegrino, James W. (2014). *Developing assessments for the next generation science standards.* Washington, DC: National Academies Press, p. 45
6. Atkin, J. M., Black, P., & Coffey, J. (2001). *Classroom assessment and the national science standards.* Washington, DC: National Academies Press.
7. Donovan, S., & Bransford, J. (2005). How students learn: science in the classroom. Washington, D.C.: National Academies Press.
8. Shwartz, Y., Ben-Zvi, R., & Hofstein, A. (2006). The use of scientific literacy taxonomy for assessing the development of chemical literacy among high-school students. *Chemistry Education Research and Practice, 7*(4): 203–225.
9. Keeley, P., Eberle, F., & Farrin, L. (2005). *Uncovering student ideas in science.* Arlington, VA: NSTA Press.
10. Harris, Phillip, et al. (2012). Standardized tests do not effectively measure student achievement. In Dedria Bryfonski (Ed.), *Standardized testing.* Farmington Hill, MI: Greenhaven Press; Opposing viewpoints in context. (2011). In *The myths of standardized tests: Why they don't tell you what you think they do* (chap. 3, pp. 33–45). Retrieved April 29, 2017, from sandhills.idm.oclc.org/login?url=http://link.galegroup.com/apps/doc/EJ3010478218/OVIC?u=uni_rodit&xid=cec59f85.

Integrating Science and Engineering

How can I integrate inquiry-based science and engineering with other subjects in a child's school day?

Yuganov Konstantin/Shutterstock

Learning Objectives

After completing the activities in this chapter, you should be able to:

6.1 Describe strategies for integrating science/engineering and language arts.

6.2 Describe strategies for integrating science/engineering and mathematics.

6.3 Describe strategies for integrating science/engineering and social studies.

6.4 Describe strategies for integrating science/engineering and art.

6.5 Describe strategies for integrating science/engineering and music.

6.6 Describe strategies for integrating science/engineering and health/physical education.

▶ GETTING STARTED

Sarah was excited to finally have her own classroom. As a student teacher, she always felt like a guest, no matter how gracious an effort her cooperating teacher made to help Sarah feel welcome. Sarah knew and the students knew that it really was not her class. Today she had a totally different feeling as she entered the school as a full-fledged faculty member. There were still several weeks remaining before the first class, but she wanted to begin planning the curriculum and preparing the room for that first day in September. As she entered the room, she noticed a vase of flowers on the desk. She was very lucky to have such a thoughtful mentor teacher. This was going to be a wonderful year. Next to the vase lay the district curriculum frameworks. Her mentor teacher suggested that she familiarize herself with the frameworks before planning the curriculum. The document seemed awfully thick as Sarah lifted it and began to read through it. An hour later, her initial excitement dampened, Sarah wondered how she was ever going to cover all the content. There were standards for language arts, history and social science, mathematics, science, and technology/engineering, as well as health, art, and English language proficiency. Sarah knew that each subject was not a separate entity, at least not in real life, and that she had to integrate the content not only to cover it but also to enrich the learning experience for her students. However, integration is easier said than done. She was going to need some help.

The good news for Sarah and all other teachers is that human knowledge is interconnected. In fact, the same strategies for discovery and inquiry used in science and engineering apply across disciplines. A historian seeking to explain the causes of the American Revolution would ask about the key issues—how they are related, their contexts, and how they merged to create conditions ripe for a revolution. A literary agent reviewing a book might ask about the characters, how they are related, and how the time period or social context come together to form the plot. These are nothing more than versions of the more general fundamental questions of inquiry: What are the elements, rules of interaction, and background space that lead to the emergent properties of the system? This way of thinking connects learning in different domains to a common process of inquiry and discovery.

As you plan science and engineering units, remember that these units can draw together a variety of subjects, acting as a kind of "superglue" that connects the learning in a range of areas and shows how human knowledge and experience fit together to form a larger, more meaningful whole. So let's consider some practical things you can do to integrate science and engineering with other subjects.

The Next Generation Science Standards[1]

Two of the three dimensions of the Next Generation Science Standards (NGSS)—Scientific and Engineering Practices and Crosscutting Concepts—provide insight regarding the broad integration of science and engineering across disciplines.

Using the crosscutting concept "systems and system models" as a theme, for example, you could teach children that a whole object, event, or interaction is made of parts; that those parts relate to each other; and that those parts affect the whole. Using the theme "models," you could teach that models are either real things or ideas that are used as tools to explain concepts, ideas, and phenomena. Patterns are recognizable in both literature and math as well as science and engineering. Using the crosscutting concept "scale, proportion, and quantity," you could help children see that things that differ from one another in terms of size, weight, or any other variable may also behave differently.

Enhanced eText Video Example 6.1

Listen to teacher Nancy Michael share her experience integrating the science curriculum. How does her example integrate language arts, math, technology, and science? Can you suggest that engineering and social studies could be integrated into a unit on plants and the environment?

Science/Engineering and Language Arts

"That cloud looks like a pregnant polar bear."

Children have a natural inclination to react to the world around them, and they absorb information from what they see, hear, taste, and touch, as well as what they read. They can also respond in many ways, talking, writing, and drawing about what they absorb. Like scientists, children develop a repertoire of specific reading and writing process skills that enable them to carefully observe and react to what they experience through their senses. The next few sections describe techniques you can use to help children expand both their science/engineering and their language arts abilities.

● The Common Core State Standards

The Common Core State Standards for English Language Arts and Mathematics were released in 2010. They were developed to help K–12 educators identify the knowledge and skills students should have upon graduation from high school to adequately be prepared for success as they enter the workplace or higher education. Most states have adopted the Common Core State Standards. These standards are informative when considering integration across disciplines. You will notice that many of these standards are complementary with science and engineering practice and skills. For example,

> English Language Arts Standards » Grade 2 » 1: "Ask and answer such questions as who, what, where, when, why, and how to demonstrate understanding of key details in a text."

And for Grade 4, "Refer to details and examples in a text when explaining what the text says explicitly and when drawing inferences from the text."[2] Asking questions, creating detailed descriptions, and drawing inferences based on evidence are practices and skills that easily cut across disciplines.

You will find the Common Core State Standards useful as you plan the integration of science with other disciplines. Many of the suggestions for integration that follow are consistent with the Common Core State Standards.

● Selecting Trade Books That Stimulate Inquiry and Discovery

One feature of your classroom should be an extensive collection of books that motivate children to think and engage in inquiry-based, discovery science.

Trade books are volumes distributed by commercial publishers that do just that. They are not textbooks. Instead, they focus on scientific adventures, the lives of scientists, and science careers and provide factual material about stars, planets, dolphins, the rain forest, and much more.

How can you select the best possible trade books for your children? Try using the following criteria, which were suggested by a distinguished panel of teachers and other science educators:

- The book has a substantial amount of science or engineering content.
- The information presented is clear, accurate, and up to date.
- Theories and facts are clearly distinguished.
- Facts are not oversimplified so as to make the information misleading.
- Generalizations are supported by facts, and significant facts are not left out.
- The book does not contain gender, ethnic, or socioeconomic bias.[3]

I won't provide you with a list of recommended science and engineering trade books because many new ones appear each month. Instead, I'll direct you to two excellent and easily accessible sources that *do* provide lists of the very best modern trade books for children and youths:

1. An annual article in *Science and Children* whose title is always "Outstanding Science Trade Books for Students K–12"
2. The site www.nsta.org, where you can select the feature "NSTA Recommends"

Three Integrating Techniques

As the children entered the classroom on Monday morning, their exclamations could be heard the length of the hallway: "Wow!" "What happened here?" "It's beautiful!"

Over the weekend, their fourth-grade teacher had transformed the classroom into a tropical rain forest. The children knew that this was going to be no ordinary day. But their teacher was no ordinary teacher.[4]

Indeed, any teacher who finds creative ways to cross subject matter barriers using language arts as the bridge is special. You can be such a teacher if you focus on actively finding techniques to tie together science/engineering and language arts. Rakow and Vasquez, who described the fourth-grade teacher in the preceding excerpt, suggest three ways to do this:

1. *Literature-based integration* is the use of fiction and nonfiction science books to help children acquire science-related information. In addition, for children who might benefit from getting science information through a storyline, many fictional books by authors such as Eric Carle and Tomie dePaola have science information and concepts threaded through them. One of my all-time favorites for engineering is *Mike Mulligan and His Steam Shovel* by Virginia Lee Burton.[5]

2. *Theme-based integration* is instruction in which a major theme or concept becomes the foundation for a learning unit that cuts across subject lines. Think in creative ways as you identify a theme such as "Ecosystems" for life sciences, "Space Neighbors" for astronomy, "What is it made of?" for physical sciences, or "How does it work?" for engineering.

3. *Project-based integration* involves children in actually carrying out a long-term activity in which they investigate a real-world problem. Here are a few examples of science- and engineering-related projects that provide excellent opportunities to tie language arts development to science content:

- Designing a method to measure the amount of paper wasted each day in a classroom or school and communicating ideas to others that will help solve the problem

- Discovering how much water is wasted at school water fountains each day or week and communicating ideas to others that will help stop the waste
- Discovering how well school hot lunch offerings and student choices match proper nutrition guidelines and communicating ideas to others that will help children choose better lunches[6]

Weaving It All Together with Language Arts

Class time overflows with children dictating stories, chanting, singing, speaking, writing, constructing "big books," and the like. These experiences help children develop and improve their language arts skills.

Language arts teaching strategies can be easily adapted to enrich and extend children's science experiences. Writing stories about butterflies and rockets, making "big books" about insects, and writing and singing songs about saving Earth's natural resources are activities that involve children in a variety of science topics and help develop their language arts skills.

I hope that you will create appropriate ways to develop each component of language arts through science. In the sections that follow, you will find some very specific ways to achieve a science/language arts synergy.

Extending the Basics: Vocabulary, Comprehension, and Writing

Someday, somewhere, some child will come up to you, look you straight in the eyes, and ask with a giggle, "What grows down while growing up?" And you will enjoy not only the joke but also what telling it has to say about that child's ability to use language.

Unfortunately, for many children, words and their meanings are *not* sources of jokes and riddles. For these children, words are mysterious combinations of ink marks that make little sense and create little pleasure. If you are not alert to the need to teach and reinforce reading skill development, the printed page of a science book can serve as a source of frustration for a child who has limited vocabulary skills. English language learners face challenges associated with learning content and language skills, both verbal and written, that enable them to express their understanding effectively. Research suggests that progress toward these two goals can be developed simultaneously by incorporating strategies used in the *Sheltered Instruction Observation Protocol (SIOP)* with constructivist learning approaches typical of discovery-centered learning.[7, 8] As suggested in previous chapters, science is particularly rich with opportunities for language demand. SIOP provides effective strategies that leverage language demand to develop language and content understanding. SIOP and its application in context of the 5E instructional strategy is addressed in more detail in Chapter 3.

Using Descriptive Modeling to Build Vocabulary   Descriptive modeling provides a meaningful context for children to use words and consequently build their vocabulary. Here are some specific strategies consistent with the SIOP model that you can use to help children broaden their vocabulary through descriptive modeling:

- *Build Background:* Introduce new vocabulary with a list of descriptive terms that children can use while developing their descriptive models. Post new science words and their definitions as they emerge in class on a piece of newsprint or poster board to create word banks. Keep the word banks posted in the room for children to refer to during the unit.

Enhanced eText Video Example 6.2

Listen to teacher Sheri Geitner discuss how she creatively integrates literature, science, and engineering for elementary school children. How does the teacher integrate literature and math into the lesson about push-pull?

- Look through science trade books and elementary science textbooks before the children work with them to *identify terms that may be too difficult to learn from the context* and then preteach those words.
- *Pronounce science vocabulary words with children* before they reach them in their science materials.
- *Have each child develop a personal word card file* that lists and defines each new science word. Each card should include the word, the sentence in which the word was found, a phonetic respelling of the word, and, if appropriate, a drawing or diagram showing the object or concept that the word defines.

Comprehension   The quest to seek explanations makes science a compelling backdrop for comprehension. If children are engaged and invested in finding an answer, then they will be more motivated to read for understanding.

You can help children build their comprehension skills in science by focusing their attention on prereading experiences. Before the children begin reading a specific text, trade book, or Internet article, focus your discussion of the material around three magic words:

1. **What?** When you distribute trade books, text material, or resource material on a science topic, take the time to discuss exactly what you expect the children to do with it. Describe how much time they will have and what they are expected to produce as a result of the reading.

2. **Why?** Take the time to explain to children why they are going to do the assignment. Do your best to describe how it will relate to work they have done before and work that will follow.

3. **How?** Describe how you expect children to learn from the material they are reading. You might say something like this: "Here are some topics you can use to organize the information you get about the planets from your reading: What is the planet's size compared to Earth? What is the surface like? How long is a day on the planet? You should list the questions in your science notebook before you start reading. That way, you will have a specific place to put the information that you find in the book."

Enhanced eText Video Example 6.3

Listen to Sheri Geitner share insights about learning strategies to meet the needs of English language learners.

Provide sentence stems for students. For instance: "Compared to Earth, the planet is . . . . . ." "The surface of the planet looks like . . . . . . " One day on the planet is the same as _____ days on Earth.

Create a T chart, label one side Earth and the other side the Planet (i.e., Mars, Neptune). Draw the planets as they appear from space.

Provide opportunities for students to express their descriptions in language, writing, and illustration. Group language-proficient students with ELL students. Coach language-proficient students to speak slowly and clearly, using body language to support communication.

REALITY check

Theme-Based Science Units and Essential Questions

When developing theme-based science units, avoid broad topics such as "The RainForest" or "The Oceans of the World." Rather, identify a science concept and essential question that will serve as the focus of inquiry, such as "RainForests and Oceans: How Can They Both Be Ecosystems?" This theme develops the concept of ecosystems, rather than the rainforest or ocean as entities in and of themselves. Most of your students will live neither in the rainforest nor the ocean, but all will live in an ecosystem.

Below are broad topics for theme-based integration. Rewrite each with an essential question that reflects a science concept.

Theme	Essential question
Volcanoes	
Adaptation	
Minerals	
Earthquakes	
The solar system	
Life cycles	

Writing

"Writing is like talking to your best friend."
—Eric, a first-grader

"Writing is a dance in the sun."
—Christi Ann, a second-grader

"Writing is meeting the person in me I never knew."
—Mike, a seventh-grader[9]

This excerpt from *Reading and Learning to Read* tells a lot about the power you give children when you help them learn how to move their thoughts to a page. Science classrooms that provide children with opportunities to explore the natural world are places that provoke thought and thus create an unending array of possibilities for communication through the powerful medium of the written word. When you are teaching science, you are offering the possibility of many "dances in the Sun."

You are quite fortunate when you teach children science because the breadth of content, processes, and affect that you teach are well matched by the range of writing forms that elementary school children need to practice. In *Language Arts: Learning Processes and Teaching Practices*, Temple and Gillet suggest that there are six basic writing forms:[10]

Description	Expression	Persuasion
Exposition	Narration	Poetry

Here are some examples of how you can help children develop their abilities with each writing form. I am sure that you can suggest many others:

- **Description.** Have the children describe in detail an animal they observe on a class trip to a zoo.
- **Exposition.** Have the children explain how to make a bulb light using just one battery, one wire, and one bulb.

- **Expression.** Have the children write thank-you letters to a park ranger who visited the class to talk about protecting the natural environment.
- **Narration.** Have the children write stories about an incident in the life of a young girl who decides to be the first astronaut to set foot on the planet Mars.
- **Persuasion.** Have the children write scripts for a children's television commercial that will convince others to eat more green, leafy vegetables.
- **Poetry.** Have the children observe and draw a seashell and then write poems that use at least three of the observations they made about the shell.

Science/Engineering and Mathematics

In The Phantom Tollbooth *by Norton Juster, Milo, the watchdog Tock, and the Dodecahedron are three characters trying to find out where numbers come from. On their quest they discover a number mine, where numbers reside.*[11]

The journey of Milo and his friends to the numbers mine has always struck me as an excellent frame of reference for both understanding the difficulties children may have with mathematics and helping them overcome those difficulties. Some children view numbers as squiggly lines on paper that have no basis in reality. For all they know, numbers come from number mines! Although there are many aspects of elementary school mathematics that can be reinforced, extended, and enriched as children do science, three are particularly important: computational skills, data collection and expression, and logical reasoning.

Computational Skills

Figure 6.1 provides examples of various ways in which computational skills can be practiced and put to real work during science. As you look over the figure, see if you can think of other ways to have children work on computation as they carry out science activities and projects.

Data Collection and Expression

Woosh—one of several paper airplanes fill the room as they dive, twist, and sail by me with excited 8-year-olds in hot pursuit. Does this chaotic scene result from a lack of discipline? It could, but this time it is characteristic of a dynamic, hands-on activity during which students design, test, and redesign to maximize the distance paper airplanes will fly.

Although I don't suggest this particular activity for either brand-new or veteran teachers with limited classroom management skills, I share it with you to focus attention on what a creative science teacher can do to build a child's science/math skills. Even though flying paper airplanes may not be your first choice of an activity to use when your school principal is observing your magnificent teaching talents, it does provide a good data-collection and data-expression experience. Notice the true sophistication of the activity:

In this experiment students test the effects of wing shape on distance. Wing shape is the independent variable and distance is the dependent variable. To keep the test fair, all other variables such as the type and amount of paper, test area, and launcher are kept constant. Data generated from repeated trials and expressed in graphs are used to assess prototypes and inform new designs, resulting in an iterative engineering design process.

Figure 6.1 A variety of science activities can be done to improve math computational skills

Computational Skill	Science-Teaching Example
• Counting	Determine the number of pieces of litter on the school lawn.
• Addition	Keep track of the number of birds that visit a feeder.
• Subtraction	Measure children's heights at the beginning and end of the year and calculate growth.
• Multiplication	Estimate the number of birds in a flock on the school lawn by first counting a small group and then multiplying by the number of groups.
• Division	Do a school survey of animals in classrooms, and find the average number in each.
• Working with fractions	Place half a collection of seeds in moist soil and half in dry soil, and compare their relative growth.
• Working with decimals and percentages	Study the list of ingredients and the nutrition chart on a box of sweetened cereal, and figure out what part of the weight of the cereal is sugar.

Even if you are not quite ready (or will never be ready) to extend science through paper airplane flights, you can do equally interesting, if not equally exciting, activities that lead to data collection and expression. For example, you can have the children observe changes in the level of water in an open container. Begin by having a child place a mark on the container to show the present water level. The children can then mark the level each day for several days. At the conclusion of the observation period, have the children measure the distance from the first mark to the new marks and make graphs to show the changes.

Can very young children express data through graphs and charts? They certainly can! By cutting paper strips that represent the distance from the water level to the original mark in the preceding example, the measurement for each day can be recorded. The paper strips can then be placed in sequence to produce a rudimentary graph of changes in water level.

Make the CASE

Following the data-gathering process, the children can be led through a discussion about the lengths of their paper strips. Probe their understanding of math concepts with questions such as these:

- Can you explain why the strips are different lengths?
- How much longer is the longest strip than the shortest?
- How do the changes shown by your strips compare with those shown by other children's strips?

Enhanced eText Video Example 6.4

Watch as students make measurements while they study sound. How could math be integrated more rigorously into this lesson?

• Logical Reasoning

An important goal of mathematics education for children is to develop an understanding of the logical structure of mathematics. In practice, this means a child is able to look at collections of items and make statements about them and the outcomes of grouping and regrouping them. This is the mathematics of sets and subsets, open sentences, and the commutative, associative, and distributive properties. Science experiences can provide children with opportunities to put their understanding of mathematical concepts to work. You could, for example, have the children in your class do these activities:

- Group collections of plants into sets and subsets.
- Devise a system for classifying organisms into the set of all plants and the set of all animals.
- Identify the similarities and differences of various elements of the set of all birds and fish.
- Use a list of characteristics to determine whether an organism is part of such subsets as fish, birds, and reptiles.

Science/Engineering and Social Studies

The children noticed a tremendous amount of food seemed to go to waste in the cafeteria. Food scraps were thrown into the trash bins along with milk cartons, wrappers, straws, and napkins. The children agreed that most of their classmates did not think about the wasted food. After deciding that the food could be put in compost bins and the resulting compost used in the school gardens or even sold during the spring fundraiser, they needed to think of a way to raise the awareness of their classmates to cooperate in separating food waste from trash.

Social studies and science/engineering can easily be integrated because societal problems, in many cases, lend themselves to real-life inquiry-based experiences for children. An engineering component can easily be added to the scenario by challenging students to propose a design for a composting process that would make it easy for students to access.

The lesson in sustainability just described shows how challenging children with meaningful projects can tie together science/engineering and social studies. Adding a social dimension raises important issues about individual and societal attitudes and values. Here is a sampling of the types of questions you can use to stimulate attitude- and value-based science discussions and to generate ideas for activities and projects that relate science/engineering and social studies:

- Should animals be kept in zoos?
- Should the town build a soccer field on the local wetland?
- Should a factory that provides many jobs for people but also pollutes the town's air and water be closed down?
- Should people be required to wear seat belts?
- Should commercials for sugar-sweetened cereals be shown during Saturday morning children's shows?

Figure 6.2 Many social studies topics can be extended through science activities

Social Studies Topic	Related Science Concept
• The natural resources of a country	The Sun as the original energy source in the solar system
	The protection of air and water resources
	The use of alternative energy sources
• The history and development of a country or part of the world	Contributions made by specific scientists and inventors
• The employment of North Americans in diverse occupations	Career awareness for occupations in science and technology
• The structure of the family and other social groups; the interaction of group members	The effect of improved technology on providing increased leisure time
• The production, transportation, and consumption of goods and services	The challenge of preserving and transporting perishable food across long distances

With any lesson or unit, clearly identify the targeted content to be taught. If you prepare a science unit on pollution, consider the science behind the pollution. For example, if you choose a lesson on oil pollution, address the effect of oil on the capacity for bird feathers to repel water or on the density of oil compared to water. Challenge the students to design a tool for cleaning oil off the surface of the water. When children address legal and social issues such as whether there should be offshore oil drilling, encourage them to use reasoning based on the science rather than pure emotion.

Also see Figure 6.2, which shows how a number of social studies topics can be extended through related science content. Integrating these two content areas will help children realize the science/social studies connection.

Science/Engineering and Art

Nature has inspired artists since the early cave paintings approximately 40,000 years ago. Keep the tradition going by encouraging your students not only to draw, photograph, and video the natural world at the micro as well as macro levels but also to look for patterns (an NGSS crosscutting concept) found in textures and colors in nature. Investigate color. Most students think color comes from the object, but the color we see originates from the reflection of white light off an object. Explore where the colors of a rainbow come from and why the sky is blue. For example, rainbows are a favorite of the fourth-graders in our classes. A simple prism demonstration provides evidence that colors are in white light that surrounds us, but raises questions about why we see things in different colors. You could follow this demonstration with lessons that help children discover that the colors of objects are results of the light reflected from objects back to our eyes.

Figure 6.3   These sample activities integrate art and science

- *Tree Stump Rubbings:* Place paper on a smooth, recently cut tree stump, and rub the paper with a pencil. Follow-up activities may include discussions about climatic changes, as reflected in changes in the annual ring pattern, and how the rings can be used to find the age of the tree.

- *Leaf Rubbings:* Place paper over a variety of leaves, and rub the paper with the side of a crayon. Follow-up activities include observation of leaf veins in the print and discussion of the variety of leaves found or defects in leaf surfaces as a result of insect activity.

- *Native Crafts:* Use natural objects to make sculptures, including mobiles or stabiles, and pictures. Examples include stone people, acorn people, applehead dolls, fruit and vegetable prints, dried flowers, and shell sculptures.

- *Sand Painting:* After studying the origin and characteristics of sand, dye the sand to use in sand paintings. This can be integrated with social studies, since it is an activity that comes from the heritage of native North Americans.

- *Moving Sculpture:* Build simple circuits to operate sculptures that have moving parts as well as blinking lights.

What Earth materials are used to make sculptures? Where does marble come from, and what are the properties of marble that make it challenging and appealing for sculptors? How are dyes and paints made from nature (plants, insects, minerals)? Let students discover dyes and make dyes from natural resources found in the schoolyard. You can find many resources online for making homemade dyes from items such as purple cabbage, onion skins, and coffee grounds. Use the dye to make a tie-dye T-shirt. Investigate how indigenous people used regional resources to produce dyes and colors. Explore connections to history and trade based on the textiles made by these dyes. Trace the impact of lapis lazuli, a rare semi-precious stone found in Afghanistan prized for its intense blue color and used by 19th-century artists to create ultramarine paint.

Figure 6.3 has more examples for integration art and science. Use your imagination, and you will find a multitude of ways to use art for teaching science and to teach the science of art.

Learn about creative ways to use visual art, drama, and songs to teach science.

Science/Engineering and Music

Music has become so much a part of our daily lives that we are sometimes oblivious to it, but the children you teach are not. Even very young children are able to hum, dance, whistle, and sing a multitude of breakfast cereal commercials and know some of the words and phrases of the most popular songs. Music has had a profound impact upon our culture, and we should be able to take advantage of its ability to attract and hold a child's attention when we teach science.

Music is a fertile topic for science and engineering. Connect the concepts of vibration, amplitude, frequency, and wavelength to familiar instruments and melodies, as well as students' own voices. Use guitar strings to explore frequencies and

Enhanced eText Video Example 6.5

Watch and listen as teacher Nicole Bay invites students to investigate properties of sound. Think about possible ways music could be integrated into this lesson. Use your imagination!

pitch. Bang drums to experience and describe vibration as it relates to sound. Design and construct instruments that play a familiar tune from popsicle sticks, rubber bands, or straw kazoos. Explore how the lengths of popsicle sticks, kazoos, or the size of rubber bands affect frequency and pitch.

Another strategy for relating music and science is to locate music that was composed to express feelings about topics that you are covering in science. For example, if you teach the four seasons, you can fill your classroom with selections from Vivaldi's Concerto in F Minor, op. 8, no. 4, "Winter," from *The Four Seasons*.

A Note about STEAM: Science, Technology, Engineering, the Arts and Mathematics

STEAM, at its core, is about integration that embraces standards from each of the respective disciplines. Arts in the context of STEAM include not just the visual arts, but music and humanities as well. STEAM challenges educators to distinguish between integration of the arts as an enhancement of science, technology, engineering, and mathematics and genuine integration intended to give equal intention to art and STEM disciplines.[12] This implies that art standards receive equal import with respect to concept development and assessment. This represents a subtle shift by both art and STEM proponents.

Proponents of STEAM often refer to the creativity and innovation afforded by the arts. While this may be true, it is also the case that STEM fields, by their very nature, are based on creativity, innovation, and the ability to think outside the box. However, it is not clear that STEM is perceived as such by much of society. STEAM, when truly understood and implemented, may serve as an invitation to creative thinking in the STEM fields. An example of goals that might integrate STEM in art and art in STEM would be understanding the geometry of design features or the science in mixing colors on a painter's pallet.

Science/Engineering, Health, and Physical Education

Sit down gently on a soft, grassy spot. Imagine you are a seed buried in the shallow ground. Pull you knees up to your chest and wrap your arms around them. Feel the cool ground begin to warm. A gentle rain moistens the soil around you. The moisture gradually penetrates your hard, dry seed coat. You become relaxed and begin to expand. Slowly unwrap your arms. Stretch out your legs. Reach for the sky and feel your shoots burst through the soil into the warm sunlight and fresh air.

Wouldn't doing this activity be a nice way to review some of the concepts taught in a unit on germination while helping a child develop his or her motor skills? The concepts that underlie physical education activities for children are clearly related to many of the topics of elementary school science. As an engineering design challenge, have students design an obstacle course that tests speed, agility, and strength or an outdoor fitness station for the school grounds they can propose to the school committee.

The physical education component of a child's day focuses on such matters as engaging in recreational activities that may be carried out over a lifetime, improving general health, and developing strength and coordination through a variety of movement activities. Thus, much of what is done during a modern physical education class actually is related to common science vocabulary terms, such as *time*, *space*, and *force*.

Fitness tracker technologies provide increasing opportunities to make relevant and meaningful connections to science and engineering. Even cell phones can track steps, distance, and calories burned. The data is compelling because it is about the students. Admittedly, few elementary schools have access to fitness trackers; however, they are being used by some physical education programs to promote wellness through healthy activity.[13] Data collected by fitness trackers has potential as a portal to engage students in both the science-related concepts that could emerge such as nutrition and energy, body systems, homeostasis, and physics (biomechanics). Analyzing and interpreting data, planning, and carrying out investigations are among potential science practices that would be supported by fitness tracker technologies.

To build your own bridge between physical education and science/engineering, you need to establish a working relationship with your school's physical education teacher. If you teach in a self-contained classroom, strive to develop each curriculum—science and physical education—in a way that emphasizes and extends the concepts common to both.

REALITY check

Choose one of the integration challenges

1. How would you integrate a social studies unit on the Pilgrims with a science unit on the weather?
2. The children are having a kickball tournament in physical education class. There is a controversy brewing about how much air to put in the ball. Some argue that the harder the ball, the farther it will go. Others argue that ball will travel farther if it is softer. How can you take advantage of this disagreement to deepen the children's science content and/or process knowledge?

Summary

The Next Generation Science Standards

Two of the three dimensions of the Next Generation Science Standards (NGSS)—Scientific and Engineering Practices and Crosscutting Concepts—provide insight regarding the broad integration of science and engineering across disciplines.

6.1 Science/Engineering and Language Arts

The Common Core State Standards for English Language Arts and Mathematics provide guidance about the content in those disciplines with which you can integrate science. Science provides many opportunities for children to ask questions, create detailed descriptions, and communicate effectively. As you deepen your knowledge and familiarity with content and strategies in science education, use your expertise in language arts to seek connections to science through stories, themes, and projects that inspire reading, writing, and verbal communication skills.

 Self-Check 6.1
Click to gauge your understanding of the concepts in this chapter.

6.2 Science/Engineering and Mathematics

As students become more proficient in seeking explanations based on evidence, math will provide them with tools to seek patterns and express relationships. At the elementary level, much can be done with basic math concepts such as counting, measurement, data collection and organization in tables and graphs, and estimations that reinforce basic computational skills involving multiplication, division, simple geometry, and fractions that are represented in the Common Core State Standards for Mathematics.

 Self-Check 6.2
Click to gauge your understanding of the concepts in this chapter.

6.3 Science/Engineering and Social Studies

Integrating social studies with science may seem challenging, but once you begin to see the connections, the possibilities seem endless. Social issues provide contexts that often make the quest for explanations or solutions to problems purposeful. Creating persuasive arguments for why the school cafeteria should incorporate recycling or working to design user-friendly recycling bins demands an awareness of social issues, scientific principles, and engineering design for integration.

 Self-Check 6.3
Click to gauge your understanding of the concepts in this chapter.

6.4 Science/Engineering in Art and Music

Nature inspires art, and much of science has been recorded and documented through art since prehistoric time. Furthermore, there is a wealth of science and engineering in the arts and music. Art is a product of raw materials and technology that lead to expressions on canvas, in sculpture, and through music. Consider the science behind elements associated with the arts and music such as the science of color (primary colors, white light, rainbows, reflection, absorption) and the science of music (frequency, pitch, amplitude, waves).

Self-Check 6.4

Click to gauge your understanding of the concepts in this chapter.

6.5 Science/Engineering, Health, and Physical Education

When the body moves, physics, biology, and chemistry are involved. And whether you are swimming, running, sliding, or even flying, Earth science is part of the equation. Most sports have equipment and therefore integrate technology and engineering. As with art and music, look for connections that capitalize on the health and physical education that is part of children's daily experiences.

Learning inquiry and discovery are at the heart of science experiences for children and can also serve as the "glue" that ties together various subjects during the school day. There is great potential for the teacher who is willing to invest the energy to integrate science across disciplines. Consider not only teaching science using art, language arts, math, social studies, and physical education, but also teaching fundamental concepts of science inherent in these subjects.

Self-Check 6.5

Click to gauge your understanding of the concepts in this chapter.

GOING FURTHER   On Your Own or in a Cooperative Group

1. Choose one topic below and describe how you might integrate math, art, history, engineering, and language arts with the topic.

   a. The seasons

   b. Sound energy

   c. Endangered animal species

   d. Rocks and minerals

   e. The role of technology in our lives

2. Do an Internet search for STEAM lessons. Find a lesson that you think represents the intent of STEAM integration described in this chapter. Justify your choice with key elements from the lesson.

3. The study of current events can provide many opportunities to relate science and social studies. Identify a recent news story that had a significant scientific or technologic dimension. For this current event, describe a scientific principle that you could teach and a series of classroom activities that would provide children with experiences that highlight the relationship of science/engineering and social studies.

4. Select a topic in science that could be used as a theme in a variety of subject areas. If you are working with a group, have each person play the role of the teacher of a specific subject in a departmentalized elementary or middle school. Discuss how a group of teachers at the same grade level might plan a teaching unit that integrates the subject areas. (If you are doing this on your own, prepare a written statement that highlights possible comments each teacher might make.)

5. Interview a teacher who works in a self-contained classroom. During the interview, determine the following:

   a. The major science topics emphasized during the year

b. The science processes that are emphasized

c. The extent to which the topics are enriched as a result of his or her efforts to relate other subjects to science

6. Interview a science teacher in a departmentalized elementary or middle school. During your discussion, determine the following:

   a. The major topics and processes emphasized during the year

b. The approximate length of a science class

c. Whether other teachers at the grade level are aware of the topics dealt with in the science curriculum

d. Whether all the teachers at the grade level ever work together to plan and teach units with interdisciplinary themes

RESOURCES FOR DISCOVERY LEARNING

- **University of Illinois at Chicago Learning Sciences Research Institute College of Liberal Arts and Sciences Teaching Integrated Mathematics and Science (TIMS) Project:**
  http://www.lsri.uic.edu/projects/tims.asp

- **Scholastic:**
  http://www.scholastic.com

- **TeachHub.com:**
  http://www.teachhub.com

- **Outstanding Science Trade Books for Students K–12:**
  http://www.nsta.org/publications/ostb/

Internet Resources

- **NSTA Recommends:**
  http://www.nsta.org/recommends/

- **Resources for STEAM:**
  https://www.edutopia.org/article/STEAM-resources

- **STEM to STEAM:**
  http://stemtosteam.org/

- **Children's Book Council: Best STEM 2017 List:**
  http://www.cbcbooks.org/best-stem/

Print Resources

Ansberry, Karen R., & Morgan, Emily. (2005). *Picture perfect science lessons: Using children's books to guide inquiry.* Arlington, VA: NSTA Press.

Kim, Y., & Park, N. (2012). The effect of STEAM education on elementary school student's creativity improvement. In Kim T. et al. (Eds.), *Computer applications for security, control and system engineering. Communications in computer and information science* (vol 339). Berlin, Heidelberg: Springer.

Kupfer, Joseph H. (2003). Engaging nature aesthetically. *Journal of Aesthetic Education, 37*(1): 77–89.

Lee, Michele, Lostoski, Maria, & Williams, Kathy. (2000). Diving into a schoolwide science theme. *Science and Children, 38*(1): 31–35.

Minton, Sandra. (2003). Using movement to teach academics: An outline for success. *Journal of Physical Education, Recreation and Dance, 74*(2): 36–40.

Mixing it up: Integrated, interdisciplinary, intriguing science in the elementary classroom. (2003). Arlington, VA: NSTA Press.

Morris, R. V. (2007). Social studies around the Blacksmith's Forge: Interdisciplinary teaching and learning. *The Social Studies, 98*(3): 99–103.

Nikitina, Svetlana. (2003). Movement class as an integrative experience: Academic, cognitive, and social effects. *Journal of Aesthetic Education, 37*(1): 54–63.

Nutta, J., Bautista, N., & Butler, B. (2010). *Teaching science to English language learners.* Boston, MA: Routledge.

Rogers, M. A. P., et al. (2007). Connecting with other disciplines. *Science and Children, 44*(6): 58–59.

Settlage, J., Madsen, A., & Rustad, K. (2005). Inquiry science, sheltered instruction, and English language learners: Conflicting pedagogies in highly diverse classrooms. *Issues in Teacher Education, 14*(1): 39–57.

Shaw, E. L., et al. (2005). From boxed lunch to learning boxes: An interdisciplinary approach. *Science Activities, 42*(3): 16–25.

Silverman, E., et al. (2007). Cheep, chirp, twitter, & whistle. *Science and Children, 44*(6): 20–25.

Stoddart, T., Pinal, A., Letzke, M., & Canaday, D. (2002). Integrating inquiry science and language development for English language learners. *Journal of Research in Science Teaching, 39*(8): 664–687.

Notes

1. Next Generation Science Standards (NGSS) is a registered trademark of Achieve. Neither Achieve nor the lead states and partners that developed the Next Generation Science Standards was involved in the production of, and does not endorse, this product.
2. Common Core State Standards Initiative. (2013). *Preparing America's students for college and career*. Retrieved June 8, 2013, from www.corestandards.org
3. National Science Teachers Association (NSTA), Children's Book Council Joint Book Review Panel. (2002). Outstanding science trade books for students K–12. *Science and Children, 39*(6): 33.
4. Rakow, Steven J., & Vasquez, JoAnne. (1998). Integrated instruction: A trio of strategies. *Science and Children, 35*(6): 18.
5. Burton, V. (1967). *Mike Mulligan and his steam shovel*. Boston, MA: Houghton Mifflin.
6. Rakow & Vasquez, p. 19.
7. Kareva, V., & Echevarria, J. (2013). Using the SIOP model for effective content teaching with second and foreign language learners. *Journal of Education and Training Studies, 1*(2). Redfame Publishing. Retrieved October 2013, from http://jets.redfame.com.
8. Nutta, J., Bautista, N., & Butler, B. (2010). *Teaching science to English language learners*. Boston, MA: Routledge.
9. Vacca, Jo Anne L., Vacca, Richard T., & Gove, Mary K. (1991). *Reading and learning to read*. Boston, MA: Little Brown, p. 127.
10. Temple, C., & Gillet, J. W. (1989). *Language arts: Learning processes and teaching practices*. Glenview, IL: Scott, Foresman, p. 231.
11. Juster, N., & Feiffer, J. (1961). *The phantom tollbooth*. New York, NY: Epstein & Carroll, distributed by Random House.
12. Riley, S. (2013, December 18). Pivot point: At the crossroads of SEM, STEAM and arts integration. *Education Trends: Edutopia*.
13. Using technology in K-12 gym classes social media and digital business. Social media and digital business. (2016). Boston College Carroll School of Management. Retrieved May 14, 2017, from http://mashable.com/2016/04/06/adidas-fitness-tracker-gym-class-students/#nSktD8_ItPqt

Part 2 addresses content in the Earth/space, life, and physical sciences. Each chapter is designed to provide elementary science teachers with key concepts and explanations to support their science teaching. Subject matter has been organized by the NGSS core disciplinary ideas addressed in each section. For example, following the section in chapter 7 titled, "Plate Tectonics and Large-Scale System Interactions," (ESS2.B) is a discussion of tectonic plate movement caused by convection currents in Earth's mantle. Multiple-choice Self-Checks at the conclusion of each chapter provide a quick review of key concepts addressed in the chapter. While it is impossible to address all the content an elementary teacher may need to know, these chapters provide foundational knowledge for the beginning teacher.

The Earth/Space Sciences

▶ History and Nature of the Earth/Space Sciences

Tonight, and every night, you have the chance to see a wondrous puzzle exactly as generations of humans before you have seen it. Tiny objects will begin to emerge, gleaming and glimmering, and darkness will envelop everything around you. This great and glorious puzzle is the night sky.

Trying to make sense of what lies above us is a mark of our humanity. Likewise, the mysteries of the Earth below make us wonder. We ask "What?" and "How?" and "Why?"

These are the same questions that guide what Earth and space scientists do. They search for answers to the puzzles of our world, so we will eventually understand what really lies above and below. The Earth/space sciences include the fields of astronomy, geology, oceanography, meteorology, and astronomy. Each requires people who wonder.

Careers in the Earth/Space Sciences

Many career paths exist for those women and men who have the required motivation, knowledge, and skills to formally explore the sky above and the Earth below. Here are a few of the wide range of possibilities:

- *Astronaut.*   Astronauts are trained to fly, or be crew members of, spacecraft. Space exploration and research are entering a new era. There are private companies such as SpaceX active in the field, and plans to carry out deep exploration that include possible trips to Mars. Astronauts are needed with a wide variety of skills including but not limited to engineering, medicine, biology, chemistry, and physical sciences.

- *Atmospheric Scientist.*   Atmospheric science is the study of the physics and chemistry of clouds, gases, and aerosols (airborne particles) that surround the planetary bodies of the solar system. Most atmospheric scientists study the atmosphere of Earth, while others study the atmospheres of the planets and moons in our solar system.[i]

- *Geologist.*   I love to tease my geologist friends by calling them "rock watchers." Of course, they tell me with great gusto that they do much more than watch rocks—and of course, they do. Geology includes the study of the origin of the Earth, the history of Earth, and the external and internal structure and movements of Earth.

- *Oceanographer.*   Not all oceanographers spend the day scuba diving in warm tropical waters, but some do! In fact, the work done by oceanographers takes them to oceans all over the world. That work might involve study of the characteristics of the seafloor, the ocean water itself, and the forms of life in, on, and under the ocean.

- *Meteorologist.*   The constantly smiling and sometimes overly excited weather people you watch on local news shows may be meteorologists or newscasters reporting the weather observed and predicted by meteorologists. A real meteorologist has taken courses dealing with atmospheric phenomena and how various weather systems affect Earth.

[i] NASA www.nasa.gov

- *Astronomer.*   If you've looked at the night sky and been enthralled by the amazing display of objects above your head, you have taken the first step that all astronomers take: to think beyond the boundaries of Earth and its atmosphere. Modern astronomers have excellent backgrounds in physics and mathematics as well as considerable computer expertise.

Key Events in the Understanding of the Earth/Space Sciences

610–425 BCE	Philosophers Anaximander, Pythagoras, Xenophanes, and Herodotus propose that fossils found inland once lived in the sea.
140	Ptolemy incorrectly concludes that Earth is at the center of the solar system.
1726–1797	James Hutton concludes that processes that were constantly occurring—such as erosion, deposition, earthquakes, and volcanic eruptions—produced the rocks of Scotland. These ideas are the foundation for the principle of uniformitarianism, which suggests that landforms developed over long periods of time through the actions of slow geological processes such as erosion and weathering.
1781	William Herschel discovers the planet Uranus, the first such discovery since ancient times.
1804	Georges Cuvier studies fossils found around Paris and suggests that they are thousands of centuries old. This meant that Earth was much older than people thought at the time.
1820–1821	Mary Anning excavates the world's first fossil plesiosaur.
1830	Charles Lyell publishes *Principles of Geology*, a book that Charles Darwin took along on his explorations.
1847	Maria Mitchell, an American astronomer and professor, discovers a comet whose path took it near the star Polaris.
1856	The first recognized fossil human, a Neanderthal, is discovered in Düsseldorf, Germany.
1912	Alfred Wegener proposes the theory of continental drift, suggesting that the individual continents were once part of one supercontinent.
1957	The Soviet Union launches Sputnik, the Earth's first artificial space satellite.
1969	American astronaut Neil Armstrong walks on the surface of the Moon.
1969	The American Apollo missions bring rocks home from the Moon to Earth.
1971	Stephen Hawking poses the hypothesis that primordial black holes might have been created in the Big Bang: a theorized explosion that marked the origin of the universe billions of years ago.
1974	Stephen Hawking applies quantum field theory to black hole space-time and shows that black holes radiate mass/energy that may result in their evaporation.
1980	Alan Guth proposes the inflationary Big Bang universe, which suggests that the universe expanded at a rate that kept doubling for a brief period of time after the Big Bang.
1980	Luis W. Alvarez, Walter Alvarez, Frank Asaro, and Helen V. Michel publish their asteroid impact theory of dinosaur extinction in *Science Magazine*.
1981	The United States launches the first space shuttle: the *Columbia*.
1990	The Hubble Space Telescope is placed in orbit; after its optical systems are improved, it sends back extraordinary pictures of the universe.

1990	The COBE (Cosmic Background Explorer) Satellite transmits data that indicate that the background radiation of the universe is what would be expected if the universe originated in a manner consistent with the Big Bang theory.
1991	The Chicxulub Crater is discovered in the Yucatán Peninsula, supporting the asteroid impact theory first suggested in 1980.
1993	J. William Schopf publishes a description of the oldest fossils known to science: 3.5 billion-year-old microfossils from the Apex Basalt in Australia.
1995	Michael Mayor and Didier Queloz identify the first planet outside our solar system.
1997	The Mars probe Sojourner lands and transmits pictures of the planet's surface to Earth.
1998	The Moon probe Lunar Prospector sends back data that indicate that some water in the form of ice lies beneath its surface.
1998	Construction begins on the International Space Station.
2001	The Mars Global Surveyor probe completes its primary mapping study of the Martian surface and reveals that there once was and now may be liquid water near the surface.
2004	The rovers Spirit and Opportunity land on Mars and begin sending back images and data of the red planet. On March 2, 2004, NASA announced that the rovers had confirmed liquid water once flowed on Mars.
2008	The orbiter spacecraft *Messenger* begins sending back a complete picture of Mercury, shedding light on its geological history.
2013	Canadian astronaut Christopher Hadfield releases the first music video from space aboard the International Space Station: "Space Oddity" by David Bowie.
2014	Scientists find evidence that most of the Grand Canyon is only 5 or 6 million years old, compared to 70 million years previously estimated.
2015	The European Space Agency's *Rosetta* spacecraft landed on Comet 67P shortly after it sent its last pictures of the comet to Earth.
2016	*SpaceX* successfully lands *Falcon 9*, a cargo resupply ship for the International Space Station, on an ocean landing platform in the Atlantic Ocean.
2017	On August 21, a total solar eclipse of the sun can be seen across a path from Oregon to South Carolina.

Women and Men Who Have Shaped the Development of the Earth/Space Sciences

PTOLEMY (ABOUT 85–165 AD) was an astronomer, mathematician, and geographer. He proposed that Earth was at the center of the universe and that the other heavenly bodies—such as the sun and planets—moved in orbits around it. He was, of course, incorrect.

TYCHO BRAHE (1546–1601), was a Danish astronomer, who gathered data that were eventually used to predict the motion and orbits of the planets. These data quashed any remaining support for the Ptolemaic, or Earth-centered, view of the universe.

SOPHIA BRAHE (1556–1643), was the younger sister of Tycho Brahe, who gathered and contributed data used to predict planetary orbits. In addition to her astronomical work, she was also a well-known horticulturalist and historian.

NICOLAUS COPERNICUS (1473–1543) was a mathematician, physician, lawyer, and perhaps priest who became known for suggesting that the Sun was at rest in the center of the universe. This is now known as the heliocentric theory.

GALILEO GALILEI (1564–1642) is credited with many discoveries related to the motion of the pendulum, the construction of compasses and telescopes, and observations of the satellites of Jupiter and the phases of Venus. He espoused Copernicus's view that the planets revolved around the Sun and was accused of being a heretic.

ISAAC NEWTON (1642–1727) provided the foundation for modern physics and mathematics. His studies of the natural world led to the development of the law of inertia, the law of action and reaction, and the relationship of force to the acceleration of a mass. He proposed the universal law of gravitation and is credited as being the co-inventor of calculus.

CAROLINE LUCRETIA HERSCHEL (1750–1848) and her brother, William, gathered data on astronomical objects. After William's death, Caroline completed their work on the creation of astronomy data sources, which were called catalogs.

MARY ANNING (1799–1847), was a self-taught paleontologist, who became known for excavating the fossil remains of an ichthyosaurus, a plesiosaur, and a pterodactyl.

MARIA MITCHELL (1818–1889), was an American astronomer, who discovered a comet whose path took it near the star Polaris; she was also known for her analysis of sunspots.

CHARLES D. WALCOTT (1850–1927) was a geologist and paleontologist who made a number of discoveries related to ancient animal and plant life. The most important of these was his study of the Middle Cambrian Burgess Shale, which had an extraordinary range of fossils.

ANDRIJA MOHOROVICIC (1857–1936), was a Croatian geologist and meteorologist, who made extraordinary discoveries related to weather and seismology. The Mohorovicic discontinuity, the boundary between the crust and the mantle of Earth, was eventually named in his honor.

ALBERT EINSTEIN (1879–1955) was a German-born physicist whose special theory of relativity and general theory of relativity provided the basis for much of what is known about the nature of time, space, and matter.

ALFRED WEGENER (1880–1930) was trained in astronomy but pursued meteorology as his profession. Curiously, he eventually became world famous for work in yet another field: geology. He first proposed the theory of plate tectonics, which is the foundation for modern ideas about continental drift.

CHARLES FRANCIS RICHTER (1900–1985) carried out work on the classification of earthquakes based on energy release. The Richter scale was developed from his careful analysis of data acquired at the Caltech Seismological Laboratory.

LUIS ALVAREZ (1911–1988) received the Nobel Prize for physics in 1968 for his study of subatomic particles. He became even more famous for his study of a thin, clay layer under Earth's surface that contains large amounts of iridium. This discovery lent support to the theory that dinosaur extinction was caused by an asteroid crashing into Earth and releasing the iridium-containing material.

WALTER ALVAREZ (1940–), is the son of Luis Alvarez, who discovered a thin, clay layer of soil that had high concentrations of iridium and also marked the end of the Cretaceous period and the dinosaurs. This research gave credence to the asteroid impact theory as the explanation for dinosaur extinction.

VERA COOPER RUBIN (1928–) has studied the orbital velocities of hydrogen clouds, and her results support the belief that there are large amounts of dark matter in the universe. (Dark matter is matter that cannot be seen or measured directly.)

STEPHEN HAWKING (1942–), is an English physicist, who has emerged as one of the most inventive scientific geniuses since Einstein. His theories about black holes and the origin of the universe guide what today's cosmologists explore. His ideas may ultimately provide physicists with a grand unified theory: one equation that will encompass all of the other equations that describe interactions in the universe.

NEIL DE GRASSE TYSON (1958–) is an American astrophysicist and author. He is an advocate for science and frequently in the media. In 1996, he became the Frederick P. Rose Director of the Hayden Planetarium at the Rose Center for Earth and Space in New York City, which is part of the American Museum of Natural History. He founded the Department of Astrophysics in 1997 and has been a research associate in the department since 2003.

▶ Personal and Social Implications of the Earth/Space Sciences

The quality of the air we breathe and the water we drink, the safety of the structures in which we work and live, and the protection of our natural resources can all be influenced by knowledge gained through the earth/space sciences. This knowledge affects us as individuals and as members of the communities in which we live.

Personal and Community Health

The work done in the earth/space sciences affects our well-being in many ways. For instance, geologists gather information about the quality of agricultural soils and the safety of recreational areas such as ski slopes and reservoirs formed behind earthen dams. The safety of our transportation system, including roads, tunnels, and bridge supports, all depends on geologists' knowledge of the rocks and rock layers underneath them.

We count on the forecasting capabilities of meteorologists to tell us how to dress for personal comfort and to provide us with a timeline for the pending arrival of violent weather. And the knowledge of the night skies provided by astronomers permits us to navigate Earth safely and even guides farmers and fishermen in their food production efforts.

Hazards, Risks, and Benefits

Today, earthquakes, volcanic eruptions, violent weather, tsunamis, and the like can all be forecast using the predictive capacities of the earth/space sciences. Given these predictions, individuals and societies can make important health- and safety-related decisions, often saving lives. In the developed nations of the world, personal housing, civic structures, and commercial buildings are all built to withstand disasters of all kinds.

▶ Earth/Space Science Technology: Its Nature and Impact

The women and men who explore the earth/space sciences solve the mysteries of nature by observing, poking at, and prodding it with technology. That technology is sometimes as simple as a compass and sometimes as complex as a radiotelescope.

Whether simple or complex, the technology used by earth/space scientists is always designed for a very specific purpose.

The Design of Earth/Space Science Technology

Astronomy, geology, meteorology, oceanography, and the other subdisciplines of the earth/space sciences depend on instrumentation: radiotelescopes that "listen" to the stars, seismographs that reveal movements within Earth, weather instruments that gather data about the atmosphere, and underwater microphones that track migration patterns of sea life. All of these instruments are designed to meet the following criteria:

1. The problem addressed with the technology has been clearly specified and is one for which data can be expected to be obtained.
2. The technology itself can reliably gather, display, and transmit data.
3. The data gathered are presented in a manner that can be easily interpreted.
4. The device or instrument provides researchers with constant feedback about the accuracy of the data being represented, errors that may have occurred in the gathering and processing of the data, and suggestions for troubleshooting malfunctions.

Examples of Earth/Space Science Technology

A variety of instruments are used to gather information about Earth, the oceans, the atmosphere, and outer space:

Hand lenses (magnifying glasses)	Seismographs
Microscopes	The global positioning system (GPS)
Optical telescopes	Weather maps
Radiotelescopes	Anemometers
The Hubble Space	Telescope barometers
High-resolution cameras	Thermometers
Satellites	Scuba equipment
The orbiting space station	Bathyscaphe (self-propelled under water
Radar	observatory)
Sonar	Computers

Long-Term Implications of Earth/Space Science Technology

Earth/space scientists seek to provide answers to basic questions about Earth—our home. Some of the data they acquire will eventually be used to improve our quality of life in ways large and small. However, earth/space scientists generally do not focus on the immediate application of new knowledge and skills to human problems. That is the work of engineers and technicians.

Engineers, who search for solutions to human problems, understand that their work has real limitations. For instance, their solutions are usually temporary, because the frontiers of scientific knowledge are constantly expanding. Their solutions may also be too costly and carry risks. For example, the use of movement-sensitive underwater microphones may disrupt whale migration patterns.

Some technological solutions may even have harmful consequences. For example, an imperfect or malfunctioning earthquake or tsunami warning device might produce information that causes people to panic—triggering the hording of food and water and producing evacuation problems—when there was really no cause for alarm in the first place. So, not all technological solutions are successful.

Earth and Space Science

Triff/Shutterstock

Learning Objectives

After completing the activities in this chapter, you should be able to

7.1 Describe ways the geosphere, biosphere, hydrosphere, and/or atmosphere interact to affect the Earth's materials and processes.

7.2 Describe how plate tectonics explain the development and ongoing changes of the Earth's surface.

7.3 Explain how solar energy, convection currents, and density influence ocean currents.

7.4 Explain how the effects of weathering or the rate of erosion by water, ice, wind, or vegetation contribute to the recycling of Earth materials.

▶ **GETTING STARTED**

You don't have to hitch a ride on the next space shuttle to treat yourself to a high-speed space adventure. You are having one right now! All living things—including you and me—are passengers on the most elaborate and marvelous spaceship that will ever hurl through space and time. It's the top-of-the-line luxury model, fully equipped with water, oxygen, and abundant food rotating at about 1,600 kilometers per hour (km/hr) (1,000 miles per hour [mph]) at the equator and orbiting the sun at approximately 107,826 km/hr (67,000 mph). And best of all, each and every seat has a fantastic view!

We can become so comfortable riding along on Spaceship Earth (otherwise known as the "third rock from the Sun") that we take its very existence and nature for granted. If you take the time to learn more about Earth, you will discover that it's just as fascinating as the Moon, planets, stars, and mysteries that lie at the far reaches of the universe.

Earth Materials (ESS2.A)

Earth, our personal spaceship, is full of surprises. One of the most extraordinary findings actually comes from the common misconception that we're walking around on some enormous, solid ball of rock. In fact, Earth is a giant, layered sphere made of materials that are as different as oil and water, rock and diamonds. Even more surprising is that at the center of Earth lies something completely unexpected—a solid inner core surrounded by a liquid outer core.

To understand the makeup of Earth, we need to figuratively peel off layers and work our way to its center. The first layer is a thin shell that ranges from 11 km (about 7 miles) to 32 km (about 20 miles) in thickness. This crust is thought to be divided into seven major sections called crustal plates. These plates are interesting for many reasons, including the fact that they are slowly moving and carrying oceans and continents along with them.

Under this first layer, we find the mantle, which is about 2,870 km (1,780 miles) deep. Figure 7.1 shows the crust and the mantle. Earthquake waves move faster in

Figure 7.1   The Upper Mantle between Hawaii and California

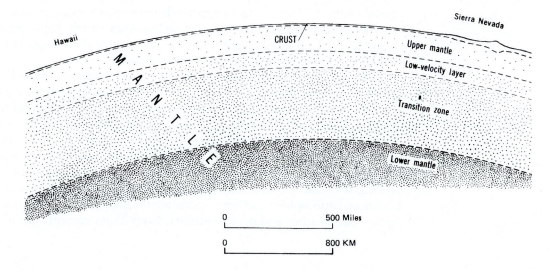

the upper mantle than in the crust. Knowing the rates at which earthquake waves travel through the different layers gives geologists important clues about the nature of the rock layers themselves.

Under the mantle, we find the core. Although no one is exactly sure of its composition, we do have an important clue: The fact that Earth has a magnetic field strong enough to turn a compass needle is evidence that a mass of molten metal exists at the center. Evidence suggests that the movement of this hot liquid metal in the outer core, which is likely a mixture of iron and nickel, creates electric currents that produce Earth's magnetic field.

Plate Tectonics and Large-Scale System Interactions (ESS2.B)

If you look outside your window, you may see mountains, prairies, a desert, a lake, or maybe other buildings. Whatever the case, the view you see creates an illusion—an illusion of permanence. In fact, all of our surroundings are in the process of gradual change, including the walls of the buildings you may see. More startling yet is the idea that even the enormous continents are in constant motion.

Most geologists now believe that all the continents were once joined in a single, large land mass. Alfred Wegener, who proposed this theory in 1912, named this land mass Pangaea. He believed that it broke apart and the pieces slowly drifted to where they are now. They are still moving but only very slowly, at rates of between 1 and 5 centimeters per year. Australia and Africa are moving northward, so sometime in the next 50 million years, Australia may strike Asia and Africa may strike Europe. Wegener's theory seems correct because geologists have discovered similar rock structures on the west coast of Africa and the east coast of South America. This similarity, along with the discovery of similar fossils in both locations, is strong evidence that the two continents were once part of the same land mass.

These massive plates of the Earth move at a steady, but extremely slow rate. If you stood between the railroad tracks in front of a freight train moving only 2 km/hr (1 mph) , you would gradually learn that powerful forces can have great consequences even though they are acting slowly. This is true for the movement of crustal plates. Violent changes happen where the plates meet, pushing and slowly grinding against one another. As they collide, they slowly build great mountain ranges as the land gets pushed up at the junction of the plates. The results are mountain ranges like the Rockies and Himalayas.

The tremendous forces that move the massive sections of the Earth's crust, known as tectonic plates, are generated by the exchange of heat energy below the Earth's surface. Heat is generated by radioactive decay that creates molten rock (magma) in the Earth's mantle. Hot magma is less dense than solid rock and rises. As the magma rises it cools, increases in density, and begins to descend. This rise and descent of magma just below the Earth's crust causes a circular motion that moves the huge continental plates. This circular motion created by heating and cooling is called a *convection current*. Convection currents are found in the oceans and atmosphere and are responsible for much of the energy exchange that creates our weather and ocean currents. Convection currents are ubiquitous in our daily lives. For example, hot water heating systems warm water in a furnace, which rises through the radiator system where it exchanges heat to the air resulting in cooler water sinks and returns to the furnace to be warmed and recirculated.

On August 24, in the year 79, the apparently extinct volcano Vesuvius suddenly exploded, destroying the cities of Pompeii and Herculaneum.[1] Vesuvius had been quiet for hundreds of years, its surface and crater were green and vine covered, and no one expected the explosion. Yet in a few hours, volcanic ash and dust buried the two cities so thoroughly that their ruins were not uncovered for more than 1,600 years!

Volcanoes form in areas where the magma burst through weaker, thin areas in the surface of the Earth. Tectonic plate boundaries create such areas where magma can reach the surface. Deep trenches form where one plate is moving below the other through a process called subduction. These trenches often expose hot magma through a process called upwelling, which reaches the surface as lava. Internal forces create volcanoes that form along plate boundaries as the result of the great amount of energy released as the plates interact. Volcanoes also form along hot spots, where molten magma comes near the Earth's surface and breaks through as the result of built-up pressure of gases and molten rock.

Molten rock below the surface of Earth that rises in volcanic vents is known as magma, but after it erupts from a volcano, it is called lava. It is red hot when it pours out of the vent, but it slowly changes to dark red, gray, or black as it cools. If lava erupts in large volumes, it flows over the surface of Earth. Generally, very hot lava is fluid, like hot tar, whereas cooler lava flows more slowly, like thick honey.

All lava that comes to the surface of Earth contains dissolved gas. If the lava is a thin fluid, the gas escapes easily. But if the lava is thick and pasty, the gas escapes with explosive violence. The gas in lava may be compared with the gas in a bottle of carbonated drink. If you put your thumb over the top of the bottle and shake it, the gas separates from the liquid and forms bubbles. When you remove your thumb, there is a miniature explosion of gas and liquid. The gas in lava behaves in somewhat the same way; it causes the terrible explosions that throw out great masses of solid rock as well as lava, dust, and ashes.

The violent separation of gas from lava may produce rock froth, called pumice. Some of this froth is so light that it floats on water. In many eruptions, the froth is broken into small fragments that are hurled high into the air in the form of volcanic ash (gray), cinders (red or black), and dust. Visit the United States Geological Survey (USGS) website[2] for resources to teach about volcanoes and other Earth Science phenomena.

The massive collision of continental plates causes earthquakes as well, which, if they occur on the ocean floor, can result in rapid displacement of ocean water causing huge tidal waves known as tsunamis. In western California, the Pacific plate is moving northwest and rubbing against the North American plate—the plate that North America rides on. Figure 7.2 shows the location of the San Andreas Fault, which runs from northern to southern California. This figure also shows the dates of major earthquakes in California and areas where rock layers are very slowly being pushed out of position.

Because of the great amounts of energy released and transferred through collisions of tectonic plates, noticeable patterns of mountain ranges, earthquakes, and volcanoes emerge around the plate boundaries.

Figure 7.2   This map shows the San Andreas Fault system and other geological faults in California.

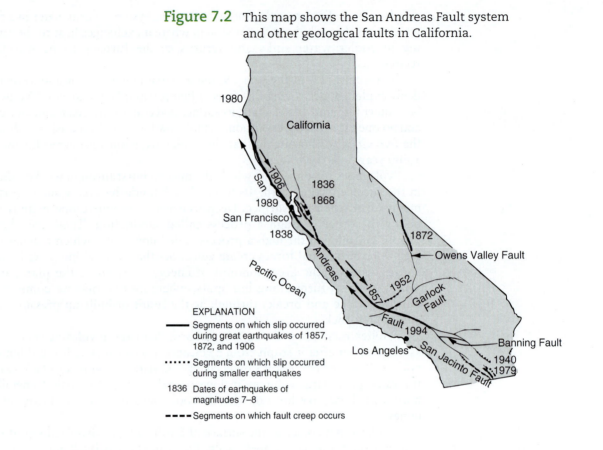

Earth Systems (ESS2.A)

The key to understanding Earth systems is to understand energy flow through the four major Earth systems: atmosphere, geosphere (also called pedosphere), hydrosphere, and biosphere. The first three spheres will be addressed in this chapter. Chapter 9 will address the biosphere in more detail. Of course, none of these systems exist in isolation. They interact in a complex web of energy flow. The ultimate source of energy is the Sun. The Sun's energy powers the Earth, affecting all four spheres.

The atmosphere consists of the envelope of gases surrounding the Earth. It consists primarily of nitrogen (78%), oxygen (21%), and carbon dioxide (0.04%). Carbon dioxide is among the most important gases with respect to energy regulation because of its ability to absorb heat that warms the atmosphere. The atmosphere is described as having five layers in ascending order: troposphere, stratosphere, mesosphere, ionosphere, exosphere. Most weather occurs in the lowest level, the troposphere, which extends about 11.2 km (7 miles) high. To get a perspective on the relative size of the troposphere, imagine a basketball as the Earth and a thin sheet of plastic wrapped around it. The plastic represents this thin layer that is the troposphere.

Energy from the Sun, called solar radiation, is absorbed by the land and water comprising the geosphere. Some of the solar radiation is reflected back into the atmosphere. The air closest to the land or water absorbs energy and is warmed. As air warms it becomes less dense and rises. As the air rises it cools, increases in density, and falls. You might recall this dynamic as convection. Convection currents play a major role in weather as they transfer energy that causes changes in temperature, wind, pressure, and humidity.

Warm air can absorb more water vapor than cool air. Air near the ocean, which has been warmed by the Sun, tends to be nearly saturated with water vapor, making the air very humid. As the hot, humid air rises, it creates an area of low pressure below it. The warm air cools as it rises and energy given off as water vapor condenses and forms around small particles such as dust (or, cloud condensation nuclei) to form clouds. Air from surrounding areas of high pressure fill in the low-pressure areas. This movement of air as it warms and rises, cools and falls, results in wind currents across the surface of the Earth. As clouds become saturated with moisture, precipitation in the forms of rain, sleet, or snow result. When the energy exchange in the atmosphere increases due to factors such as warm ocean water over the tropics, the cycle of heating/cooling, rising/falling air becomes energized to form severe weather such as hurricanes.

● Weathering and Erosion

Weather causes constant changes in the Earth. Weathering is the wearing down of the Earth's surface structures, loosening and breaking surfaces such as rocks and minerals. Weathering can be chemical or physical (also referred to as mechanical). Chemical weathering occurs when rocks react with a chemical, such as water that is acidic. Acid rain, often the result of pollutants such as sulfur dioxide, is a common cause of chemical weathering. Mechanical weathering occurs when a force breaks down rocks and minerals. Ice that forms in rock crevices can force rocks to crack and splinter. Wind and waves can grind rock particles together in a process called abrasion. Perhaps you have seen smooth stones in a river bed or on a beach that have been weathered by the mechanical action of current or waves. Have you ever seen a plant grow in the crevices of rocks? Plant roots can slowly break down the rock, which is another example of mechanical weathering caused by living things. Plants and animals can also cause chemical weathering by releasing fluids that react with and break down rocks and minerals.

Erosion is not the same as weathering, although the two terms are often used in conjunction. Erosion is the process that removes the rock and minerals broken down by weathering to a new location. Wind and water are the most common agents of erosion.

Enhanced eText Video Example 7.1

Watch and listen as Ashley Welch leads children to discover concepts about erosion. What science practices do the students demonstrate? How does Ashley use questions, prompts, and discourse to think with students?

The Roles of Water in Earth's Surface Processes (ESS2.C)

Humans are land animals, but it is important to remember that most of the Earth, about 70%, is composed of water. The vast system of water is interconnected as the hydrosphere. It includes all the lakes, seas, oceans, rivers, ponds, and streams as well as the water beneath the ground. About 97% of all water is salt water found in oceans. Approximately 3% of water is fresh water, most of which is locked up in ice or in the ground. Only about 1% of fresh water is found on the surface of the Earth in lakes, streams, ponds, and rivers. All of these bodies of water are connected by the water cycle: Solar energy heats the water, which rises as vapor, condenses into clouds that become saturated to form precipitation, which returns the water to the surface of the Earth where it continues the water cycle.

The Ocean Floor

When we look at the ocean, we see nothing but water. Imagine for a moment that the water disappeared. What would you expect the floor of the ocean to look like? With the water gone, you would see gently sloping areas, known as continental shelves, along the edges of the continents. These areas extend outward to a region of ocean floor that slopes steeply to a flatter part of the ocean floor called the abyssal plain. Not all continents have a gradually sloping continental shelf. In some places, the shelf extends hundreds of kilometers; in other places, the coastline drops immediately into deep water.

The continental shelf receives the sediment carried by rivers from the land surface. The sediment is called the continental deposit. The edges of the continental shelf mark the beginning of a steeply sloping region known as the continental slope. The continental slope extends until it reaches the ocean floor, which is lined with ridges known as midocean ridges. Between the ridges lie the abyssal plains. The ridge that rises from the Atlantic Ocean floor is called the Mid-Atlantic Ridge. The islands known as the Azores are the peaks of the Mid-Atlantic Ridge that have risen above the water. Although there are ridges in the ocean floor beneath the Pacific Ocean, they are not as tall as the Mid-Atlantic Ridge.

The ridges in the ocean floor are made by molten rock from deep within Earth pushing upward and slowly spreading out to the east and west. Thus, the ridges indicate places where the ocean floor is actually expanding. The movement of continents away from these areas is known as continental drift. Because Earth is not becoming larger, there must be an explanation for what happens as new land is created at the ridges and pushed outward. The explanation can be found in ocean trenches. At other places on the ocean floor, Earth's crust is being pushed downward, creating large trenches. Ocean trenches are the most striking feature of the Pacific Ocean floor. The trenches are thousands of kilometers long and hundreds of kilometers wide.

Ocean Currents   Throughout history, sailors have used their knowledge of ocean currents to move from place to place quickly and efficiently. But what causes the currents in the first place? The answer is complex, but most explanations must begin with energy from the Sun. The Sun's energy creates convection currents in the troposphere, which causes winds that contribute to surface currents in the ocean. Deeper currents are influenced by temperature differences between warm, less dense water and cool, denser water. The equatorial regions of Earth receive more sunlight than other places on the planet's surface. Because they do, the oceans in the equatorial regions absorb an enormous amount of energy and become warm. Water in the northern regions of Earth tend to be cooler and denser. Ocean water that is frozen loses salt, which remains in the cool water making it even denser. As the cool, dense water sinks, warmer water replaces it, which in turn cools and sinks creating a current. You might recognize this as yet another example of a convection current. This movement of ocean water away from the Equator results in major ocean currents. Earth's rotation turns these currents clockwise in the Northern Hemisphere and counterclockwise in the Southern Hemisphere. Along the eastern coast of North America, a powerful current called the Gulf Stream carries warm waters from the Equator northward and then eastward toward England.

Although many people are familiar with the major ocean currents at the water's surface, few people realize that there are currents far beneath the surface. There is, for example, a deep current that flows out of the Mediterranean under the surface current that flows into the Mediterranean at the Straits of Gibraltar. It is said that ancient sailors familiar with this unseen current sometimes took advantage of it by putting weighted sails into the deep water. Let your students explore the properties of ocean currents using the National Aeronautics and Space Administration's (NASA's) "Go with the Flow" game.[3]

Seasonal changes in the strength, direction, and temperature of currents produce a variety of effects. Fish dependent on the movement of currents to carry food to the area of the ocean in which they live may perish if the current changes. Variations in the temperature of a current can affect the hatching of fish eggs. These effects impact humans because we depend on the ocean's resources.

The oceans of our planet are a source of food, minerals, water, and energy. The challenge we face is to harvest the ocean's resources without diminishing their richness. The living resources of the ocean begin with phytoplankton—tiny, one-celled plants that carry out photosynthesis. Their capturing of sunlight is the first step in creating the food chains and webs found in the oceans. Phytoplankton serve as food for microscopic animals known as zooplankton. Zooplankton are then eaten by larger organisms, and these organisms are eaten by still larger organisms. Thus, the energy originally received by the phytoplankton is passed along through the ocean food chains and webs (Figure 7.3).

The food chains and webs of the oceans can be thought of as a vast repository of protein-rich foods, and many modern technologies are used to locate and acquire fish, mollusks, and crustaceans for human consumption. Hopefully, international agreements concerning overfishing and water pollution control measures will permit future generations to benefit from these food resources.

The adage "Water, water everywhere and not a drop to drink" may have been true once with respect to salty seawater, but it is not true any longer. One important ocean resource is the water itself. Modern desalinization plants make it possible for communities that do not have access to fresh water to get it from salt water. This is accomplished by evaporating seawater, which yields fresh water as vapor. The water vapor then condenses to form liquid water, which can be used for drinking, farming, or industrial uses. Sodium chloride and other substances are left behind as solids. The process is somewhat costly in terms of the energy required to evaporate seawater; however, as the technology improves and becomes more efficient, more of Earth's population will get its fresh water from seawater.

Figure 7.3 If you examine this ocean food chain closely, you will discover how the energy consumed by phytoplankton eventually sustains life for the shark.

The ocean is a vast resource for humankind. With technological advances and a sensitivity to maintaining the quality of the water in Earth's oceans, humans will no doubt find and use other valuable ocean resources.

Real Teaching: Clouds

I invited fourth-graders to become official cloud observers for GLOBE (Global Learning Observations to Benefit the Earth). GLOBE provides teachers and students opportunities to learn by doing authentic science as citizen scientists. The GLOBE program works closely with NASA, which uses the data collected by students all over the world in conjunction with satellite data to gain insight into the dynamics of Earth systems.

The invitation to fourth-graders to become cloud observers for GLOBE serves two main purposes: It is an opportunity to engage students in the culture of science through participation in an authentic science-related endeavor. It also provides a meaningful and purposeful context about which to learn more about clouds and fundamental core ideas including but not limited to temperature, evaporation, condensation, weather, and the water cycle.

I invited students to be part of the GLOBE team and briefly explained that we need them to join people from around the world in describing clouds. We began simply by asking students what they know about clouds (prior knowledge—i.e., K-W-L). Using pictures of various types of clouds, we asked students to describe the characteristics of clouds in their own words. We duplicated the projected pictures on sheets so students could write their descriptors. [MULTIPLE MODES OF ENGAGEMENT] I asked them to share some words that describe clouds. With answers like "they are fun," "interesting," and "scary," I realized that I was not clear about the type of characteristics I wanted. [FORMATIVE ASSESSMENT] I then asked for words that describe what clouds look like. After some false starts, we began to come up with descriptors such as "big," "fluffy," "thin," "white," and "gray." We posted these words on the Clouds Word Wall [UDL/SIOP]. We watched a brief cartoon about Luke Howard, the man credited for naming clouds. We only watched a few minutes, up to the part where the narrator told us how the names for three basic cloud shapes were derived—stratus, cumulus, and cirrus—and the characteristics used to identify them—layered, puffy, and eye lash. I handed out cloud charts with these three types of clouds. I chose to keep the task and new knowledge limited to avoid cognitive overload. Had I handed out altocumulus, nimbostratus, among others, it would be too much information too quickly. I knew we would take a deeper dive into the content as the unit progressed. We used the charts to associate names of clouds with characteristics.

The next day we briefly reviewed what we had learned and then went outside to observe the clouds. To do so, we had to identify the cardinal compass points: N, S, E, and W, so we would be able to work as a team to observe four quadrants of the sky. This was one more layer of content knowledge introduced based on a need. We marked the compass points in chalk on the playground, with an X depicting where to stand.

Students were given an observation sheet with a place to draw a picture of the cloud and write the type and description along with the compass point they represented. [UDL, MULTIPLE MODES OF REPRESENTATION] After making their observations, students sat, legs crossed, to complete their observation sheet, which was on the clipboard provided to each student. [REFLECTION TIME/ METACOGNITION]

We returned to the classroom to debrief. I projected the quadrants on the smartboard. All of the children who collected data looking north got together in a group. Likewise, for groups who made observations from the south, east, and west. I asked them to reach agreement (consensus) on the types of clouds they wanted to report. Then we had a discussion about their observations. Each compass point group reported out. I wrote their descriptions in the corresponding quadrant on the smartboard.

The discussion brought up several questions: Can stratus clouds be dark and white? Why do we sometimes see different types of clouds at the same time? What types of weather do we usually experience with each type of cloud cover?

The discussion helped us reach some important realizations about science: clouds change—science often studies change over time. Clouds seem related to the weather—science looks for relationships and patterns. [NGSS CROSS CUTTING CONCEPT]

The discussion about whether stratus clouds can be dark or white led us to the need for modifiers to describe clouds: nimbus, in this case. As a teacher, I know we eventually need to describe clouds in more detail and that children will learn names like nimbostratus, altocumulus, and cumulonimbus. These names reflect precipitation and altitude associated with clouds as well as shape. I did not plan to address these names or weather associated with types of clouds for five more lessons. However, the students generated some questions and ideas that create a teachable moment. I will adjust the next lesson to build on the students' ideas about the need to identify and describe clouds in greater detail. [AMBITIOUS TEACHING] We will address heights of clouds, which just might lead to other hook questions that I plan to address: How much does a cloud weigh? Why do they float? Both of which lead to, "What is a cloud made of, anyway?" I also know that we will be addressing weather and the water cycles. My class is building connections and permitting me to practice responsive teaching: building concepts through student-centered progression in response to student questions and interests.

The History of Planet Earth (ESS1.C)

To track various changes during Earth's history, scientists have created a geologic time scale. The largest division in the scale is the era. Each era is named for the type of life that existed then. Here are the four eras of geologic time and the approximate beginning of each:

Precambrian era	4,500,000,000 years ago
Paleozoic era	600,000,000 years ago
Mesozoic era	225,000,000 years ago
Cenozoic era	70,000,000 years ago

Table 7.1 gives an overview of some of the most important characteristics of each era.

For most of Earth's history there was no one to record it. So how do we know the history of the Earth? Scientists look for clues in the Earth that reveal changes over time. For example, sedimentary rocks reveal the types of environments that existed long ago in a particular region. Rounded pebbles deposited in the shape of a channel suggest a river once ran through the area. Thin layers of rock with ripple marks indicate where a beach once was. Former swamps leave behind think organic material that eventually becomes coal.

Fossils also provide clues to the age of rocks. Fossils change as the life forms they represent change with time. Recall that fossils form along with rocks as mineral deposits build up over time. Therefore, rocks that have the same types of fossils represent rocks of approximately the same age.

Table 7.1 The four eras

Era	Living Things Present	General Characteristics
Precambrian: 4,500,000,000 years ago	Single-celled and multicelled life appear.	This era represents about 90% of all geologic time. The earliest rocks on Earth are found in Precambrian deposits. They are about 4.5 billion years old.
Paleozoic: 600,000,000 years ago	The first land plants, reptiles, fish, spiders, and insects appear.	This was a time of great change. Sheets of ice covered much of the land in the Southern Hemisphere. Seas and oceans formed in the Northern Hemisphere. In time, much of the ice melted and land masses emerged from the oceans.
Mesozoic: 225,000,000 years ago	The first mammals, frogs, flowering plants, and dinosaurs appear. The dinosaurs also become extinct.	The Appalachian Mountains, Rocky Mountains, and Sierra Nevada Mountains were all formed. Great seas in the middle of North America disappeared, and these areas formed plains. The levels of the oceans dropped, and the climate became colder.
Cenozoic: 70,000,000 years ago	Mammals flourish, including humans, dogs, horses, and cattle.	Movement of the seven crustal plates pushed up mountains and increased earthquakes and volcanic activity. Glaciers from both polar regions spread out toward the Equator. At one point, glaciers covered North America between the Appalachian Mountains and the northern Rocky Mountains. Eventually, the glaciers receded into southcentral Canada.

Weather and Climate (ESS2.D)

The thin layer of air surrounding Earth—the atmosphere—changes continuously. When we use the term *weather,* we are describing the condition of the atmosphere at a given time. That condition may be hot, cold, windy, dry, wet, sunny, or cloudy. The term *climate* is used to describe the average weather in a region over many years.

Because Earth receives almost all its heat energy from the Sun, we can say that the Sun is the principal cause for changes in the weather. Heat energy from the Sun causes the air to warm and move upward, water to evaporate into the atmosphere, and air to flow throughout the Earth. These changes play a part in determining the extent and type of weather and climates on Earth.

Scientists who study the weather and predict weather changes are called meteorologists. Every country has meteorologists who gather weather data from a variety of sources, summarize it, record it using various symbols on a weather map, and make predictions.

Because changes in the conditions of the atmosphere (the weather) tend to move in regular patterns above Earth's surface, the weather we will experience tomorrow will likely be much the same as the weather someplace else today. As a result, the most important tool that a weather forecaster has is a weather map. He or she studies the most recent weather map and tries to predict both the strength of the disturbances observed and their path. The forecaster also studies the map to see where and how new disturbances are being formed.

Meteorologists in North America know that in the middle latitudes, the upper air moves from west to east. Storms tend to enter from the west, pass across the middle of the North American continent, and move toward the North Atlantic.

Thus, the weather that is likely to affect a local area is predicted on the basis of the larger-scale weather movement depicted on a weather map. The map is created by first recording symbols representing the data gathered at weather stations—pressure, temperature, humidity, wind direction, wind velocity, and cloud types.

Meteorologists use a variety of instruments to collect this data. The pressure of the air above us is measured with a barometer. A wind vane is used to determine the direction of the wind at Earth's surface. Wind speed is measured with an anemometer, an instrument consisting of a set of cups mounted so that they can easily be rotated by the wind. The amount of moisture in the air is determined by a hygrometer. The amount of moisture that reaches the ground as precipitation is measured by rain and snow gauges.

Natural Hazards (ESS3B)

● Violent Weather

Earth is not always a peaceful place, and the same is true of its atmosphere. Under the right conditions, violent weather—including thunderstorms, tornadoes, winter storms, and hurricanes—can have a great impact on the surface of Earth and all of the life on it! Table 7.2 describes some common violent weather phenomena.

Table 7.2 Violent weather phenomena

Phenomenon	Characteristics
Thunderstorm	Upward and downward air movements (convection) produce a thunderstorm. Denser air sinks, and warmer, less dense air rapidly rises. The downdraft produces winds and heavy rain or hail. Some thunderstorms even produce tornadoes.
	Thunder is produced by the explosive expansion of air heated by a lightning bolt. The lightning is seen before the thunder is heard. The distance from lightning in miles can be estimated by counting the time in seconds between seeing lightning and hearing thunder and then dividing by 5.
	Lightning is caused by the movement of charged particles in a thunderstorm that produces electric fields. These cause currents (lightning) to flow within a cloud, from cloud to cloud, from cloud to ground, and, in some cases, from ground to cloud.
Tornado	A short-lived storm that has high-speed winds that rotate counterclockwise. These winds may appear as a funnel attached to a thundercloud, which can pick up and move dust and debris if it nears or touches the ground.
Snowstorm	A storm in which snow falls for several hours without letting up.
Freezing rain, freezing drizzle, and ice storm	Freezing rain or freezing drizzle occurs when the surface temperature is below 0°C (32°F). The rain falls as a liquid but freezes in an ice glaze on objects. If the glaze is thick, it's called an ice storm.
Cold wave	A time period in which the temperature falls far below normal.
Hurricane	A violent rain and wind storm that gets energy from the heat of seawater. The quiet core, or eye, is surrounded by blowing winds. The thunderclouds of a hurricane sometimes cause tornadoes. Learn how hurricanes are formed.

The characteristics of the air high above Earth are commonly determined by the use of radiosondes. These are miniature radio transmitters to which are attached a variety of weather instruments. Radiosondes are carried aloft by balloons or small rockets. Data gathered by the instruments are transmitted back to Earth by the radio transmitter.

In recent years, weather satellites have greatly improved the accuracy of weather forecasts. Their photographs and infrared detection of conditions such as cloud cover, ocean temperature, relative humidity, and a host of data reveal a great deal about weather phenomena and Earth systems. Such satellite data are of great assistance to meteorologists as they develop their weather forecasts for a particular area.

Summary

7.1 Describe ways the geosphere, biosphere, hydrosphere, and/or atmosphere interact to affect the Earth's materials and processes.

Earth can be understood by a complex relationship of systems, all of which are ultimately driven by energy from the Sun. A thin layer of gases comprises Earth's atmosphere. The water and land make up the geosphere. The biosphere consists of all life on the plant, and the hydrosphere is made up of all the water on the planet. All of these systems interact and impact one another to constantly shape and change the Earth and the life that inhabits the planet.

7.2 Describe how plate tectonics explain the development and ongoing changes of the Earth's surface.

7.3 Earth is a dynamic planet, constantly changing through immense forces.

Heat energy circulating through Earth's mantle creates convection currents that move massive continents, creating land-forms such as mountain ranges and deep ocean trenches. Occasionally the energy is released in violent bursts creating volcanoes, earthquakes, or tsunamis. Earth is constantly changing as energy flows through all its systems.

7.4 Explain how solar energy, convection currents, and density influence ocean currents.

Patterns can be discerned in the flow of energy through Earth's systems that are largely driven by heat energy and result in convection currents. The transfers of energy in the form of heat account for winds, ocean currents, and forces that move massive continental plates. The steady and unstoppable movement creates great mountain ranges and deep ocean trenches, as well as earthquakes, volcanoes, and tsunamis. Explain how the effects of weathering or the rate of erosion by water, ice, wind, or vegetation contribute to the recycling of Earth materials.

Weathering by mechanical and chemical means break down the Earth's surface. The cycles of freezing and thawing allow water to flow into crevices and cracks in solid rock that widen and weaken each time water expands as it changes state to solid ice, eventually breaking off pieces of the rocky surface. Chemicals in rain and organic chemicals from organisms break down rocks and minerals. Wind and waves constantly buffet and pound the land, wearing it down and carrying it away through the process of erosion. Together, weathering and erosion contribute to the constantly changing face of the planet.

Understanding the Earth systems helps us predict patterns of weather and climate. Our planet Earth is susceptible to human actions. The more we understand how Earth systems interact to influence our planet, the more we can live in harmony with our planet and learn to harness the renewable sources of energy as they flow through our planet in the forms of wind, current, and sunlight.

Chapter 7 Self-Check
Click to gauge your understanding of the concepts in this chapter.

Notes

1. The discussion of volcanoes was excerpted with minor modifications from *Volcanoes*, a pamphlet prepared by the U.S. Geological Survey, U.S. Department of the Interior. http://pubs.usgs.gov/gip/volc/text.html#people
2. https://www.usgs.gov/
3. Go with the Flow: https://spaceplace.nasa.gov/ocean-currents/en/

The Cosmos

NASA images/Shutterstock

Learning Objectives

After completing the activities in this chapter, you should be able to:

8.1 Reflect on the origins of the universe.

8.2 Describe the relationships among the Earth, Moon, and Sun that explain observable patterns such as day/night, tides, and seasons.

8.3 Explain why the Sun appears bigger and brighter than other stars.

8.4 Describe the mechanisms for natural climate change.

8.5 Describe a brief history and the anticipated future of modern space exploration.

▶ **GETTING STARTED**

Are we all alone in the vastness of space? Are other planets in orbit around distant stars?

Although we still don't have an answer to the first question, we do have an answer to the second. Humankind has made an extraordinary discovery: There *are* planets around other stars!

Powerful telescopes, the careful study of light spectra from stars, advanced computer software, new techniques for studying the wobbles in the movements of stars (an important clue for the presence of a planet), and diligent work by astronomers have revealed that there are stars in the evening sky that do have planets. The names of three of them are 51 Pegasi in the Pegasus constellation, 70 Virginis in the Virgo constellation, and 47 Ursae Majoris in the Big Dipper. Even more amazing, a family of planets has been discovered orbiting Upsilon Andromedae, a star similar to our Sun and 44 light-years away. New **planet candidates** continue to be discovered.

So, now we know that planets may be far more common in the universe than we would have ever believed. But where does that leave us? Will we *ever* get the answer to that first question: *Are we alone?* Perhaps, but as we use powerful radiotelescopes to search the sky for signals sent by intelligent life, we can also pursue answers to other questions that are just as interesting. For instance: How did the universe come into existence? When did the universe come into existence? What is the real meaning of *time?* and Did time exist before the universe came into being? There are even more mind-wrenching questions, such as whether universes parallel to ours exist and whether matter that enters a black hole can pop out somewhere else in our universe or another universe—if there are other universes.

All these questions bring us very close to the edge of what people call *science fiction*, yet each day very respectable scientists search for the answers. These esoteric questions, as well as those focused more closely on our planet and solar system, will eventually produce answers. We are moving closer and closer to the time when we'll finally be able to answer the question, *Are we alone?*

Earth's Place in the Universe (ESS1)

The universe is all the matter, energy, and space that exists. But how did this matter, energy, and space begin? Scientific debate over how the **universe began** seems to be endless. One important theory, known as the *Big Bang theory*, suggests that the universe had a definite beginning. According to the theory, approximately 13.8 billion years ago, the universe was created as a result of a fiery explosion. Astronomical observations reveal that all galaxies have been moving apart from one another at enormous speeds, and other evidence supports this theory. By reasoning backward from the present outward movement of galaxies, we can assume that all the matter of the universe was once packed tightly together in an incredibly hot, dense point.

Astronomers believe that the Sun, Earth, and other planets were formed from an enormous contracting cloud of dust and gas that formed after the Big Bang. All parts of this cloud did not move uniformly. Some parts formed local condensations that eventually became our planets, moons, comets, and asteroids. Gradually, the main cloud, which was to become our Sun, became spherical. Gravitational contraction increased its temperature. Eventually, the core temperature rose to a point at which the cloud's hydrogen nuclei began to fuse. Nuclear energy then produced enough outward pressure of heated gas to balance the inward force of gravity and maintain the Sun as a glowing star. The formation of our Sun is thought to have occurred about 900 million years after the Big Bang, a relatively short astronomical time. The Earth and planets in our solar system are thought to have formed about 8.3 billion years after the formation of the Sun.

The theory of a cosmic explosion is also supported by a discovery made in 1965 by Arno Penzias and Robert Wilson of Bell Laboratories. Penzias and Wilson discovered and measured the strength of faint radiation that came from every direction in the sky. The entire universe seems to be immersed in this radiation. Measurements of the strengths and forms of radiation coincide with the strengths and forms that would have resulted from an enormous explosion that occurred billions of years ago.

Maps of the sky made from data gathered by the *Cosmic Background Explorer* (COBE) satellite showed slight differences in the background radiation discovered by Penzias and Wilson. Advocates of the Big Bang theory claim that the data are exactly what a scientist would predict if the universe began with a Big Bang.

Although the Big Bang theory offers many explanations for astronomical phenomena, some recent discoveries have strongly challenged it. Observational studies of galaxies by Dr. Margaret J. Geller and Dr. H. P. Huchra of the Harvard–Smithsonian Center for Astrophysics and others have found some organized patterns of galaxies. However, according to the Big Bang theory, these patterns or structures, including an enormous chain of galaxies about 500 billion light-years across and known as the *Great Wall*, should not exist because galaxies should be homogeneously distributed.

Perhaps future studies will be able to explain the organized pattern of galaxies within the confines of the Big Bang theory. On the other hand, future studies may provide data that suggest alternate theories that better explain the nature of the universe we observe today.

Magnetars

A new type of star was discovered through an effect it had on our environment for one brief moment. Called a *magnetar*, it is believed to be a neutron star that has a magnetic field billions of times more powerful than Earth's magnetic field. A neutron star is a remnant of a collapsed star and is extremely dense. The forces that form a neutron star are so powerful that the original star's protons and electrons were compressed together to form neutrons.

Some scientists thought for a while that this strange type of star existed, but there was no proof until 1979, when an intense pulse of X-rays and gamma rays entered our solar system and set off detectors on spacecraft orbiting our Earth and surveying other planets. The intensity of the radiation was powerful enough to cause some spacecraft to automatically shut down their instruments to prevent them from being damaged. Fortunately, the radiation didn't penetrate our atmosphere any further than a distance of 48 kilometers (km) (about 30 miles) from our planet's surface. The burst of radiation probably occurred when something caused the magnetic field around the magnetar to become rearranged. No real harm was done, except to disappoint those scientists who were confident that magnetars didn't exist in the first place.

Quasars, Pulsars, and Black Holes

Magnetars aren't the only fascinating objects in the universe. There are faint blue celestial objects that are thought to be the most distant and luminous objects in the universe. There are rotating neutron stars thought to be remnants of *supernovas*, exploding stars that at peak intensity can outshine their galaxies. Astronomers have even found evidence that some stars have collapsed, forming such a powerful gravitational field that no light or any other radiation can escape. These objects, known as *black holes*, along with quasars and pulsars, raise many interesting questions about the universe in which we exist.

Table 8.1 gives a brief summary of the characteristics of quasars, pulsars, and black holes.

● Galaxies

Within the universe are billions of clusters of stars, known as *galaxies*. Each galaxy contains hundreds of millions of stars, clouds of dust, and gas. (Figure 8.1).

The galaxy of stars that contains our Sun is known as the *Milky Way*. The stars in the Milky Way are so far from one another that measurement in kilometers (or miles) would be impossible to imagine. As a result, astronomers use a measuring unit called the *light-year*. A light-year represents the distance that light travels in 1 year. Light travels 299,792 km (about 186,000 miles) in just 1 second, so 1 light-year represents a distance of 9,450,000,000,000 km (about 6,000,000,000,000 miles). Astronomers have estimated that the Milky Way is tens of thousands of light-years in length and one-eighth that distance in width. Their evidence seems to indicate that our galaxy has a spiral shape. The closest star to our Sun, Alpha Centauri, is more than 4 light-years away. The distance from the Milky Way to the nearest galaxy is 1,500,000 light-years.

● Constellations

Constellations are groups of stars that seem to form specific patterns when viewed from Earth. Ages ago, people on Earth looked up at the night sky and saw that the

Table 8.1 Characteristics of quasars, pulsars, and black holes

Object	Characteristics
Quasar	The name *quasar* comes from the term *quasi-stellar objects.* Quasars are extremely bright objects in the universe that shine with an intensity that's much more powerful than that of hundreds of galaxies. Their energy seems to come from gas and the remnants of stars spiraling into black holes. Quasars are thought to be at the centers of galaxies. Quasars are some of the oldest objects in the universe and are billions of light-years from Earth.
Pulsar	A pulsar is a dense, rapidly spinning remnant of a supernova explosion. (A supernova is the explosive end to the life of a massive star.) The pulsar consists solely of neutrons and produces intense magnetic fields that sweep across space like lighthouse beacons. When the first pulsar was discovered, its extremely regular rate of pulsing was thought to be a signal from another intelligent civilization.
Black hole	Black holes cannot be seen, but their presence is detected by studying the behavior of objects near them. Black holes are often thought of as vacuums that take in all that is around them, but that is not completely true. Some black holes emit radiation as matter is drawn in. Observable X-rays and radio waves are then emitted. A black hole is formed by the collapse of an old star into an extremely dense state surrounded by a powerful gravitational field. It is thought that some black holes may contain the masses of millions or billions of stars. These supermassive black holes may begin as ordinary black holes and over a long period of time take in the masses of large numbers of surrounding stars. Another theory is that they were formed during the Big Bang.

Figure 8.1 The Andromeda spiral galaxy, which is visible as a faint patch in the constellation Andromeda, is about 2 million light-years from Earth.

DVIDS/NASA

stars that make up the Milky Way seemed to be organized into patterns. Each area of the sky containing such a pattern was identified as a constellation, and all the stars within the pattern were considered to be part of it. Many constellations were given names from mythology. Others were named for their apparent resemblance to familiar animals and objects. At present, there are 88 named constellations.

The easiest constellations to recognize are the polar constellations, groups of stars located around the North Star (Polaris). To locate the North Star, find the constellation known as the Big Dipper. By sighting along an imaginary line between the two stars at the rim of the Big Dipper, you should be able to locate the North Star.

Our Solar System

Our Sun, the planets revolving around it, and associated clouds and bodies of matter make up what we call the *solar system*, which scientists believe was formed about 4.5 billion years ago. The Sun's gravitational pull is the dominant force in the **solar system**, and the Sun itself is the most massive part of the solar system.

● Our Sun, a Star

The Sun is one of the estimated 10^{24} stars in the universe! It is the source of energy that maintains our planet. Although it appears as the largest and brightest star in the universe, it is considered just average in size and brightness. Because it is by far the closest star to Earth, it appears as the biggest and brightest star.

The Earth's atmosphere and its distance from the Sun are just right to sustain life. Among all the stars in the universe, the Sun is ideal for supporting life on Earth.

The relationship of the Sun and Earth is responsible for the patterns of night, day, and seasons to which we have become accustomed. The Earth rotates in a counterclockwise, or easterly, direction. Every point on the planet will pass through the Sun's rays and be shielded from the Sun's rays approximately every 24 hours (23 hrs., 56 minutes), resulting in our experience of day and night.

The tilt of the Earth, 23.5 degrees, as it orbits the Sun has an effect on day length. When a hemisphere is angled toward the sun, the days tend to be longer as one heads toward the pole inclined toward the Sun. The circumference of the Earth is smaller toward the poles, and therefore the region remains illuminated by the Sun longer during the Earth's rotation, resulting in longer days and shorter nights. The opposite occurs as one moves toward the pole oriented away from the Sun.

The tilt of the Earth also has an effect on seasons. As the Earth orbits the Sun, the Earth's axis maintains its orientation. This is easily overlooked and can lead to misunderstanding. The result is that there are times during the year when a hemisphere is angled more toward the Sun (summer) or angled more away from the Sun (winter). The Earth's tilt causes the Sun's rays to encounter the Earth at different angles as the Earth orbits the Sun. The more directly the Sun's rays encounter the Earth (closer to perpendicular), the more concentrated the energy. The more indirectly the Sun's rays encounter the Earth, the more spread out and less concentrated the energy. This can be illustrated by shining a beam of light perpendicular to a black piece of paper and slowly tilting the paper away from the perpendicular. As the paper tilts away from the source of light, the area illuminated becomes larger and less concentrated. The patterns of night, day, and seasons repeat on a predictable basis as the Earth rotates and orbits the Sun. The elliptical orbit of the Earth varies from 91.5 million miles in early January, called "perihelion," to 94.5 million miles in early July, called "aphelion." Perihelion is the term used to describe the Earth's closest point to the Sun; aphelion describes Earth's most distant point from the Sun. The average distance between the Sun and Earth is 93 million miles. The elliptical path causes only small variations in the amount of solar radiation reaching the Earth. Distance is not a determining cause of the seasons.

Day, night, and the seasons are relatively short-term repetitive patterns created by the interactions of the Sun and Earth. Longer term patterns affect natural climate change. These patterns result from properties of the Earth called wobble, eccentricity, and tilt. The interaction of these three variables impacts the variation in climate and seasons over *thousands* of years.

Wobble   The Earth also wobbles on its axis, much like a spinning top wobbles. For example, we see the North Pole pointing toward the North Star, Polaris. But Polaris has not always been and will not always be the North Star. The Earth completes a wobble about every 21,000 years. During that wobble, the North Pole will point toward other stars as well.

Eccentricity   The eccentricity of the Earth's orbit means that its orbit, while nearly circular, varies over long periods of time (about 100,000 years to complete one cycle). The changing shape of the Earth's orbit impacts the intensity of the seasons over long periods of time.

Tilt   The tilt of the Earth does not remain constant at 23.5 degrees. It varies from about 22.5 degrees to a maximum of 24.5 degrees and takes 41,000 years to complete one cycle.

The complex interaction of these three properties of the Earth influence the climate and seasons over *thousands* of years, causing global warming and ice ages. The combined effects of these variables are referred to as the *Milankovitch cycles* after Milutin Milankovitch, a Serbian scientist who proposed the influence of these variables on climate in the 1920s.

These factors that impact climate change are *natural* and gradual, occurring over long periods of time. They are *not to be confused* with the rapid changes in climate currently taking place. In fact, the rapid change in climate during the past 100 years is alarming because it is indeed unnatural and clearly associated with human behaviors.

As we learn more about the Sun, it is proving to be a more complex star[1] than we ever realized. Most scientists seem to agree on how the Sun was formed and how it will die. They have even calculated how much longer it has to exist: 5 billion years as a normal, or main-sequence, star.

About 5 billion years from now, the Sun will have depleted the hydrogen fuel in its core. Its thermonuclear reactions will then move outward where unused hydrogen exists. At the same time, the tremendous nuclear heat at the Sun's core will also move outward, expanding the Sun by as much as 60 times. As the Sun cools by expansion, its surface color will become a deep red. It will then be a *red giant*—not a main-sequence star. Looming across much of our sky, it will boil off our water and air and incinerate any remnants of life.

When the Sun exhausts its hydrogen fuel, it will no longer be able to withstand gravitational contraction. Eventually, it will shrink to a *white dwarf*, no bigger than Earth but so dense that a piece the size of a sugar cube would weigh thousands of kilograms. Eventually, after billions of years, our Sun will cool and dim to a *black cinder*. Only then will eternal night fall upon the solar system.

● Types of Interactions (PS2.B)

Earth has a single natural satellite: the Moon. The Moon orbits the Earth on a regular basis, once approximately every 28 days. The moon is one of many celestial bodies that orbit a closer, larger celestial body. What is the explanation for orbits?

All objects exert a gravitational force on each other. This phenomenon is referred to as Newton's law of universal gravitation. The larger the objects and the closer they are, the greater the attraction. The Moon and Earth are large enough to attract each other. So why doesn't the Moon collide with the Earth? The Moon is a satellite. It is constantly falling, but it is moving so fast it does not become drawn into the Earth. This can be a difficult concept to grasp. You can model the phenomenon by attaching a ball to a pole with a length of string, like a tetherball. The string models the force of gravity. As long as the ball is moving fast enough, it will not fall into the pole. If the Moon moved too fast, it would leave Earth's orbit just as the tetherball would if it moved so fast it broke the string.

The Moon in turn exerts a gravitational force on the Earth. We see this by the ocean shore in the form of tides, which result from gravitational force of the Moon on the massive ocean waters. The Sun also has an influence on the tides, but less so because of its distance from the Earth.

The first human footsteps on the Moon were made by American astronauts, who explored its dusty surface in 1969. Six two-man crews brought back a collection of rocks and soil weighing 382 kilograms (842 pounds) and consisting of more than 2,000 separate samples.

Rocks collected from the lunar highlands date from 4.0 to 4.3 billion years ago. The first few million years of the Moon's existence were so violent that little trace of this period remains. As a molten outer layer gradually cooled and solidified into different kinds of rock, the Moon was bombarded by huge asteroids and smaller objects. Some of the asteroids were the size of Rhode Island or Delaware, and their collisions with the Moon created huge basins hundreds of kilometers across.

The catastrophic bombardment died away about 4 billion years ago, leaving the lunar highlands covered with huge overlapping craters and a deep layer of shattered and broken rock (Figure 8.2). Heat produced by the decay of radioactive elements began to melt the inside of the Moon at depths of about 200 km (124 miles) below its surface. Then, from 3.1 to 3.8 billion years ago, great floods of lava rose from inside the Moon and poured over its surface, filling the large impact basins to form the dark parts of the Moon, called *maria*, or seas. Surprisingly, recent analysis of data from the Moon has suggested the presence of water trapped as ice at its polar regions.

Figure 8.2 This lunar landscape photo was transmitted to Earth by a *Surveyor* spacecraft.

DVIDS/NASA

● The Planets

Eight planets, including Earth, revolve around the Sun. Three of these planets—Mercury, Venus, and Mars—resemble Earth in size, density, and chemical composition. The other four—Jupiter, Saturn, Uranus, and Neptune—are larger and have thick, gaseous atmospheres (Figure 8.3).

In 2006 the International Astronomical Union redefined the definition of the term *planet* as a celestial body that (a) is in orbit around the Sun, (b) has sufficient mass for its self-gravity to overcome rigid body forces so that it assumes a hydrostatic equilibrium (nearly round) shape, and (c) has cleared the neighborhood around its orbit.[2] "Cleared the neighborhood" means that the planet is the dominant gravitational force and that any other bodies of similar size in the area of the planet are under its gravitational influence. The Moon is an example of a body under the gravitational force of Earth. Hence the Moon is not a planet, whereas Earth is a planet. Under the new definition, Pluto has lost its status as a planet and is now considered a dwarf planet. A dwarf planet needs to meet the same first two criteria as a planet; however, it has not cleared the neighborhood around its orbit, and it is not a satellite. To make matters more complicated, as of June 11, 2008, Pluto became a special type of dwarf planet called a "plutoid."[3] Plutoids are Pluto-like dwarf planets.

It's important to be aware of the key physical characteristics of each planet in our solar system, the nature of any atmosphere that exists, and the kind and number of satellites it has. Table 8.2 provides a considerable amount of detail for each planet, including its distance from the Sun, diameter, and rotation period. The following sections detail some of the key characteristics of each planet.

Mercury   This is a small, heavily cratered, rocky planet. Dried gullies on and in the surface may indicate the presence of streams and seas millions of years ago. There is possibly water under the surface now. In fact, scientists are reasonably sure they have found water under Mercury's north and south poles. Mercury has a very thin atmosphere that's composed of carbon dioxide and small amounts of nitrogen. No natural satellites orbit this planet.

Venus   The planet's surface is covered with lava flows from ancient volcanoes, quake faults, and impact craters. One of the lava-filled basins is larger than the continental United States. There is even one volcano that is taller than Mt. Everest. The atmosphere is a poisonous mixture of carbon dioxide and sulfuric acid. Thick clouds hide the Venusian surface. No natural satellites orbit Venus.

Earth   Earth's atmosphere contains oxygen, nitrogen, carbon dioxide, and other gases. There is also an ozone layer, which protects living things from solar ultraviolet radiation, and clouds, which are part of Earth's water cycle. Earth has one natural satellite: the Moon.

Figure 8.3   The Relative Sizes of the Planets

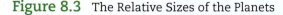
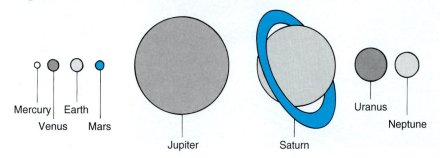

Table 8.2 Characteristics of the planets

Characteristic	Mercury	Venus	Earth	Mars	Jupiter	Saturn	Uranus	Neptune
Mean distance from Sun (millions of kilometers)	57.9	108.2	149.6	227.9	778.3	1,427	2,871	4,497
Period of revolution	88 days	224.7 days	365.3 days	687 days	11.86 years	29.46 years	84 years	165 years
Equatorial diameter (kilometers)	4,880	12,100	12,756	6,794	143,200	120,000	51,800	49,528
Atmosphere (main components)	Virtually none	Carbon dioxide	Nitrogen Oxygen	Carbon dioxide	Hydrogen Helium	Hydrogen Helium	Helium Hydrogen Methane	Hydrogen Helium Methane
Moons	0	0	1	2	47	30+	20+	8
Rings	0	0	0	0	3	1,000 (?)	11	4
Inclination of orbit to ecliptic	7°	3.4°	0°	1.9°	1.3°	2.5°	0.8°	1.8°
Eccentricity of orbit	.206	.007	.017	.093	.048	.056	.046	.009
Rotation period	59 days	243 days retrograde	23 hours, 56 min.	24 hours, 37 min.	9 hours, 55 min.	10 hours, 40 min.	17.2 hours retrograde	16 hours, 7 min.
Inclination of axis*	Near 0°	177.2°	23° 27'	25° 12'	3° 5'	26° 44'	97° 55'	28° 48'

*Inclinations greater than 90° imply retrograde rotation.

Figure 8.4 *Sojourner* on the Surface of Mars

DVIDS/NASA

Mars A tiny, toylike robotic vehicle called *Sojourner* was sent to Mars in 1977 (Figure 8.4). It successfully traveled over a small portion of the Martian surface and sent back pictures to Earth. Although *Sojourner* showed us some Martian rocks, our telescopes and other instruments have provided a larger view of the Martian landscape. The surface has dried gulleys, which may indicate that Mars had running water and streams at one time. In addition, geological features resembling shorelines, gorges, riverbeds, and islands have also been observed. Mars has polar ice caps, which likely consist of water. Following up on the *Sojourner* mission, the *Phoenix Mars Lander* arrived on the planet on May 25, 2008. One of its main objectives was to collect and test surface samples for evidence of liquid water on the planet. The second objective was to search for evidence of a habitable zone that could support life at the microbial level. More recently, the **Mars Science Laboratory**, carrying the Mars rover *Curiosity*, landed in the Gale Crater on August 5, 2012. The mission of this rover is to look for evidence of microbial life now or in the past on Mars.

The Martian atmosphere, like that of Venus, is composed primarily of carbon dioxide with small amounts of nitrogen, oxygen, and argon. The small amount of water vapor in the air condenses to form clouds along the slopes of volcanoes. Some fog even forms in Martian valleys. Mars has two moons—Phobos and Deimos—and each has a heavily cratered surface.

Jupiter   This planet, the largest in our solar system, has an atmosphere that is mostly hydrogen and helium, whirling above a ball of liquid hydrogen. Jupiter's extraordinarily large atmosphere includes the Great Red Spot: a giant storm that is at least three times the size of Earth.

A number of natural satellites travel around Jupiter. The four largest are Ganymede, Callisto, Io, and Europa, and two of next largest are Amalthea and Himalia. The moon Europa has a deep ocean of liquid water under an icy crust.

Saturn   This planet seems to have no solid surface and is composed of hydrogen gas. The sixth planet from the Sun, Saturn is known for its intricate ring system. The rings are made of ice and rock particles, which vary in size from being as small as dust to as large as boulders. The rings appear to be held in their respective orbits by the gravitational attraction of the planet and its satellites (Figure 8.5).

Saturn has at least 30 moons. Titan is the largest, and the next six in size are Rhea, Iapetus, Dione, Tethys, Enceladus, and Mimas. The moon Titan has an atmosphere rich in nitrogen, similar to Earth's atmosphere in its early days. Consequently, this moon holds great interest to scientists searching for extraterrestrial life.

Uranus   This, the third-largest planet in our solar system, rotates on its side! It has no solid surface, although it may have a small, silicate-rich core. The atmosphere of Uranus contains hydrogen, helium, water, ammonia, and methane. The blue-green color of the planet is due to the presence of methane gas above the cloud layers. Astronomers have detected a system of faint rings around the planet. Uranus has more than 20 moons. Five of the largest are Miranda, Titania, Oberon, Umbriel, and Ariel.

Neptune   This gaseous planet is composed of hydrogen, helium, and methane, and these gases are thought to surround an Earth-sized liquid core. Like Uranus, Neptune has sufficient methane to give it a slightly bluish color. Winds in the atmosphere of Neptune are the fastest anywhere. They are three times stronger than any winds on Earth and nine times more powerful than the winds of Jupiter.

Neptune has several faint rings. The farthest ring has been named Adams, and within it are arcs named Liberty, Equality, and Fraternity. The moons of Neptune include Naiad, Thalassa, Despina, Galatea,

Figure 8.5   This photo montage of Saturn and its rings and moons was created by an artist who juxtaposed a series of photographs transmitted by the *Voyager* spacecraft.

DVIDS/NASA

Larissa, Proteus, Triton, and Nereid. The largest of these moons, Triton, travels in an orbit opposite to the planet's rotation direction. This means that Triton is continually getting closer to the planet and will crash into it in about 10 to 100 million years!

Exploring Space

Voyager 1 and *2* are rocket probes launched in 1977 to observe phenomena on Jupiter, Saturn, Uranus, and Neptune. It is hoped that one or both of these probes will be able to reach the edges of our solar system and beyond. At present, the probes are sending back an enormous amount of data about the outer planets. Data gathered by *Voyager 2*'s flyby of Uranus in 1986 provided extremely sharp pictures of its major satellite. At the time of publication **Voyager probes** were in the heliosheath (The *heliosheath* is the outer region of the heliosphere or region of space dominated by the sun. Far beyond Pluto!) and continue to generate valuable data.

If they are not destroyed, the *Voyager* spacecraft will escape the solar system at a speed of 62,000 km (about 38,700 miles) per hour. Onboard each spacecraft are a phonograph record, sound-reproduction equipment, and playing instructions. The records include music, spoken languages, and common sounds from nature. Also included is a plaque that shows pictures of humans and describes, in scientific symbols, Earth, its location, and its people. The *Voyager* spacecraft will reach the first star in their interstellar voyage in about 40,000 years. Perhaps someone or something will interrupt them before then and learn about our planet and its people from the information, equipment, and pictures onboard.

The *Magellan* spacecraft was deployed by the space shuttle *Atlantis*. Its interplanetary journey includes a careful study of Venus. *Magellan*'s onboard instruments, which include radar imaging systems, have transmitted rather spectacular images of the Venusian surface. Early radar images include that shown in Figure 8.6, which shows 75-km-long (46-mile-long) valleys that photoanalysts have nicknamed "Gumby."

The Hubble Space Telescope

The Hubble Space Telescope (HST) was deployed from a space shuttle launched on April 24, 1990, and just 1 month later, on May 20, humans saw the first pictures transmitted from the telescope. The HST was designed to gather the sharpest pictures ever of astronomical objects (Figure 8.7). Unfortunately, defects in one of the Hubble's mirrors limited its effectiveness. To correct this problem as well as upgrade related equipment, astronauts from the space shuttle *Endeavor* carried out the most complicated space repairs ever attempted. They secured the HST in the shuttle cargo bay, replaced its solar panels, installed a device to correct the mirror defects, replaced gyroscopes (instruments that sense the telescope's orientation in space), replaced one of its cameras, and released the upgraded HST into orbit. The Hubble Space Telescope is continually repaired and upgraded and is now able to detect stars that are 13 billion or more light-years away.

Figure 8.6 This *Magellan* radar image of Venus shows a set of valleys nicknamed "Gumby."

DVIDS/NASA

Figure 8.7   Compare these photographs of the nearest starburst spiral galaxy, NGC-35. The image on the left was taken with a land-based telescope. The detailed area shown on the right is an image from the Hubble Space Telescope (HST). The HST's high resolution allowed astronomers to quantify complex structures in the starburst core of the galaxy for the first time.

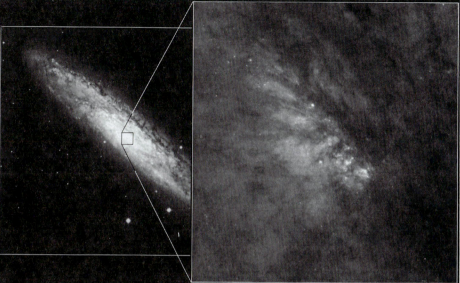

DVIDS/NASA

● The Space Shuttle

After 30 years of exploration in outer space, the first reusable spacecraft was retired in 2011. NASA's space shuttle could orbit Earth like a spacecraft and land like an airplane. The shuttle was designed to carry heavy loads into orbit around Earth. Other launch vehicles have done this, but unlike those vehicles, which can be used only once, each space shuttle orbiter could be reused more than 100 times (Figure 8.8).

The shuttle permitted the checkout and repair of satellites in orbit and the return of satellites to Earth for repairs that cannot be done in space. Thus, the shuttle made possible considerable savings in spacecraft costs.

Principal Components   The space shuttle had three main units: the *orbiter*, the *external tank*, and two solid rocket *boosters*. The orbiter served as the crew-carrying and payload-carrying unit of the shuttle system. It was 37 meters (122 feet) long, had a wingspan of 24 meters (79 feet), and without fuel weighed about 68,000 kilograms (150,000 pounds). It was about the size and weight of a DC-9 commercial airplane.

The orbiter could transport a payload of 29,500 kilograms (65,000 pounds). It carried its cargo in a cavernous payload bay 18.3 meters (60 feet) long and 4.6 meters (15 feet) in diameter. The bay was flexible enough to provide accommodations for unmanned spacecraft in a variety of shapes and for fully equipped scientific laboratories.

The orbiter's three main liquid rocket engines were fed propellants from the external tank, which was 47 meters (154 feet) long and 8.7 meters (28.6 feet) in diameter. At liftoff, the tank could hold 703,000 kilograms (1,550,000 pounds) of

Figure 8.8 A Successful Shuttle Launch

DVIDS/NASA

propellants, consisting of liquid hydrogen (fuel) and liquid oxygen (oxidizer). The hydrogen and oxygen were in separate pressurized compartments of the tank. The external tank was the only part of the shuttle system that was not reusable.

A Typical Shuttle Mission In a typical shuttle mission, lasting from 7 to 30 days, the orbiter's main engines and the booster ignited simultaneously to rocket the shuttle from the launch pad. Launches were made from the John F. Kennedy Space Center in Florida for east–west orbits and from Vandenberg Air Force Base in California for north–south orbits.

At a predetermined point, the two solid rocket boosters separated from the orbiter and parachuted to the sea, where they were recovered for reuse. The orbiter continued into space, jettisoning its external propellant tank just before orbiting. The external tank entered the atmosphere and broke up over a remote ocean area.

The orbiter then proceeded on its mission in space. When its work was completed, the crew directed the orbiter on a flight path that took it back to Earth's atmosphere. Various rocket systems were used to slow its speed and adjust its direction. Previous spacecraft followed a direct path from space to the predetermined landing area. The orbiter was quite different. It could maneuver from the right to the left of its entry path a distance of about 2,035 km (about 1,265 miles). The orbiter had the capability of landing like an airplane at Kennedy Space Center or Vandenberg Air Force Base. Its landing speed was about 335 km (about 208 miles) per hour.

Successes and Tragedies The NASA space shuttle program enjoyed many successes during its 20-plus years. Its first success was in April 1981, when the orbiter *Columbia* carried out a 2-day mission that proved the shuttle could put a spacecraft in orbit and return safely. Missions that followed included the deployment of satellites, scientific explorations, the deployment of the Hubble Space Telescope, and flights to assist in the building and servicing of the *International Space Station*.

These successes have not been without human costs, however. On January 28, 1986, the orbiter *Challenger* exploded just 73 seconds after liftoff. This accident took the lives of all seven crew members, including the first teacher-astronaut, Christa McAuliffe. On February 1, 2003, the space shuttle *Columbia* suffered a catastrophe on reentry into Earth's atmosphere. Again, all seven crew members were killed. Each of these tragedies was followed by an intense investigation to determine the cause and to hopefully prevent similar events from happening in the future. To be sure, the exploration of space will continue and the mysteries of the universe will continue to be revealed.

Exploring Space: The Next Steps

Would you sign up for a trip to Mars? It is a question that your students, or possibly even you, may have a realistic chance of answering in the future. NASA is working on solving problems to challenges that will make human journeys to Mars possible. These challenges represent the integration of science, engineering, and technology to their fullest. Some challenges include creating habitation for living and working for long periods in space (up to 1,000 days); and transporting humans and cargo safely, efficiently, and reliably over distances never traveled by humans.

Some of the projects under development of a possible Martian mission include those discussed next.

● Space Launch System (SLS)

The SLS is an advanced space vehicle with the world's most powerful rocket to launch astronauts into deep space. It will carry the *Orion* spacecraft on missions to Mars. Production of the SLS is now underway.

The *Orion* Multipurpose Crew Vehicle (MPCV)   Deep space exploration is the next frontier. The *Orion* MPCV is designed to support astronauts on missions up to 6 months. It includes both crew and service modules that could pave the way for manned space flights to Mars. In the meantime, the current mission being carried out by the Mars Science Laboratory and a rover mission planned for 2020 will contribute valuable information in preparation for landing humans on the red planet.

● The *International Space Station:* A Rest Stop on the Road to Mars?

High above our heads, men and women are at work in and on the *International Space Station.* This space laboratory is permanently orbiting Earth at a distance of 323 km (200 miles). As you read these words, scientists in the space station are conducting an intensive study of how the human body and other biological systems respond to prolonged time in space. They are also at work constructing additional internal and external parts for the space station, using 21st-century materials and techniques adapted for use in space.

The *International Space Station* is a cooperative venture of a number of countries. Each is making its own unique contribution to this, the largest cooperative scientific and engineering effort in human history. When it is complete, the space station will contain facilities for biotechnology, fluids and combustion, a space station furnace, gravitational biology, and human research.

Crews are continually onboard the space station and busily at work. The United States and Russia have delivered people, equipment, and supplies to the station, including materials created by other nations. In addition, unmanned rockets have been used as "freighters" to carry equipment and supplies to the *International Space Station.* So, the science fiction of our childhood has become today's reality: We have space "ferries"!

What will humankind accomplish next, as today's science fiction frontier becomes tomorrow's rest stop on our journey to Mars and beyond?!

Summary

8.1 **Reflect on the origins of the universe.**

The universe is all the matter, energy, and space that exists. It can be difficult to comprehend the extraordinary vastness of the universe, how it may have begun, and what existed prior to the universe. Theories such as the Big Bang theory suggest that all the matter of the universe was combined in a single, extremely dense unit the size of a pebble that exploded on a scale hardly imaginable, giving rise to a continually expanding universe in which the matter formed into celestial bodies such as stars and planets. Recent discoveries of patterns of galaxies pose a challenge to the Big Bang theory.

8.2 **Describe the relationships among the Earth, Moon, and Sun that explain observable patterns such as day/night, tides, and seasons.**

The Earth, Sun, and Moon interact through gravitational attraction that results in orbits of the Earth and Moon around the Sun and the Moon around the Earth that are responsible for regular cycles such as night, day, seasons, and tides.

8.3 **Explain why the Sun appears bigger and brighter than other stars.**

From our perspective on Earth, the sun appears as the largest and brightest star in the universe. In fact, it is considered just average in size and brightness. Because it is by far the closest star to Earth, it appears as the biggest and brightest star.

8.4 **Describe the mechanisms for natural climate change.**

Climate change is a natural phenomenon that occurs over thousands of years due to variations in the Earth's wobble, eccentricity, and tilt—the combination of which is referred to as Milankovitch cycles.

8.5 **Describe a brief history and the anticipated future of modern space exploration.**

The 1950s to 1980s saw a rapid growth in space exploration that involved astronauts traveling as far as the Moon and spending extended time on the *International Space Station*. The 21st century promises to be a time of deep space probes and peopled exploration with the growth of private space industries and technologies that could put humans on Mars.

 Chapter 8 Self-Check
Click to gauge your understanding of the concepts in this chapter.

Notes

1. The discussion of the Sun was excerpted with modifications from *Our Prodigal Sun*, a pamphlet prepared by the National Aeronautics and Space Administration. This pamphlet (stock number 3300-00569) can be purchased from the Superintendent of Documents, Government Printing Office, Washington, DC 20402. http://ntrs.nasa.gov/archive/nasa/casi.ntrs.nasa.gov/19750004813_1975004813.pdf
2. International Astronomical Union News Release - IAU0603: IAU 2006 General Assembly: Result of the IAU Resolution votes Aug 24, 2006, Prague. www.iau.org (accessed 06-30-08).
3. Courtland, Rachel. June 2008. NewScientist news service. http://space.newscientist.com/article/dn14118-plutolike-objects-to-be-called-plutoids.html (accessed 06-30-08).

The Life Sciences

▶ **History and Nature of the Life Sciences**

Life always has been and always will be a wondrous mystery. The tiniest ocean creature sneaking up on an even tinier prey, a grizzly bear growling as she dips a giant paw into a river full of salmon, and the human sitting down to a meal are all trying to get energy as efficiently as possible. If they are successful, they will be able to move through their individual life cycle and possibly bring forth more life.

Biologists, zoologists, botanists, medical researchers, and others strive to understand how and why living things capture energy, cells grow, and species reproduce. What they learn provides the foundation for the everyday work of people in a wide range of careers in the life sciences. The results of that work touch all our lives.

Careers in the Life Sciences

Many career paths are available for women and men who have the required knowledge, skills, and motivation to explore the nature of life and how life, in all its forms, can be protected and enriched. Here are a few of the many possibilities:

- *Physician.* Physicians undergo training that will bring them knowledge and skills in a variety of the life sciences. And that training will ultimately support their practice in any of a wide variety of specialties: internal medicine, emergency room care, orthopedics, reconstructive and cosmetic surgery, ophthalmology, nervous system disorders, obstetrics and gynecology, oncology, and cardiology.

- *Biomedical Engineer.* Consider all the technology you might encounter during a medical visit from a digital thermometer to a functional MRI machine. Prostheses that interface with the human nervous system and can be controlled by the individual's thoughts (myoelectric interfaces). These are examples of work by biomedical engineers.

- *Medical Technologist.*   Medical technologists are assistants to physicians, pharmacists, laboratory scientists, and others who perform medical research. Technologists are usually employed in physicians' offices, hospitals, blood banks, pharmacies, and laboratories—all places where blood and cell specimens are analyzed for the presence of bacteria, parasites, fungi, cancer, and so on.

- *Molecular Biologist.*   Molecular scientists apply knowledge of biology, chemistry, physics, and even engineering at the molecular level. A molecular biologist could be engaged in any form of research that involves life particularly at the cellular level: drug development, genetic engineering, environmental protection, biofuel production to name few.

- *Horticulturalist.*   If you've ever wondered why the flowers in a flower shop or the fruits and vegetables in a supermarket are so abundant and appear to be so perfect, then you've seen the results of work done by horticulturalists. They are trained in certain aspects of the life sciences and use their knowledge and skills to improve the quality and production of plant life.

- *Marine Biologist.*   About 70% of Earth's surface is covered by water teeming with life. The people who study life in the water are marine biologists. Imagine the wide range and diversity of topics one could study as a marine biologist, from the migration of whales to the effects of climate change on zooplankton.

Key Events in the Development of the Life Sciences

350–341 BCE	Aristotle classifies the animals on Earth into eight distinct groups.
350 BCE	Diocles writes a book on anatomy and a book on herbal remedies.
190–209	Galen, a Greek physician, organizes all the medical knowledge of that time into a coherent work that will be used by physicians until the Middle Ages.
1665	Robert Hooke publishes *Micrographia*, which displays drawings of natural objects he has studied with a microscope.
1673	The Royal Society of London receives correspondence from Dutch naturalist Antoni van Leeuwenhoek, describing his discoveries using a tool called a *microscopia*.
1735	Carl von Linné (whom we refer to as *Linnaeus*) publishes *Systema Naturae*, which proposes the system of binomial nomenclature (i.e., the use of a genus and species name for each organism) that is still used today.
1837	Charles Darwin begins work that will, after many years, lead to the development of the theory that changes in species over time are the result of *natural selection*, which is the fundamental idea of evolution. His thoughts were based on both his personal study of plants and animals gathered along the coast of South America and his study of the work of Thomas Malthus. Unfortunately, Darwin feared that others would react negatively to his ideas and delayed publishing his conclusions.
1858	Alfred Russell Wallace concludes, as Darwin did, that natural selection propels the evolution of species. Wallace's and Darwin's papers are both presented at a meeting of the Linnaean Society.

1859	Charles Darwin, provoked by Wallace's work, finally publishes a complete book that puts forth his theories. *On the Origin of Species* will become one of the most important books in the history of science.
1860s	Louis Pasteur disproves the idea that flies and other small living things can spontaneously arise from living matter. He shows that new living things can be created only through the reproduction of existing living things.
1866	Gregor Mendel, an Austrian monk, proposes the basic laws of heredity.
1871	Charles Darwin publishes *The Descent of Man*.
1902	Walter Sutton discovers that chromosomes separate for reproduction, an idea that will become the foundation for other scientists' work as they attempt to fully understand inheritance.
1925	Tennessee schoolteacher John Thomas Scopes is brought to trial for teaching evolution. William Jennings Bryan is the lead prosecutor, and Clarence Darrow defends Scopes.
1938	Fishermen find a *coelacanth*, a fish that was thought to be extinct, off the coast of South Africa.
1953	James D. Watson and Francis H. C. Crick publish their paper on the molecular structure of deoxyribonucleic acid (DNA) in journal *Nature*.
1959	In Africa, Mary Leakey, a paleontologist, finds a hominid skull belonging to *Australopithecus boisei*.
1971	Stephen Jay Gould and Niles Eldredge propose their theory of punctuated equilibrium, which states, essentially, that evolution often occurs in short bursts followed by longer periods in which no or only very modest changes occur in a species.
1974	Donald Johanson and others discover the fossils of a female fossil hominid, *Australopithecus afarensis*. The team names her *Lucy* and proposes that hominids walked upright before they developed large brains.
1974	Bob Bakker proclaims that birds are the descendants of dinosaurs.
1978	Mary Leakey discovers fossil footprints at Laetoli in Africa, which demonstrates that hominids walked upright 3.6 million years ago.
1990	Headed by James D. Watson, the 13-year Human Genome Project formally begins, representing an effort to "find all the genes on every chromosome in the body and to determine their biochemical nature."
1992	A yeast chromosome (*S. cerevisiae*) gene sequence is published.
1993	Biologist E. O. Wilson concludes that there may be as many as 30 million species of insects on Earth.
1995	The *Haemophilus influenzae* genetic sequence is published by Venter, Smith, Fraser, and others.
1996	The yeast genome sequence is investigated and published by an international consortium.
1997	The Roslin Institute, in Edinburgh, Scotland, successfully clones a sheep, producing Dolly the Lamb. She is the first mammal to be cloned from an adult.

1999	Gunter Blobel, a cell and molecular biologist at Rockefeller University, receives a Nobel Prize for identifying how and where proteins move in the cell. He shows that new proteins move to their correct locations by using a molecular "bar code" that the cell can read.
1999	The DNA of the first human chromosome, chromosome 22, is sequenced.
2000	A "draft" of the human genome is completed. Researchers essentially receive a road map that will result in the identification of the entire human genome DNA sequence.
2003	Sequencing of the human genome is finished, and researchers celebrate the completion of the Human Genome Project, begun in 1990.
2006	Craig Mello and Andrew Fire are awarded the Nobel Prize for their discovery of RNA interference-gene silencing by double-stranded RNA.
2012	Sir John B. Gurdon and Shiya Yamanaka are awarded the Nobel Prize in Physiology for discovering that mature cells can be reprogrammed to behave as stem cells.

Women and Men Who Have Shaped the Development of the Life Sciences

ANDREAS VERSALIUS (1514–1564) secured corpses for the earliest scientific dissections. As a professor at the University of Padua in Italy, he conducted many of these dissections for the benefit of future medical students. He summarized and categorized his lifetime of work in *De humani corporis fabrica libri septem*, which, when translated from Latin, means "The Structure of the Human Body in Seven Volumes."

CARL VON LINNE (CAROLUS LINNAEUS) (1707–1778) was known for his careful study and classification of plants, animals, and minerals. Although he was a physician, he is most famous for his book *Systema Naturae*, which still provides the foundation for the methods used to observe and classify natural objects.

JEANNE VILLEPREUX-POWER (1794–1871), a French-born woman, was a self-taught naturalist who studied in Sicily. She was one of the first scientists to use aquariums for experimentation with living organisms. In honor of this and other scientific achievements, a crater on the planet Venus was named for her.

ELIZABETH BLACKWELL (1821–1910) received the first medical degree granted to a woman in the United States. She specialized in the treatment of women and children and established what came to be the New York Infirmary for Women and Children.

REBECCA LEE CRUMPLER (1831–1895) was the first African American woman to become a physician in the United States. She wrote *A Book of Medical Discourses* in 1883, one of the first written about medicine by an African American.

ALEXANDER FLEMING (1881–1955) spent much of his life searching for an effective antiseptic and ultimately discovered that a sample of mold from the *Penicillium* family was extraordinarily effective in killing microbes.

GEORGE WASHINGTON CARVER (1896–1943) experimented widely in the field of plant genetics. He crossed plants of various types to produce new flowers, fruits, and vegetables and was known as an expert in the study of molds and fungi. His work did much to speed the progress of agriculture in the United States.

PERCY LAVON JULIAN (1899–1975) received his bachelor's degree from DePauw University, his master's in chemistry from Harvard University, and his Ph.D. in chemistry from the University of Vienna. Although trained as a chemist, he devoted most of his life's work to the development and refinement of chemicals that could be used as medicines.

BARBARA MCCLINTOCK (1902–1992) was a biologist who specialized in the study of genetics. She received the Nobel Prize for medicine in 1983 for the analysis of mechanisms that affect genes and, in fact, evolution itself.

RITA LEVI-MONTALCINI (1909–), an Italian-born biologist, came to St. Louis, Missouri, where she studied cellular reproduction and growth in the human body at Washington University. Her research led to her sharing of the Nobel Prize for physiology and medicine in 1986.

FRANCIS HARRY COMPTON CRICK (1916–2004) was trained as a physicist but is known for his work with James D. Watson, in which they proposed that DNA has a double-helix structure and then explained how it is replicated. With Watson and Maurice Wilkins, Crick received the Nobel Prize for medicine and physiology in 1962.

JONAS SALK (1914–1995), as head of the Virus Research Laboratory at the University of Pittsburgh, worked to improve a previously developed influenza vaccine; his synthesis of data from other scientists led to strategies that would create a vaccine to stop the polio virus. His work led to the large-scale vaccination of schoolchildren and the reduction of polio as a threat to public health worldwide.

GERTRUDE BELLE ELION (1918–1999) focused her scientific research on the creation of drugs to treat cancer, malaria, leukemia, and other diseases. She shared the 1988 Nobel Prize for physiology.

JAMES DEWEY WATSON (1928–), who had earned a Ph.D. in genetics, joined Francis H. C. Crick, Maurice Wilkins, and Rosalind Franklin in the study of the structure of DNA. Watson, Crick, and Wilkins shared the Nobel Prize for medicine and physiology in 1962. The year 2003 marked the fiftieth anniversary of the Watson/Crick discovery and the successful completion of the Human Genome Project, of which Watson was the head.

PATRICIA BATH (1942–). An American ophthalmologist known for being the first African American physician to receive a patent for a medical invention.

► Personal and Social Implications of the Life Sciences

No area of scientific exploration has clearer implications for our health and well-being than the life sciences. But along with progress comes certain risks and benefits. Let's consider a few areas of our personal and societal lives that are affected by developments in the life sciences.

Personal and Community Health

Many life scientists spend their careers in search of the causes and cures of illnesses and injuries. Some of that work has looked at the roles of proper nutrition and sanitation. And other research has led to the discovery that some illnesses and predispositions for particular illnesses may come from a person's genetic makeup. The discovery has led to enormous strides in biomedical research.

The study of the sources and effects of pollution is another area of study that has implications for personal and community health. The effects of water pollution, acid rain, and the depletion of ozone in the atmosphere are a few examples of topics that have drawn the attention of life scientists.

Hazards, Risks, and Benefits

The life sciences have brought us new knowledge about natural hazards in the environment, including the risks of emerging and reemerging infectious diseases, the effects of eating food containing parasitic organisms, and even ways for coexisting with large predators. How well we cope with these natural hazards is, to some extent, grounded in how well we understand the life sciences in all of its forms. Each of us must make careful decisions, assessing the risks and benefits associated with the choices we have about the kinds of food we eat, whether to smoke, and whether to use alcohol or potentially dangerous drugs.

We have enjoyed great benefits as the result of pharmaceutical technologies, surgical procedures, and even organ transplantation. But these benefits have sometimes been achieved through medical research that has used human subjects. Individuals who volunteer for treatment with new drugs and procedures must be made aware of the possible risks and benefits of doing so.

▶ Life Science Technology: Its Nature and Impact

You might not think of the life sciences as having a significant technological component, but they do! Moreover, that technology touches you in some very specific ways.

Modern health care—from making eyeglasses to performing cardiovascular surgery—overflows with instrumentation that has been brought to your health care provider (and ultimately to you) by engineers who have applied their expertise to the life sciences. Even something as banal as a visit to the dentist will give you a visual display of electromechanical devices to probe, unearth, and repair cavities; carry out root canal procedures; and even administer anesthetics. Recent developments in myoelectric controlled interfaces link the human nervous system to robotic limbs that can be controlled by thoughts.

Of course, biomedical research is only one aspect of the life sciences that receives the attention of engineers. Other engineering challenges include improving crop production, removing contaminants from water supplies, and designing facilities to help preserve endangered species.

The Design of Life Science Technology

Whether they work in environmental protection, criminal investigation, horticulture, or health care, life scientists require devices whose design meets the following criteria:

1. It does no harm or as little harm as possible to living things and the environment.
2. It addresses a problem that has been clearly identified and for which data can reasonably be expected to be obtained.

3. It presents data in a manner that is readily interpretable by life science researchers or health care providers, as appropriate.

4. If it is a tool, it can be easily used and safely operated.

5. It provides the users of life science technology with constant feedback about the accuracy of the data being represented and/or the health and welfare of the living things being treated.

Examples of Life Science Technology

A variety of technologies are used to gather information about living things and to improve their health and welfare:

Binoculars

Optical microscope

Electron microscope

Autoclave (sterilizing device)

Heart/lung machine

Blood pressure monitoring devices

Conventional pharmaceuticals

Genetically engineered pharmaceuticals

Prosthetic devices

Cardiac pacemaker

CAT (computerized axial tomography) scan devices

MRI (magnetic resonance imaging) devices

Safe capture traps (to study living things)

Technologies to convert biomass into biofuels

Myoelectric controlled artificial limbs

Long-Term Implications of Life Science Technology

The technology that has come from the wellspring of life science research has done much to improve the quality of our lives and our environment. We now have the tools to analyze and solve a multitude of problems.

But along with this capability comes concern about how to reduce the biological dangers new technology sometimes creates. This is truly a double-edged sword, as these examples point out:

- Antibiotics are widely available, but their use may have as an unintended consequence an increase in antibiotic resistant bacteria such as Methicillin-resistant *Staphylococcus aureus*, or MRSA.

- X-ray technology permits exploration of the human body and the treatment of some cancers, but it may lead to increased health risks—including a risk for cancer.

- False-positive results on medical tests can lead to unnecessary treatment regimens.

- The biological control of some insects can result in the increased population of other more harmful insects who have lost their natural predators.

- The use of antibiotics to treat infections that do not have bacteria as a root cause may inadvertently result in increasing the number of species of bacteria that are resistant to antibiotics.

Finally, the increased use of technology in all fields of the life sciences traditionally brings increases in the costs of goods and services. The implications of these increases for the consumer—whether a farmer calculating the cost of the foods he or she produces or a patient dealing with increases in the costs of his or her health care—must be considered as new technologies are invented and applied.

Living Things

Dark Moon Pictures/Shutterstock

Learning Outcomes

After completing the activities in this chapter, you should be able to:

9.1 Distinguish living from nonliving systems.

9.2 Describe relationships among structure and function.

9.3 Understand the flow of energy as a unifying theme of life systems.

9.4 Describe the interdependence of organisms in an ecosystem.

9.5 Explain how inheritance, variation of traits, and natural selection impact evolution.

9.6 Discuss how connecting children with the planet and Earth systems precedes and supports education about climate change.

▶ **GETTING STARTED**

A large figure is silently moving through the depths of the ocean, gliding effortlessly past huge underwater cliffs and ledges. As it nears the

Figure 9.1 Remoras benefit from scraps of food left by the whale shark.

Zeamonkeyimages/Fotolia

surface, you feel a slight movement in the water like a giant pressure wave moving toward you. Slowly a massive dark shape begins to rise from the depths of the ocean. It seems undisturbed by your presence as it glides quietly past with its broad gaping mouth wide open waiting to devour everything in its path. Looking up, you see the huge underbelly of a whale shark. Swarming around the gigantic shark are many smaller fish, apparently unconcerned about becoming a meal for the whale shark (Figure 9.1). The small fish are called remora. They eat scraps of food from the whale shark's diet of plankton and small fish. They also use the shark's bulk for transport and protection. This type of relationship is called commensalism. One organism, in this case the remora, benefits, while the other organism gains little or nothing but remains unharmed.

What makes the cliffs and ledges fundamentally different from the whale shark and remora? When scientists make observations to determine whether something is living or nonliving, they search for these eight characteristics, or *functions*, of life:
    All living things have or do the following:

1. Are composed of cells[1]—the smallest structural unit of an organism that is capable of independently carrying out the processes listed below.

2. Use energy that they produce or acquire. They use this energy to carry out energy-requiring activities such as movement, growth, and transport.

3. Grow.

4. Are able to reproduce, either by sexual or asexual means (an individual organism does not need to reproduce to be alive).

5. Inherit traits from the parent organisms.

6. Respond to stimuli in their environment.

7. Maintain a state of internal balance called homeostasis.

8. Adapt to their environment and evolve as a species.

From Molecules to Organisms: Structure and Processes (LS1-1)

All living things have unique internal and external structures to help them grow, survive, and reproduce as a species. Believe it or not, you have a lot in common with a cactus plant! This hopefully doesn't apply to your outward appearance, but it most definitely applies to your inside appearance. Both you and the cactus plant have specific structures that help you survive.

You, the cactus plant, and every other living thing are made up of one or more *cells*. Within every cell is a gelatin-like, colorless, semitransparent substance called *protoplasm*, which is made up of a variety of elements: carbon, hydrogen, oxygen, potassium, phosphorous, iodine, sulfur, nitrogen, calcium, iron, magnesium, sodium, chlorine, and traces of other elements. The cell also includes many structures called organelles. Each structure functions to support the cell's ability to live. Some organelles, such as vacuoles, serve primarily as storage areas. Others, such as mitochondria, carry out chemical reactions that support life. All cells contain DNA, which holds the genetic information that is organized into genes and chromosomes. Genes are sometimes referred to as the blueprints of the cell, as they hold the instructions in the arrangement of four key molecules called adenine, cytosine, thymine, and guanine that code for proteins, which carry out most of the essential functions of the cell. Less than 10% of the 3 billion molecules of DNA code for protein.

Scientists are working to understand the function of the remaining 90% of the DNA. The Human Genome Project, which succeeded in mapping the human genome in 2003, was among the most important scientific accomplishments. The ENCODE project, Encyclopedia of DNA Elements, began in 2003 and continues its mission to understand the functions of DNA.

A list of some of the common organelles found in cells are as follows:

Nucleus: is a membrane-bound organelle that stores DNA. It is often referred to as the control center of the cell.

Cell membrane: surrounds the cell and defines its boundaries with the outside world. It is selective and semipermeable, meaning it permits only certain molecules to enter or exit the cell

Cytoplasm: material between the cell and nucleus. It can be loosely thought of as the packing material of the cell, maintaining the cell's shape and anchoring organelles.

Mitochondria: often referred to as the powerhouse of the cell. Mitochondria are where chemical reactions take place that provide energy for the cell.

The cells that make up living things also differ. Those that have clearly defined nuclei and organelles are known as eukaryotes. All animals and plants have eukaryotic cells. Many one-celled organisms, known as prokaryotes, have neither nuclei nor other membrane-bound organelles. Bacteria are prokaryotes; and although plants and animals are both eukaryotic, the cell walls of plants contain cellulose, while the cells of animals are bound by membranes that do not contain cellulose.

In living things that contain more than one cell, any group of cells that performs a similar function is called a *tissue*. A group of tissues that function together is called an *organ*. And a group of organs that work together to perform a major function is known as a *system*. For instance, in plants, the various cells and tissues that enable the food made in the leaves to be transported to stems and roots make up the vascular system. Plants contains many different systems that perform different functions, as does the human body. In humans, those systems include the skeletal, muscular, respiratory, nervous, excretory, and reproductive systems.

Organization for Matter and Energy Flow in Organisms (LS1.C)

All living things have the same basic needs to survive; they need to acquire energy, grow, and reproduce. Each organism has unique adaptations in structure, function, and behavior to meet these needs. There are basically two methods to acquire energy: (1) convert the energy of the Sun into organic material that stores energy through photosynthesis, or (2) break down some organic material that has been produced by a photosynthetic organism. Ultimately, all energy for life originates from the Sun.[2]

Because harnessing energy from the Sun is foundational to life on the planet, a brief description of photosynthesis is helpful. You probably have encountered the familiar chemical equation for photosynthesis: carbon dioxide plus water fueled by sunlight produces carbohydrate and oxygen (CO_2 + H_2O — sunlight energy → $C_6H_{12}O_6$ + O_2). It is not unlike cooking, in which carbon dioxide and water are the ingredients, sunlight the energy, and carbohydrate the product. Carbohydrate stores the energy of the Sun, which both plants and animals use for growth, movement, metabolism (the chemical reactions in organisms), and reproduction. A typical question posed to students is to ask where the mass of a tree comes from. The mass does not come from the soil, as is often thought. The answer is in the equation for photosynthesis. The mass of the tree comes primarily from carbon dioxide.

Structure and Function (LS1.A)

Most organisms depend in some way, either directly or indirectly, on the carbohydrate created by photosynthetic organisms to store energy. Therefore, all organisms have structures to help them tap into the stored energy initially created through photosynthesis. Some organisms feed directly on photosynthesizers such as plants or algae: cows, horses, many fish, and a host of other organisms. These organisms in turn store the energy they acquired from photosynthesizers. Every organism is uniquely suited to get to acquire energy: Tigers have claws, powerful jaws, and can run very fast to catch their prey, for example. Some algae can absorb light energy at depths that other algae cannot. And plants have a wide variety needles, leaves, stems, and roots that serve as natural solar panels to capture energy from the Sun. Each structure evolved to help a particular organism survive in its unique environment.

Acquiring food is essential but not the sole requirement for survival. Nature has myriad strategies for protection from predators and the elements. Turtles have hard shells into which they can retreat to protect their soft bodies from injury and attack. Stick insects are almost indiscernible from the plants on which they live. Have you ever wondered why a penguin's feet do not freeze? Arteries in a penguin's legs can adjust the flow of blood to the feet to keep them a few degrees above freezing, not unlike a radiator exchanges heat with the cold air in a home to keep the house warm.

Information Processing (LS1.D)

Organisms also have developed unique structures that function to help them respond to their environment. Have you wondered why your dog seems to know you arrive home before any human in the house? A dog's sense of hearing is much more acute than a human's hearing. Dogs can perceive frequencies in a range of about 40 to 60,000 hertz (Hz), whereas humans have a range of about 20 to 20,000 Hz. Cats, horses, and even some moths have similarly extraordinary hearing. Hearing, touch, and vision are senses that enable organisms to interact with and interpret physical signals. Taste and smell enable organisms to sense the world through chemical clues. Both physical and chemical properties of the environment are sensed by organisms using specialized receptors. Receptors receive stimuli and send signals to the brain and nervous system that in turn interpret the signals and give them meaning. Therefore, if an animal eats something that may be poisonous, chemical receptors in the tongue send a message to the brain. The brain interprets the particular signal caused by the chemical in the food as dangerous, and the animal is deterred from ingesting a potentially lethal substance. Organisms from the smallest single cell to the blue whale all have specialized receptors to help them sense and respond appropriately to their environment.

Growth and Development of Organisms (LS.B)

Individual organisms do not have to reproduce in order to survive, but the species does. Organisms all possess special structures to support reproduction. Most organisms reproduce sexually, combining genetic information in the form of genes from both male and female parents. Other organisms reproduce asexually, without the mixing or genes from different parents. All reproduction occurs at the cellular level. Cells have specialized structures such as spindle fibers that organize and separate chromosomes during cell division. Plants can reproduce sexually, exchanging genes through the dispersal of pollen, or asexually like the spider plant that produces plantlets from stolons that branch out from the parent plant.

Living things grow and develop in predictable cycles, called life cycles. Most mammals, including humans, begin growth inside the parent (viviparous). In viviparous organisms, the fetus is nourished directly from the mother via a placental connection. Others organisms, such as birds, many reptiles, amphibians, and fish lay eggs in which the organism develops externally (oviparous). Unborn ovoviviparous organisms are nourished by a yolk in the egg prior to hatching. Some sharks, reptiles, insects, amphibians, and fish use a combination of both, with eggs hatching in the mother's body (ovoviviparous) prior to live birth.

Once born, nature has several versions of life cycles for organisms on their journey through life. The simplest life cycle consists of three stages: birth, growth, death. The young are born looking like little adults, with all the major features they will have throughout life. Most mammals, fish, and bird have simple life cycles.

You are no doubt familiar with more complex life cycles such as those experienced by butterflies and frogs. They undergo big changes (metamorphosis) during their lives. Many insects, such as butterflies, undergo complete metamorphosis. Complete metamorphosis typically has four stages: egg, larva, pupa, and adult. The larva (i.e., caterpillar) hatches from an egg. It looks and behaves completely different from the adult butterfly. The larva crawls and eats leaves rather than flies, and drinks nectar. Most if not all of the larva's time is spent eating and storing food in preparation for the next big change in its development, the pupa. During the pupa stage, the larva builds a cocoon (also known as a chrysalis) for its change to a butterfly. This is a period when the organism is stationary, but internally very active. The complex biochemical changes a caterpillar undergoes as its body morphs into a completely different form are extraordinary. Eventually, an adult organism emerges fully prepared to enter a new dimension of its life.

Amphibians also undergo a form of complete metamorphosis, but with only three stages. They are born either alive (ovoviviparous) or hatched from eggs (oviparous). Once born, they spend their childhood under water, without the major features of the adult. During this time, they grow and differentiate, meaning they slowly develop new, adult structures such as legs and lungs with functions that will enable them to survive as an adult. This is considered complete metamorphosis. As with the butterfly, the hatchling has a completely different body type and eating habits as the adult. Therefore, the degree to which hatchlings resemble the adult determines if metamorphosis is complete. If the hatchling is completely different from the adult, then complete metamorphosis occurs.

Another version of metamorphosis has only three stages. It is called incomplete metamorphosis. After hatching from an egg, the organism goes into a nymph stage. Nymphs are very close in body type and eating habits to the adults, but not so much like an adult as is the case with a simple life cycle. The nymph molts its exoskeleton several times during development. As it does so, new structures, such as wings, begin to emerge. After the final molt, the adult is formed, which looks like the nymph with a few modifications. Grasshoppers and dragonflies are examples of organisms that exhibit incomplete metamorphosis.

Behaviors play a significant role in survival as well. Some animals are nocturnal, becoming active only at night for a variety of reasons: Cooler nights mean less competition for food from other organisms and the cover of darkness may provide protection. Birds fly south in the fall to warmer climates where they can avoid the risks of cold weather and a shortage of food supplies. All organisms possess structures and unique behaviors that enable them to survive by acquiring energy, growing, reproducing, and responding to the environment.

Ecosystems: Interactions, Energy, and Dynamics (LS2)

Interdependent Relationships in Ecosystems (LS2.A)

As stated earlier, all organisms need to acquire energy and ultimately the energy comes from the Sun. Photosynthetic organisms convert carbon dioxide and water into carbohydrates that can be used by the plants themselves or other organisms. Some organisms eat the plants directly. Other organisms eat the organisms that ate the plants. Thus, the original energy from the Sun is passed on through successive meals by different organisms. Each time the energy is consumed and passed on to another organism, some of the energy is lost. When we eat meat about 90% of the energy it took to produce the meat has been lost, primarily as heat.

We call the photosynthetic organisms that produce the original carbohydrate *producers*. The first organism that consumes the producer is called a *primary consumer*. Rabbits, cattle, chipmunks, and horses are primary consumers. An organism that consumes the primary consumer is a *secondary consumer*, and so on. A single stream of consumers is called a food chain. When food chains overlap and intertwine, a food web results. For example, grasshoppers eat grass; frogs eat grasshoppers; mice also eat grasshoppers; snakes eat frogs; hawks also eat frogs and mice. Food webs can become quite complex.

As energy travels through the food web, organisms take in materials from the environment to support their growth and return materials to the environment. Photosynthetic organisms take in carbon dioxide and water but also give off oxygen as a waste product. Of course, oxygen is an essential element for most life. It is interesting to note that oxygen was at one time absent from the atmosphere and only began being produced about 3.5 billion years ago by a type of bacteria called cyanobacteria, which are understood to be the first photosynthetic organisms. Initially oxygen was toxic to all life forms until adaptations occurred that enabled organisms to use oxygen to release energy, which is much more efficient than the production of energy without oxygen and gave oxygen using organisms a distinct advantage. Oxygen is important for most forms of life because it is necessary to break down stored energy and make it usable, very much like gasoline or logs are burned to release energy in usable forms. This process is called cellular respiration. You may be more familiar with the term *respiration* in the physiological context as another term for breathing. Cellular respiration is a chemical process that breaks down the stored energy in molecules such as carbohydrates and fats. Note that a byproduct of cellular respiration is carbon dioxide. Recall that carbon dioxide is used by plants, which in turn produce oxygen. This is one of many examples in nature that demonstrate the recycling of materials among organisms and the Earth such as carbon, oxygen, nitrogen, and sulfur cycles.

Every life cycle ends in death. When death occurs, the organism ceases to consume energy. But there remains stored energy in the deceased organism. Nature has a way to recycle this energy with specialized organisms called decomposers. Bacteria, worms, slugs, snails, and fungi like mushrooms are all decomposers. They use the energy derived from breaking down the dead organism for their life cycle and return the resultant minerals and compounds back to the soil where they can be reused by the next generation of organisms.

Ecosystem Dynamics, Functioning, and Resilience (LS2.C)

Organisms can only survive in environments where all of their needs for energy, growth, and reproduction are met. A fish will not survive in the desert, neither will a cactus survive in the ocean. There is a balance among the interactions between the environment and the organisms that live in the environment. This interaction of environment and organisms is called an ecosystem. The balance is often very delicate, depending on flowers to bloom and ponds to fill with regularity each year. Imbalances can be due to natural causes such as flooding or fires, and to human intervention such as pollution or the introduction of invasive species. There are many instances of imbalances in ecosystems resulting from a rapid change in climate. As average temperatures begin to change, even slightly, large changes in plant and animal life can result. Winters become warmer, snowpack in mountains decreases, and spring seasons last longer. In regions that depend on the water stored in snowpack, this puts a strain on the water supply that results in drought. Drought in turn weakens forests and makes them more vulnerable to natural pests, such as the bark beetle, which survive mild winters, thus extending their range and making them more plentiful. As a result, more trees are stressed and die, which creates more fuel for forest fires. As forests are depleted, all the organisms that depend on the stability afforded by the forests also are affected.

Similarly, as average ocean temperatures increase and levels of carbon dioxide rise, life cycles and chemical balances are affected. Warmer water holds less dissolved gas, such as oxygen. (Cold fluids hold more dissolved gas. That is why it is better to store carbonated beverages cold.) As average ocean temperatures change, fish such as cod move northward to cooler waters necessary for survival. As carbon dioxide increases in the atmosphere, it also increases in the oceans, increasing the acidity of the ocean water. Acidic water interferes with the ability of coral, which is an animal, to absorb the calcium carbonate needed to make their hard exoskeleton and therefore die. Coral reefs support many organisms, all of which need to relocate to another coral reef or perish.

Social Interactions and Group Behavior (LS.D)

Organisms of the same species often depend on each other to acquire energy, grow, and survive. Honeybees and other social insects such as ants are excellent examples of organisms working together to survive. Each member of the honeybee colony has a specific role in the hive. There is usually only one queen bee at a time. The role of the queen bee is solely to lay eggs for the community. She can lay more than 1,500 eggs per day! But she needs the support from the rest of the hive community to survive. As their name implies, worker bees build and maintain the hive. They build the honeycomb-shaped cells in which honey and pollen are stored and eggs are laid. Workers also gather pollen, nectar, and water as well as serve as defenders of the hive. They even fan their wings to ventilate the hive! Drones have one job only, to fertilize the eggs produced by the queen. Consequently, drones do not have stingers, pollen baskets, glands for producing wax, or mouthparts equipped to gather nectar. Nature tends not to waste energy and materials on structures and functions that are not necessary.

Heredity: Inheritance and Variation of Traits (LS3)

● Inheritance of Traits (LS3.A)

Sexual reproduction contributes to biodiversity by ensuring the redistribution of genes that carry traits. Recall that DNA codes for proteins that determine physical traits. Some proteins are identical across organisms in a species or even across species. Hemoglobin and insulin are two proteins whose structure and function are very specific for transporting oxygen and metabolizing (breaking down) sugar. Any variance, even a slight variance, in those molecules can have devastating effects on their functions. Hence, they are said to be highly conserved. That is why insulin from pigs was given to people with diabetes before human insulin could be genetically engineered. Other traits, such as eye color, shape of nose, height, and a host of traits, can vary among individuals with little or no negative consequences.

During fertilization, half the genes come from the male and half from the female. Even prior to fertilization the genes go through a shuffling process during the formation of sperm and egg. As a result, each sperm and egg bring a unique contribution of genetic information to the offspring. This shuffling and reorganization of genetic information results in the unique physical traits of individuals (except for identical twins, who shared the original set of genes from the same fertilized egg).

● Variation of Traits (Environment)

Traits are not solely dependent on genes. The environment can influence the expression of genes. For example, temperature can affect the gender of alligators. Alligator eggs that are kept at 33°C produce mostly males. Eggs kept at 30°C result in mostly female alligator hatchlings. When Himalayan rabbits are raised in temperatures above 30°C, they are all white. When they are raised in temperatures below 20°C, they are white with black noses, feet, tail, and ears. The gene that produces pigmentation for black fur is inactive above 30°C. Therefore, the gene does not produce black fur on the midsection of the rabbit in climates where the main body of the rabbit remains above 30°C. However, the gene is active and produces black fur in parts of the body that tend to be below 30°C, such as the feet, ears, nose, and tail. This is an evolutionary advantage, because dark coloring will absorb more light energy and therefore keep the parts of the body that are usually cold warmer.

Biological Evolution: Unity and Diversity (LS4)

Evolution is change in species over time through genetic inheritance, referred to as descent with modification. Evolution is based on the premise that all life shares a common ancestor, which, over billions of years, gave rise to the great diversity of life today. There are several mechanisms that drive evolution. The most common is natural selection, which occurs through random mutation of genetic material and/or changes in the environment that favor particular structures and functions. Evidence for evolution is found in the fossil records and in patterns of the genetic information found in species.

Fossils are formed in different ways. When organisms die in conditions that are watery or muddy, minerals slowly seep into bones or shells as they begin to decay in a process called petrification. Alternatively, the bones may decay completely before petrification, leaving a hollow space in the mud that becomes filled in with minerals and turns to stone. Even footprints can be fossilized in this manner. Other fossils are formed when insects are trapped and preserved in tree sap. Hot lava flows can trap animals, leaving a cast of the shape of the animal.

Fossil records are important because they show a history of changes in the structures of organisms over time and how different species shared common ancestors. Paleontologists, scientists who study fossils, look for fossils that are closely related but show changes over time. One of the more common examples is the evidence for the descent of birds from dinosaurs. Archaeopteryx is a fossil with structures such as a long bony tail, three claws on each wing, and teeth that suggest it is clearly a dinosaur estimated to have lived about 150 million years ago. However, it also has feathers on its tail, a characteristic not seen in earlier dinosaurs. Archaeopteryx is an example of a transitional fossil, which is a fossil containing traits of both its ancestor group and an emerging new descendant group of organisms. In this case, Archaeopteryx possesses traits of both dinosaurs and birds.

Extinction

Fossil evidence reveals that the peak of the dinosaurs' development occurred near the end of the Cretaceous period, in the Mesozoic era. However, no one is sure why the dinosaurs became extinct. Some scientists have suggested that a catastrophe such as an earthquake, a volcano, or a sunlight-blocking cloud resulting from a comet strike killed the dinosaurs. However, this theory does not explain why *only* the dinosaurs were destroyed, while other life forms survived. Scientists have also conjectured that the apatosaurus and its vegetarian relatives eventually became extinct because their huge bulk made it difficult for them to move to new environments as changes occurred in their natural habitat, but this does not explain the extinction of all the dinosaurs. Changes in climate may have changed the vegetable and animal life upon which dinosaurs fed, but there were places where such climatic changes did not occur, so some species of dinosaurs should have survived. The point is that some species do not evolve quickly enough to survive, resulting in extinction. Perhaps one of the children you teach will someday develop a theory that explains the extinction of dinosaurs satisfactorily.

Natural Selection (LS4.B)

Central to changes due to genetic inheritance is the shuffling and recombination of genes that result from sexual reproduction, random mutations, and interactions with ecosystems. Sexual reproduction results in variation within species. Mutations result in the emergence of unique traits among individuals, adding to potential diversity within species and the emergence of new species. Traits associated with structures and functions that support survival provide advantages to the individuals with those traits. As more of those individuals survive to reproduce, the probability that those favorable traits will be inherited by the next generation increases. Different groups of the same species can evolve different traits, usually due to selective pressures in different ecosystems. When the groups become so different that they can no longer breed together, a distinct species emerges.

The coloration of a deer mouse is an example of interactions among sexual reproduction, random mutation, and ecosystems. The deer mouse is found throughout North America. Most deer mice are brown. Deer mice are considered primary consumers in the food web. They in turn are prey for secondary consumers such as owls and hawks. Coloring is a trait that provides camouflage. In Nebraska, there are regions where glaciers left deposits of light-colored sand. These regions are known as the Sand Hills. In these regions, dark brown mice stand out in contrast on the lightly colored surfaces, making them easy prey for hawks. Consequently, light brown deer mice living in the sand hills survive better than dark brown mice, resulting in a higher frequency of the gene for light brown. Researchers at Harvard University were able to identify a mutation in a single gene that results in lighter colored fur. This is an example of natural selection, a process in which genetic variation results in traits that benefit survival and the production of more offspring.

It should be noted that variations themselves, such as brown fur, are not caused by the environment. Traits vary as a result of random mutations that by chance are favorable for a given species in a given environment. The classic example is the giraffe's neck. It did not become longer because giraffes developed a gene for long necks in response to a need to reach leaves. Rather, giraffes born with genetic information that randomly mutated to code for longer necks had a better chance of survival because they had an advantage for accessing food over shorter necked giraffes.

Classifying Living Things

Long ago, biologists classified all living things into just the two categories: plants and animals. With further study and more sophisticated equipment, biologists were surprised to discover living things that really didn't fit into either group.

● The Six Kingdoms

Modern biologists use a classification system that includes six distinct kingdoms:

1. **Archean**—This kingdom includes one-celled living things that don't have a membrane around the cell's genetic material. In other words, none of these organisms have nuclei. You will recognize this as a property of bacteria, too. For a long time, scientists did not recognize Archaea as a distinct kingdom. With the advancement of technology, scientists are able to distinguish significant differences among bacteria at the genetic and biochemical levels that compelled them to create a new kingdom. For example, Archaea have more complex RNA polymerases and their cell walls have a slightly different composition than bacteria. Archaea are often found in extreme conditions such as hot springs or highly saline waters such as the Dead Sea or Great Salt Lake.

2. **Bacteria**—Like Archaea, bacteria are unicellular and lack a membrane around the cell's genetic material. These include many beneficial bacteria as well as pathogenic bacteria that inhabit our world. Bacteria are ubiquitous with species found in every ecosystem of the Earth. Most bacteria cannot produce their own food. However, cyanobacteria, commonly known as blue-green algae, can produce food through photosynthesis. You may be familiar with cyanobacteria as the cause of algal blooms that occur in fresh or marine water. Did you know cyanobacteria are considered the first organisms to

photosynthesize and therefore produce oxygen about 3.5 billion years ago? Prior to that, all life was anaerobic (living in the absence of oxygen).

3. **Protista**—This group includes single-celled organisms that have a membrane surrounding the cell's genetic material—for example, diatoms, protozoa, and euglena. Common amoebas and paramecia are also protozoans. All protists are found in moist or aquatic habitats and get their nutrition in a variety of ways. Protists are believed to be early examples of the types of life forms that eventually became the fungi, plants, and animals that live on Earth today.

4. **Fungi**—This group of living things may be single celled or multicellular. They gain their nutrition by absorbing nutrients from their surroundings, and they store energy in the chemical compound glycogen, which makes them different from plants that store food as starch. Fungi can reproduce sexually or asexually. Asexual reproduction is carried out through the production and release of tiny spores that can be carried long distances through the air. Sexual reproduction occurs from the fusion of cell material from two types of fungi competing on the same food source.

5. **Plantae**—This kingdom includes living things that are multicellular and have true cell nuclei and cell walls. Most use photosynthesis to produce food. The green plants in this kingdom—mosses, ferns, grasses, trees, and so on—reproduce sexually or asexually.

6. **Animalia**—This group is made up of multicellular organisms that are able to ingest food directly from their environments. Animal cells contain nuclei. Members of this kingdom reproduce sexually, with a few exceptions. Sponges, for example, reproduce asexually by forming buds that can break free of the parent sponge and be carried to a place where they can develop into a complete sponge. Although some animals, such as sponges, are sessile (i.e., they remain in one specific place during their life cycle), most are able to move freely from place to place.

The Plant Kingdom: A Closer Look

Recent classification systems have grouped the organisms of the plant kingdom into two major phyla: The Bryophytes (Bryophyta) and the Tracheophytes (Tracheophyta). *Bryophytes* are small plants that lack conducting vessels for transporting water and nutrients. This phylum includes mosses, liverworts, and hornworts. The phylum *Tracheophyta* includes all vascular plants—that is, plants that have vessels for transporting water and nutrients.

Ferns, conifers, and flowering plants are all tracheophytes. Ferns do not produce true seeds. Both conifers and flowering plants are seed-producing tracheophytes. These seed-producing plants are grouped into two classes: the gymnosperms and the angiosperms. Most gymnosperms do not produce flowers; they produce cones. Evergreen trees such as pines, redwoods, and spruces are all gymnosperms. Angiosperms produce flowers. Fruit trees, rose plants, and daisies are all examples of angiosperms.

● The Structure of Flowering Plants

Incredibly, there are more than 250,000 species of flowering plants, or *angiosperms*. As the most advanced form of plant life on Earth, this class can survive and even thrive in a variety of climates and soil types. The structure of these plants is what enables them to survive (see Table 9.1).

Table 9.1 The structure of flowering plants

Element	Characteristics	Function(s)
Roots	Roots grow downward and outward into the soil. Tiny root hairs behind the root tip absorb water and minerals.	Anchor the plant. Absorb water and minerals. May store food.
Stems	*Monocot* stems emerge from seeds with one cotyledon or seed leaf (such as corn, grasses). *Dicotyledonous* stems emerge from seeds with two cotyledons (such as tomatoes, roses). *Herbaceous* (soft and green) stems are found in short-lived plants (such as dandelions, tomatoes, grasses). *Woody* stems are found in longer-lived plants (such as forsythia, lilac, trees).	Serve as a pipeline, carrying produced foods downward and water with dissolved minerals upward. Display the leaves to sunlight.
Leaves	Leaves come in many shapes and sizes. *Monocot* leaves are narrow and have smooth edges and parallel veins. *Dicot* leaves are broad and have veins that spread out. Water vapor leaves the plant through leaf openings called *stomata.*	Carry out photosynthesis (food making) because they contain chlorophyll. Assist the plant in losing excess water through transpiration.
Reproductive organs	A typical flower has sepals, petals, stamens, and a pistil. *Sepals* form the leaflike outer covering of the developing flower bud, which is usually green. *Petals* are usually bright colored, have an odor that's attractive to insects, and produce a sugary nectar (a food source for insects and birds). *Stamens* are male reproductive organs that produce pollen containing a sperm nucleus. At the top of each stamen is an *anther*, or pollen box, that releases pollen. The *pistil* is the female reproductive organ. At the top of the pistil is the *stigma*, to which pollen can stick.	Produce fruits containing seeds, which produce new plants.

● Sexual and Asexual Reproduction in Flowering Plants

Most flowering plants have both male and female organs, Thus, in angiosperms, reproduction is generally accomplished by the union of sperm and egg cells to form seeds. This is called *sexual reproduction.* However, fruit and vegetable growers are able to produce new plants without using seeds. *Asexual reproduction* can happen

Table 9.2   Sexual and asexual reproduction in flowering plants

Type of Reproduction	Characteristics
Sexual	The sperm and egg nucleus unite in the process known as *pollination.* Pollen grains are carried to the *stigma* and produce a tube that grows downward to the *ovary,* or enlarged bottom part of the pistil. The sperm nucleus travels down the tube and unites with egg cells in the ovary to eventually produce seeds.
Asexual	Parts of plants—such as leaves, stems, and roots—are used to produce new plants. Examples include "cuttings" (containing a stem with leaves) from begonias, bulbs (which have large, food-storing, underground stems) from lilies and tulips, and potato pieces that contain buds, or "eyes."

in the natural world when separated plant parts reach soil and moisture. They will grow into a new plant that has the exact genetic makeup of the original plant. Table 9.2 presents key points about sexual and asexual reproduction in flowering plants.

The Animal Kingdom: A Closer Look

Animals are multicellular organisms that obtain food from their environments. Most have systems that allow them to move, and most reproduce sexually. Almost 1 million different kinds of animals inhabit Earth. In order to keep track of them, biologists have found it useful to classify them into two major groups: animals without backbones and animals with backbones. Animals without backbones are called *invertebrates.* They include sponges, jellyfishes, starfishes, worms, mollusks, lobsters, spiders, and insects. The second major group, those with backbones, are called *vertebrates.* This group includes fishes, frogs, snakes, birds, and mammals. Vertebrates and invertebrates are divided into various phyla.

Vertebrates: Mammals

Mammals are vertebrates that nourish their young with milk produced by mammary glands. Their bodies are usually covered with hair or fur, although in some mammals, the hair takes the form of a few whiskers around the mouth. Although many mammals have four legs, some mammals—for example, whales, dolphins, and manatees—do not. In other mammals, the forelegs and rear legs are modified to perform particular functions. For instance, the forelimbs of kangaroos enable them to grasp food, whereas their strong, enlarged back legs enable them to hop.

The eggs of mammals are usually fertilized internally, and most mammals produce young by giving birth to them (although the duck-billed platypus, which is a monotreme mammal, does lay eggs). Female mammals suckle their young and care for them as they mature. The amount of time for a young mammal to mature into an adult varies greatly. Mammals seem able to teach their young to perform functions that will ensure their survival. Some mammals care for their young until they are fully grown and able to survive on their own.

Female opossums and kangaroos are marsupial mammals. They have pouches in which they place their young as soon as they are born. Although bats appear to be birds, they have hair rather than feathers. Bats can fly through the use of a leathery membrane stretching between their forelimbs and hind legs.

Although whales look like fish, they are really sea-living mammals. The hair on their bodies takes the form of whiskers around the mouth. The blue whale can reach almost 30 meters (about 100 feet) in length and weigh more than 140,000 kilograms (about 150 tons).

The primates, which include monkeys, apes, and humans, are the most intelligent of the mammals. They have the best-developed brains of all animals, fingers that are able to grasp objects, opposable thumbs, and nails instead of claws. (An opposable thumb can be positioned opposite the other fingers, making it possible to manipulate objects with one hand.) The largest of all apes is the gorilla, which can weigh as much as 180 kilograms (about 400 pounds). The gorilla is able to walk upright and to support itself by placing its hands on the ground. Except for humans, one of the most intelligent of all animals is probably the chimpanzee, though some people feel that a sea mammal, the dolphin, may be more intelligent than the chimpanzee and perhaps as intelligent as humans.

Biologists usually group the human species with the primates. The characteristics that have traditionally differentiated humans from other primates include the ability to reason, the use of complex communication systems, and the use of tools. In recent years, the observation of chimpanzees and gorillas in the wild, as well as laboratory research, has revealed that primates may have capabilities that challenge traditional views.

Real Teaching

The children at an urban elementary school were planting a garden for the first time in the small green space between the sidewalk and the northeast-facing brick wall of the school. Funding for the garden supplies came from a small community grant. I knew the enthusiasm for being outside, spreading loam, and planting seeds would provide a fertile context for learning about plant life cycles.

The next day I stood before the class, holding a small pumpkin seed, and wondered aloud what happened to the seed after it was planted underground. [HOOK QUESTION] I asked the children to draw in their science notebooks a sketch of what they thought was happening to the seed and some words to describe it. After a few minutes, I let them turn and talk to share ideas and asked the children to report out by group: "It grows roots," "It has to have sun and water," "It eats the soil to grow." I wrote their ideas on the board, silently noting some of the preconceptions. [PRIOR KNOWLEDGE]

"Those are interesting ideas," I said. "I see that many of you have roots in your drawings. Some drawings have small plants underneath the soil with flowers on them. Some have seeds with roots. What gave you the ideas for your drawings?

Some students referred to what they see when they pull plants out of the ground. Most children had no response.

"Now I am very curious. I wonder how we could see what happens to the seeds underground. Do you have any ideas?" The answers included: "Bury a camera" [good that they are thinking about technology!] and "Dig them up every day." My plan was to create seed chambers out of plastic bags. But I suppose we could dig up a seed each day, but we would need to think through the design of the investigation. Because it was a student idea, and I had the materials to easily set up the investigation, I thought it worthwhile to pursue with the students. It was another opportunity to work on the NGSS science practice "Planning and Carrying out Investigations." [AMBITIOUS TEACHING]

"Let's think about an investigation to dig the seeds up each day. How should we plan it?" [DISCOURSE]

C: "We need seeds."

T: "What kinds of seeds, what properties should they have?

C: "They should be big so we can see them."

C: "Pumpkin seeds, like we planted in the garden."

C: "Sunflower seeds, those were big."

T: "Both seeds fit our needs. We have only a few pumpkin seeds left, but a lot of sunflower seeds. Let's use sunflower seeds."

I asked for next steps. We had a lively discussion about how many seeds to plant. I wanted the students to make an informed decision, not just a wild guess. We decided to look on the package to see how long the seeds usually take to sprout. [OBTAINING INFORMATION] Someone also suggested we check it on Google. We did both and determined the seeds took 7 to 10 days to sprout. I realized *sprout* was not a familiar term, so I wrote it in the "New Words and Phrases" section of the board, had a brief discussion, some examples, and posted a definition we all agreed on. [LANGUAGE DEMAND]

I asked students to work in small groups that included L2 students with native English speakers. [SIOP] "Given the information at hand, decide how many seeds should be planted, when we should dig each seed up, and state your reasons." This took longer than I anticipated, and I was beginning to question my decision to follow the idea generated by the class to dig up seeds rather than impose my plastic baggie seed chamber on them. Finally, we decided that each group would plant 12 seeds, just to be sure, and dig up one seed each day to examine. [EVALUATING INFORMATION, REASONING BASED ON EVIDENCE] We would tape the seeds on a chart with our observations below. Before we began, I asked whether it matters if the seeds are all planted and taken care of with the same conditions. Collectively the class agreed that yes, the conditions should be the same. So, I asked what conditions should be kept the same. Amount of water, time of watering, depth, container, and location were chosen. Some students still insisted on keeping them in the sunlight. Should I challenge that misconception now? I decided to use the plastic baggie seed chambers at a different time to address the need for sunlight during germination. We were running out of time for the day. Tomorrow we will begin our investigation.

Climate Change and Stewardship of Earth

That the climate is changing at a rapid pace is no longer an issue of significant debate within the scientific community. Science seeks explanations based on evidence, and the evidence that **climate change** is occurring is exceedingly strong. Most of the debate about climate change is in the arena of politics and the economy. As elementary science teachers, we look to our community of scientists and educators for guidance about what and how we should teach about climate change. Most recently, the Next Generation Science Standards (NGSS) indicate that climate change be taught at the middle and high school levels. I suppose that it may seem like we elementary school teachers are off the hook for teaching about climate change. However, the NGSS does encourage elementary educators to teach about impacts on Earth systems and ways that science ideas can be used to protect Earth's resources and environment.[3] Perhaps our responsibility is to lay a foundation for children to learn about Earth and how humans interact with Earth so they can later understand the meaning, causes, and consequences of climate change.

We have an opportunity to teach children about our relationships with and interdependence on Earth, thereby fostering a sense of stewardship toward our environment. Many children are disconnected from Earth and the ecosystems that are responsible for our survival. That carrots grow in the ground, milk comes from animals such as cows, and photosynthesizing by plants and microorganisms provides the oxygen for us to breathe is not readily apparent to all children. Better than telling students about stewardship, we can strive to provide opportunities for students to practice stewardship. A school garden is rich with connections to Earth while creating meaningful contexts to practice science and develop core concepts. Children experience the cycle of life while caring for plants as they germinate, grow, produce seeds, and die. Children can experience firsthand the effects of weather on plants and animals. They encounter evidence of interdependence among many different forms of life: plants, insects, animals, and microorganisms. Children realize that they are part of the ecosystem and that the actions of their community affect the ecosystem in both positive and negative ways.

In addition to gardens, children can participate in counting the local flora and fauna, tracking the waste generated in the cafeteria, and designing ways to decrease the waste. Citizen science projects are also ways for students to connect to local habitats and explore the diversity of life and Earth systems that connect us with the planet.

The generations of children you teach will no doubt be confronted with the reality of climate change. By cultivating an understanding of Earth and our interconnectedness with it through a scientific worldview, they stand a better chance of making informed decisions on which future generations will depend.

Summary

9.1 Distinguish living from nonliving systems.

Life is fascinating and magnificently diverse. It may seem overwhelming to study and understand the life sciences because of the seemingly endless variations. However, consideration of several big ideas can help us understand life and its complex interactions through reasoning rather than memorization. While there is great biodiversity, all living things have or do the following:

1. Are composed of cells[4]—the smallest structural unit of an organism that is capable of independently carrying out the processes listed below.
2. Use energy that they produce or acquire. They use this energy to carry out energy-requiring activities such as movement, growth, and transport.
3. Grow.
4. Are able to reproduce, either by sexual or asexual means (an individual organism does not need to reproduce to be alive).
5. Inherit traits from the parent organisms.
6. Respond to stimuli in their environment.
7. Maintain a state of internal balance called homeostasis.
8. Adapt to their environment and evolve as a species.

9.2 Describe relationships among structure and function.

Fundamental to understanding life is to acknowledge the basic needs all living organisms share: energy to grow and reproduce. The acquisition of energy is either through capturing stored energy primarily from the Sun during photosynthesis or consuming the stored energy of photosynthesizers directly or indirectly. Growth and reproduction benefit from specific adaptations in structures and functions of organisms that help them survive in their environments. Individual organisms do not need to reproduce to survive, but each species requires a robust reproductive strategy to survive. These adaptations include structures and functions for acquiring food, protection, and shelter.

9.3 Understand the flow of energy as a unifying theme of life systems.

The diversity of life on Earth is astounding. Looking at life systems through the lens of energy flow helps us make sense of the wide range of adaptations found in life forms to acquire energy, use energy for life processes, and deal with the byproducts of energy use.

9.4 Describe the interdependence of organisms in an ecosystem.

Every form of life is intimately connected to its environment and the neighboring life forms that share life sustaining resources. Any imbalance in one component of the ecosystem has consequences for the entire ecosystem.

9.5 Explain how inheritance, variation of traits, and natural selection impact evolution.

Variation among organisms within a species occurs through the shuffling of genes during the formation of egg and sperm and the combination of genetic information during fertilization. Random mutations occur that may result in a structure, function, or behavior that affords a favorable advantage for survival in a particular environment, as exemplified by the deer mice in the Sand Hills. This process is known as natural selection.

9.6 Discuss how connecting children with the planet and Earth systems precedes and supports education about climate change.

Prior to teaching children about climate change, it is beneficial to connect children with the planet and our close ties with the Earth systems so that they may appreciate and understand the need to be stewards of the planet. If children appreciate and understand our dependence on a healthy planet then the need to actively address human-induced climate change as adolescents and adults will be meaningful.

Chapter 9 Self-Check
Click to gauge your understanding of the concepts in this chapter.

Notes

1. Scientists have argued about whether viruses are alive.
2. There are other chemosynthetic organisms, such as those that live deep in the ocean around black smokers, but ultimately one can argue the energy used also came from the Sun.
3. NGSS Lead States. Next Generation Science Standards: For States, By States. Disciplinary Core Idea 5 ESS3-1. Achieve, Inc. on behalf of the 26 states and partners that collaborated on the NGSS. 2013.
4. Scientists have argued whether viruses are alive.

10

The Human Body

dotshock/Shutterstock

Learning Outcome

After completing the activities in this chapter, you should be able to

10.1 Describe and identify primary structures and functions of major human body systems.

▶ **GETTING STARTED**

In the cold gray light of dawn, a runner moves briskly along the pavement. The rowhouses look quietly on as her footsteps echo off their walls. Her stride is steady and firm. Her breathing barely reflects the strain of 4 miles of running. Her gaze is clear and her ears are sensitive to the sounds of the neighborhood awakening. The blood courses through her arteries, bringing oxygen and nourishment to her body's cells and carrying away byproducts produced by the cells. The runner's body systems are functioning well when she arrives home. Within minutes, her body has recovered from this morning's ritual run. She feels refreshed and alive.

The well-functioning systems of the runner's body enable her to concentrate on the things that matter in her life. The discipline of her body is matched by the discipline of her mind, which wills her to rise early each day to run. To understand fully how the human body is able to perform, we need to consider its basic systems. *Body systems* are groups of organs that work together to carry out a particular function. For example, the heart, arteries, and veins each perform specific tasks that together enable the bloodstream to transport oxygen, nutrients, and waste products. This system of heart, arteries, and veins is called the *circulatory system*. The other basic body systems are the *digestive*, *skeletal-muscular*, *respiratory*, *nervous*, *excretory*, and *reproductive systems*. To understand them, you need to know both their structures and their functions.

The Digestive System

Thinking a thought, blinking an eye, and taking a step are not possible without energy. The basic source of this energy is the food we eat. The process of digestion changes food from its original form to a fuel that can release energy when it reacts with oxygen. Digestion also breaks down and transforms proteins—the materials necessary for building new cells and repairing old ones. The hamburger, potato salad, and ear of corn on your plate at a late-summer picnic are the raw materials that transfer energy and supply the building materials of life itself.

Structure and Function

Digestion is the process through which the body breaks down the molecules that make up the food that has been eaten and prepares them to react with oxygen to produce energy. Digestion begins in your mouth. As you chew food, glands in your mouth secrete *saliva*, a digestive juice that mixes with the food particles. Saliva contains water, mucus, and an enzyme that begins the process of breaking down the food.

As food moves through the digestive system, *enzymes* continue to act on it. Each enzyme breaks down a particular material found in food. The seeds of certain fruits, the cellulose in vegetables, and some meat tissues are indigestible. Such material passes into the large intestine and is eventually excreted.

Food and Nutrition

Figure 10.1 MyPlate[2]

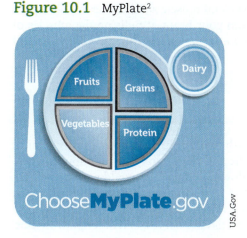

All food contains *nutrients*, specific substances that provide the energy and materials the body requires to function properly. The nutrients in the food we eat are used in one of two basic ways by the body. Some are converted into energy and used immediately. Others are used to build new cells. Six specific nutrients are necessary for health and growth: carbohydrates (starches and sugars), fats, proteins, minerals, vitamins, and water. The foods we eat contain different amounts of these nutrients.

The U.S. Department of Agriculture recommends that we all eat more grains, fruits, and vegetables and less meat, fat, and sweets (see Figure 10.1). To convey this view of appropriate nutrition, the Department of Agriculture has created a guide called **MyPlate** that can help you make wise decisions about what you eat.

The Skeletal-Muscular System

Bones: Structure and Function

Your bones and muscles work together to give your body its form and structure. The bones provide support, protection for vital organs, a place in which red blood cells and some white blood cells are produced, a storage area for minerals, and surfaces to which muscles are attached. Although many people think that bones are hard, dry objects within the body, they are really alive.

Bone tissue is composed of living bone cells (which require food and oxygen, just as other body cells do), the products of bone-cell respiration, and deposits of minerals. Most bones in the human body originate from softer bonelike structures, or *cartilage*. As you age, the cartilage present in your body when you were very young becomes strong bone. This process continues until you are 20 to 25 years old.

A *joint* is a place where two bones meet. There are five types of joints in the human body: immovable, hinge, ball-and-socket, pivot, and gliding. Each provides flexibility of movement. In some joints—such as the one that connects the upper arm to the shoulder—bands of strong connective tissue, called *ligaments*, hold the bones of the joint together.

Muscles: Structure and Function

The muscles in your body provide you with the ability to move. This results from the ability of muscle cells to contract. There are three types of muscles in your body: smooth muscle, cardiac muscle, and skeletal muscle. *Smooth muscles* are those that act involuntarily. For example, the muscles that line the stomach and intestinal walls and the arteries are all involuntary muscles. This means they are able to operate quickly and without the direct control of the brain.

The involuntary muscle found in your heart is called *cardiac muscle*. When the fibers in this muscle contract, the chambers of the heart are squeezed and blood is forced out through blood vessels. If the cardiac muscle were not involuntary, your brain would have to tell your heart to beat each time blood was needed to be pumped through your circulatory system.

Skeletal muscles are voluntary muscles. They work because the brain tells them to bend or flex or stretch. Skeletal muscles attach directly either to bones or to other muscles. *Tendons* are bands of connective tissue that attach the ends of some skeletal muscles to bones. When a skeletal muscle such as one in your upper arm contracts as a result of a message from your brain, it pulls on the muscles of your lower arm. The movement of the lower arm results from the contraction of the voluntary skeletal muscle.

The Respiratory System

The food you eat supplies your body with energy through a series of chemical reactions that take place in the body's cells and require oxygen. Without oxygen, the food molecules could not be broken down, and energy would not be released. Although some of this energy is released as heat, much of it is stored in chemical form. Carbon dioxide and water are given off during this energy-producing process. The stored energy is used by body cells, tissues, nerves, and other body organs.

This simple model shows the process by which energy is produced in your body cells: food + oxygen → carbon dioxide + water + energy. Note the similarity of respiration, the release of stored energy, to photosynthesis, the storage of energy: carbon dioxide + water + energy (solar) → food (carbohydrate) + oxygen. The term *respiration* is used in two related contexts. Respiration often means the process of breathing. Cellular respiration is the biochemical process referred to above that releases stored energy from food.

The Diaphragm, Windpipe, and Lungs: Structure and Function

The oxygen your body needs to produce energy from food is contained in the air you breathe. Air is about 21% oxygen and about 78% nitrogen. When you inhale, both oxygen and nitrogen enter your lungs. The nitrogen, however, is not used by the body. The in-and-out action of your lungs is controlled by the *diaphragm*, a large curved muscle that lies underneath them. As the diaphragm contracts, it moves downward. At the same time, the rib muscles separate the ribs and move them forward. These actions increase the amount of space in your chest and allow the lungs to expand, creating negative pressure that draws air into the lungs.

After the air space in your chest has been enlarged, increasing the volume, outside air pressure forces air through your nose and throat, down your windpipe, and into your lungs. After you have inhaled air, the action of your diaphragm and rib muscles increases the pressure within your chest and pushes air out through your windpipe, throat, and nose. This occurs each time you exhale.

The *windpipe* is a tube that stretches from your throat to your lungs. At your lungs, it divides into two branches. Each of these branches subdivides into smaller and smaller branches within the lungs. These small branches end in tiny air sacs, each of which is surrounded by tiny blood vessels called *capillaries*. The air sacs have very thin walls that permit the oxygen to pass through them and into the capillaries.

Oxygen Transport

Once oxygen has entered the air sacs of the lungs and diffused into the capillaries, it is picked up by hemoglobin in red blood cells and carried to all parts of the body, where it reacts chemically with food to produce energy, carbon dioxide, and water. Carbon dioxide produced in the cells enters the bloodstream and is carried back by the same hemoglobin in red blood cells to the air sacs in the lungs. There it leaves the bloodstream, enters the lungs, and is exhaled. The paper-thin walls of the air sacs are continually allowing oxygen to pass from the lungs to the bloodstream and carbon dioxide to pass from the bloodstream to the lungs.

The Nervous System

A chirping bird catches your attention during a quiet morning walk along a wooded path. You stop and turn your head in an attempt to locate the source of this early morning joy. Your ears help focus your attention on the uppermost branch of a nearby tree. The song seems to come from somewhere behind a clump of leaves and twigs attached to the branch. Suddenly, your eyes pick out a slight movement and come to rest on a brownish head that pokes its way over the nest top and looks directly at you.

Your sight and hearing are precious gifts that, along with your other senses, gather information about the surrounding world. These sense organs are the farthest outposts of your nervous system. It is your nervous system that permits you to see, hear, touch, smell, taste, and of course become aware of and enjoy the existence of chirping birds on quiet morning walks through the woods.

Nerves: Structure and Function

The nervous system consists of the brain, the spinal cord, and many nerve cells. A *nerve cell* has three parts: a cell body; short, branchlike fibers that receive impulses from the brain; and long, thin fibers that carry impulses away from the cell body. Bundles of either short or long fibers are known as *nerves*. Nerves carry messages from the brain to other parts of the body and from other parts of the body to the brain. Messages are carried by nerve *impulses*, chemical changes that cause electrical charges to be transmitted through the nervous system.

Twelve pairs of nerves directly connect the brain to the eyes, ears, nose, and tongue. These nerves are called *cranial nerves*. Branches of some of these nerves leave the head and connect with the variety of muscles and other internal organs in other parts of your body.

The principal way in which messages are sent from the brain to the body is through the *spinal cord*, a column of nerves that extends from the base of the brain down through the backbone. Thirty-one pairs of nerves directly connect the spinal cord with such organs as the lungs, intestines, stomach, and kidneys. These organs usually function without voluntary control. Thus, the nerves that control these functions make up what is known as the *autonomic nervous system*. Actions over which the individual has some control or awareness of are controlled by the *somatic nervous system*.

A *reflex* is another type of automatic action controlled by the nervous system. A reflex, the simplest way in which your nervous system operates, occurs when some part of the body is stimulated. The knee-jerk reaction is a good example of a reflex. If a person taps the tendon below your kneecap with an object, your lower leg swings upward. The tapping of the tendon stimulates a nerve cell in your lower leg. The nerve impulse travels along nerves to the spinal cord. When the impulse reaches the spinal cord, a message is immediately sent to the leg muscle, which causes the jerking movement. In this and many other reflex reactions, the response is not controlled by the brain. Reflex reactions are completed well before the brain is aware of their occurrence. Other reflexes are coughing, blinking, and laughing when you're tickled. Reflexes enable our bodies to respond very quickly to avoid potentially threatening situations.

The Senses

The sense organs, the farthest outposts of the human nervous system, contain specialized nerve cells that receive stimulation from the outside world and carry messages to the brain. Nerve cells that are capable of receiving information from the external environment are called *receptors*. Each of your sense organs has special receptors.

The Skin Sensors
Your skin is able to sense a variety of stimuli, including touch, pressure, pain, heat, and cold. Whenever a receptor is stimulated, an impulse (nerve message) begins traveling along the nerve to which the receptor is connected and eventually arrives at the central nervous system. Receptors for the various skin senses are distributed at different locations and different depths in the skin. The touch receptors are close to the surface of the skin. Your fingertips contain many touch receptors. Pressure receptors are deeper in the skin.

Taste   Your ability to taste results from specialized nerve receptors on your tongue. The areas containing these receptors are called *taste buds*. There are specialized taste buds for each of the following flavors: sour, sweet, salt, umami, and bitter. What you interpret as taste is actually a combination of taste and smell, for when you chew food, vapors from it reach your nose. Thus, you simultaneously taste and smell the food you're eating. You may have noticed that when you have a cold, food does not taste as good as usual. This is due to the fact that you cannot smell it as you eat it.

Smell   The principal nerve that carries information about smell to the brain is the *olfactory nerve*. Branches of this nerve are contained in a cavity in your nasal passage. Vapor from the food you eat enters your nasal cavity, is dissolved in a liquid, and stimulates the endings of the olfactory nerve.

Hearing   The ear is the principal organ through which sound waves enter the body. Sound waves enter the opening in your external ear and travel through a tube called the *auditory canal*. This canal ends at a membrane called the *eardrum*. The sound waves stimulate the eardrum, causing it to vibrate. On the other side of the eardrum, a group of tiny bones—the hammer, the anvil, and the stirrup—transmit energy in the form of vibrations from the eardrum to the cochlea and the semicircular canals, located in the inner ear. These organs relay the vibrations to the sensitive receptors at the end of the auditory nerve, which send signals to the brain that we interpret as sound.

Sight   Your eyes receive information in the form of light from the external world (see Figure 10.2). Light passes through a transparent covering called the *cornea* and enters the *pupil*, a small opening at the front of the eyeball. The size of the pupil is controlled by the opening and closing of the *iris*, the colored portion of the eyeball. Directly behind the pupil is the *lens*, which focuses your sight. Focusing is achieved by a muscular contraction that changes the shape of the lens. Between the lens and the cornea is a watery liquid known as the *aqueous humor*. Within the eyeball is a thicker, transparent substance called the *vitreous humor*. The structures at the front of the eyeball all serve to focus light on the *retina*, the rear portion of the eyeball containing light receptors. These receptors are of two types: cones and rods. The cones are responsible for color vision; the rods produce a material that helps you see in dim light. Focused light rays, or images, that reach the retina stimulate the receptors, which in turn transmit information about them to the brain via the optic nerve. In interpreting these messages, the brain gives us the sense we call sight.

Figure 10.2   The human eye receives information from the external environment

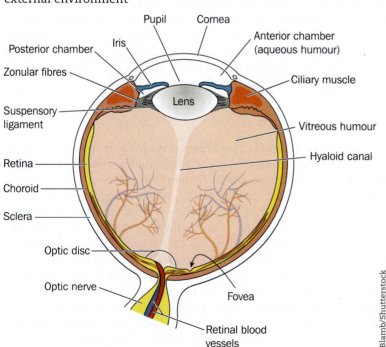

Pupil
Cornea
Iris
Anterior chamber (aqueous humour)
Posterior chamber
Zonular fibres
Ciliary muscle
Lens
Suspensory ligament
Vitreous humour
Hyaloid canal
Retina
Choroid
Sclera
Optic disc
Optic nerve
Fovea
Retinal blood vessels

Blamb/Shutterstock

The Excretory System

The process by which your body rids itself of wastes is called *excretion*. Virtually all forms of energy production create waste by-products. The human body produces both energy and an abundance of gaseous, liquid, and solid wastes. These wastes result from the production of energy and the process through which complex food materials are changed to simpler, more usable ones. If, for some reason, wastes cannot leave the body, sickness and death are certain to follow. The human body is able to rid itself of wastes by means of a very efficient group of organs.

● The Kidneys: Structure and Function

Wastes from your body's cells enter the bloodstream and are carried to specific excretory organs. The major excretory organs are the kidneys and the skin. The kidneys lie on each side of the spine in the lower back. Each kidney is protected by a layer of fat. Waste-containing blood enters the kidneys and is divided into smaller and smaller amounts as the arteries transporting it branch into capillaries. From the capillaries, the blood flows through filters that separate the wastes from the blood and combine them into urine. *Urine* is a liquid that contains, in addition to the body's waste by-products, water and excess mineral salts that have also been filtered from the blood by the kidneys. Tubes called *urethras* carry the urine from the kidneys to the *urinary bladder*. This muscular organ then expels the urine from the body through the *urethra*. Meanwhile, the cleansed blood exits the kidneys through the renal veins.

● The Skin and Lungs: Function

You may be surprised to learn that your skin is an important excretory organ. Its principal role is the removal of excess heat. When the body becomes too warm, blood vessels in the skin open wide, increasing the flow of blood to the capillaries, which allows heat to be given off to the air. Through pores in the skin exit water, salts, and small amounts of *urea*, a waste found principally in the urine. The liquid that contains these body wastes is *perspiration*. As perspiration evaporates, it helps cool the body by transferring heat energy away from your body. The lungs are considered part of the excretory system because they rid the body of carbon dioxide and excess water in the form of water vapor.

● The Liver and Intestines: Function

Although the liver is principally a digestive organ, it is also able to form urea and secrete it into the bloodstream. Bacteria, some drugs, and hormones are removed from the blood in the liver and converted into less harmful substances. For example, alcohol is broken down in the liver by the enzyme alcohol dehydrogenase. These substances are returned to the blood and eventually excreted from the body by the kidneys. The liver enzymes can become overwhelmed by the volume of harmful substances, resulting in toxic effects. Such is the case when alcohol consumption overwhelms the rate at which alcohol dehydrogenase can break it down.

The large intestine performs an important excretory function by removing from the body food that has not been digested by the small intestine. Solid waste that moves through the large intestine is composed largely of undigested food and bacteria. It is eliminated from the body through the *anus*—the end of the digestive tract. The *rectum* is that portion of the large intestine that lies directly above the anus.

The Circulatory System

A complex system consisting of a pump and conducting vessels keeps you alive. This system, known as the *circulatory system*, operates efficiently whether you are sitting, standing, walking, running, or sleeping. The circulatory system is an extraordinarily complex system but so efficient and automatic that you are able to carry out the activities of living without even an awareness of its existence.

● The Heart and Blood Vessels: Structure and Function

The heart is the powerful pump that moves blood through your body's blood vessels. It has four chambers: a right atrium, a left atrium, a right ventricle, and a left ventricle. Blood enters this marvelous pump through the *atria* (the upper chambers) and is pumped out of the heart by the *ventricles* (the lower chambers). Between the atria and the ventricles are *valves* that prevent the blood from flowing backward. Once blood passes from the atria to the ventricles, it is impossible for it to return through these controlling valves. The opening and closing of the heart valves produce the sound that a physician hears when he or she uses a stethoscope to listen to your heart. The "lub-dub, lub-dub" is simply the opening and shutting of the valves. If the heart valves are damaged and blood is able to leak backward from the ventricles to the atria, a health problem results. Physicians can usually detect this problem by listening through their stethoscope for the sound produced by blood moving in the wrong direction. This sound is called a *heart murmur*.

The vessels that carry blood from the ventricles to various parts of the body are called *arteries*. The vessels that return blood to the heart are called *veins*. Within the body tissues, the major arteries branch into smaller and smaller arteries and small veins merge to form large veins. A series of microscopic *capillaries* connect small arteries and veins and permit the exchange of dissolved nutrients, oxygen, wastes, and other substances.

The right side of the heart receives blood from the body and pumps it to the lungs. This blood contains the carbon dioxide produced by the cells as they convert nutrients to energy. In the lungs, the carbon dioxide is removed from the blood, and oxygen from inhaled air is added. The oxygen-rich blood is then carried to the left side of the heart, which pumps it to the remaining organs of your body (see Figure 10.3). To understand the circulatory system, you must remember that the heart seems to act like two pumps. On the right side, blood that contains carbon dioxide is pumped to the lungs. On the left side, blood that is rich in oxygen, as a result of having passed through the lungs, is pumped to all parts of the body.

● Blood

Human blood is made of a variety of materials. One such material is *plasma*, which is 90% water and 10% various dissolved substances. Among the most important of these substances are *antibodies*, which help your body fight diseases.

Red blood cells are another component of blood. They contain *hemoglobin*, the iron-rich substance that receives oxygen from the lungs and carries it to the tissue cells. It also binds carbon dioxide produced as a by-product of cellular respiration and carries it to the lungs where it is exhaled.

Another type of cell found in the bloodstream is the *white blood cell*. White blood cells do not contain hemoglobin. Rather, they are your body's first line of defense against infection. If you have an infection, the number of white cells in your blood increases very rapidly. White blood cells are able to surround disease-causing bacteria and kill them.

Figure 10.3   The human heart consists of two pumps lying side by side to form a single organ. The right side of the heart sends oxygen-poor blood to the lungs; the left side of the heart sends oxygen-rich blood to the rest of the body

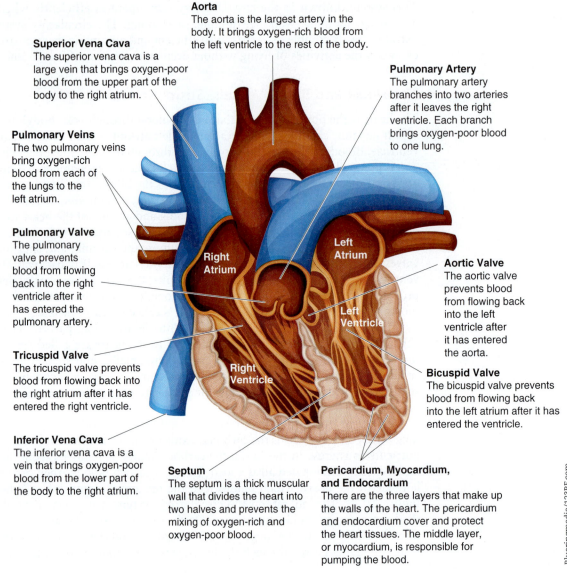

Aorta
The aorta is the largest artery in the body. It brings oxygen-rich blood from the left ventricle to the rest of the body.

Superior Vena Cava
The superior vena cava is a large vein that brings oxygen-poor blood from the upper part of the body to the right atrium.

Pulmonary Artery
The pulmonary artery branches into two arteries after it leaves the right ventricle. Each branch brings oxygen-poor blood to one lung.

Pulmonary Veins
The two pulmonary veins bring oxygen-rich blood from each of the lungs to the left atrium.

Pulmonary Valve
The pulmonary valve prevents blood from flowing back into the right ventricle after it has entered the pulmonary artery.

Aortic Valve
The aortic valve prevents blood from flowing back into the left ventricle after it has entered the aorta.

Tricuspid Valve
The tricuspid valve prevents blood from flowing back into the right atrium after it has entered the right ventricle.

Bicuspid Valve
The bicuspid valve prevents blood from flowing back into the left atrium after it has entered the ventricle.

Inferior Vena Cava
The inferior vena cava is a vein that brings oxygen-poor blood from the lower part of the body to the right atrium.

Septum
The septum is a thick muscular wall that divides the heart into two halves and prevents the mixing of oxygen-rich and oxygen-poor blood.

Pericardium, Myocardium, and Endocardium
There are the three layers that make up the walls of the heart. The pericardium and endocardium cover and protect the heart tissues. The middle layer, or myocardium, is responsible for pumping the blood.

Right Atrium

Left Atrium

Left Ventricle

Right Ventricle

Blueringmedia/123RF.com

Fibrinogen, which makes possible the process of clotting, is found in plasma. If you cut yourself, substances called *platelets* release a chemical that causes fibrinogen to turn into needlelike fibers that trap blood cells and form a clot. It is this clotting process that allows the bloodstream to repair itself in the event of a cut. It simply restricts the flow of blood to an open cut or puncture.

As blood passes through the body, it distributes necessary nutrients picks up wastes . . . nutrients in the blood are carried to the various body cells, where, in combination with oxygen, they are converted to energy. This energy production results in carbon dioxide, water, and other waste by-products. These wastes leave the cells and are carried by the bloodstream to organs that are able to rid the body of them.

The Reproductive System

The egg or sperm cells within your body are so tiny that they can be seen only with a microscope, yet within each reposes half of a blueprint for a new human being, who may one day contribute one of its own reproductive cells to the process of creating a new person. We are bound backward in time to our parents, grandparents, and all those who have preceded us.

● Structure and Function

The male reproductive organs produce *sperm*, or male reproductive cells. The female reproductive organs produce female reproductive cells, or *eggs*. Through sexual intercourse or by artificial means, a sperm cell and an egg cell may unite to form a human embryo. The embryo has the potential for becoming a new human being.

Sperm are produced in an organ called the *testis*. A pair of testes is contained in a pouch called the *scrotum*. Because this scrotum is outside the body wall, the temperature of the testes is somewhat lower than the body temperature. The production of healthy sperm cells requires this lower temperature. Within each testis are numerous coiled tubes. The cells that line the walls of these tubes produce sperm. These tubes merge to form a larger tube, the *sperm duct*. The sperm duct carries sperm and fluids produced by other glands (Cowper's gland, the prostate gland, and the seminal vesicles) into the body and then through the external sexual organ, the *penis* (see Figure 10.4). The penis is used to deliver sperm to egg cells in a female.

Figure 10.4   The Human Male Reproductive System

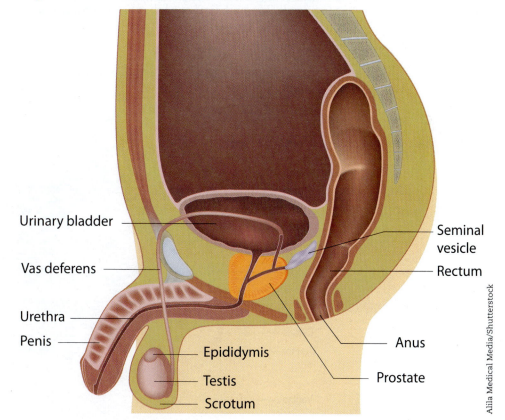

Alila Medical Media/Shutterstock

Human egg cells are produced in a pair of *ovaries* in the female body. During a human female's lifetime, about 500 eggs, or *ova*, will mature and be released by the ovaries. Usually one ovum matures and is released at one time. A mature ovum leaves the ovary and passes into a tubelike organ known as an *oviduct*, where it is pushed along by hairlike projections to a large hollow muscular organ called the *uterus* (see Figure 10.5).

The *vagina* is a tube that connects the uterus with the outside of the body. During intercourse, sperm cells placed here may swim through the uterus and reach the oviducts. If a healthy sperm cell reaches a healthy, mature egg cell, fertilization occurs. The sperm and egg each contribute half of the genetic material—genes containing DNA genetic code packaged in chromosomes—to the embryo. The nucleus of the female egg cell and the nucleus of the male sperm unite to form a human embryo. The fertilized egg then attaches to the uterine wall.

Within 1 week of fertilization, the cell produced by the union of the sperm and egg will divide into about 100 cells. Eight weeks after fertilization it is generally recognized that the embryo becomes a fetus. About 9 months later,[1] the embryo will consist of more than 200 billion cells, each designed to carry out a particular life function.

The developing embryo gets its food through a membrane called the *placenta*. Nutrients and oxygen in the mother's bloodstream pass from the uterus into the blood vessels of the placenta and from there into the embryo, by way of blood vessels in an umbilical cord. The belly button, or *navel*, marks the place where the umbilical cord entered the developing embryo's body. Wastes produced by the cells of the developing embryo enter the embryo's bloodstream and are eventually carried by the placenta to the mother's bloodstream. However, the blood of the mother and the embryo do not naturally mix.

When the embryo reaches maturity, birth occurs. At birth, the embryo is forced through the vagina and out of the mother's body as a result of contractions of the uterine wall. The umbilical cord that had connected the embryo with its mother is cut. The baby is born.

Figure 10.5   The Human Female Reproductive System

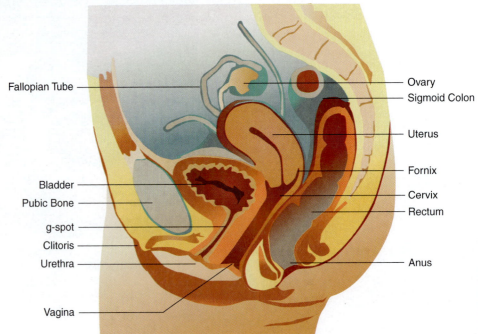

Charobnica/Shutterstock

Every month the uterine wall thickens in preparation to receive the fertilized egg (implantation) to provide nutrients to the developing embryo after fertilization. If fertilization does not occur, the thickened part of the uterus and unfertilized egg is released in a process called menstruation.

Reproduction and Heredity

Heredity is the transmission of the physical traits of parents to their offspring. Your physical traits result from the transmission of hereditary information that occurred when a sperm and egg united to produce you. The nucleus of the sperm cell and the nucleus of the egg cell contain material that determines the embryo's physical traits. The part of the nucleus that contains hereditary information is the *gene*. Genes occupy distinct places on ribbonlike structures called *chromosomes*. The nuclei of all human cells contain chromosomes. Although the nuclei of most cells contain 46 chromosomes, the nucleus of a human sperm cell and the nucleus of a human egg cell contain only 23 chromosomes. When a sperm cell and an egg cell unite, the resulting cell has 46 chromosomes. Twenty-three chromosomes carry genes from the male parent, and 23 carry genes from the female parent. Therefore, the fertilized cell contains hereditary information from both parents. The genes on the chromosomes and their particular pairings give the offspring its inherited traits.

Identical twins result when an embryo splits in two, creating two embryos with identical hereditary information. The two embryos develop into individuals who have the same physical traits. *Fraternal twins* result when two ova are each fertilized by different sperm. They are simply siblings who happened to be conceived and born at the same time.

Summary

10.1 Describe and identify primary structures and functions of major human body systems.

Note that the theme of energy transfer is inherent in all the life support systems. The digestive system converts food into energy or cell-building material. The skeletal-muscular system transfers the energy into mechanical energy that provides the body with its shape and structure and gives it the ability to move. The respiratory system secures the oxygen necessary for the conversion of food to energy and eliminates carbon dioxide. The nervous system receives stimuli and carries them to the brain; it then transmits the brain's messages to various parts of the body by means of electrical energy through nerve impulses. The excretory system rids the body of energy by-products: gaseous, liquid, and solid wastes. The circulatory system moves a variety of substances that supply stored energy and building materials from place to place in the body. The reproductive system uses energy to ensure the continuation of the species.

Chapter 10 Self-Check
Click to gauge your understanding of the concepts in this chapter.

Notes

1. Average human gestation is estimated as 40 weeks from the first day of the woman's last menstrual period.
2. MyPlate graphic is produced by the United States Department of Agriculture. Used with permission.

The Physical Sciences

▶ ## History and Nature of the Physical Sciences

What makes that arching band of colors appear from nowhere in the distant sky and then, in the blink of an eye, disappear? What are *you* really made of? How can we communicate with satellites millions of miles away? How can a cardiac surgeon tell exactly where my elderly uncle has a blocked coronary artery?

The answers to these questions and more come from the most fundamental of the sciences: the physical sciences. In fact, *all* science emerges from our knowledge of matter and energy. These topics are at the center of physics and chemistry.

Careers in the Physical Sciences

A range of career paths are open to those women and men who have the required knowledge, skills, and motivation to explore the nature of matter and energy. Here are a few of the possibilities:

- *Chemist.* The chemist's work, in general, involves assembling atoms to form new molecules or breaking down complex molecules to explore the numbers and types of atoms they contain. The results of this work include improved processed food products, cosmetics, fuels, household products, industrial chemicals, pollution control, weapons systems, and drugs.

- *Physicist.* Through careful experimentation, the physicist tries to find explanations for natural phenomena such as the action of forces on matter, as well as for the behavior of energy in all its diverse forms. *Theoretical physicists* explore phenomena that are impossible to represent on Earth, such as the nature of space and time, the formation of black holes, and the interactions that occur as stars pass through their life cycles.

- *Engineer.* Engineers apply the knowledge produced by physicists and chemists to the development of products and procedures that solve human problems. The subspecialties of engineering include the development of electronic circuits on chips; the creation of machines to fabricate products; the design of bridges, aircraft, and satellites; and the creation of new drugs to improve our health and well-being, and methods to generate clean energy that will preserve the planet.

Key Events in the Development of the Physical Sciences

500 BCE	Sometime during the fifth century B.C.E., Empedocles proposes that everything comes from four *elements*: earth, air, fire, and water.
440 BCE	Democritus observes and reflects upon the matter around him and concludes that it is made of fundamental particles he calls *atoms*.
260 BCE	Archimedes uses mathematics to propose the principle of the lever. He also discovers the principle of buoyancy, which states that the upward force on an object in water is equal to the weight of the volume of water displaced by that object.
1490	Leonardo da Vinci observes and then describes capillary action in detail.
1581	Galileo Galilei observes that the movement of pendulums displays a time-keeping property.
1589	By observing rolling balls on an inclined plane, Galileo Galilei shows that objects of different masses fall with the same acceleration.
1687	Isaac Newton publishes *Principia Mathematica*.
1781	Joseph Priestly creates molecules of water by combining hydrogen and oxygen and igniting them.
1786	Luigi Galvani discovers what he refers to as *animal electricity* and concludes that the bodies of living animals contain electricity.
1808	John Dalton proposes the theory that each element has its own type of atom and that every compound is made of a particular combination of atoms.
1820	Hans Oersted observes that a current in a wire can affect a compass needle.
1852	James Joule and Lord Kelvin show that a gas that expands rapidly cools while it does so.
1862	Dmitri Mendeleyev summarizes his research about the properties of elements by creating a chart known as the *periodic table*, which places elements into groups and rows. The elements of each group have similar properties.
1873	James Clerk Maxwell concludes that light is an electromagnetic phenomenon.
1895	Wilhelm Roentgen discovers X-rays.
1897	Joseph Thomson discovers electrons and calls the particles *corpuscles*.
1897	Marie Curie begins research on so-called uranium rays, which eventually leads to the discovery of radioactivity.
1905	Albert Einstein explains the photoelectric effect.
1905	Albert Einstein states the theory of special relativity as well as the law of mass/energy conservation.
1907	Albert Einstein states that gravitation and inertia are the same and uses this to predict the gravitational red shift of starlight.
1907	Albert Einstein infers from his studies that time is slowed in a gravitational field.

1911	Ernest Rutherford conducts experiments that indicate that particular types of atoms radiate particles and discovers that alpha particles are helium atoms without electrons and beta particles are high-speed electrons.
1912	Albert Einstein concludes that the space/time continuum is curved and that gravity is caused by that curvature.
1913	Niels Bohr proposes that when electrons move from a high-energy level to a lower energy level around an atom, photons ("packets") of light are released. He also states that the movement of electrons from a low energy level to a higher energy level is the result of photons being absorbed.
1915	Albert Einstein puts forth his complete theory of general relativity and also proves that the excess precession of the planet Mercury is a result of general relativity.
1932	The first atom is split with a particle accelerator.
1934	Irene Joliot-Curie and Frederick Joliot-Curie bombard aluminum atoms with alpha particles and create artificially radioactive phosphorus-30.
1934	Leo Szilard concludes that nuclear chain reactions may be possible.
1939	Lise Meitner and her nephew, Otto Hahn, reveal that uranium nuclei can disintegrate through a process called *fission*.
1943	The first all-electronic calculating device (computer) is developed by a team led by Alan Turing and used to crack German codes during World War II.
1945	On July 16, the first atomic bomb is successfully tested in the United States.
1949	William Bradford Shockley and his research team invent the transistor.
1952	The first hydrogen bomb is tested.
1969	Murray Gell-Mann wins the Nobel Prize for physics for his work on classifying elementary particles.
1994	Kyriacos Nicolau and Robert Holton create a synthetic molecular form of the naturally occurring cancer treatment compound Taxol.
1997	Steven Chu, Claude Cohen-Tannoudji, and William D. Phillips win a Nobel Prize for developing a way to trap and study individual atoms using laser technology.
1998	Robert B. Laughlin, Horst L. Stormer, and Daniel C. Tsui win a Nobel Prize for discovering a new form of matter known as *quantum fluid*.
2001	Carl E. Wieman, Wolfgang Ketterle, and Eric A. Cornell win the Nobel Prize in physics for work on an exotic state of matter that results from cooling down an alkali gas to 0.00000002° above absolute zero.
2002	Raymond Davis, Jr., Mastoshi Koshiba, and Riccardo Giacconi win a Nobel Prize for their study of the nearly undetectable cosmic radiation that reaches Earth.
2005	Roy J. Glauber, John L. Hall, and Theodor W. Hänsch receive the Nobel Laureate in Physics for their contributions to the development of laser-based precision spectroscopy, including the optical frequency comb technique.
2006	Nobel laureate, Carl E. Wieman, renowned for his leadership in science education, joins The University of British Columbia to boost science education.
2007	The Nobel Prize in physics is awarded to two European scientists—Albert Fert and Peter Grünberg—for their discovery of a physical effect, known today as Giant Magnetoresistance or GMR.

2012	A Higgs-like particle is discovered at the Large Hadron Collider near Geneva Switzerland.
2014	The Borexino experiment detected the presence of low energy neutrinos, deepening scientists' understanding of how the sun generates energy through nuclear fusion
2016	The Nobel Prize in Chemistry is awarded to three scientists who figured out how to build nano-sized machines out of molecules.

Women and Men Who Have Shaped the Development of the Physical Sciences

ISAAC NEWTON (1642–1727) is known as the founder of modern physics and mathematics. His studies of the natural world led to the laws of inertia, action and reaction, and the acceleration of a mass being proportional to force applied. He also proposed the universal law of gravitation and is considered to be the inventor of calculus.

COUNT ALESSANDRO VOLTA (1745–1827) was an Italian nobleman who conducted research into the nature of electricity. The unit of electricity known as the volt is derived from his name.

MICHAEL FARADAY (1791–1867) was a bookbinder whose intense curiosity led him to read every book that he bound, particularly those that dealt with energy. Later in life, he became a chemist and a physicist. His accomplishments included the separation of benzene from petroleum and experiments with electromagnetic induction (the production of current in wires moved through a magnetic field).

LADY AUGUSTA ADA BYRON, COUNTESS OF LOVELACE (1815–1851) wrote in 1843 what we now refer to as the code, or the program to operate the first mechanical computer. The U.S. Navy named the computer language *Ada* in her honor.

THOMAS ALVA EDISON (1847–1931) was perhaps the greatest inventor in history. His patents led to development of the phonograph, the motion picture camera, electric lights, and power plants to produce electricity. He received over 1,000 patents in his lifetime.

LEWIS H. LATIMER (1848–1928) invented, among other things, a method for producing the carbon filaments used in the electric lamps of his time. He was an engineer at the Edison Electric Light Company and the only African American in Edison's engineering and invention group. Latimer authored *Incandescent Electric Lighting*, the first book describing the installation and operation of lighting systems.

GRANVILLE WOODS (1856–1910) was an African American whose early work as a fireman/engineer on railroads provided a foundation for his later studies of electrical and mechanical engineering. His inventions included devices that could send telegraph messages between moving trains and an automatic airbrake system.

MARIE CURIE (1867–1934) was a Polish-born scientist whose work touched both physics and chemistry. An indication of her extraordinary contribution to the sciences is the fact that she won the Nobel Prize twice! She and her husband, Pierre, shared the Nobel Prize in 1903 for their discovery of radium and polonium, and in 1911, she won it by herself for the research that led to the isolation of pure radium.

ERNEST RUTHERFORD (1871–1937) was known for his exploration of many phenomena related to atomic structure, energy release, and the nature of particles, including alpha, beta, and gamma radiation and the proton and neutron. He is credited with discovering the nucleus of an atom and with proposing a model of the atom in which electrons orbited the central nucleus.

ALBERT EINSTEIN (1879–1955) stands as one of the true geniuses in the history of civilization. His theories shaped the development of modern science and have had profound implications on science and society. Among his many accomplishments, he explained Brownian motion and the photoelectric effect, and he developed both the special and general theories of relativity. Born in Germany, he emigrated to the United States while in his fifties. He joined the Institute for Advanced Study in Princeton, New Jersey.

NIELS BOHR (1885–1962), a Danish physicist, provided an explanation for the structure of the atom that included a description of how electrons absorb and lose energy. His theory provided the best explanation for experimental results gathered by atomic physicists from around the world. Bohr received the Nobel Prize for physics in 1922.

LUIS FEDERICO LELOIR (1906–1987) was an Argentine physician and biochemist who isolated a new class of substances call sugar nucleotides that was a major breakthrough in the understanding of metabolic reactions. Her received the Nobel Prize in chemistry for his work in 1970.

GRACE HOPPER (1906–1992) was an active-duty U.S. Navy lieutenant who was key in developing computer programs. Her programming skills were used in one of the earliest computers, the Univac I. She is credited with invention of the term *computer bug*.

CHIEN-SHIUNG WU (1912–1997) received her Ph.D. in physics from the University of California, Berkeley. She is most well known for her work in developing an experiment that confirmed a theory related to particle physics proposed by T. D. Lee and C. N. Yang. Lee and Yang received the Nobel Prize for their work on the theory but Wu did not. She did receive the Comstock Award from the National Academy of Sciences in 1964 and was the first woman to do so.

RICHARD FEYNMAN (1918–1988) won the Nobel Prize in Physics in 1965 for his work on quantum electrodynamics, or QED. In 1986, he served on the presidential commission investigating the explosion of the space shuttle *Challenger*. He is known for his 1985 memoir, *Surely You're Joking, Mr. Feynman*, which portrayed him as whimsical character. He earned a bachelor's degree at MIT in 1939 and a doctorate from Princeton in 1942. During World War II he worked at the Army research center at Los Alamos, New Mexico, helping design the first atomic bomb. *The Feynman Lectures on Physics*, a collection of his lectures to Caltech freshmen, remains a popular text in the field.

ROSALIND FRANKLIN (1920–1958) received her doctorate in physics from Cambridge University in 1941 and developed great expertise in the study of crystals. She analyzed the behavior of fine beams of X-rays through DNA (deoxyribonucleic acid).

ROSALYN SUSSMAN YALOW (1921– 2011) shared the Nobel Prize for medicine in 1977, which was awarded for development of a method to detect minute traces of substances in blood and other body fluids.

MURRAY GELL-MANN (1929–) is most famous for proposing a theory that grouped atomic particles into eight "families." This grouping was grounded in his belief that all particles are composed of smaller particles that he called *quarks*. He won the Nobel Prize for physics in 1969.

STEVEN WEINBERG (1933–) is known as one of the twentieth century's most talented theoretical physicists. He is best known for his work on a unified field theory, or a single explanation that ties together the laws of physics dealing with gravity, electromagnetism, the strong force holding the atom's nucleus together, and the weak force (which results in the breaking apart of the nucleus). He shared the Nobel Prize for physics in 1979 with Sheldon Glashow and Abdus Salam.

CHARLES K. KAO (1933–) is an electrical engineer and physicist who won the Nobel Prize in Physics in 2009 for his research into the transmission of laser light through glass fibers in optical cables, which has led to the widespread use of fiber optics in modern telecommunications.

▶ Personal and Social Implications of the Physical Sciences

Personal and Community Health

Maintaining your personal health depends, in large part, on the work of physicists and chemists. Does that sound a bit surprising? Just think about it for a moment. Every medication was most likely created by chemists, any instrument used to fix broken bones or repair other body parts uses metals and plastics that came from a physical scientist's laboratory, and many of the diagnostic procedures used to identify the causes of illnesses emerged from the laboratories of physical scientists. To be sure, scientists from other disciplines are obviously also heavily involved in the development and delivery of personal health care, but in many ways, chemists and physicists carry out the fundamental research upon which health-related work is done.

Your health, and that of those around you, also depends a great deal on the environment in which you live. And knowledge about that environment emerges, in part, from the work of physicists and chemists. The quality of land surfaces, oceans, and atmosphere is constantly being assessed (and hopefully improved) as a result of the basic research done by physical scientists and the engineering of diagnostic instruments, clean energy technology, and medical equipment done by engineers.

Hazards, Risks, and Benefits

The degradation of natural resources—whether the land, water, or atmosphere—poses a severe threat to the health and well-being of *all* populations of living things. Many scientists work to acquire knowledge that will serve as the basis for inventing devices and systems to measure changes in environmental quality and to use chemical agents and physical processes to retard or correct problems that affect life in its many forms.

One example of work in this area is that done to stop or at least slow down depletion of the ozone layer, which is a part of the atmosphere that shields us from certain radiant energy. The free movement of ultraviolet radiation through the atmosphere and to the skin surfaces of living things can cause serious harm. The instrumentation for monitoring the ozone layer, the modification of industrial processes to slow down ozone depletion, and even the creation of chemicals to retard sunburn have all emerged from work done in the physical sciences.

Personal safety for workers as well as travelers can be increased by the use of certain technologies, such as air pollution measurement devices, built-in sprinkler systems, and procedures and equipment that permit the rapid exiting of individuals from factories, businesses, homes, automobiles, trains, and airplanes. Technology has also brought us increased surveillance techniques that can be used to safeguard our personal and societal well-being. Of course, with these surveillance techniques comes the potential for risk to our privacy. As with any technology, we must carefully weigh the benefits against the risks.

▶ Physical Science Technology: Its Nature and Impact

If you've eaten a slice of toast today or traveled in a car or turned on a light, you have used technology that came from the physical sciences. The study of matter and energy has not only revealed some of the deepest secrets of our natural world but has also provided the basis for most of the world's technology. Engineers have used the principles of physics and chemistry to produce items as varied as disposable diapers, long-lasting lipstick, cell phones, augmented reality, and nuclear bombs.

Even your personal recreation possibilities have been affected by the technology that's rooted in the physical sciences. Plastic kayak hulls, indoor ice rinks, roller coasters, snowboards, specialized shoes, and, of course, the aluminum softball bat have all come from work in the physical sciences.

The Design of Physical Science Technology

The engineers who create technology based on the findings of the physical sciences develop measuring devices, materials, and tools whose design usually meets the following criteria:

1. It addresses a problem that has been clearly identified and for which data can reasonably be expected to be gathered.

2. It serves as a data-gathering tool to assist in physical science exploration or as a device to be used in the fabrication of a material or product.

3. It can withstand a wide range of external environmental conditions.

4. It presents data in a manner that is readily interpretable by chemists or physicists, as appropriate.

5. If it is a tool, it can be readily used.

6. It preserves the safety and health of individuals who use it.

7. It provides constant feedback about the accuracy of the data being represented or the efficiency of the tool.

Examples of Physical Science Technology

Many devices have been developed from the foundation of knowledge produced from work in physics and chemistry, and they can be used to produce further knowledge about the physical world or to improve the quality of life:

Radiation-measuring devices	Wind tunnels
Computers	Lasers
Circuit testers	Solar energy collectors
Particle accelerators	

Chemical reagents (molecules that can split or combine other molecules)

Oscilloscopes (convert sound waves to electrical signals that can be viewed on a screen)

Spectrophotometers (measure the intensity of light absorbed at different wavelengths)

Chemical indicators (for example, a solution that can identify the presence of hemoglobin)

Calorimeters (can measure the amount of energy released during a chemical reaction)

Long-Term Implications of Physical Science Technology

The technological implications of the physical sciences are profound. In the area of medicine, knowledge of the behavior of elements, including how they may be combined to form molecules, has led to the development of pharmaceutical agents that have done much to reduce pain and suffering. In the area of food production, the application of scientific techniques to the measurement of trace amounts of substances has provided government and other agencies with the capability of analyzing food products to determine if they meet certain standards of purity.

Technology has led to the creation of an amazing array of brand-new materials. In addition to some rather extraordinary synthetic materials—including plastics, nylon, and nanocarbon fibers—there are some very specialized materials used to construct recreational boats and automobiles, replacement devices for joints and organs, and even aircraft that are invisible to radar.

In this early part of the twenty-first century, we have seen how discoveries related to digital electronics have been used to develop widespread use of the Internet, computerized manufacturing, computing for personal and business uses, and the ubiquitous cellular phone. Looking ahead, we can see truly extraordinary technology emerging, including miniature robotic devices, made of only a few hundred or thousand molecules, that can be injected into the bloodstream and travel to specific sites, where they will repair damaged tissues or organs! And while this may sound like science fiction, nanomedicine is already part of our lives.

Consider all of the technological innovations that seemed like utter fantasy at one time but have become real—very real. It seems that what the human mind can imagine, the physical sciences can create!

Matter and Motion

Sergey Nivens/Shutterstock

Learning Objectives

After completing the activities in this chapter, you should be able to:

11.1 Explain how the kinetic molecular theory of matter can be used to explain fundamental properties of matter.

11.2 Describe distinctive attributes of chemical reactions.

11.3 Provide examples for Newton's laws of motion.

11.4 Explain how mass and distance relate to gravitational force.

▶ **GETTING STARTED**

Imagine getting in a car, stating your destination, and reading a book or watching your favorite movie while the car navigates the roads and traffic to your destination. Self-driving car technology is no longer a dream of the future. Prototypes of these cars have already been on roads in the United States for several years.

Our ability to accomplish such amazing things as online meetings with people around the world or remotely controlling vehicles on Mars is possible because of the technology available to us. We have mobile devices in our pockets that rival computers used to put people on the moon; we have drugs that can prevent or cure illnesses; we have automobiles, airplanes, unbelievable weapons of destruction, and wonder of wonders—sonic toothbrushes. The rapid pace of technological development is a direct result of our increased knowledge of the nature of matter, motions, and our ability to harness energy from nature.

Matter and its Interactions (PS1)

Silly Putty, a chicken, and pistachio ice cream all have something in common. They are all *matter*. Anything that occupies space and has mass is matter. Everything in our universe that has mass and occupies space—Earth, the planets, the Sun, and so on—is composed of matter. Most properties of matter can be understood based on these characteristics:

- Matter is made up of small particles called *molecules*.
- Spaces exist among the molecules.
- The molecules of matter are in constant motion.

Changes in the states of matter can be explained by the motion of molecules. A solid has a definite shape because its molecules are arranged in a pattern. Although the molecules hold this pattern, they also vibrate. If heat is applied to a solid, the rate at which its molecules vibrate becomes so fast that they break away from one another in the pattern. If we add sufficient heat, the solid melts and becomes a liquid. If we add even more heat, the molecules in the liquid may move fast enough to escape from the surface of the liquid and enter the air. These molecules have gone from the liquid state to the gaseous state—the process known as *evaporation*.

If we reverse this process, if we take the heat from gas, its molecules may slow down sufficiently to form a liquid. If we take away more heat, the molecules may begin forming the patterns in which they exist in their solid state. These types of changes in matter are physical changes. No new types of molecules are created. The description of matter as molecules in motion is referred to as the kinetic molecular theory of matter.

The kinetic molecular theory of matter can be used to explain the expansion and contraction of matter. When the speed of the molecules in matter increases, they bump into one another more and tend to spread apart. *Expansion* of matter thereby occurs. If heat is removed, the molecules move more slowly and tend to come closer to one another. When this occurs, matter *contracts*.

We usually describe matter by its physical properties. We say various types of matter are *solids*, *liquids*, or *gases*. These forms of matter are known as *states*, or phases, of matter. Rocks and soils are solids. Water may be found as a solid, a liquid, or a gas. The state that matter is in can be determined by observation. A solid has a definite shape. A liquid takes the shape of its container. Both solids and liquids have a definite volume: They occupy a certain amount of space. A gas takes the shape of its container, but it also expands to fill all of the container. Thus, gases do not have a definite volume: Their volume is the volume of the container.

We can also describe matter by describing its color, how hard or soft it is, the extent to which it dissolves in liquid, and whether it is easily stretched or broken. Another specific physical property of matter is its *density*. Unlike units of weight, which represent a gravitational attraction for that matter, units of mass, such as grams and kilograms, represent the amount of matter in something. Density is commonly measured as mass per unit of volume and is expressed in grams per cubic centimeter. To find the density of something, we can simply divide its mass by its volume.

Conservation of Matter

If one were to add 10 grams of ice to 100 grams of water, the total mass will remain at 110 grams even after the ice melts. The same would be true if the water evaporated. There would still be 110 grams of water vapor, even though the water seems to have disappeared. This is characteristic of the law of conservation of matter, which states that matter cannot be created or destroyed, it can only change its form.

A Closer Look at Matter

Matter is made up of small units called atoms, whose arrangement impacts the properties of matter. Scientists know a great deal about the way in which atoms interact with one another as well as the way in which they absorb and release energy. With this knowledge, scientists have constructed a model of what they believe an atom to be. Keep in mind that the protons, neutrons, and electrons that make up an atom are not really the round objects they are depicted to be in diagrams. Even so, diagrams can help us understand atomic interaction. Figure 11.1 illustrates six different atoms. The electrons in these atoms exist in the outer rings, or shells. Electrons are negative electrical charges that orbit around the atom's nucleus. A *shell* is an energy level on which an electron exists.

The center of an atom is called the *nucleus*. This is the place where *protons*, heavy particles having a positive electrical charge, and *neutrons*, heavy particles having no electrical charge, are found. It is the protons and neutrons that make up most of the atom's mass. An *electron* has only $\frac{1}{1837}$ the mass of a proton. Atoms are electrically neutral—that is, an atom contains as many positive charges (protons) in its nucleus as there are negative charges (electrons) around the nucleus. Some atoms do not have neutrons. The hydrogen atom, for example, has one proton and one electron but no neutrons. The helium atom consists of two protons and two neutrons in the nucleus surrounded by two orbiting electrons.

The *atomic number* of an element is the number of protons it contains. The *atomic weight* of an element is the weight of its protons plus the weight of its neutrons. An element's atomic weight is also determined in relation to the weight of a carbon atom, which is 12 units. A hydrogen atom has about $\frac{1}{12}$ the weight of a carbon atom. Therefore, hydrogen has an atomic weight of about 1.

Figure 11.1 Models like these are used to keep track of the number and placement of protons, neutrons, and electrons in atoms.

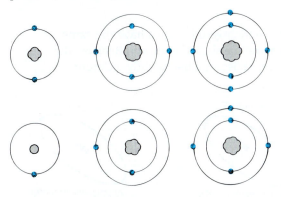

Magnesium is about twice as heavy as carbon; its atomic weight is 24. Here are the atomic weights of some elements:

Element	Atomic Weight
Aluminum	27.0
Carbon	12.0
Chlorine	35.5
Copper	63.5
Gold	196.9
Hydrogen	1.0
Lead	207.2
Oxygen	16.0
Silver	107.0
Sulfur	32.1

Some atoms of an element are slightly heavier than most atoms of the same element. These atoms are known as *isotopes*. Isotopes differ in atomic weight because they have a different number of neutrons. For example, the most common sulfur atom has an atomic weight of 32. However, some sulfur atoms have a weight of 36. Both types of atoms are sulfur atoms since they have an atomic number of 16. The average atomic weight of sulfur atoms is about 32.1. The 0.1 results from the atoms that have slightly different atomic weights. These isotopes of sulfur have the exact chemical properties of the element sulfur. Their physical properties, however, may differ from those of the predominant sulfur atoms. There are at least three isotopes of hydrogen in nature: hydrogen 1, hydrogen 2, and hydrogen 3. Study Figure 11.2 and note that most hydrogen atoms have one proton and one electron. However, hydrogen isotopes may have one proton, one electron, and one neutron (hydrogen 2) or one proton, one electron, and two neutrons (hydrogen 3). The atomic weight of hydrogen represents the average weight of all hydrogen atoms, including the isotopes.

● Chemical Reactions (PS1.B)

Some types of matter are capable of uniting with one another to form very different types of matter. This characteristic is known as a *chemical property of matter*. A chemistry teacher holds a piece of magnesium with tongs and places it in the flame of a Bunsen burner. Bright light is produced, and the metallic magnesium changes to a white powder: magnesium oxide. Changes resulting in substances that

Figure 11.2 The nuclei of these hydrogen isotopes have the same number of protons but not the same number of neutrons. Because the number of neutrons is different, each isotope has slightly different physical properties.

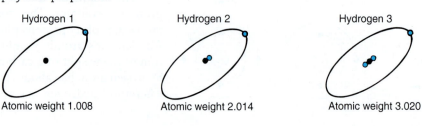

Hydrogen 1   Hydrogen 2   Hydrogen 3

Atomic weight 1.008   Atomic weight 2.014   Atomic weight 3.020

differ from the original substance are known as *chemical changes*. The rusting of iron and the burning of wood or paper are other examples of matter changing and combining with other types of matter (in these examples oxygen) to produce new forms of matter.

Although we can describe these changes in many ways, to fully understand the chemical properties of matter, it is helpful to think about specific chemical changes. The roasting of a marshmallow and the phenomenon of fire are two good examples.

The Roasting of a Marshmallow   A marshmallow is made of sugar. Sugar contains carbon, hydrogen, and oxygen. You've probably noticed that when you heat a marshmallow over an open flame, the surface of the marshmallow darkens. It does so because the sugar undergoes a chemical change. The heat added to the sugar breaks the sugar into carbon, hydrogen, and oxygen. The dark material on the outside of the marshmallow is carbon. Hydrogen and oxygen leave the heated marshmallow in the form of water.

Fire   The flickering candles atop a birthday cake, the ring of blue flame on a gas stovetop, and a raging forest fire are all examples of matter undergoing a rapid chemical change that gives off both light and heat. In each case, three things are present: (1) a material that will burn (a fuel), (2) oxygen, and (3) something that heats the fuel to a temperature at which it will burn.

All common fossil fuels contain carbon. When these fuels burn, they undergo various chemical changes. The carbon within them combines with oxygen to form the gas carbon dioxide. If there is insufficient oxygen, however, carbon monoxide, a very dangerous gas, is released. If the fuel contains hydrogen as well as carbon, during *combustion* (another word for "burning"), oxygen in the air also combines with the hydrogen in the fuel to form water vapor. In each of these examples, matter undergoes chemical changes to become a new type of matter, and in each example, it is the presence of oxygen that allows the changes to occur quickly.

● Elements, Compounds, and Mixtures

An *element* is a substance that cannot be separated into simpler substances by chemical changes. Carbon, hydrogen, and oxygen are elements. Through chemical changes, elements can be combined into *compounds*. Table salt is a compound composed of the elements sodium and chlorine. Its chemical name is *sodium chloride*. Elements and compounds can be represented as *formulas*. The formula for table salt, for example, is NaCl. This combination of symbols indicates that there is one part sodium (Na) and one part chlorine (Cl) in salt. The formula H_2O stands for a combination of two parts hydrogen and one part oxygen.

If we break down a molecule of water or a molecule of salt, we will produce hydrogen and oxygen or sodium and chloride. These parts of a molecule are called *atoms*. When we write the chemical formula H_2O, we are indicating that a molecule of water contains two atoms of hydrogen and one atom of oxygen. When we write CO_2, we are saying that one molecule of carbon dioxide contains one atom of carbon and two atoms of oxygen. The number written below the line in the formula tells us how many atoms (if more than one) of the preceding element are present in the molecule.

Chemists use chemical equations to describe chemical changes in matter. Let's see how this is done. If we place a clean iron nail in a solution of copper sulfate, a chemical change will occur: The iron nail will become coated with a reddish covering, which is copper. As this occurs, the blue color of the copper-sulfate solution becomes less intense. In the chemical change that occurs, iron in the nail changes places with some of the copper in the copper sulfate. The equation that describes this reaction is as follows:

$$Fe + CuSO_4 \rightarrow FeSO_4 + Cu$$

Fe represents iron. $CuSO_4$ represents copper sulfate. The arrow means "forms" or "yields." On the right side of the arrow are the products of the chemical change: $FeSO_4$ (iron sulfate) and Cu (copper). Notice that the number of atoms on each side of the arrow is the same. No atoms are gained or lost during a chemical change.

Not all combinations of elements form compounds. The principal test is whether the various substances can be separated from one another. For example, if you were to mix a small amount of sand with a small amount of salt, no chemical change would occur. If you had patience and a strong lens, you could probably separate the two materials. It would take time, but it could be done because the salt and sand do not chemically unite with each other. Any combination of materials that can be separated from one another is known as a *mixture*. The air we breathe is a mixture of various gases. The soil we walk on is a mixture of various rocks and minerals.

Forces and Motion (PS2.A)

"How long 'til we get there?"

This question commonly punctuates long family drives to distant destinations, regardless of the frequency of the parents' response. The driver, if he or she is patient enough, will try to give the child a response that is based on the speed of the automobile, its present location, and the location of the destination.

The *speed* of an automobile is determined by the distance it travels in a given unit of time. The units commonly used to express the speed of automobiles are *kilometers per hour* and *miles per hour*. We can fairly easily use our knowledge of speed to answer the child's question about how long it will take to reach a destination. Because speed is the distance divided by the time, we can multiply the speed of the object by a given time to find how far we will travel in that time. If you know the destination is 100 kilometers (about 60 miles) away and the average speed during the journey will be 50 kilometers (about 30 miles) per hour, you can divide the distance by speed and remark calmly that the journey will take about 2 hours.

If you specify the speed of an object and the direction in which it is traveling, you are talking about an object's *velocity*. We call changes in velocity *acceleration*. An automobile speeding up is accelerating. The rate of acceleration is equal to the change in velocity divided by the time it took for the change. If your car stops at a red light during your trip and then gains a speed of 50 kilometers (about 30 miles) per hour in 10 seconds, traveling in a straight line, the change in velocity is 50 kilometers per hour and it occurs in 10 seconds. Therefore, the rate of acceleration of the car is 5 kilometers (3 miles) per hour per second.

Because scientists define velocity as both speed and direction, an object that moves with constant speed yet changes direction is accelerating. For example, a racing car traveling around a track at a constant speed is accelerating because its direction is constantly changing.

With this information in mind, we can now consider objects in motion. To understand why objects in motion behave as they do, we need to understand the laws that govern them.

Newton's Laws of Motion

Have you ever blown up a balloon, held its end shut, and then released it to watch it rocket around the room? You may not have realized it, but you were demonstrating a phenomenon described about 300 years ago by Isaac Newton. Newton's observations of the motion of objects led him to reach conclusions that we now refer to as *laws of motion*. Newton's three laws of motion help us explain the motion of objects that are subjected to forces.

Newton's first law of motion, sometimes called the *law of inertia*, states that an object at rest will remain at rest and a body moving with a constant velocity in a straight line will maintain its motion unless the bodies are acted upon by an unbalanced external force. This law tells us that in order to change the position of an object at rest, we must apply a force to it. Similarly, if we wish to change the speed or direction (velocity) of a moving object, we must apply a force. To move a golf ball from the grass of a putting green to the hole, we apply a force with the putter. To increase the speed of an automobile, we cause the engine to increase the forces that turn the wheels. To slow down a bicycle that is moving along at a constant velocity, we apply frictional forces by using the brakes.

Newton's second law of motion states that the force varies with the acceleration and mass of the object. For example, suppose you push a 10-kg wagon with a dog on the wagon that weighs 20 kg. You push the wagon with a constant force to maintain a speed of 5 kilometers per hour (the forces you apply overcome friction). If the dog jumps out of the wagon and you continue pushing with the same force, then the wagon will accelerate (change its velocity). If a heavier dog, say 30 kg, jumps into the wagon and you continue pushing with the same force, then the wagon will slow down or decelerate. In both cases, there is a change in acceleration. Similarly, if the force on an object is increased (push harder) and no mass is added to or taken away from the object (dog stays in the wagon), the object (wagon) will accelerate. Specifically, this law tells us that an object will accelerate in the direction in which an applied force is acting and that the acceleration will be proportional to the applied force. You may be familiar with Newton's second law expressed in mathematical terms as Force = Mass × Acceleration (F = MA).

Newton's third law of motion states that for every action, there is an equal and opposite reaction. The air escaping from the blown-up balloon mentioned earlier moves in one direction; it is the action force. The balloon moves in the opposite direction as a reaction to the action force.

In summary, forces can be thought of as pushes or pulls. Pushes/pulls have two components: strength and direction. If the push/pulls are equal and opposite, no change in motion will occur. If they are unbalanced, a change in motion will occur. Changes can be observed in speed, direction, or both.

Types of Interactions (PS2.B)

Scientists have found that all matter in the universe exerts an attractive force on all other matter in the universe. The matter in this book is exerting an attractive force on you, and you are exerting an attractive force on the matter in the book. This attractive force is called *gravitation*, and it exists regardless of the location of the matter. The strength of the force depends on the amount of matter in both you and the book, for example, and your distance from the book. The force that gravity exerts on matter is called *weight*. The weight of an object on Earth is a measurement of the extent to which Earth pulls on the object and the object pulls on Earth.

• Gravity and Motion

Whether you live in Beijing, China, or Paramus, New Jersey, you know that what goes up must come down, and the downward path is always the same: All objects fall toward the center of Earth. After studying the behavior of falling objects, Newton concluded that the cause for the path of a falling object was the attractive force that exists between masses. This force of attraction depends on two variables: the mass of each attracting object and the distance between them.

Very precise scientific instruments have revealed that Newton was correct in his conclusion that all masses exert attractive forces. Newton's conclusion is called the *law of universal gravitation*, and it is a fundamental law of the universe. Every mass in the universe attracts every other mass with a force that varies directly with the product of the masses of the objects and inversely with the square of the distance between them. In simpler terms, this means that distance has an increasingly larger effect on gravitational attraction between objects. The gravitational attraction between two masses is exponentially weaker as the distance increases. This becomes more evidence by looking at the relationship written as an equation:

$$F = G\, m_1\, m_2 / r^2$$

Although it may not look it, this is actually an easy equation to understand. The variable m represents the masses of the two objects. The r is the distance between the centers of the objects. The G is a constant. In other words, the same value of G is used every time the equation is solved. F stands for the actual force of attraction between objects.

As noted earlier, the force of attraction between an object and Earth is the object's weight. Earth's gravitational pull causes falling objects to accelerate at the rate of 9.8 meters (32 feet) per second per second. This means that an object increases its speed 9.8 meters (32 feet) per second during each second it falls. Strictly speaking, this rate applies to objects falling through a vacuum because the presence of air retards the acceleration of objects that have a large surface area compared with their mass.

Gravity is not the only force that changes with distance. Electric and magnetic forces between objects depend on distance and the forces they exert. In general, the further objects generating force are apart, the weaker the attraction. Magnetic forces have the added characteristic of orientation; like poles repel, opposites attract.

• Air Pressure and Flight: An Example of Physics and Technology

"Just pull the yellow oxygen mask toward you. Then cover your mouth and breathe normally."

Each time a flight attendant says that prior to takeoff, I begin to wonder: How exactly do you breathe *normally* when an aircraft is having a serious problem that may soon give it the aerodynamic characteristics of a rock? I understand the physics of flight, but I am always astonished that masses of metal can become airborne. It is most amazing!

What causes an airplane to rise? The answer is a force called *lift*. A plane's wings are shaped so that air going across the upper surface moves at a higher velocity than the air going across the bottom surface. This causes a region of low pressure to form above the wing. The air pressure below the wing is greater than the air pressure above the wing, causing an unbalanced upward force. But in order to understand lift, children need to understand air pressure.

Real Teaching: Air pressure

If you live at sea level, there is about 15 pounds per square inch (psi) of air pressure on you every moment. If you live at 5,000 feet above sea level, the pressure is about 12 psi. So, if your hands measure roughly 7 in × 4 in, there are approximately 420 psi on each hand as you eat your sandwich at the beach. But we do not notice the pressure on us because we are acclimated to it. Consequently, it is often a challenge for students to grasp the concept of air pressure.

Today I explored air pressure with third-graders. They had just returned to school after 2 days off because of a snowstorm, which caused school to be cancelled. I thought the recent snowstorm would serve as a good hook for the class. [RELEVANCE] I began by asking whether they knew the storm was coming and if so, how did they know. [PRIOR KNOWLEDGE] Most replied they were told by their parents or teachers, or they heard about the pending storm on the news. I was hoping they would tell me about changes in weather that they experienced. I changed the question slightly, "Is anyone able to sense a storm is coming even before being told by someone else?" I received several affirmatives in the form of head nods and yesses. Great, now I was getting some traction. But I asked them a very convergent question. I had to get beyond yesses and head nods. "So tell me, what hints do you get from nature that a storm is coming?" I asked. [QUESTIONING] "The clouds get dark. The temperature goes down. It gets windier," were some of their answers. Meanwhile my colleague was writing the children's responses on the board. I nodded in agreement with their answers. The students were engaged and participating. Now was the time to transition to the topic of the day. "You know," I said, "There are other hints nature gives us. Sometimes they are not so obvious." [TRANSITION TO HOOK QUESTION] I projected a typical weather map on the interactive Smartboard depicting high and low pressure areas. "Do these look familiar?" I asked. Again, some head nods, one or two blank stares, and one enthusiastic student bouncing in their seat bursting to tell me about her aunt whose knee aches right before it rains. Okay, I thought, there is some evidence that joint conditions such as arthritis are affected by changes in air pressure. It is not too far-fetched, considering that even a slight change of 15 psi could easily be felt, especially in sensitive areas such as fluid in arthritic joints. It was important that I acknowledge children's contributions, so we added her aunt's knee to the list of hints about impending storms. [VALUING STUDENT RESPONSES] I was concerned about the blank stares. So I asked, "What is air pressure?" Not surprisingly, a student responded, "It is the pressure caused by the air." Hmm, not what I really wanted, but it is what I asked for. "Right," I said, "It is the pressure caused by air," and I thanked the students for their contributions. We needed a deeper dive into air pressure. Time for the challenge.

"Let's investigate air pressure. I have a challenge for you. I will give you a cup of water and a straw. Without using your mouth, try to pick up the water using the straw." The third-graders immediately put the straw in the water, placed their thumb on the end of the straw, and picked up the water. A few bent the straws and scooped up the water. Both strategies were valid. Although I did not expect the latter. I validated both strategies, but wondered aloud about the finger method: "Wait," I said. "The scooping method makes sense to me, but how does the finger method work?" Some hands went up, but this was a big idea I wanted them to think about. I asked them to turn and talk. [REFLECTION] Listening to the conversations I realized they were thinking about air pressure, but were having difficulty articulating the relationship and role of air pressure to make sense of the phenomenon. I asked them what would happen if they covered the end of the straw with their finger before putting it in the water, would the straw still pick up water. [GUIDED EXPLORATION]

I asked for a thumbs-up if they agreed that the straw would pick up water, a thumbs-down if they disagreed, and a neutral thumb if they were undecided. Responses were varied. "Let's try it," I said. We discovered that the straw did not pick up water when we placed our thumb on the end before putting it in the water. I followed up by saying, "Tell me your ideas about the role of air pressure in this demonstration." I wrote the big ideas they expressed on the board: Air pressure somehow keeps the water in the straw. Air is pushing.

I told them that I liked the way they were thinking. "Let's see what we can learn from another demonstration," I said. I filled a plastic cup as much as possible with water, and placed a piece of noncorrugated cardboard (a playing card or index card works well) over the mouth of the cup, and asked the students to predict what would happen when I turned the cup over. They predicted unanimously that the water would fall out. It did not! [DISCREPANT EVENT] A lot of "ooohs" and "aaahs" confirmed the demo grabbed their attention. Without much prompting from me they offered explanations. I prompted them to think about where the air was pushing. Again, a turn and talk was in order. It did not take long for Carlota to report out that the air was pushing on the cardboard. I asked Raul to restate what Carlota said. [TALK TOOLS] I asked the class whether they wanted to add to Carlota's explanation. Ezekiel added that the air pushed hard enough to keep the water from falling out. I asked him to come to the front of the room and point in the direction the air was pushing. He pointed to the cardboard. "Is the air pushing anywhere else?" I asked. "From the top, too," shouted one child. "And from the sides," offered another. We determined that the air was putting pressure on all sides of the cup, and the cardboard, too. But the air was blocked by the cup from pushing down on the water.

"I like your explanations," I said. "Please take out your science notebooks. Draw a diagram of the cup, water, and cardboard. Use arrows to show where the air pressure is. Complete this sentence: "The water stays in the cup because . . . ."

After writing, I asked the students to turn, talk, and compare answers. I asked for volunteers to report out. April volunteered, "The water stays in the cup because the air is pushing on it."

I asked whether students had any questions or comments about April's response. Some said they agreed. I asked April if she could explain what she meant by "it." What was the air pushing on? [TALK TOOL—SEEKING CLARIFICATION] April explained the air was pushing on the cardboard. Choral responses from the class were strongly in favor of April's claim.

Moving the lesson along, I projected a table of air pressure spanning the days prior to, during, and after the most recent storm (see Table 11.1). I used millimeters of mercury, another unit of barometric pressure, because the differences would be more pronounced and easier for students to see patterns. Units in this case are not as important as recognizing trends. "Look at the air pressure before, during, and after the storm. Tell me what trends you see." [CROSS CUTTING CONCEPT—PATTERNS] To help them visualize trends, I projected a graph of the data (Figure 11.3). "The pressure goes down when the storm comes," was the choral response. [SCIENCE PRACTICES: USING MATHEMATICS, ANALYZING AND INTERPRETING DATA]

Table 11.1 Air Pressure

	Air Pressure (mmHg)
Before Storm	1536
During Storm	1520
After Storm	1541

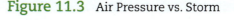

Figure 11.3   Air Pressure vs. Storm

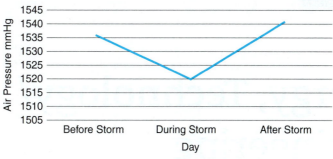

Summary

11.1 Explain how the kinetic molecular theory of matter can be used to explain fundamental properties of matter.

Anything that occupies space and has mass is matter. A change in matter from one state, or phase, to another is a physical change. The kinetic molecular theory is used to explain a variety of changes in matter.

11.2 Describe distinctive attributes of chemical reactions.

A change in matter that produces a new substance is a chemical change. Matter exists as elements, compounds, and mixtures. Atoms are composed of smaller particles. Matter is neither created nor destroyed, it changes form.

11.3 Provide examples for Newton's laws of motion.

Newton's laws of motion describe how the motion of an object will change as a result of the application of forces. Forces can be thought of as pushes or pulls. Push/pulls have two components: strength and direction. If the push/pulls are equal and opposite, no change in motion will occur. If they are unbalanced, a change in motion will occur. Changes can be observed in speed, direction, or both.

When objects come in contact, they exert forces on each other. The size of the forces depends on their masses and acceleration.

11.4 Explain how mass and distance relate to gravitational force.

The law of universal gravitation states that all masses are attracted to all other masses by a force that varies directly with the product of the masses and inversely with the square of the distance between them.

Chapter 11 Self-Check
Click to gauge your understanding of the concepts in this chapter.

Energy, Technology/ Engineering

Dmytro Zinkevych/Shutterstock

Learning Objectives

After completing the activities in this chapter, you should be able to:

12.1 Develop a working definition of energy.

12.2 Explain relationships between energy and forces.

12.3 Explain how energy transfer is related to potential energy, kinetic energy, and work.

12.4 Describe the meaning of the law of conservation of mass and energy.

12.5 Describe how waves relate to energy.

12.6 Identify properties of electrical, sound, light, and heat energy.

▶ **GETTING STARTED**

"Psssst. Drop your pencil at exactly 9:15. Pass it on."

A little mischief is going to take place, and a substitute's teaching day is about to take a turn for the worse. It's an old prank, but it will work once again. At precisely 9:15, 25 pencils fall from desktops to the floor, and innocent faces gaze about, waiting for the substitute's reaction.

I'll bet that the conspirators in the old drop-the-pencils-on-the-floor routine don't realize that they are demonstrating an important scientific phenomenon: the process of energy change. Imagine that the substitute teacher outsmarted the class by not reacting to the tap, tap, tap of the pencils, and the class decided to try a repeat performance. Follow the energy changes as the prank is recycled.

When you pick up the pencil from the floor and place it on your desk, you do work and use energy. Your body uses some of the energy created by the chemical breakdown of the food you eat. This energy enables you to move, grasp, and lift. It may surprise you to learn that when you pick up the pencil, some of the energy that you use increases the pencil's potential energy. The pencil resting on the desk has some potential energy. When it is lifted above the desktop, it has even more. It is higher above Earth than it was before, and if you drop it again, you will hear a sound when it hits the floor. That sound is produced when the potential energy of the falling pencil is converted to the energy of motion.

Conservation of Energy and Energy Transfer (PS3.B)

Energy is defined as the capacity to do work. This begs the question, "What is work?" Work occurs when force is applied to an object and the object moves. Wherever there is movement of an object resulting from a force acting on it, there is energy. Work always involves a transfer of energy. Electricity, light, sound, heat, and magnetism are all considered forms of energy.

Most systems, living and nonliving, can be understood by following the flow of energy. The flow of energy through food webs, the flow of energy in the atmosphere, the flow of energy into your home in the form of electricity, or the flow of energy in a river roaring through a gorge all involve motion and the transfer of energy from one form to another.

One way to think about energy transformation is to consider pulling a wagon up a hill. As the wagon gets higher up the hill, its potential to come down the hill increases. If you release the wagon and let it go down the hill, the force of gravity will act on it, accelerating it as it descends. The energy (capacity to do work or produce change) transferred as the wagon descends depends on the mass of the object and the height from which it is released. The higher the mass is lifted, the more potential it has to transfer energy and do work on its way down. Hence this stored energy is referred to as potential energy. Potential energy is dependent on the height and mass of objects. As height increases, the *potential* to transfer energy increases. In practical terms, a ping pong ball will not do as much damage as a bowling ball when both are dropped from the same height. For those of you who are interested in the mathematical expression of potential energy, you might appreciate Potential Energy = Mass*Gravity*Height ($PE = mgh$).

Earlier we suggested that energy is present whenever there are moving objects. Once the potential energy is transferred through movement, it is referred to as kinetic energy. Kinetic energy varies with mass and velocity. The heavier and faster an object is moving the more energy (capacity to do work or produce change) it can transfer. Think of the bowling ball and ping pong ball. The faster and heavier the ball, the more damage it does upon impact. The mathematical expression for kinetic energy is $\frac{1}{2}$ Mass * Velocity^2 (KE $= \frac{1}{2}$ mv^2).

The Conservation of Energy

The ability of energy to change its form is the basis of the *law of conservation of energy*. This important law simply states that energy is neither created nor destroyed. But it can be transformed from one form to another.

Whenever we use energy, we change its form, but we do not use it up. The energy we use may be changed to a less useful form, but it still exists. In the example of the pencil being picked up, placed on a table, and dropped again, some of the Sun's energy was initially stored in food. Your digestive and cellular-respiration processes released some of this energy, and you used this energy to lift the pencil. In the process, the pencil acquired potential energy from its new position, and as it fell, it displayed increasing kinetic energy. The kinetic energy was changed to heat and sound. It is at least theoretically possible, if difficult in practice, to recapture this heat and sound energy and reuse it. All the energy you used to pick up the pencil still exists. It has just changed to other forms of energy.

According to Albert Einstein, energy and matter are related. In fact, they can be considered one and the same, because each can be converted to the other. Einstein's equation $E = mc^2$ does not contradict the law of conservation of energy because mass can be viewed as stored energy. Scientists no longer say that energy is never used up; instead, they prefer to say that the total amount of energy and mass in the universe is never used up. The interchangeability of mass and energy has resulted in the use of a more general law than either the law of conservation of energy or the law of conservation of mass. Now it is generally agreed that we should think in terms of a *law of conservation of mass and energy*.

Relationship Between Energy and Forces (PS3.C)

Energy can be transferred from one object to another. When a bowling ball strikes pins, some energy is transferred on contact to the bowling pins, resulting in a change in motion of both the bowling pins and bowling ball. Energy is also transferred to the air, resulting in the sound of the ball hitting the pins. If we could measure the air temperature around the ball, we would record a slight increase in temperature as well.

Energy in Chemical Processes and Everyday Life (PS3.D)

You may be wondering how other forms of energy such as electrical, solar, or chemical energy apply to the idea of energy as the capacity to do work or effect change. At the risk of oversimplifying, these energy transformations occur through movement as well, not of bowling balls, but movement of much smaller particles.

For example, during photosynthesis solar energy changes the positions of electrons (where electrons are said to enter an excited state) by moving them farther away from the atomic forces attracting them, similar to a bowling ball being lifted farther from the ground. The electrons gain potential energy as they move away from the atomic force. When they return to their initial position (ground state), energy is transferred. In photosynthesis, solar energy excites electrons. The energy transferred is used to create chemical bonds that stored energy (carbohydrate). When the carbohydrate is digested by an organism, the stored energy is again transferred and used by the organism for any number of functions such as growth or movement.

The concept of energy flow is a unifying theme that applies across domains. Whether it be weather, ocean currents, ecosystems, or flight, looking at the system through the lens of energy flow can make understanding the principles underlying these phenomena easier to understand.

● Waves and Their Applications in Technologies for Information Transfer (PS4)

Waves are fundamental to understanding energy transfer. Energy waves travel through matter, such as air, water, or space. But the medium itself does not travel. Rather, the medium is displaced. An example would be "the wave" done by spectators in a sports stadium. As the wave moves around the stadium, each person moves up and down perpendicular to the direction of the wave, but no one moves forward with the wave. Their position in the direction of the wave does not change.

Recall that energy is related to motion. As each person stands up, they generate potential energy, which is transferred as kinetic energy when they sit down and return to a more stable state. A similar pattern can be observed by waves in the water. When energy waves move across the water, molecules of water move up and down, thereby transferring energy. Sound waves similarly displace air molecules as energy travels through air.

Electrical and magnetic waves are a bit more difficult to envision, but they transfer energy similarly through displacement of electric or magnetic fields. The energy released can be transformed to other forms of energy such as light, heat, or mechanical energy. Digital devices such as cell phones, computers, and satellites send signals as wave pulses that are converted into useful information such as sound or pictures.

Waves are usually described by their height, the distance from the lowest part of the wave (trough) to its highest part (peak), and wavelength, which is the distance between wave peaks. Height and wavelengths can range from several meters in ocean waves to nanometers for light waves.

Electrical Energy

The bright flash of lightning jumping across the night sky and the subdued light coming from a desk lamp are both produced by electrical energy. They are similar to each other in their transmission of electrical charge through electrons, which can be thought of as charge carriers. Lightening differs, however, in that lightning is a form of static electricity, and the light from a desk lamp is a form of current electricity.

● Static Electricity

Lightning, a spark jumping from your fingertip to a metal doorknob, and the clinging together of articles of clothing when they are removed from a clothes dryer are all forms of *static electricity*. In order to understand them, you need to review your knowledge of atoms. An atom consists of protons, neutrons, and electrons. Each proton has a positive charge—one unit of positive energy. Each electron has a negative charge—one unit of negative energy. Neutrons have no charge. Because atoms normally have the same number of electrons as protons, the positive and negative charges cancel each other out. As a result, atoms usually have no netcharge; they are considered neutral.

If, however, an electron is removed from a neutral atom, the atom is left with a positive charge. If an electron is added to a neutral atom, the atom acquires a negative charge. When certain materials are rubbed together, electrons are transferred from one surface to the other. In other words, one surface gains electrons and acquires a negative charge. The other surface, having lost electrons, is left with a positive charge. When a surface has acquired a strong negative charge, the extra electrons may jump to a neutral or positive object. You see this jump of electrons when you see a spark. A spark is a rapid movement of a number of electrons through the air.

You may have had the exciting adolescent experience being shocked by a spark during a kiss. The excitement may have come from the kiss, but the shock was the result of static electricity. Electrons were probably inadvertently rubbed from the fibers of a rug or other floor covering by the soles of the "kisser" or "kissee," giving that person's body a surplus negative charge. The extra charge was removed by the spark jumping from the negatively charged person to the neutrally charged person.

Lightning is a giant spark that sometimes occurs when clouds that have acquired a charge suddenly discharge electrons. The rapid outward movement of the air heated by the lightning causes the sound wave that reaches our ears as thunder.

Current Electricity

Sometimes it seems that my doorbell never stops ringing, and, if I am busy, I get grumpier each time it rings. If I get grumpy enough, sometimes I curse Benjamin Franklin, Thomas Edison, and my local electric company all in one breath for bringing electrical energy to my home. Even so, I know we are living at a time when electricity is a necessity, not a luxury. Occasional electrical blackouts bring activities to a grinding halt: Traffic lights don't work; elevators stop wherever they happen to be; heating and cooling equipment stops functioning; lights go out; and food in refrigerators begins to rot. Electricity has become a necessity for us because it is an excellent and convenient form of energy. It can be converted to heat, to light, and to sound. It can also be used to operate electric motors that cause objects to move.

Electricity has become an integral part of our lives. It would be very difficult to live without it. But it is often misunderstood. We often learn that *current electricity* is the movement of charge along a stream of electrons moving through a conductor. The rate at which the charge moves through the conductor is called *current*. But what do charge and current really mean? What is happening in a wire as current flows through it? Contrary to popular belief, electrons move very slowly through wire, typically about 1 meter per hour! One way to think of charge and current is to imagine thousands of snails packed together on a 1-meter race course. The snails fill the entire course. Each snail moves very slowly, but every second, hundreds of snails cross the finish line. In this analogy, snails are the electrons. The current is measured by the number of snails that cross the finish line per second. Therefore, the current can be high although the electrons move slowly. The unit for measuring electrical current is the *ampere* (amp). It is equal to the flow of 6.25×10^{18} electrons (snails) past a point (finish line) in a conductor (race course) in 1 second. Electron current that moves in just one direction is termed *direct current*. Electricity from dry cells (batteries) is direct current. Current that changes direction is known as *alternating current*. Electricity for home or industrial use is alternating current.

A *conductor* is any material with available electrons that can transmit charge easily. Such a material offers little *resistance* to the charge or current. The amount of resistance to the flow of electrical energy is measured in *ohms*. Examples of materials that are good conductors include copper, silver, gold, and aluminum. Electrical charge moving through a conductor results in many collisions of electrons that transfer the energy down the line. Think of a long chain of marbles in a tube. When the marble at one end is pushed, the marble at the other end moves.

Not all substances are good electrical conductors. Wood, rubber, plastic, and dry air are examples of substances that do not carry electrical energy very well. Because these materials are poor conductors, they offer high resistance to the flow of charge and are called *insulators*.

Some substances—for example, germanium, silicon, and selenium—are neither conductors nor insulators. They are *semiconductors* that can be used to make tiny electrical devices to control the flow of electrons. Semiconductors are widely used in the fabrication of computer chips.

Electrical Circuits

Figure 12.1 illustrates a simple electrical circuit. In an electrical circuit, electrons with a great deal of energy leave a source (in this case, a dry cell), move through a conductor (a wire), lose some energy in a load or resistance (a lightbulb), and return to the source. As long as the switch is closed (the wires are connected), energy is transmitted through the circuit. The lightbulb—the resistance—converts some of the electrical energy to light energy.

In the types of electrical circuits illustrated in Figures 12.1 and 12.2, chemical reactions in the dry cell provide the push that starts and keeps high-energy flowing into the conductor. The charge leaves the negative pole, or port, and returns to the dry cell at the positive pole, or port. The force with which the charge moves through a circuit is called the *voltage*. The voltage that a dry cell can produce is measured by determining the amount of work a charge can do as it goes through a circuit. The unit of measurement for voltage is *volts*.

Although there are many ways to attach sources of high-energy charges, conductors, and loads to each other, we usually concern ourselves with two basic circuits: series circuits and parallel circuits. A *series circuit* has only one path for current. A circuit that has more than one path for the current is a *parallel circuit*. Figure 12.1 shows a series circuit. Figure 12.2 shows a parallel circuit.

Because there is only one path, the current is the same throughout a series circuit. In a parallel circuit, however, the current is divided among many paths. If one lightbulb in a series circuit burns out, all the lightbulbs will go out because only one path for electrons exists. If a lightbulb in one branch of a parallel circuit burns out, the bulbs in the other branches will remain lit.

Figure 12.1 In this electric circuit, the lamps are wired in series.

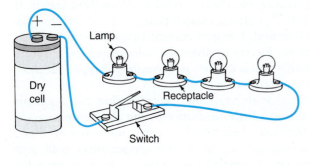

Figure 12.2 When lamps are wired in parallel, as shown here, the bulbs will remain lit even if one goes out.

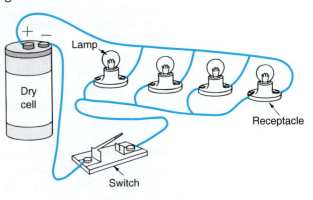

● Magnets, Generators, and Motors

Although chemical reactions in dry cells can start current flowing through a conductor, moving a conductor through a magnetic field or moving a magnet so that the lines of force in the magnetic field cut through the conductor can also start a flow of current. Metals that have the ability to attract iron, steel, and some other metals are said to have a property called *magnetism*. Magnetite, or lodestone, is a naturally occurring iron ore that has such magnetic properties. Alnico—a material that contains aluminum, nickel, cobalt, and iron—can be used to make a permanent magnet, even though aluminum, nickel, cobalt, and iron are not naturally magnetic. When these substances are brought near a strong magnet, they become magnetic.

All magnets have two poles: a north pole and a south pole. A bar magnet suspended at its center by a string will rotate until one end points north. The magnet end that points north is known as the *north-seeking pole*. The other end of the magnet is the *south-seeking pole*. If two N poles or two S poles are brought near each other, they will repel. When unlike poles are brought near each other, they attract. The rotation of a freely suspended bar magnet until it is oriented north and south is evidence that Earth itself is a magnet. Earth's magnetic pole attracts the pole of a magnet.

Around all magnets is a region that we call a *magnetic field*. If we move a conductor through a magnetic field so that it cuts through the lines of force in the field, an electric current will be produced in the conductor. An electrical generator produces electrical energy either by spinning a coiled conductor between the poles of a magnet or by rotating a magnet or series of magnets around a coiled conductor. Of course, a source of energy is needed to spin the coiled conductor or rotate the magnets. For commercial electrical generators, that source may be moving water; fossil fuels such as coal, gas, and oil; or nuclear fission.

An electrical generator permits us to produce electricity. An electric motor permits us to put electricity to work moving objects. A **simple electric motor** converts electrical energy into the energy of motion by means of a coil of wire wrapped around a metal core. This wire-wrapped core is suspended between the magnetic poles of a permanent magnet. When current flows through the coil, it becomes a magnet. The coil's N and S poles are repelled by the N and S poles of the permanent magnet. As a result of this repulsion, the coil turns. If we change the direction of flow of electricity through the coil, the location of its N and S poles will change. The coil will continue to spin as its ends are continually repelled by the poles of the permanent magnet.

Real Teaching: Simple Circuit

I observed as a team of preservice elementary teachers taught a lesson about simple circuits to a diverse class of fourth-graders. The lesson began when one member of the teaching team announced that she wanted to show the class a demonstration of reflection using a flashlight. She deliberately used a flashlight that did not work and feigned surprise that it was inoperative. She wondered aloud why the flashlight did not work. She asked the children for their thoughts on the matter. "Check for batteries," "Bulb's out," "Return it to the store," "Just use your phone," were some of the answers. The teacher nodded and replied, "Those are some interesting ideas. I have another idea. Could you all draw some diagrams of how you understand a flashlight works?" Most of the students answered in the affirmative, so other members of the teaching team passed out blank sheets of paper for the students to make their diagrams (Figure 12.3).

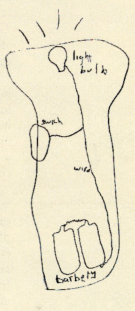

Figure 12.3
Example of student flashlight diagram

The students posted their diagrams around the room and were given 5 minutes to do a gallery walk. They received post-it notes and were tasked with writing one question they had after looking at the diagrams. This activity resulted in a bit of chaos, as there was minimal direction provided to organize gallery walk. The children tended to congregate around the same diagrams, which were closely spaced and did not allow for students to distribute themselves. [CLASSROOM MANAGEMENT]

Eventually the teaching team was able to get the students back in their seats. About half of the students generated questions. The diagrams revealed students' conceptions of simple circuits. It became clear that while students generally identified the basic components such as energy sources (batteries), energy converter (bulb), and conductors, most were not aware of the properties of these components and how they interacted to form the emergent properties of a simple circuit system. [PRIOR KNOWLEDGE/ FORMATIVE ASSESSMENT]

The teaching team acknowledged that the students identified some key components of the flashlight. They asked the students, "How do these pieces work together to make the light bulb light?" [HOOK QUESTION] The children were grouped in teams of two. Each team was given the components they all agreed were in a flashlight: one battery, two wires, and light bulb. They were challenged to use these components to make the bulb light. The teachers were skeptical during their planning that such an unstructured activity would be doable for the students. Therefore, they were ready with question prompts to coach groups. As it worked out, some groups did get the bulb to light up. News of how they did so spread from group to group, until eventually all groups succeeded.

Time allotted for the class was running out at this point. The teaching team asked the students to make another diagram of how the battery, wires, and bulbs were arranged to make the bulb light. They would compare this post exploration diagram with the diagram of the flashlight done during class engagement. Subsequent lessons would address the properties of each component and their interactions to complete the circuit.

Sound Energy

Sounds affect us in many different ways. The purring of a kitten brushing against your leg may make you feel wanted. The chirping of baby birds may make you feel joyful. The uproarious and chaotic sounds of sanitation workers waking up your neighborhood with an early morning symphony of bangs, crunches, screeches, and shouts may annoy you immensely. But what causes the sounds that bring you pleasure or irritation?

● What Causes Sound?

All sounds, whether they come from a garbage-can orchestra or a kitten, are produced by vibrating matter. A vibrating object receives energy from a source (a kitten or a dropped garbage can) and transfers energy to a *medium*, such as air. The medium carries the energy away from the vibrating object. Sound travels in all directions from its source. In other words, you can hear a sound whether your ears are above it, to the side of it, or below it.

A vibrating tuning fork is a good example of a source of sound. When a tuning fork is struck, its prongs move back and forth rapidly. When a prong moves in one direction, it presses together the modules in the air ahead of it. This pressing together of air is known as a *compression*. As the tuning fork moves in the opposite direction, it causes a portion of air to pull apart. This area is known as a *rarefaction*. The movement of each prong back and forth alternately produces compression and rarefaction.

The molecules in the air disturbed by the vibration of the tuning fork during compression transfer energy to adjacent molecules before returning to their original positions during rarefaction. The newly disturbed molecules pass some of their energy on to still other molecules, and the process is repeated. If you could see the molecules being disturbed, you would see areas of compression and rarefaction, or *sound waves*, being continuously created and moving away from the source of the vibration. A full sound wave consists of one compression and one rarefaction.

Sound waves require a medium for transmission. They travel most rapidly through solids and least rapidly through gases. At a temperature of 0°C, sound travels at a speed of 340 meters (about 1,090 feet) per second in air. In water, sound travels at about 1,420 meters (4,686 feet) per second. Sound waves cannot travel through a vacuum, so, if you are wondering how astronauts communicate with one another in the vacuum of space, they do so using radio transmissions. Radio waves do not require a medium.

The *wavelength* of a sound wave is the distance between the centers of two rarefactions. The amount of energy contained in a wave is interpreted by our ears as the loudness or softness of a sound. The loudness, or *amplitude*, of a sound is measured in decibels. The *pitch* of a sound—how high or low the sound is—depends on the number of complete vibrations that the vibrating object makes in one second. This rate of vibration is known as the *frequency*.

● Sound Can Be Absorbed or Reflected

Sound waves that strike a surface may be so strong that they travel through the object struck. However, some surfaces absorb little sound and cause the sound wave being received to bounce off the surface, or be reflected. Reflected sound waves that can be distinguished from the original sound are known as *echoes*. Although echoes are interesting to hear, they can be distracting. Therefore, many classrooms are fitted with sound-absorbing tiles or draperies.

Some of the energy carried by a sound wave causes the surface of the object it strikes to heat up slightly. Usually, the amount of heat produced cannot be detected without the use of special instruments.

Light Energy

Light energy, like sound energy, travels in waves, but a light wave is very different from a sound wave. Light waves travel at a speed of 300,000 kilometers (186,000 miles) per second and do not require a medium. Thus, light waves, unlike sound waves, can travel through a vacuum.

Light energy is produced from other types of energy. If we burn a substance, one of the products of combustion is light energy. The light is released as a result of the electrons in the substance changing energy levels as new compounds are formed. Electric lightbulbs change electrical energy to light energy. The light energy that reaches us from the Sun and other stars is the result of nuclear fusion. In stars, huge amounts of matter are converted to energy as a result of nuclear fusion. In nuclear fusion, hydrogen atoms are fused together to form helium atoms, a process accompanied by the release of light energy as well as other types of energy.

Light energy can be transformed into other forms of energy, such as heat or electricity. If you've ever had a sunburn, you've experienced both the conversion of light energy into heat (as your skin became warm) and the effect of light energy on the molecules of substances that make up your skin (as it turned red or blistered).

The Reflection and Refraction of Light

Light is able to pass through some materials, such as clear plastic or glass. A material that light can pass through is called *transparent*. Materials that light cannot pass through are called *opaque*. Materials that permit some, but not all, light to pass through are called *translucent*. Windows made of frosted glass are translucent.

As light passes from one medium to another, it is bent, or *refracted*. Light traveling through air bends as it enters water, glass, or clear plastic. This bending, or refraction, of light waves can be put to good use. A lens, for example, changes the appearance of objects because the image we see through the lens is produced by rays of light that have been bent. Eyeglasses, microscopes, hand lenses, and telescopes all provide images formed by light rays that have been refracted.

A *convex* lens is thicker in the middle than it is at its edges. Such a lens pulls light rays together. The point at which rays of light are brought together by the lens is called the *focal point*. The distance from the focal point to the center of the lens is the lens's *focal length*. When light is reflected from an object through a convex lens, the rays of light are brought together at the focal point, and an image is formed. The size, position, and type of image formed depend on the distance of the object from the lens. If the object is more than one focal length from the lens, the image is inverted and formed on the opposite side of the lens. This type of image is called a *real image*, and it can be projected onto a screen. If the image is two focal lengths away, the image is the same size as the object.

If the object is less than one focal length from the lens, the image formed is magnified and right-side up. This type of image is called a *virtual image*. It is formed on the same side of the lens as the object and can be seen by looking through the lens toward the object, but it cannot be placed on a screen. When you use a convex lens as a magnifier, the image you see is a virtual image.

The refraction of light through a lens can be illustrated with a *ray diagram*. Look at the ray diagrams in Figure 12.4. As you study them, note that the *principal axis* is an imaginary line passing perpendicular to the lens through its center. The *virtual focus* is the point on the axis at which the light would converge if you passed the light through the lens to the object, rather than from the object to the lens.

A lens that is thicker at its edges than at its center is a *concave lens*. A concave lens causes light rays to bend toward its edges. This type of lens can produce only virtual images that are smaller than the real objects (see Figure 12.5).

● Light, Prisms, and Color

Have you ever been surprised to see an array of colors projected on a wall or ceiling as a result of sunlight passing through a crystal glass? This band of colors is called a *spectrum*. Some pieces of glass are made to separate sunlight or artificial light into a spectrum. A triangle-shaped piece of such glass is called a *prism*.

Figure 12.4 These ray diagrams for convex lenses illustrate how a convex lens focuses light. Light passing through the lens converges to form an image that can be seen on a screen when the object is more than one focal length from the lens. When the object is less than one focal length from the lens, a virtual image is formed. It cannot be projected on a screen.

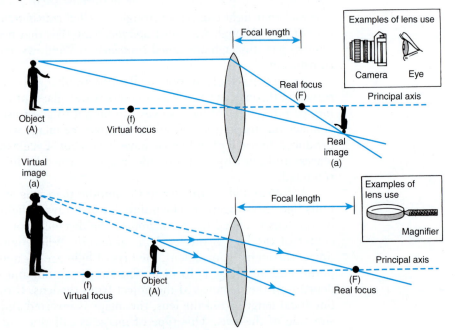

Figure 12.5 As this ray diagram for a concave lens illustrates, the lens disperses light, and the image produced cannot be seen on a screen.

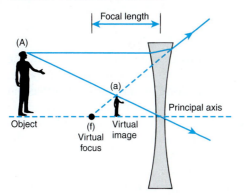

The colors of a spectrum represent the components of a light wave that enters a prism. As the light wave is refracted by the prism, the light is separated according to wavelengths. Each wavelength corresponds to a different color. The colors of a spectrum caused by the refraction of light by a prism are red, orange, yellow, green, blue, indigo, and violet.

The color of an object we see is a property of the wavelength reflected from the object. *Pigments*—the chemical substances that we usually think of as the sources of color—actually produce their effects because they absorb some light waves and reflect others. Grass is green to our eyes because pigments in grass absorb the red, orange, yellow, blue, indigo, and violet wavelengths and reflect the green.

Heat Energy

Suppose that one hot summer afternoon, you decide to buy a double-dip chocolate ice cream cone and sit in the park while you eat it. As you walk toward the park clutching your cone, you will certainly notice the effect of heat on ice cream. Heat from the hot surrounding air will flow to the colder ice cream, causing an increase in the temperature of the ice cream, a lowering of the temperature of the surrounding air, and the immediate need for a napkin as the change in the temperature of the ice cream results in a change in the ice cream's state—from solid to liquid. The phenomenon of melting can be a good starting point for understanding heat and how it brings about change.

● What Is Heat?

Heat is energy that travels from a warm substance to a cool substance. Keep in mind that all substances are made of molecules, and molecules, even in solids, are in constant motion. The motion and positions of these molecules determine the internal energy of (the energy within) a substance. If the molecules in a substance move slowly, the substance has a low level of internal energy. If the molecules move rapidly, the substance has a high level of internal energy. *Temperature* is an indication of the internal energy of a substance. The higher the temperature of a substance, the greater its internal energy and the more heat it releases to a cool substance. The temperature of a substance is measured in *degrees*. There are two temperature scales in wide use: the Celsius (centigrade) scale and the Fahrenheit scale.

A *thermometer*, which measures temperature, consists of a narrow column of tinted alcohol sealed in a glass tube. (You may remember mercury thermometers, which have largely been replaced by alcohol or digital thermometers.) Changes in temperature cause the liquid in a thermometer to expand or contract. Because the alcohol within the thermometer expands and contracts more than the surrounding glass with each degree of temperature change, we can see changes in the alcohol level.

Two important markings on all thermometers are the freezing and boiling points of water. The Celsius thermometer shows the temperature at which water freezes as 0° and the temperature at which water boils as 100°. The Fahrenheit scale shows the temperature at which water freezes as 32° and the boiling temperature as 212°. Wherever possible, use a Celsius thermometer and Celsius measurements in the classroom.

● How Is Heat Measured?

Because it is virtually impossible to add up the individual energies possessed by the millions of individual molecules found in even a very small amount of a substance, heat energy must be measured indirectly. This is done by measuring its effect on a substance. The standard unit of heat is the *calorie*, the heat required to raise the temperature of 1 gram of water 1° Celsius. Because this is a very small amount of heat, the *kilocalorie*, which equals 1,000 calories, is a more practical unit. The energy contained in foods is expressed in kilocalories.

In the English system of measurement, the British thermal unit (Btu) is the standard unit of heat. This is the amount of heat required to raise the temperature of 1 pound of water 1° Fahrenheit.

Summary

12.1 Develop a working definition of energy.

Earth systems are about energy flow. Energy is expressed in a variety of ways by the scientific and engineering communities. At a basic level, energy can be thought of as the capacity to do work or effect change.

12.2 Explain relationships between energy and forces.

The transformation as well as the transfer of energy allows us to harness the energy to sustain life, move mountains, and run our computers.

12.3 Explain how energy transfer is related to potential energy, kinetic energy, and work.

Potential energy refers to objects, large or small, that are in a state to release energy when forces act upon them. Potential energy increases with its distance from the source of the force. We are perhaps most aware of potential energy that results from the height of an object above the ground. Kinetic energy is associated with motion and results from the movement of an object as a force acts upon it. Most people are familiar with the force of gravity acting on objects dropped from heights.

12.4 Describe the meaning of the law of conservation of mass and energy.

The law of conservation of energy reminds us that energy cannot be destroyed. Fortunately, it can be changed from one form to another.

12.5 Describe how waves relate to energy.

Energy travels in waves, which can be described by their amplitude and wavelength. Energy is transmitted through media, such as water and air without moving the media in the direction of the wave, but rather displacing the media perpendicular to the wave. Electrical and magnetic energy displace electrical and magnetic fields, respectively.

12.6 Identify properties of electrical, sound, light, and heat energy.

Static electricity results from the movement of electrons between atoms that build up charge that is ultimately discharged to another object. Current electricity is the constant flow of electrons through conductors. Sound and light energy can both be described by waves. Sound energy requires a medium whereas light energy can travel through a vacuum. Heat energy is a function of the internal energy of a substance due to the movement of molecules within the substance.

Chapter 12 Self-Check
Click to gauge your understanding of the concepts in this chapter.

Introduction to Appendices

Each appendix includes examples of discipline-specific ideas for putting content into action. The activities and suggested articulation with disciplinary core ideas are by no means comprehensive or exhaustive. In and of themselves, they do not represent 3-D learning. They are intended to provide you with some ideas to create your own innovative science learning experiences for children.

> Appendix A: Earth/Space
> Appendix B: Life Sciences
> Appendix C: Physical Sciences

Each appendix is organized into five sections:

Unit Plan Ideas and Questions

Unit plan ideas are organized by Disciplinary Core Idea Arrangements of the NGSS. They include a unit title, a question, and a brief unit overview.

MAKE THE CASE: An Individual or Group Challenge

This section challenges the reader to reflect on the use of phenomena in 3-D teaching and identify potential phenomena for disciplinary core ideas.

Classroom Enrichment Ideas

This section makes suggestions for discovery centers, bulletin boards, and field trips that could enrich each content area. Suggestions for articulation with disciplinary core ideas are listed in parenthesis for each enrichment idea.

Examples of Topics and Phenomena

Suggested phenomena are given for selected topics in each discipline along with motivating questions, activities, and science content that support the topic for teachers.

Discovery Activities

These are activities that you may find helpful to support teaching in the content area. Each activity includes objectives, science processes, materials, a motivation (engagement), directions, discussion questions, and science content for the teacher.

Earth/Space Science

Putting the Content into Action

Unit Plan Ideas and Questions

● **Earth Systems**

UNIT TITLE: *Our Earth Changes*

QUESTION: Is Earth the same place today as it was yesterday, last year, when I was born, when dinosaurs roamed?

UNIT OVERVIEW: Using observations over a short period along with photographs, illustrations, and interviews for longer periods, children recognize changes in Earth's landforms, weather, and climate.

UNIT TITLE: *The Earth Is a System*

QUESTION: What is beneath the surface of Earth?

UNIT OVERVIEW: Students describe the layers of Earth, its core, and how the core and layers interact.

UNIT TITLE: *Solid or Not?*

QUESTION: What are the forces that shape Earth?

UNIT OVERVIEW: Students present evidence that supports the hypothesis that the solid Earth beneath their feet is constantly changing. Their descriptions will include references to the movements of plates, constructive and destructive forces, and the rock cycle (i.e., the change of old rocks to particles and their eventual reformation into rocks).

UNIT TITLE: *Gradual Changes in the Earth*

QUESTION: How is Earth changing from day to day?

UNIT OVERVIEW: Students identify modern Earth processes—such as plate movement, erosion, and atmospheric changes—and make hypotheses about whether these processes have also occurred in the past.

UNIT TITLE: *Weather Prediction*

QUESTION: How do we know a storm is coming?

UNIT OVERVIEW: Students identify the forms of technology used by meteorologists and build a model of at least one instrument used to gather weather observations.

UNIT TITLE: *My Rock Collection*

QUESTIONS: Could you pick your rock out of a group? What is the same and different about rocks?

UNIT OVERVIEW: Students gather rocks outdoors, observe them, learn that they are made of different substances, and classify them.

UNIT TITLE: *Soils Here/Soils There*

QUESTIONS: What is the dirt on dirt? What are properties of soils, and what do they tell us about where the soil comes from?

UNIT OVERVIEW: Students collect soil samples from various locations, observe them, and classify them on the basis of color, particle size, texture, and how they react with water.

● Earth's Place in the Universe

UNIT TITLE: *Look to the Sky*

QUESTION: What do you see when you look in the sky?

UNIT OVERVIEW: Through observations of the sky during the day and at night, children describe objects in the sky, near and far (e.g., clouds, stars, Moon, Sun [do not observe the Sun directly], planes, and birds). They identify the general properties, relationships in space, and movements of the objects.

UNIT TITLE: *The Planets and the Stars*

QUESTION: Where are the planets and the stars?

UNIT OVERVIEW: Children learn the relative spatial relationships of the planets within our solar system and the visible stars.

UNIT TITLE: *The Sun, Moon, and Earth*

QUESTION: How do cycles of the Sun, Moon, and Earth create years, months, and days?

UNIT OVERVIEW: Through actual observations, charts, diagrams, and simulations, children learn that Earth revolves around the Sun in approximately

365 days and rotates on an axis once per day. The Moon revolves around Earth in approximately 30 days (one month).

UNIT TITLE: *The Solar System*

QUESTION: Where are we, really?

UNIT OVERVIEW: Students create charts, graphs, and drawings that demonstrate their knowledge of the position of Earth in the solar system and the locations of the other seven planets, moons, asteroids, and comets.

UNIT TITLE: *Children of the Sun*

QUESTION: How is Earth solar powered?

UNIT OVERVIEW: Students give evidence that supports the hypothesis that the Sun is the major source of energy for phenomena such as plant growth, winds, ocean currents, and the water cycle.

● Earth and Human Activity

UNIT TITLE: *Understanding Climate Change*

QUESTION: What changes are taking place in the climate?

UNIT OVERVIEW: Students use evidence to determine what is changing in the climate. In the process, they learn more about what climate is and the relationships among climate factors affecting change. *Hint:* Learn how to use NASA's Global Climate Change website in your classroom.

Make the CASE *An Individual or Group Challenge*

● The Problem

Three-dimensional teaching often begins with a phenomenon. It can be challenging to find a suitable phenomenon that inspires students, in their quest to figure out an explanation, to dive deeply into a topic that leads them to uncover core science concepts.

● Assess Your Prior Knowledge and Beliefs

1. Write your interpretation of the following statement:
   Phenomena do not need to be phenomenal to be academically productive.
2. Discuss your interpretation with colleagues.

● The Challenge

Identify phenomena that you might use to anchor a unit about the roles of water in Earth's surface processes (ESS2.C).

Justify the phenomena by explaining how they could drive students to uncover core science concepts.

Classroom Enrichment Ideas

● Discovery Centers

A well-prepared in-class learning center offers children many opportunities to make their own discoveries. To be well-prepared, such a center must provide a wide range of materials that encourage hands-on, discovery-based learning, ranging from print and audiovisual resources to art supplies and games. The learning center must be located where children have ready access to it yet can be somewhat removed from the larger classroom setting while doing independent activities. The following starter ideas for in-class discovery centers should get you thinking about how to create centers in your own classroom. Suggestions for connections with disciplinary core ideas are included in parentheses.

CENTER TITLE: *Spaceship Earth* (**ESS1.B: Earth and the Solar System**)

IDEA: Place this center in a location where students can turn out the lights when necessary (see Figure A.1). Make available space for working with clay, assembling models, and making large murals. In the center, arrange a library section containing books about the Sun, Earth, seasons, stars, planets, and the solar system. If you have a computer with relevant software and internet access, place it in or near the center as well. Provide activity cards or guide sheets that give directions for activities based on the following ideas:

- **Globe Explorations** Children locate where they live on the globe along with nearby bodies of water and a place to which they have traveled.

Figure A.1   This learning center—Spaceship Earth—provides enough activities and materials to hold the children's interest throughout the unit.

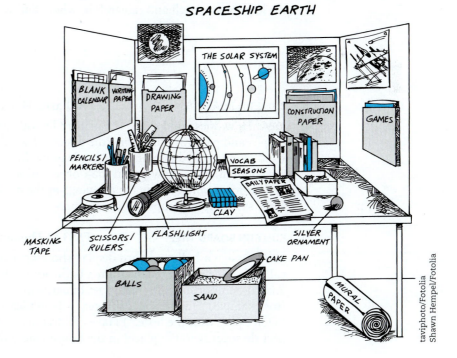

taviphoto/Fotolia
Shawn Hempel/Fotolia

- **Seasons Murals** Children draw or paint murals that show seasonal changes.
- **Phases of the Moon** Children take home calendars and draw the nightly shape of the Moon over the course of four weeks.
- **Clay Planets** Children make labeled models of the Sun and planets.
- **Reflection** Children observe how the visibility of a ball of foil or a silver ornament changes when light from a flashlight strikes the surface of the ball or ornament in bright light and in total darkness.
- **Surface of the Moon** Children model the Moon's surface by shaping sand in a pie plate.

CENTER TITLE: *Wild Weather* (ESS3.B: Natural Hazards)

IDEA: Identify characteristics of violent weather phenomena, make related drawings, and illustrate the safety precautions to be followed for each.

CENTER TITLE: *Wet and Wonderful* (ESS2.C: The Roles of Water in Earth's Surface Processes)

IDEA: Make models of mountains and riverbeds with sand and soil, pour water on them, and observe how the water travels through and changes each model.

CENTER TITLE: *What's a Land Form?* (ESS2.A: Earth Materials and Systems)

IDEA: Use art materials to create various landscapes, then label mountains, hills, plateaus, and valleys.

CENTER TITLE: *Constellation Celebration* (ESS1.A: The Universe and Its Stars)

IDEA: Use art materials to make diagrams of the major constellations. Label the key stars in each and research if, when, and where they will be visible.

Bulletin Boards

BULLETIN BOARD TITLE: *Wind* (ESS2.A: Earth Materials and Systems)

IDEA: How does wind shape the planet? Provide and display various photographs and pictures illustrating the effects of wind (e.g., dunes changed by wind, wind-eroded mountains, trees leaning due to prevailing winds). Have the children make drawings of their observations about the impact of wind on landforms and include the drawings in the display. Children may also write stories to accompany their pictures.

BULLETIN BOARD TITLE: *Save Water* (ESS3.C: Human Impacts on Earth Systems)

IDEA: Design a bulletin board display showing a cutaway view of a typical house. Include in the diagram a bathroom, a kitchen, a laundry room, and an outdoor hose. Prepare a set of cards that list ideas for saving water (for example, "Take a short shower," "Don't leave the water running," and "Don't play with the hose.") Have children use yarn and push pins to connect these ideas to the places in the house where they should be carried out.

BULLETIN BOARD TITLE: *Shadows on the Moon* (**ESS1.B: Earth and the Solar System**)

IDEA: Use cutouts representing Earth, the Moon, and the Sun to depict why the Moon appears to be crescent-shaped. Prepare other cutouts to represent the various phases of the Moon, and have the children arrange them on the bulletin board in the proper sequence.

BULLETIN BOARD TITLE: *Natural Features* (**ESS2.B: Plate Tectonics and Large-Scale System Interactions**)

IDEA: Provide a set of labels for land types, including grasslands, mountains, hills, lakes, rivers, and so on. Attach pictures showing examples of each land type to the board. Challenge the children to attach the pictures under the correct headings.

BULLETIN BOARD TITLE: *Land Shapes* (**ESS2.A: Earth Materials and Systems**)

IDEA: Place on the bulletin board a large topographical map that includes a key. Then place cards on the board representing different physical features that can be found on the map. Have the children attach the cards to the proper locations on the map.

BULLETIN BOARD TITLE: *Our Changing Earth* (**ESS3.C: Human Impacts on Earth Systems, ESS2.A: Earth Materials and Systems**)

IDEA: Prepare a bulletin board so it has two distinct halves. Title one side "Changes Caused by Humans" and the other "Changes Caused by Nature." Attach an envelope containing a random assortment of pictures that depict an example for one half or the other. Have the children attach each picture to the proper half.

● Field Trips

Field trips provide amazing opportunities for discovery learning, as they take children out of the classroom and immerse them in the real world. Whether you teach in a city, suburban, or small-town school, you can find ideas for field trips all around you. Here are ideas for field trips for all schools.

FIELD TRIP TITLE: *The Weather Station* (**ESS2D: Weather and Climate**)

IDEA: Even the smallest communities have locations where you can observe the operation of weather measurement and forecasting equipment. Find out ahead of time what equipment is used so you can familiarize your class with it. Contact the person who will show you around to let him or her know the abilities and interests of your students. Prior to the trip, discuss or review topics such as cloud types, precipitation, violent weather, and weather forecasting. During the visit, be sure that you or the guide explains the purpose of the weather station, and discuss the instruments and procedures used in long-range forecasting. There are many follow-up activities for this trip, including the construction of simple instruments for a classroom weather station, the giving of daily weather reports, and long-range forecasting. As with any field trip, look for ways students can be active participants in the discovery of knowledge rather than passive recipients of knowledge.

FIELD TRIP TITLE: *Touch Earth* (ESS2.A: Earth Materials and Systems)

IDEA: This field trip is helpful if your class is studying changes in Earth's surface. The destination should be any place where the surface of the land is being disturbed, such as a construction site, a beach, or the edge of a stream or river. Institute appropriate safety procedures depending on the location. Students should have notebooks, magnifying glasses, and something for carrying samples. Follow-up activities could include presenting topic reports, making displays of collected items, and preparing charts that show the results of soil and water testing.

FIELD TRIP TITLE: *What Cracks the Sidewalks?* (ESS2.E: Biogeology)

IDEA: Children survey the sidewalks on the school grounds to find large and small cracks, and make hypotheses about what causes the cracks.

FIELD TRIP TITLE: *What Happens to the Rain (Snow)?* (ESS2.A: Earth Materials and Systems)

IDEA: Children search for evidence that will tell how rain or melted snow is absorbed by the soil or carried off.

FIELD TRIP TITLE: *What Clouds Are Those?* (ESS2.D: Weather and Climate)

IDEA: Children go outside regularly to draw clouds, classify them, and track their movements.

FIELD TRIP TITLE: *Trash and Treasure* (ESS3.C: Human Impacts on Earth Systems)

IDEA: Children walk around the block on recycling day (i.e., the day households and businesses use special blue or green plastic boxes to dispose of recyclables) to determine the extent to which apartment houses, homes, and businesses participate in recycling.

Examples of Topics and Phenomena for the Physical Sciences

PHENOMENA ARE "observable events that occur in the universe and that we can use our science knowledge to explain or predict."[1] They don't need to be flashy or sensational, but they should generate compelling questions that create real opportunities for students to develop an explanation or solve a problem. Some examples of phenomena and associated activities arranged by topic are listed below.

• Topic: Night and day

Phenomenon: Day and night lengths vary.

Materials   Tennis ball
Steel knitting needle
Small lamp without lamp shade
Chalk
One meter (about three feet) of string
Marking pen

Figure A.2 Earth in orbit in the classroom

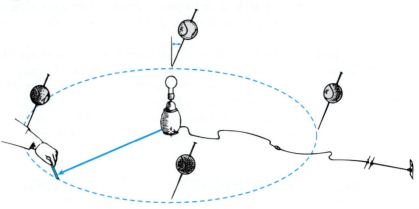

Motivating Questions

- If you didn't have to go to school, would you have more time to play outside in the summer months or in the winter months?
- Are the lengths of the days and nights the same all year?

Directions

1. Before class, carefully push the knitting needle through the tennis ball from top to bottom. Use a marking pen to make a dot that represents your city or town on the tennis ball.

2. Use the string to make a circle on the classroom floor. Put the lamp at the center of the circle. Use the chalk to label the farthest-left part of the circle *June 21*. Label the farthest-right part of the circle *December 21*, the topmost point *March 21*, and the bottommost point *September 21*.

3. At the start of class, have the children gather around the model. Explain that the circle *almost* represents the path of Earth.

4. Tell the children that the path is really a flattened-out circle called an *ellipse*. The elliptical path of Earth around the Sun is relatively insignificant with respect to seasons. Therefore, do not overemphasize the elliptical pattern to avoid misconceptions when students later learn about the reason for the seasons. Convert the circle to a slight ellipse by using the original circle as a guideline and drawing an ellipse with chalk.

5. Incline the tennis ball approximately 23 degrees from the vertical and have a child hold it at the spot marked March 21 and slowly rotate it. The children will note that their town gets light for half the rotation (12 hours). When this procedure is repeated at June 21, the children will note that the town is lit for approximately two-thirds of a rotation (16 hours). At the December 21 spot, the children will note their town gets few hours of sunlight (8 to 10 hours). To make this more obvious, have a child sit at the Sun's location and tell whether she or he sees the town for a long or short period of time on June 21 and December 21.

It may be a difficult concept for young learners to reconcile the actual length of days with the immediacy and scale of the model. After initiating this model with the students, keep the model in the classroom and have the students keep track of each day's length throughout the year. Enlarge the model by hanging a larger ball representing the Sun from the center of the ceiling. Suspend another ball with a

23-degree tilt so it inscribes a circle extending to the edges of the room. Adjust the model each week to represent the relative position of Earth as it revolves around the Sun. Label the date and length of day on the model.

Science Content for the Teacher   Spring and fall are times when Earth's axis is not tilted toward or away from the Sun. At these times, day and night are of equal length. During summer in the Northern Hemisphere, Earth's axis is tilted in the direction of the Sun, so any location in the Northern Hemisphere has longer days. There are several animations on the internet that model the rotation of Earth on its axis to model day/night as well as animations that model the orbit of Earth around the Sun to illustrate seasons.

• Topic: Sedimentary rock formation

Phenomenon: Some rocks have visible layers.

Objectives
- Children make a model and use it to discover the order in which particles of different sizes settle to the bottom.
- Children make drawings to document the results of their experimentation and discuss their results.

Sciences Processes Emphasized
Observing
Using models
Interpreting data
Communicating
Asking questions
Making predictions

Materials for Each Child or Group
Large glass jar with lid
Source of water
Pebbles
Gravel
Soil
Sand

Motivation   This is a good activity to do before the children begin studying how various types of rocks are formed. Display several variations of sedimentary rocks. Ask the children to predict how these rocks were formed. Let the students examine the rocks, and encourage them to look for patterns, textures, and colors that they have in common. After some initial discussion, provide the materials and challenge the students to use those materials to test their ideas. Anticipate that the students will need some guidance. Use the directions below to scaffold the activity as needed.

Directions
1. Have each group fill one-third of a large glass jar with equal amounts of soil, pebbles, gravel, and sand.
2. Have the groups fill the jars the rest of the way with water and screw on the lids.
3. Have the groups shake the jars so that all the materials are thoroughly stirred in the water.
4. Ask the groups to let the materials settle.
5. Have the groups observe the settling and make drawings of the layers they observe.

6. Engage the class in a discussion of the results of the activity.

7. Present students with an assortment of rocks, including sedimentary rocks. Ask the students to identify the rocks they think formed in a streambed.

Key Discussion Questions

1. Which of the materials settled to the bottom of the jar first? *The gravel.*

2. How can you explain the results in this activity? *The large pieces of gravel settled first because they were heavier than the other materials. The heaviest materials are at the bottom and the lightest materials are at the top.*

3. What type of rock is formed from layers of Earth materials that settle out of water? *Sedimentary*

Science Content for the Teacher

When water moves across the surface of Earth, it picks up tiny rocks, pebbles, grains of sand, and soil. This flow of water and materials eventually reaches streams, rivers, and the ocean, and the particles within the water become known as *sediment*. Whenever a flow of water is slowed, some of the sediment is deposited on the bottom of the flow. Layers of sediment pile up under the water. After hundreds of years, the weight of these layers may be so great that the bottom layers are turned into rock.

Extension

If available, take students to a local stream or streambed. If the former, have them predict where the sediments may be finer (slower-moving water) and where the sediments may be larger (fast-moving water). Help them test their results: Allow them to take samples if it is safe to do so or take samples for them.

● Topic: Earthquakes

Phenomenon: There is a pattern to the location of earthquakes.

Objectives

- Children will be able to locate regions of Earth that have more earthquake activity than others.
- Children will study earthquake occurrence data and seek explanations for patterns they observe.

Sciences Processes Emphasized

Interpreting data
Making hypotheses
Asking questions

Materials for Each Child or Group

Note: This is a long-term activity in which children plot data from current government information on earthquakes. (Use the United States Geological Survey's [USGS] latest earthquakes data.)

Paper
Pencil
Access to the internet
World map with latitude and longitude marked

Motivation

Ask the children if they have ever been to part of the country that has a lot of earthquake activity, such as San Francisco. If any have, encourage them to discuss anything they may have heard about earthquakes from people who live there. If no one has, engage the children in a discussion about earthquakes. Stress their cause and possible hazards. Explain that scientists are able to study information about previous earthquakes to predict the general locations of future earthquakes. Tell the children they will work with some of the same information that scientists use, then display the collection of epicenter charts and world maps.

Directions

1. Using the internet, access government information on latest earthquakes provided by the USGS.[2] Be sure to click on "options" and choose the "30 days, magnitude 2.5+ worldwide" option. This will provide a color-coded map of epicenters during the past 30 days. Explain that the information on the charts shows where scientists believe the source of an earthquake was located, then explain the information. Explain that magnitude indicates the strength of the earthquake.

2. Have the children use Google Earth to find the locations of each representative earthquake or cluster of earthquakes, then mark their copy of the world map with a symbol for the earthquake.

3. When they have recorded data from the epicenter chart, ask the students to describe the patterns of earthquakes and whether the pattern suggests possible explanations for the cause of earthquakes. This is a difficult question to answer without knowledge of continental plates. You may want to introduce the idea of continental plates now or leave the explanation of earthquakes open.

4. Have the children maintain their maps for a few months and repeat the activity when you study plate tectonics.

Key Discussion Questions

1. What parts of Earth seem to have the most earthquakes? Where are they? *Along the western portion of the Pacific Ocean, from the Mediterranean Sea across Asia, and along the west coast of North and South America.*

2. Describe patterns you see between earthquake locations and tectonic plates. *Earthquakes are more likely to occur at the boundaries of tectonic plates.*

3. What relationship do you think earthquakes have to tectonic plates? What are the reasons for your claim?

Science Content for the Teacher

An *earthquake* is a shaking of the ground caused by shifting plates that make up Earth's surface and the release of pressure through faults in Earth's crust, which results in the movement of blocks of rocks past each other. The vibrations at ground level are sometimes strong enough to damage buildings and threaten life. The shaking of the ocean floor can produce gigantic waves that roll across the ocean. Scientists record the presence of an earthquake with an instrument known as a *seismograph*. To pinpoint the source of an earthquake's vibrations, scientists gather data from seismographs all over the world. The *epicenter* is thought to be directly above the place where the initial rock fractures occurred. When the locations of epicenters are plotted on a map, they roughly mark the places on Earth where crustal plates grind against each other.

Extension

Science/Social Studies: Have children research the effects of the San Francisco earthquake of 1906. Ask the children what effects the earthquake likely had on community life immediately after it occurred and its effect after a few years had passed.

• Topic: Gradual formation of landforms

Phenomenon: Collisions of tectonic plates have tremendous power that create massive landforms such as mountains.

Objectives
- Children will observe the occurrence of folds and faults in simulated rock layers.
- Children will infer the causes of changes in rock layers.

Sciences Processes Emphasized

Observing
Inferring
Using models

Materials

two blocks of wood
four sticks of modeling clay, each a different color

Motivation

Ask the children how they could use clay to model rock layers. Flatten each stick of clay into a strip that is about one centimeter (less than one-half inch) thick and eight to ten centimeters (about three to four inches) wide.

Directions

1. Place the clay strips on top of one another. Ask the children to suggest whether the strips represent sedimentary, igneous, or metamorphic rocks.
2. Gently press the wood blocks against the ends of the clay layers and have the children observe changes.
3. Eventually, small cracks will appear on the layers, and the layers will be forced into a hump. *Note:* If the clay is too soft or too warm, the fractures will not occur. You may want to allow the layers to dry or cool for a day before performing this part of the demonstration.

Key Discussion Questions

1. How does this demonstration help explain the formation of mountain ranges? *The collision moves land upward.*
2. If the clay layers were layers of rock, which layer would probably be the youngest? Why? *The top one because the material in it was deposited last.*
3. What causes the bends and breaks in real rock layers? *Answers will vary. Some children may be aware that when the plates of Earth's crust push together, the action produces great forces that change and fracture rock layers.*

Science Content for the Teacher

Mountain ranges are formed by the upwelling of the Earth's crust as tectonic plates slowly collide over millions of years. Layers of sedimentary rock provide important clues about the relative ages of rocks. Top layers are *usually* younger than lower layers. Sometimes, however, layers of rocks are turned upside down as a result of the collision of the crustal plates and the movement of molten rock beneath the surface.

Extension

Challenge students to find evidence of this type of movement in their schoolyard or town. Chances are good that you can find evidence of rock layers, especially in road cuts.

• Topic: Cloud formation

Phenomenon: Clouds seem to come out of nowhere.

Materials
One liter, heat-resistant glass beaker
Warm (just below boiling) water
Matches
Ice
Aluminum pan (large enough to cover the top of the beaker)

Motivating Question
What are clouds made of?

Directions
1. Heat the water to a temperature just below boiling (about 90°C).
2. Pour about an inch of water into the bottom of the beaker.
3. Light a match, hold it in the beaker, and blow it out to create smoke.
4. Fill the aluminum pan with ice and place it over the top of the beaker.

Science Content for the Teacher
The hot water evaporates, creating water vapor that condenses near the top of the beaker where the ice cools the air. Smoke particles create condensation nuclei on which the water condenses to simulate the formation of a cloud. Shine a flashlight beam through the beaker to highlight the cloud.

Discovery Activities: Use the Following Activities to Support Discovery Experiences with Your Students.

• How to Find the Relative Humidity

Objectives
• Children will observe how to construct a wet/dry bulb hygrometer.
• Children will measure the relative humidity.

Sciences Processes Emphasized
Observing
Using numbers

Materials
Two identical Celsius thermometers
Small piece of gauze
Small rubber band
Baby food jar full of water at room temperature
Small board or piece of heavy cardboard
Relative humidity table

Motivation
Ask the children whether they feel hotter on a hot muggy day or an equally hot but drier day. Ask them to propose a reason for their claim. Tell them they will conduct an investigation to seek an explanation.

Directions

1. With the help of a student volunteer, tape the two thermometers about 6s centimeters (about 2.4 inches) apart on a piece of cardboard. The bulb end of one thermometer should extend 6 centimeters beyond the edge of the cardboard.

2. Wrap the extending end in gauze. Fasten the gauze with the rubber band, but leave a tail of gauze that can be inserted into the baby food jar.

3. Place the tail in the baby food jar filled with water and moisten the gauze around the bulb. The tail will serve as a wick to keep the bulb moist.

4. Fan both thermometers vigorously. In a few minutes, the volunteer will observe that the thermometers display different temperatures. Use the wet/dry bulb table to find the relative humidity. (Example: If the dry bulb reading is 24°C and the wet bulb reading and dry bulb reading is 20°C, the difference is 4°C. Using the chart below, we determine that the relative humidity is 69%.)

Relative humidity expressed as a percentage:

Dry Bulb Reading (°C)	Difference Between Wet Bulb Reading (°C) and Dry Bulb Reading (°C)									
	1	2	3	4	5	6	7	8	9	10
0	81	64	46	29	13					
2	84	68	52	37	22	7				
4	85	71	57	43	29	16				
6	86	73	60	48	35	24	11			
8	87	75	63	51	40	29	19	8		
10	88	77	66	55	44	34	24	15	6	
12	89	78	68	58	48	39	29	21	12	
14	90	79	70	60	51	42	34	26	18	10
16	90	81	71	63	54	46	38	30	23	15
18	91	82	73	65	57	49	41	34	27	20
20	91	83	74	66	59	51	44	38	31	24
22	92	83	76	68	61	54	47	41	34	28
24	92	84	77	69	62	56	49	44	37	31
26	92	85	78	71	64	58	51	47	40	34
28	93	85	78	72	65	59	53	48	42	37
30	93	86	79	73	67	61	55	50	44	39

Key Discussion Questions

1. Why do you think the wet bulb showed a lower reading than the dry bulb? *Water evaporated from the gauze and cooled the thermometer.*

2. Would more or less water evaporate on a drier day? *More, because water enters the air faster if there is little water in the air to begin with.*

Science Content for the Teacher

Hygrometers are used to measure relative humidity. The evaporation of water lowers the wet bulb temperature. The amount the temperature decreases depends on a variety of factors, including the amount of water vapor already in the air. On hot muggy days, the air is saturated with water vapor. Therefore, the rate of evaporation (drying) is slower. On hot muggy days, our sweat does not evaporate as quickly and consequently does not cool us by evaporation as quickly.

Extension

Science/Social Studies: Have the children interview adults to find out if they lived in places where the relative humidity is high or low. The interviewers can find out how this affected the way of life in each place. Children can practice geography skills by locating various high and low humidity regions on a world map.

● How to Find the Dew Point

Objectives

- Children will find the temperature at which water vapor in the air condenses.
- Children will analyze their data and offer an explanation of how changes in treatment of air moisture will affect dew point readings.

Sciences Processes Emphasized

Observing
Gathering data
Analyzing and interpreting data
Constructing explanations

Materials for Each Child or Group

Empty soup can with one end cut out
Outdoor thermometer that will fit into the soup can
Supply of ice cubes
Rag

Motivation

Begin a discussion with the children about invisible water vapor present in the air. Ask them if they have ever observed evidence of water vapor in the air. They will probably share such observations as the steaming up of mirrors in bathrooms and the steam that seems to come out of their mouths when they breathe on a cold day. Tell the children that water vapor in the air is usually not observed because the air temperature is sufficiently high to keep the water vapor in a gaseous state. As a gas, water vapor is invisible. Display the equipment for this activity and tell the children they will use it to find the temperature at which the water vapor in the air condenses. Explain that this temperature is known as the *dew point*. The dew point is the temperature at which water vapor changes from a gas to a liquid.

Directions

1. Distribute the soup cans to the children and have them remove the labels, scrub the outside of the cans with soap and water, and polish the surfaces. (Be sure to remove sharp edges prior to distribution of the cans to children.)

2. Demonstrate the following procedure for the children: Fill the shiny can about two-thirds full of water at room temperature and place a thermometer in it. Add small amounts of ice and stir the mixture until the ice melts. Have the children observe the outside of the can as you add small amounts of ice and stir. Eventually, the outside will begin to lose its shine and a layer of moisture will be observable.

3. Have the children do this activity on their own. Ask them to keep track of the temperature on the thermometer and pay close attention to the outside of the can as the temperature drops. Stress the importance of observing the precise temperature at which the film forms.

4. After the children have found the dew point inside the classroom, you may want to have them find it outside.

Science Content for the Teacher

The air's capacity to hold moisture is determined by its temperature. The temperature at which air can no longer hold water vapor is known as the *dew point*. *Condensation*, the change from water as a gas to water as a liquid, is usually observable in the atmosphere as dew, fog, or clouds. Condensation occurs when the air is saturated with water vapor. *Saturation* occurs when the temperature of the air reaches its dew point. In this activity, the air near the outside surface of the can is cooled to its dew point. The moisture in that layer of air condenses on the available surface—the outside of the can.

Key Discussion Questions

1. Why do you think we use a shiny can for this activity? *It makes it easy to tell when the moisture condenses. The moisture makes the shiny can look dull.*

2. Why do you think knowing the dew point might be important to weather forecasters? *If they know the dew point, they will know the temperature at which the moisture in the air will condense. Then they can more easily predict when fog, clouds, or rain will happen.*

3. Why do you think dew forms only at night? *During the night, the temperature of the air falls. Sometimes, the temperature falls so low that the dew point is reached. When this happens, the moisture condenses on grass and on the leaves and branches of plants.*

Extension

Have students measure dew points weekly throughout the year. Ask them to predict whether the dew point will differ from season to season. As the data are collected, have them look for patterns in the dew point and relationships to the season.

● You've Heard of Rock Musicians, but Have You Heard of Rock Magicians?

Objectives

• Children will observe one unusual characteristic each in five rocks.

• Children will describe each characteristic observed.

• Children will name each of the rocks used in the demonstration.

Sciences Processes Emphasized

Observing
Communicating

Materials

Bowl of water
Sheet of paper
Matches
White vinegar (*Safety note*: Use safety glasses when dealing with acids and bases)
Samples of rocks: pumice, anthracite, or calcite
Very optional: Top hat and/or cape

Motivation

Because of the nature of this demonstration, it will take little to get the children's attention. You may want to be the rock magician yourself or you may have a child who is perfect for the part! Be sure all the children have a good view of what is to transpire. Be clear that science is not magic, although all magic is based on science.

Directions
1. The rock magician should use the materials in the list to demonstrate the following:
   a. The floating rock: Pumice will float in water
   b. The writing rock: Anthracite will write on paper
   c. The fizzing rock: A few drops of vinegar will cause calcite to fizz
2. Before each demonstration, the magician should name the rock, spell it, and write its name on the chalkboard. The children will thereby learn the name of each rock displayed.
3. Have the children write down their observations.

Key Discussion Questions
1. Why do you think geologists are interested in the special characteristics of these rocks? *They can tell a lot about the rock from its properties.*
2. Why do you think the pumice floated? *It has a lot of air trapped in it.*
3. Do you think the material in your pencils might be something like anthracite? Why? *Yes, both can make marks on paper. Note:* The material in pencils these days is not lead, but graphite. Graphite is essentially carbon. Anthracite is also carbon.

Science Content for the Teacher
Pumice is magma (molten rock) that trapped bubbles of steam or gas when it was thrown out of a volcano in liquid form. When magma solidifies, it is honeycombed with gas-bubble holes. This gives it the buoyancy to float on water. *Anthracite* is a type of coal that results from the partial decomposition of plants. The carbon in the plants is the primary constituent of anthracite and other forms of coal. *Calcite* is a mineral found in such rocks as limestone and marble. Geologists test for its presence by placing a few drops of warm acid on the rock under study. If calcite is present, carbon dioxide gas is released with a fizz by the chemical reaction.

Extension
Science/Social Studies: Follow this demonstration with a map or study exercise in which the children find out where the various rocks come from. They will need some Earth science reference books and an atlas.

● Can You Move Like the Planets?

Materials
Eight sheets of 8½-by-11-inch pastel paper, one sheet for each group
Larger sheet of orange paper
Crayons or water-based markers for each group

Motivating Questions
• What are some things you see in the sky on a bright day?
• Display a globe and ask: Do you think our Earth moves or stays still?

Directions
1. Write the planet names on the whiteboard, distribute the paper, and assign a planet name to each group.
2. Write the word *Sun* on the orange sheet, and have each group write the name of its planet on the paper it received.

3. Have volunteers from each group join you at a central place in the room. Arrange the volunteers in proper sequence from the Sun (the orange sheet that you are holding) and have the children circle around you.

4. Indicate that the planets spin (rotate) as they move (revolve) and have the children do the same, slowly.

Science Content for the Teacher
Eight major planets travel around the Sun in orbits. These planets do not emit light; they reflect the Sun's light. The Sun is a star whose apparent motion is due to Earth's rotation. Seasonal changes are due to the change in the relative position of Earth as it orbits around the Sun.

● Can You Move Like the Moon?

Materials
Orange sheet of paper
White sheet of paper
Blue sheet of paper
Crayons or water-based markers

Motivating Questions
- Do you think Earth moves around the Sun or do you think the Sun moves around Earth?
- Do you think the Moon moves around Earth or do you think Earth moves around the Moon?

Directions
1. Write the word *Sun* on the orange sheet of paper, the word *Earth* on the blue sheet, and the word *Moon* on the white sheet. (You may want to have children copy the words from the board.)

2. Select one student to stand and hold the orange sheet to represent the Sun.

3. Select another student to hold the blue sheet and move in orbit around the Sun.

4. Select a third student to hold the white sheet and orbit Earth as it travels around the Sun.

Science Content for the Teacher
The Moon is a satellite of Earth. This means the Moon revolves around Earth as the Earth rotates and revolves around the Sun. The Moon also rotates as it orbits Earth.

● Where Does the Sun Appear to Rise and Set?

Materials
Two sheets of drawing paper for each child
Pencils, crayons, or markers

Motivating Questions
- Where does the Sun set?
- Where does the Sun rise?

Directions
1. Have each child place the drawing paper so that the long side runs from left to right in front of him or her.

2. On one sheet of paper, have each child draw some of the objects he or she would see while looking toward the east of where he or she lives (e.g., buildings, trees, fields, forests, parks, etc). On the other sheet, have each child do the same for the west.

3. Have each child draw a rising Sun on the sheet at the place that represents where the Sun rises and a setting Sun at the place they think represents where the Sun sets.

4. Have the children take both papers home for a few days to correct, if they need to, the locations of their Suns. *Safety note:* Remind the children to never look directly at the Sun.

Science Content for the Teacher

It seems to us that the Sun is moving across our sky every day, rising in the east and setting in the west. However, the sunrise and sunset that we see are due to Earth's rotation. In this activity, the children simply compare their memories of where the Sun rises and sets to the evidence.

● Planets on Parade

Objective
- Children will place the planets in sequential order from the Sun.

Science Processes Emphasized

Using numbers
Using space/time relationships

Materials for Each Child or Group

One deck of eight index cards, each labeled with a different planet name

Motivation

Tell the children they are going to play a game that will help them learn about the planets. Display the eight index cards you will distribute.

Directions

1. Before beginning this activity, create a set of clues for each planet, such as "I am Venus; I am closer to the Sun than the Earth," and "I am Neptune; I am farther from the Sun than Mars."
2. Distribute a randomly sequenced deck of index cards to each group. Explain that each card represents a planet that is traveling around the Sun but that the cards are not in the proper order. Challenge the groups to rearrange the cards based on the clues you give.
3. Read each clue and encourage the children to rearrange the cards on the basis of the clues.

Key Discussion Questions

1. Which planet is closest to the Sun? *Mercury*
2. Which planet is farthest from the Sun? *Neptune*
3. Which planet is just before Earth, and which planet is right after Earth? *Venus, Mars*

Science Content for the Teacher

The eight known planets of our solar system in order from the Sun are Mercury, Venus, Earth, Mars, Jupiter, Saturn, Uranus, and Neptune.

Extension

Science/Math: After the children put their zero in order, have them turn the decks over and number each card sequentially from one to eight. Have pairs of children play a game in which one child removes one of the numbered cards and the other child has to guess the planet name that is on the reverse side.

● Making a Simple Sundial

Objectives
- Children use numbers to write time measurements.
- Children predict the time from the position of the shadow on a sundial.

Science Processes Emphasized

Using numbers
Predicting
Constructing explanations

Designing solutions
Arguing from evidence

Materials for Each Child or Group Sheet of light cardboard measuring a 25 centimeter (10 inch) square
Masking tape
Straw

Motivation Display the materials and tell the children that they will make their own clocks. Indicate that they will be strange clocks, because they will only work when the Sun shines.

Directions 1. Prior to class, make a 20-centimeter (about 8-inch) circle on each sheet of cardboard and punch a small hole at the center of each circle. Have a compass available for step 3.

2. Distribute the straw and a few strips of masking tape to each group. Have the groups insert one end of the straw into the cardboard circle's hole and tape the straw so that it can stand upright. Tell them to write the letter N at any point along the edge of the circle.

3. On a sunny day, take the groups and their sundials outside. Using the compass, point north and have the children orient their sundials so that the N are pointed north. Have them mark the location of the straw's shadow, then tell the children the actual time. Have them write the time on the cardboard at the end of the shadow.

4. After repeating this procedure at various times on consecutive days, have the children predict where the straw's shadow will be at a given time and take them outside at that time to check. As a final step, take the children outside and have them use their sundials to tell you the time.

Key Discussion Questions 1. There is one time of the day when the shadow is shortest or does not exist at all. What time is that? *When the Sun is directly overhead.*

2. What are some problems with using sundials to tell time? *You can't tell the time on a cloudy day or at night.*

Science Content for the Teacher Because Earth is constantly changing its position in relation to the Sun, the sundials made in this activity will be fairly accurate for only a few days. Sundials in gardens or parks are designed to compensate for Earth's changing position. They usually do not use a vertical object for the shadow but rather a rod that is inclined at the angle of the location's latitude and pointed toward the North Star.

Extension *Science/Engineering:* Have students try their sundials over an extended period to discover that they become more inaccurate. Challenge the students to propose a design for a sundial that is accurate over a longer period. Let them look at other sundial designs for ideas to modify their designs. Allow them to test their sundials and redesign them. Finally, challenge them to explain why their first design only worked for a limited time and how the new design attempts to address the problem.

● Sunlight in Winter versus Summer

Objective • Children will observe that light striking an inclined surface does not appear as bright as light striking a surface directly.

Science Process Emphasized Measuring

Materials for Each Child or Group	Black construction paper Chalk Book Tape Flashlight

Motivation Ask the children if they have ever wondered why it is colder in winter than in summer. Tell them they will discover one of the reasons in this activity.

Directions

1. Have a globe available before beginning this activity. Darken the classroom and distribute a book, tape, chalk, paper, and flashlight to each child or group.

2. Have each child or group tape the paper to the book and hold the book vertically on a flat surface. Ask them to shine the flashlight perpendicular to the paper and use the chalk to draw a circle outlining the illuminated area.

3. Tell the children to keep the flashlight at the same distance and angle to the book while tilting the book away from the flashlight and outlining the lit area.

4. Turn the lights on and display the globe. Use a flashlight to represent the Sun and tilt the globe to show that Earth's tilt causes the Northern Hemisphere to be angled away from the Sun during the winter. Relate this to the light striking the paper that was tilted away from the light source.

Key Discussion Questions

1. How are the drawings you made different from one another? *The first was smaller.*

2. Was the patch of light brighter the first or second time you had the light strike the paper? *The first*

Science Content for the Teacher Although many people believe that winter occurs because Earth is farther from the Sun at that time of year than it is in summer, the principal cause for winter is Earth's tilt and the resulting indirect light, not its distance from the Sun. This tilt serves to disperse and decrease the intensity of the Sun's energy more in the Northern Hemisphere during the winter. Sunlight strikes the Northern Hemisphere more directly in June than in December.

Extension *Science/Social Studies:* Have the children look at the globe and consider how their lives would be different if they lived in an equatorial region, which receives a great deal of direct sunlight all through the year, or in a polar region, which receives much less sunlight. Relate the concept of direct and indirect light to the developing classroom model described in the attention-getter *Is Day Always as Long as Night?*

● Make a Solar System Mobile

Objective • Children construct mobiles showing the eight planets of the solar system.

Science Processes Emphasized	Measuring Scale Proportion Using space/time relationships

Materials	Wire coat hanger String Crayons

Three or four straws
Scissors
Tape
Eight circles of oak tag board measuring eight centimeters (about three inches) across

Motivation   Tell the children they are going to create an art project that illustrates some of their science knowledge. You may want to display a sample planet mobile at this point.

Directions   1. Prior to class, create a mobile using a coat hanger as a base and an arrangement of strings and horizontal straws. Attach the eight oak tag board circles to the strings that dangle from the straw ends.

2. Display the mobile and explain that each circle represents one of the planets in the solar system. Write the names of the planets on the chalkboard and distribute the materials. Tell the children to write the name of a planet on each circle.

3. Once the circles are labeled, have the children construct the mobiles. Assist children who need help tying knots to attach string to straws or to oak tag circles. (Some children may find it easier to tape the parts of their mobile together.) You may suggest that the children construct some of the subparts of the mobile first—for example, a straw with two or three planets hanging from it. If you have parent volunteers or assistants in the classroom, urge them to help children who have limited psychomotor abilities.

4. When the children are finished, have them hang their mobiles in the classroom.

Key Discussion Questions   Because this activity is focused on the construction of a mobile, the questions you raise should facilitate the children's use of psychomotor skills.

1. If you wanted to hang two planets from a straw, where would you tie them? *One at each end*

2. If you hung one planet from each end of a straw, where would you tie the string that attaches the straw to the hanger? *At the center*

Science Content for the Teacher   Remind the children that although their planets are all the same size, the real planets are of different sizes.

Extension   *Science:* The scale of distances in space can be a difficult concept to grasp, especially for young children. You can introduce the idea of scale and distances in our solar system by creating a model that approximates the relative distances of planets from the Sun. Use astronomical units (AU) to create a scale model of the solar system in your schoolyard. One AU is the distance between the Sun and Earth. Once you establish a distance to represent one AU, you and your students can develop a solar system model based on AU distances. See the solar system website provided by NASA for AU distances of planets from the Sun.

● **How to Build an Altitude Finder (Astrolabe)**

Objectives   • Children construct a simple device for measuring the heights of planets and stars above the horizon.

• Children measure how many degrees an object is above the horizon.

Science Processes Emphasized	Observing Using mathematics Measuring

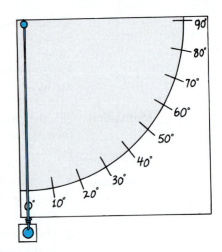

Figure A.3 An altitude finder

Materials for Each Child or Group	Piece of cardboard measuring 25 by 25 centimeters (about 10 by 10 inches) Length of string measuring 25 centimeters (10 inches) Small weight, such as a washer or nut Protractor Tape

Motivation   Tell the children they will build an instrument that the Greeks invented long ago to discover how far above the horizon the planets and stars are. Explain that scientists call this instrument an *astrolabe* but that they can call it an *altitude finder,* because it finds altitudes. You may need to explain that *altitude* is the term for height above the ground (or sea level).

Directions
1. Distribute a protractor to each child or group. Show the children that the protractor scale can be used to measure angles from 0 degrees to 180 degrees.

2. Distribute a cardboard square to each group and have the children place a 0-degree mark at the lower-left corner of the cardboard. Have them place a 90-degree mark at the upper-right corner.

3. Have the children attach one end of the string to the upper-left corner of the cardboard with the tape and tie a pencil to the free end of the string. Now they can use the string and pencil as a compass to draw an arc from the lower-left corner to the upper-right corner.

4. Have the children divide the arc they have drawn into 10-degree intervals from 0 degrees to 90 degrees—that is, 0°, 10°, 20°, . . ., 90°. The protractor can be used to help mark these divisions.

5. The children should now untie the pencil and tie the nut or washer to the string. The string should cross the 0-degree mark when the upper edge of the cardboard is held horizontally. Tell the children that they will be sight objects along the top of the cardboard with the string on the edge of the cardboard that is farthest away from them.

6. When the children have constructed their altitude finders, you may want to take them outside to find how many degrees such things as chimneys, tree tops, or lamp posts are above the horizon. Be sure they do not try to sight the Sun with their altitude finders.

7. Encourage the children to take their altitude finders home and measure the number of degrees the visible heavenly bodies are above the horizon.

Key Discussion Questions
1. Why do you think we attached a weight to the string? *To pull the string straight down*

2. Sometimes people use the term *angle of elevation* when they use an astrolabe. What do you think the term means? *How many degrees the object is above the horizon*

3. Does the altitude finder tell you anything about the direction the object is from you? *No*

4. How could you find the direction? *Use a compass. Note:* The next activity in this chapter involves creating an instrument that measures the angle of a heavenly body from true north.

Science Content for the Teacher

The astrolabe was invented by the Greeks to observe heavenly bodies. It consisted of a movable rod that was pointed at a star or planet. The position of the rod against a circle indicated the altitude of the Sun, Moon, and stars. The astrolabe was eventually refined for use as a navigational tool. The sextant, a more accurate device that fulfills the same purpose, came into use in the eighteenth century. It uses a small telescope and a system of mirrors to compare the position of a heavenly body with the horizon.

Extension

Science/Social Studies: Have a group of children do some library research to find out more about the extent to which the ancient Greeks were involved in astronomy. This group can also research the importance of the astrolabe and sextant in the exploration of the world by seafaring countries.

● Moon Watcher

Objectives
- Using a model, children will observe the phases of the Moon.
- Children will explain why the Moon seems to change its shape.

Science Processes Emphasized

Observing
Communicating

Materials

Small lamp with ordinary light bulb and removable shade
Orange
Paper and pencil
Signs with the labels *Earth*, *Moon*, and *Sun*

Motivation

Ask the children to describe and draw the various shapes that the Moon seems to take. (As a preparatory experience, instruct students to keep a Moon journal for a month in which they will record the shape of the Moon each night. If possible, they could also photograph the Moon at night. Consider assigning each student three or four days to take photos of the Moon for the class.) Collect the data and discuss it as a class. Ask if they think the Moon really changes shape. After some discussion, display the materials for the demonstration and tell the children that they will observe a model of the Moon in orbit around Earth that will help them understand the changes in its shape.

Figure A.4 What phase of the Moon is this?

DVIDS/NASA

Directions

1. Remove the lamp shade and place the *Sun* label on the lamp. Place the Sun at the center of the front of the room. Select one child and affix the *Earth* label to him or her.

2. Darken the room by drawing the shades and shutting off the classroom lights.

3. Attach the *Moon* label to the orange. Have the child with the Earth label hold the orange so that his or her hand is fully outstretched. Have the child first stand so that he or she is facing the Sun and holding the Moon directly in line with it. The child should be about one meter (a little more than three feet) from the Sun.

4. The lamp should be turned on at this point. Have the child holding the orange describe how much of the orange's lit surface is seen. None of the lit surface should be seen; the Moon is not visible in the sky.

5. Have the child turn sideways and ask him or her how much of the lit surface of the orange he or she can see. Half of the lit surface should be visible; the child sees a half-Moon.

6. Have the child stand so that his or her back is to the lamp and the orange is about 30 centimeters (1 foot) away from his or her eyes and slightly to the left of the head. Ask how much of the lit surface of the Moon can be seen. All of it should be visible; the child sees a full Moon.

7. Repeat the demonstration so that the crescent Moon and three-quarters Moon can be seen.

Key Discussion Questions

1. Does the Moon produce light? *No, it just reflects light from the Sun.*

2. What name do we give to the shapes that the Moon seems to take? *Phases*

3. Does the Moon really change in shape? Why? *No, the only thing that changes is the pattern of the light we can see bouncing off the Moon.*

Science Content for the Teacher

The Sun shines on only half of the surface of the Moon. This entire lit surface is not always visible from Earth. The apparent shape of the Moon at any given time is really the portion of the lit surface that is visible. The different portions of the surface that are lit at different times are the phases of the Moon. The *full Moon* is the phase in which we see the entire lit surface. When full, the Moon appears as a round disk in the sky. We refer to the phase in which we see half the lit surface as the *half Moon*. The *crescent Moon* is a phase in which we see only a sliver of the lit surface. The *new Moon* is the phase in which none of the lit surface can be seen.

Extensions

Science: Encourage a group of children to use the lamp, orange, and other round objects to demonstrate other astronomical phenomena, such as lunar and solar eclipses.

Science/Arts: Have a group of children draw a sequence of pictures to represent an imaginary incident that occurs as astronauts explore a mysterious crater on the Moon.

● The Shoebox Planetarium

Objective

• Children will observe the Big Dipper constellation projected in the classroom and locate it in the night sky.

Science Processes Emphasized	Observing
Materials	Shoebox with lid Index card Flashlight Electrical tape Scissors
Motivation	Tell the children they will observe something that they can then ask a parent or another adult to help them find in the night sky.

Directions

1. Tape the lid to the shoebox. At one end, cut out a hole large enough to insert the lamp end of a flashlight. Cut a rectangular window the size of a small index card in the other end.

2. Using the electrical tape, seal one end of the box around the flashlight so that the switch is not in the box.

3. Poke small holes in an index card in the shape of the Big Dipper. Attach the index card to the window in the shoe box. *Note:* For somewhat older children, you may want to prepare additional index cards to project images of other constellations.

4. Darken the room, turn on the flashlight, and project the Big Dipper on a screen or wall. Have the children note the shape of the handle and the cup. Encourage the children to ask an adult to help them find it in the night sky.

Key Discussion Questions

1. Look at the sides of the Big Dipper. What do you notice about them? *Answers will vary. If no one mentions that the sides of the dipper slope inward, do so.*

2. Look at the handle of the Big Dipper. What do you notice about it? *Answers will vary. If no one mentions that the handle is curved, do so.*

Science Content for the Teacher

We are able to observe thousands of stars with the naked eye. Groupings of stars that seem to move together in an apparent path around the North Star are known as *constellations*. The following is a sample of the many constellations visible from the northern latitudes at various times of the year: *spring*, Leo, the lion; *summer*, Cygnus, the swan; *fall*, Andromeda, the maiden; and *winter*, Orion, the hunter. This demonstration focuses on the constellation known as the Big Dipper, which is visible throughout the year. The Big Dipper is part of another constellation known as Ursa Major, the bear, with the tail of the bear made from the handle of the Big Dipper.

Extension

Science/Math: Have the children create their own connect-the-dots puzzles that include numbers representing the seven stars of the Big Dipper. Have them exchange papers so each can complete a puzzle made by someone else.

There are several astronomy apps that help students explore space. Use them as a guide, but not as a substitute for looking at and observing the real night sky.

● Space Journey

Note: Due to the unique nature of this demonstration, Motivation, Directions, Key Discussion Questions, and Extensions have been integrated under one heading.

Objectives
- Each child will take the role of a member of a space exploration team and describe his or her imaginary adventure.
- Children will explain the similarities and differences between their imaginary journeys and a possible real journey into outer space.

Materials

A classroom that can be darkened by shutting off the light and adjusting the blinds

Motivation, Directions, Key Discussion Questions, and Extensions

Through this simulation of a journey into outer space, children have an opportunity to use their knowledge of the solar system to form mental images of the planet on which their spaceship lands. The experience encourages children to use their imagination, communicate orally with the remainder of the class, and, at a later time, use their creative writing and artistic abilities.

Prior to the simulated space journey, divide the class into teams of space explorers. Each team will have four members: a pilot, a navigator, a scientist, and a medical officer. Allow group members to select their roles and change the classroom seating arrangement so that team members can sit side by side. Have various team members explain what their jobs will be at the time of launch and during planetary exploration. With the assistance of the class, you may redecorate the classroom so it looks like the interior of a spacecraft. To add realism to the experience, play rocket launch sound effects during blastoff.

Have each team prepare for the launch by sitting quietly in their seats for a few seconds. Indicate that you will soon begin the countdown for blastoff. Tell them that they should shut their eyes and listen to your words.

Begin the countdown. Tell the children that the rocket engines are beginning to work. When you reach 0, tell them that the rocket is lifting off the launch pad. Use descriptions such as the following to guide their thinking during the flight:

"You are being pressed backward. . . . You are in the most dangerous part of the flight, a time when a group of astronauts once lost their lives. . . . Your journey will be a safe one. Imagine that you are looking back at Earth. . . . You are flying higher and higher. . . . Earth is getting smaller and smaller. . . . It is a tiny blue dot. Ahead of you is the blackness of space. . . . The stars are bright. Brighter than you have ever seen them before. . . . Way ahead, you see a tiny reddish-colored dot. . . . The pilot puts the spacecraft on automatic pilot, and all the members of the crew go to special sleeping compartments, where they will sleep as the spacecraft approaches its target. . . . You are sleeping.

"You awake to the sound of a buzzer. You return to your seats and see that the planet is now a large reddish ball directly ahead. As the spacecraft gets closer, the pilot prepares for a landing. The spacecraft gently lands. You look out the windows and see the surface of the planet. . . . Think about the way it looks. Is it flat or bumpy? Does it have mountains? Don't answer. Just think about how it seems to you.

"The science officer checks some instruments that tell about the planet's surface and atmosphere. The science officer says it is safe to explore the planet if you wear spacesuits.

"Imagine that you put the bulky spacesuits on. You check each other's suits to be sure they are working properly. Imagine that the pilot opens the door and you go down a ladder to the surface of the planet.

"You look around and then look back at one another. You check that your radios are working. Now each of you starts out in a different direction. After you've walked for a few minutes, you stop and look around to see if you can still see the other crew members. You can see each of them. Keep walking and making observations. . . . You notice something very interesting at your feet. You bend down, pick it up, and gently place it in your collection bag. You reach a large boulder and walk behind it. On the ground, you see something in the shadows. You are amazed at what you see. You try to it, but you can't. You pull and pull, and finally get it free. Just as you are getting ready to call the other crew members to tell them what you have found, you hear the pilot's voice: 'Emergency, get back to the ship immediately.' You take what you discovered and race back to the ship. You and the other crew members are safely on board.

"Relax. . . . The pilot makes a safe liftoff. You begin the long journey back to Earth. . . . A few months later, you see a tiny blue speck straight ahead. It gets larger and larger. . . . It is Earth, your home. The pilot makes a safe landing. . . . You may open your eyes. Welcome home!"

When all the spacecraft have made safe landings, engage the participants in discussions of what they observed and how their observations compare with what they have learned about the solar system and planets. You may want to have the children prepare illustrated written reports about their adventures.

Science Content for the Teacher Prior to this demonstration, study the physical characteristics of the various planets in our solar system as well as the stars. This knowledge will enable you assist the children when they discuss their experiences. Don't forget to check NASA resources about future space exploration that you can use in your classroom.

Earth/Space Sciences Sample Lesson

Title: The Power to Move Continents: Convection Currents and Plate Tectonics Suggested practices, core ideas, and crosscutting concepts related to Next Generation Science Standards:[3]

- Science practices: using models, carrying out investigations, analyzing and interpreting data, using mathematics
- Core idea: plate tectonics and large-scale system interactions
- Crosscutting concept: energy and matter[4]

Background for Teachers The movement of the continents is appropriately referred to as *continental drift*. Fundamental to the understanding of this incredible system we call Earth is an understanding of the powerful forces within Earth that can move continents. As stated earlier, Earth's crust, which consists of the ocean floors and continental land masses, sits on a mantle that has a consistency similar to hot asphalt that acts like a slow-moving fluid. The movement is caused by the heating and cooling in the mantle, which creates a temperature differential of hot, molten rock near the liquid outer core and cooler rock material closer to the crust. The circulation created by hot, less dense rock material rising toward the crust that in turn cools and becomes denser and sinks toward the outer core is called a *convection current*. Imagine large chunks of crust that make up the oceanic and continental plates floating on this cyclical convection current. The slow, powerful force created by the convection current moves the plates sitting on top of them.

Materials   One beaker (500-milliliter or 1 liter)
Glitter
Ice cubes made with blue food coloring
Red food coloring (optional)
250-milliliter Erlenmeyer flask (optional)
Clear plastic container about the size of a shoebox (the deeper the better)
For teams of two students:
One thermometer per team of two
Computer
LCD projector

● Element 1: Content to Be Taught

Content Analysis: Convection and Plate Tectonics

Students learn that convection currents occur where there is a temperature difference in gases or liquids. Warm matter rises and cooler matter sinks. Convection currents in the mantle cause the crustal plates on the surface of Earth to move.

● Element 2: Prior Knowledge and Misconceptions

Children may perceive of Earth as a solid rock consisting of one giant, homogenous layer.

● Element 3: Performance Objectives

Given a diagram of a cross-section of Earth that includes temperatures in Earth's mantle, students explain in writing the movement of the mantle and crustal plates earning satisfactory or better on the accompanying rubric.

● Element 4: Concept Development

Engagement   Introduce the phenomenon of continental drift to students by using an animation depicting continental drift from the US Geological Survey as a phenomenon to engage the students.[5] Pause the animation at the beginning (740 million years ago) and ask the children what they think the picture represents. After the children express their ideas, run the animation again. Ask them again what they think the animation represents. When they recognize the animation as a depiction of moving continents, tell them many scientists have discovered evidence that the continents are indeed moving. Raise the essential question, "What force of nature could actually move continents?"

Exploration   *Safety note:* Create a safety splash zone around the boiling water during the demonstration in Part II of the exploration. Direct children to stand behind the zone boundary. Set the zone boundary to prevent spillage of hot water on the children. Alternatively, use a Plexiglas shield around the boiling water to prevent spillage.

Part I: Activity—Tell the students that the following activity[6] provides some information that might help them answer the essential question.

Student Instructions   Fill a clear plastic container about the size of a shoebox three-fourths full with tap water. Do *not* fill it to the very top. You will add something to the container that will raise the water level.

Using the thermometer, measure the temperature of the water at the bottom and top of the water level. Record the values in the chart, "No Ice."

Place a blue ice cube *gently* on the surface of the water in one end of the container. (For a more dramatic effect, gently lower a 250-milliter Erlenmeyer flask with warm water colored red in the opposite end of the container.) Once the ice cube is in the container, do not shake the table.

Measure the temperature of the water at the bottom and top after one and five minutes with ice.

As the ice melts, record the movement of the colored water in your science notebook.

Data Table

Location of Thermometer	Initial Temperature No Ice (°C)	Temperature 1 minute With Ice (°C)	Temperature 5 minutes With Ice (°C)
Bottom			
Top			

Write your explanation for the movement that you observed in the cup.

Part II: Demonstration—Place a beaker of cool water on a hot plate. Sprinkle glitter into the water. Direct the children to make a descriptive model of the system that you have created. Ask the students to predict what will happen when the water is heated. Point out that the water will get warmer on the bottom of the beaker first.

Heat the water (but do not boil) until the glitter begins to move vertically. Ask the children to explain the movement of the glitter based on their observations of the prior investigation they did using colored ice cubes in water. Encourage them to use diagrams and/or a graphic organizer.

Part III: Diagram—Post a diagram of Earth's layers. Based on prior lessons, review the properties of the mantle with The children: the mantle is viscous, like hot asphalt. The lower mantle is warmer (2,200°C) than the upper mantle (871°C). Ask the children to predict the effect of the difference in temperature of the mantle.

Explanation   Ask the children to try to answer the essential question, "What force of nature could actually move continents?" Have the children write individual responses in their science notebooks. Ask them to share their responses with two other children. Have each group of three devise a way to record and share their group explanation. This is an opportunity to offer multiple means of expression: diagram, text, simulation, PowerPoint, or verbal report.
Allow the groups to present their answers to the essential question, then go to the USGS website for an explanation of convection currents in the context of continental drift. Use the explanation to explain that the warmer lower mantle heats the rock, which rises to the upper mantle, where it cools and sinks back to the lower mantle. (If children understand density, you can explain that heat energy makes the particles in the rock move faster and expand, decreasing the density, and making the rocks rise.) Identify this process as *convection*. Convection is the movement of particles with high heat energy to areas with less heat energy.

The movement creates a circular motion in the mantle that moves Earth's crustal plates floating on top of the mantle.

Elaboration   Show children a weather map with warm and cold fronts. Ask them to use their knowledge of convection to predict what will happen when the two fronts meet.

● Element 5: Evaluation

Show the children a diagram of Earth's mantle and crust and include the temperatures, 1,000°C (1,832°F) near Earth's boundary with the crust, to nearly 4,000°C (7,232°F) near its boundary with the core.

Ask the children to explain in writing how the continents move. Assess children based on the following rubric:

Well Done	Satisfactory	Needs Improvement
Children include all five relationships in their explanation:	Children include any three out of five relationships in their explanation:	Children include fewer than three relationships in their explanations:

Relationships

- The lower mantle is hotter than the upper mantle.
- The hotter lower mantle rocks rise and then cool in the upper mantle.
- The cooler upper mantle rocks sink to the lower mantle.
- The rising and sinking of rock particles causes a circular movement.
- The movement of the mantle moves crust floating on top.

● Element 6: Accommodations

English Language Learner

1. The teacher will state directions and procedures verbally as well as in writing.
2. The teacher will create a word bank with definitions to remain posted in the room.

Attention-Deficit/Hyperactivity Disorder

1. There are several coherent transitions to engage students and minimize the time spent on one particular task.
2. The students will be given a checklist for the activities to keep track of their progress and accomplishments.
3. The teacher will explicitly state the directions prior to each activity.

Emotional and Behavioral Disorder

1. Criteria for class participation and considerate group work (such as raising one's hand and giving everyone in the group an opportunity to participate) will be reviewed before the lesson.

RESOURCES FOR DISCOVERY LEARNING

Internet Resources

Websites for Earth/Space Science Units, Lessons, Activities, and Demonstrations

- **NASA:**
  www.nasa.gov

- **US Geological Survey:**
  www.usgs.gov

- **National Weather Service:**
  www.weather.gov/education.php

- **National Oceanic and Atmosphere Administration (NOAA):**
  www.noaa.com

Print Resources

Suggested Reading

Ashby, Suzanne. "NASA Quest." *Science Scope* 33, no. 1 (September 2000): 40–43.

Barker, Marianne. "Student Centered Seismology Activities." *Science Scope* 23, no. 4 (January 2000): 12–18.

Booth, Bibi, et al. "Energy: Fuel for Thought." *Science and Children* 39, no. 8 (May 2002): 35–42.

Comstock, D. "A Week for Space." *Science and Children* 46, no. 1 (September 2008): 25–29.

Corder, Greg, and Reed, Darren. "It's Raining Micrometeorites." *Science Scope* 26, no. 5 (February 2003): 23–25.

Danaher, Edwin. "Science 101: How Do Snowflakes Form?" *Science and Children* 40, no. 1 (January 2003): 53.

Giacalone, Valerie. "How to Plan, Survive, and Even Enjoy an Overnight Field Trip with 200 Students." *Science Scope* 26, no. 4 (January 2003): 22–26.

Gibb, Lori. "Second Grade Soil Scientists." *Science and Children* 38, no. 3 (November/December 2000): 24–26.

Hemmenway, Mary Kay. "Our Star, the Sun." *Science and Children* 38, no. 1 (September 2000): 48–51.

Lester, Dan, et al. "The Sun Tower." *Science and Children* 38, no. 3 (November/December 2000): 14–17.

Lucking, Robert A., and Christmann, Edwin P. "Tech Trek: Technology in the Classroom." *Science Scope* 26, no. 4 (January 2003): 54–57.

Mohler, Robert J. "More Space Shuttle Experiments Take Flight." *Science and Children* 38, no. 2 (October 2000): 38–43.

Newhouse, Kay Berglund. "What Lies in the Stars?" *Science and Children* 39, no. 6 (March 2002): 16–21.

Paty, Alma Hale. "Rocks and Minerals: Foundations of Society." *Science Scope* 23, no. 8 (May 2000): 30–31.

Riddle, Bob. "Scope on the Skies: The Brightest Stars in the Sky." *Science Scope* 26, no. 4 (January 2003): 60.

Riddle, Bob. "Scope on the Skies: Scintillating Stars." *Science Scope* 26, no. 5 (February 2003): 56–57.

Smith, Shaw. "Turning Bread into Rocks." *Science Scope* 24, no. 2 (October 2000): 20–23.

Sorel, Katherine. "Rock Solid." *Science and Children* 40, no. 5 (January 2003): 24–29.

Waters, M., et al., "Science Rocks! A Performance Assessment for Earth Science." *Science Activities* 45, no. 1 (Spring 2008): 23–28.

Wiig, Diana. "A Week with the Stars." *Science and Children* 39, no. 7 (April 2002): 22–25.

Wiley, David, and Royce, Christine Anne. "Crash into Meteorite Learning." *Science and Children* 37, no. 8 (May 2000): 16–19.

Notes

1. Using Phenomena in NGSS-Designed Lessons and Units. www.nextgenscience.org.
2. USGS. earthquake.usgs.gov/earthquakes/map/.
3. Next Generation Science Standards (NGSS) is a registered trademark of Achieve. Neither Achieve nor the lead states and partners that developed the Next Generation Science Standards was involved in the production of, and does not endorse, this product.
4. Achieve, Inc., on behalf of the 26 states and partners that collaborated on the NGSS. (2013). *Next Generation Science Standards*.
5. Alternatively, use diagrams from the US Geological Survey at www.nature.nps.gov/geology/usgsnps/pltec/scplseqai.html.
6. Adapted from a lesson titled "Make Convection Currents!" from *Climate Discovery Teacher's Guide*. National Center for Atmospheric Research. http://eo.ucar.edu/educators/ClimateDiscovery/ESS_lesson3_10.19.05.pdf.

Life Sciences Lesson Ideas

Putting the Content into Action

Unit Plan Ideas and Questions

● From Molecules to Organisms: Structures and Functions

UNIT TITLE: *Taking Care of Plants*

QUESTION: What conditions are needed to keep a plant alive and healthy?

UNIT OVERVIEW: Children care for classroom plants for a two-week period, then prepare charts and drawings to show how structures of plants help the plants meet their requirements for life (e.g., air, water, nutrients, and light).

UNIT TITLE: *Taking Care of Animals*

QUESTION: What conditions are needed to keep an animal alive and healthy?

UNIT OVERVIEW: Children care for classroom animals such as dwarf frogs, millipedes, goldfish, or geckos and identify through diagrams and written explanations how they helped the animals meet their requirements for life (e.g., air, water, and food).

UNIT TITLE: *Cycles in a Garden*

QUESTION: How does a full-grown plant grow from a tiny seed?

UNIT OVERVIEW: Children maintain an outdoor garden, observe plants growing into adulthood from seeds, and maintain records that show the changes that occur as the plants go through their life cycles.

Figure B.1 Children's curiosity about plants makes this topic an excellent source of starter ideas.

frantisek hojdysz/Fotolia

UNIT TITLE: *Plant Cycles/Animal Cycles*

QUESTION: How are the life cycles of animals and plants similar and different?

UNIT OVERVIEW: After raising plants from seeds and frogs from eggs, children compare plant and animal life cycles, including attention to birth, adulthood, reproduction, and death.

UNIT TITLE: *Cells—The Basis of Life*

QUESTION: What makes a cell so special to life?

UNIT OVERVIEW: Each child or team of children is given a sample of cells that are easily observable using a microscope (e.g., paramecium, euglena, volvox, or ameba). They will be charged with taking care of the cell culture for two weeks, periodically estimating the number of organisms in the culture, graphing the data, and figuring out how they survive based on observations and research. *Note:* A digital microscope can help students visualize their cultures.

UNIT TITLE: *Our Senses, Windows to the World*

QUESTION: How do we know the world around us?

UNIT OVERVIEW: Children will use each of their five senses to solve a mystery. Put a popcorn popper in a mystery box. Hand out popcorn kernels in a black bag so the children can touch but not see them. Turn on the popcorn popper and let the children try to describe what is in the box. They will need to use their sense of hearing and smell. Hand out popped corn for them to see. If you choose, let them taste the popcorn to use the sense of taste.

● Ecosystems: Interactions, Energy, and Dynamics

UNIT TITLE: *Ecosystems in Balance*

QUESTION: Why are there more mice than hawks in the state park?

UNIT OVERVIEW: Through data collected or provided and direct observation, children make and justify a claim in response to the question.

UNIT TITLE: *Nature's Incredible Solar Chefs*

QUESTION: How did the Sun make an apple?

UNIT OVERVIEW: Children identify organisms that capture the Sun's energy in a desert, a woodland, a meadow, and an ocean ecosystem.

● Biological Evolution: Unity and Diversity

UNIT TITLE: *Incredible Life in the Lawn*

QUESTION: What is life like in the lawn?

UNIT OVERVIEW: Children are assigned a plot of lawn that is left unmowed. They make careful descriptive models of life in the lawn during the school year, recording their observations in their lab notebooks, raising questions, and conducting experiments throughout the year.

UNIT TITLE: *Life in a Log*

QUESTION: How many different forms of life can there be in a log?

UNIT OVERVIEW: Children explore a rotting log for all the different forms of life they can find. (Review safety: Wear gloves, check logs for stinging organisms, and do not handle organisms.) This can be coordinated with "Incredible Life in the Lawn."

● Heredity: Inheritance and Variation of Traits

UNIT TITLE: *Is That My Puppy?*

QUESTION: What makes puppies with the same parents look the same or different?

UNIT OVERVIEW: Children compare parents and offspring of animals and look for traits that might be inherited from the mother or father (puppy pictures are popular, but try a variety of organisms).

Make the CASE *An Individual or Group Challenge*

● **The Problem**	Three-dimensional teaching often begins with a phenomenon. It can be challenging to find a suitable phenomenon that inspires students, in their quest to figure out an explanation, to dive deeply into a topic that leads them to uncover core science.
● **Assess Your Prior Knowledge and Beliefs**	1. Write your interpretation of the following statement: Phenomena do not need to be phenomenal to be academically productive. 2. Discuss your interpretation with colleagues.
● **The Challenge**	Identify phenomena that you could use to anchor a unit about interdependent relationships in ecosystems (LS2A). Justify the phenomena by explaining how they could drive students to uncover core science concepts.

Classroom Enrichment Ideas

● Discovery Centers

A well-prepared in-class learning center offers children many opportunities to make their own discoveries. To be well prepared, such a center must provide a wide range of materials that encourage hands-on, discovery-based learning, ranging from print and audiovisual resources to art supplies and games. The learning center must be located where children have ready access to it yet can also be somewhat removed from the larger classroom setting while doing independent activities. The following starter ideas for in-class discovery centers should get you thinking about how to create centers in your own classroom. Suggestions for connections with disciplinary core ideas are included in parentheses.

> **CENTER TITLE:** *The Wonder Machine* (**LS1.A: Structure and Function**)
>
> **IDEA:** A corner of your classroom is a good location for this learning center. Allow enough floor space for children to make outlines of themselves by rolling out shelf paper and tracing around their bodies. You may want to cover part of the floor with newspapers on which the children can work with clay and paste. If you have computer software or videos related to the human body, make them available in this center, too (see Figure B.2).

Prepare activity cards or guide sheets that give directions for activities based on the following ideas:

- *Find Your Pulse* Children use a stopwatch or the second hand of a clock to count heartbeats, do mild exercises, and count heartbeats again. The children should graph their results.

Figure B.2   This in-class discovery center—the Wonder Machine—holds a host of activities to interest children.

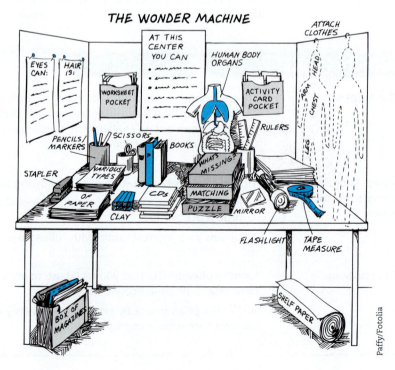

THE WONDER MACHINE

Paffy/Fotolia

- *Take a Breather* Children breathe on a mirror and record what they observe.
- *Bright Eyes* Children observe changes in their partner's eyes when they briefly shine a flashlight at them.
- *Different Bodies* Children trace each other while lying on shelf paper and then, after referring to materials on the principal organs of the body and their locations, draw the organs on the shelf paper. Some children may use a tape measure to gather data for a chart on foot sizes.
- *What's Inside?* Children use clay, construction paper, and other art materials to construct models of organ systems.

CENTER TITLE: *Worm Wonders* (**LS1.A: Structure and Function**)

IDEA: Identify the body parts of an earthworm, describe the function(s) of each, and carry out research using books and the internet to discover the nature of the earthworm's life cycle. If possible, also provide living earthworms at the center.

CENTER TITLE: *Something Fishy* (**LS1.A: Structure and Function**)

IDEA: Using a whole, dead (but refrigerated) fish, identify its body parts and adaptations that enable this species to swim efficiently, respire, capture prey, reproduce, and carry out its life cycle. If possible, also provide living fish at the center.

Bulletin Boards

BULLETIN BOARD TITLE: *Flower Power* (**LS1.A: Structure and Function**)

IDEA: Create vocabulary word cards for the words *stem, leaf, roots, petals, soil, air, Sun,* and *water*. Make construction paper cutouts of a plant stem, leaves, petals, roots, the Sun, clouds, soil, and raindrops, and display them on the bulletin board with the word cards. After the children become familiar with the vocabulary on the word cards, provide an age-appropriate method for attaching the cards to the appropriate parts. Provide a self-correcting key.

BULLETIN BOARD TITLE: *Desert Animal Homes* (**LS4.D: Biodiversity and Humans**)

IDEA: Cover the bulletin board with easel paper and use colored paper, crayons, pastels, paint, and other art supplies to create, with the children's assistance, a desert scene without animals. Include cacti, sand, rocks, a blue sky, a shining Sun, and so forth. Copy 10 pictures of desert animals (e.g., a hawk, a rattlesnake, a scorpion, and a lizard), and place them in a folder or envelope at the bottom of the bulletin board. Provide an age-appropriate method for children to attach the pictures to the bulletin board. Encourage children to use their free time to work on putting the animals in their proper places.

BULLETIN BOARD TITLE: *Plant Munchers* (**LS1.A: Structure and Function**)

IDEA: Create a large, generic plant that includes a flower, seed, fruits, leaves, stems, and roots. Add unlabeled arrows that point to each part. Put pictures of commonly eaten fruits and vegetables in a large envelope attached to the bulletin board. In their free time, have children attach the pictures to the appropriate arrows.

BULLETIN BOARD TITLE: *Producers, Consumers, and Decomposers* (**LS2.A: Interdependent Relationships in Ecosystems**)

IDEA: Cover the bulletin board with easel paper. Divide it into three equal-sized parts and label each with one of these headings: *Producer, Consumer,* or *Decomposer.* As the children have free time, ask them individually or in groups to draw and label an example of each type of organism following this rule: "The three organisms must interact with one another."

BULLETIN BOARD TITLE: *Body Systems* (**LS1.A: Structure and Function**)

IDEA: Place a large drawing of the human body at one side of the bulletin board. Each week, place a large index card with the name of a body system (e.g., digestion, circulation and respiration) at the top of the other side of the bulletin board. Challenge children to attach smaller cards with labels to show the sequence of steps that occur in the identified system. For example, if the system is digestion, the children might attach cards under it that say, "Food eaten," "Food enters stomach," and so on.

● Field Trips

Field trips provide amazing opportunities for discovery learning, as they take children out of the classroom and immerse them in the real world. Whether you teach in a city, suburban, or small-town school, you can find ideas for field trips all around you. The field trip may be to the regional aquarium or the pond down the street, but either way, children will be eager to see what the day will hold (see Figure B.3). Take advantage of local museums, nature centers, and discovery centers in your region. Many of these organizations have field trip guides for teachers and will work with you to customize your field trip. The National Park Service also provides resources for field trips for those fortunate enough to teach near a national park. Also consider mini-field trips to ecosystems in your own schoolyard.

Figure B.3   A field trip to an aquarium gives children the chance to see animals up close that they would otherwise see only in books or on television.

Andy Dean/Fotolia

FIELD TRIP TITLE: *Animal Study* (LS1.A: Structure and Function)

IDEA: Visiting a zoological park, an aquarium, or a farm gives children an opportunity to observe some of the animals they have seen only through media. Consider having individual children or cooperative learning groups become "experts" on one animal they will see during the trip and have them compare their research with what they actually observe during the trip. A nearby stream, field, or park also can offer children a chance to obtain first-hand knowledge about animal life. Because such trips can also provide opportunities for students to draw and write about interesting animals, art materials and notebooks should be available. If the location is easily accessible, visit it at different times of the year so variations in animal life can be observed.

FIELD TRIP TITLE: *Plants on Parade* (LS4.D: Biodiversity and Humans)

IDEA: A nature walk focused on plants may reveal a great deal to children about the types and quantities of plants that live on or near school grounds. Prior to the trip, have children predict the number of different plants they will see. During the trip, have them keep track of the kinds of plants they observe.

FIELD TRIP TITLE: *Mud Puddle Life* (LS4.D: Biodiversity and Humans)

IDEA: Children observe living things in and at the margins of a mud puddle after a rainstorm.

FIELD TRIP TITLE: *Dandelion Detectives* (LS1.A: Structure and Function)

IDEA: Children count dandelions, note where they are found, and observe their structures.

FIELD TRIP TITLE: *Squirrel Detectives* (LS3.B: Variation of Traits)

IDEA: Children count the squirrels they see on a nature walk and try to tell them apart by their unique characteristics.

FIELD TRIP TITLE: *Local Birds* (LS4.D: Biodiversity and Humans)

IDEA: Children record the types of birds that live in their city or town.

FIELD TRIP TITLE: *Bug Business* (LS4.D: Biodiversity and Humans)

IDEA: Children take a nature walk to locate (without touching) as many insects as they can and note what the insects are doing.

FIELD TRIP TITLE: *Is There Life in That Lot?* (LS4.D: Biodiversity and Humans)

IDEA: Under close supervision and at a vacant lot that is safe in every respect, children note the presence of such living things as ragweed and milkweed plants, fungi, moths, butterflies, and so forth.

Examples of Topics and Phenomena for the Life Sciences

PHENOMENA ARE "observable events that occur in the universe and that we can use our science knowledge to explain or predict."[1] They don't need to be flashy or sensational, but they should generate compelling questions that create real opportunities for students to develop an explanation or solve a problem. Some examples of phenomena and associated activities arranged by topic are listed below.

Topic: Adaptation

Phenomenon: Some animals seem invisible, e.g., zebras, uroplatus geckos, willow ptarmigans, baron caterpillars, seahorses, and stick insects.

Materials for Each Child or Group
Sheet of green construction paper
Sheet of brown construction paper
Scissors
Paper leaf pattern

Motivating Questions
- Why do zebras have stripes?
- How do colors and patterns help animals survive?

Directions
1. Distribute the materials and have the children use the leaf pattern to draw and then cut out one brown leaf and one green leaf. Have them cut out a few small green and brown squares that measure about 2.5 centimeters (1 inch) on each side.
2. Tell the children that they should pretend the squares are insects. Have them place the green insects on the brown leaf and the brown insects on the green leaf.
3. Ask the children how hard they think it would be to find the insects if they were birds.
4. Have the children put the green insects on the green leaf and ask the question again.
5. Take students into the schoolyard to look for evidence of organisms that use coloration to hide.

Science Content for the Teacher
Many animals have protective coloration that increases their chances of escaping predators. Insects that have the same color as their background stay still when predators are near and blend into their background, which increases their chances of survival.

Topic: Biodiversity

Phenomenon: A shovelful of soil is teeming with life, e.g., earthworms, mites, millipedes, centipedes, springtails, pillbugs, and grubs.

Materials
Sheet of easel paper
Marking pen

Motivating Questions
- Where do you think these animals live?
- How many animals do you think we will see?

Directions
1. Take the children on an expedition around the school grounds to look for animals in the soil and under rocks around the school. (Check out the locations first to ensure safety.)

2. On your return to the classroom, prepare a three-column chart and list the children's recollections of the types and quantities of animals observed. Also note where the animals were seen—for example, under a rock.

Science Content for the Teacher

Life is both diverse and widespread. Any lawn, playground, or natural area on or near the school will have an abundance of soil animals. Search for insects and other small creatures under rocks and near moist areas such as the ground near a water fountain or a mud puddle as well as on the bark of trees. Caution students not to handle insects and animals.

Topic: Variation among seeds

Phenomenon: Seeds come in a variety of shapes and sizes.

Materials for Each Child or Group

One common fruit per group (*Note:* Try to have a variety of fruits available, including oranges, apples, pears, grapefruit, peaches, and plums.)
Lightweight plastic serrated knives (if working with older children)
Paper towels
Drawing paper
Hand lens

Motivating Questions

- Do you think your fruit has a seed?
- Do you think your fruit has more than one seed?
- What do you think the seed or seeds in your fruit will look like?
- Do you think different fruits will have seeds that are the same or different?

Directions

1. Distribute the materials and give each group one or more fruits. Before they cut open their fruits, have the groups predict the number, shape, size, and color of the seed or seeds, then draw what they think their seed or seeds will look like.

2. Have the groups cut open the fruits and examine the seeds. *Safety note:* Cut open the fruit for younger children after the groups complete their drawings.

3. Have the groups compare the seeds and discuss the variety of the number and types of seeds in fruits.

Science Content for the Teacher

Although there is great variety in seeds of common fruits, fruits of the same type have the same type of seeds. An interesting addition to your discussion would be consideration of the great size and variation in seeds, with the coconut as one of the largest seeds in the natural world. You may wish to point out to the children that many types of seeds are important to humans, such as corn, oats, and wheat.

Topic: Growth and reproduction

Phenomenon: Some plants grow from roots.

Materials

Small sweet potato
Glass wider than the potato's diameter
Six toothpicks
Water

Motivating Questions	• Where are the sweet potato seeds?
	• Where does a new potato plant come from?

Directions
1. Distribute the materials and have the children wash the sweet potatoes to remove excess dirt.
2. Have each group of children stick the toothpicks into the potato so it can be suspended in the glass with the narrow end submerged in water. (About one-fourth should be in the water.)
3. After each group prepares its potato, put the potatoes in a warm, well-lit area of the room.

Children will need to add water periodically to replace that used by the growing potato plant and lost through evaporation.

Science Content for the Teacher   Unlike the white potato, which is a tuber, or underground stem, the sweet potato is a root. The rapid root and leaf growth that will occur is partially due to the availability of starch in the fleshy material within the sweet potato root.

Topic: Biodiversity

Phenomenon: Insects are very different and very similar.

Materials   Collection of common insects (or photographs), e.g., grasshoppers, crickets, butterflies, flies, and ants
Hand lens
Drawing paper

Motivating Questions
• How are these animals alike?
• How are they different?

Directions
1. Have the groups observe the insect or insects in each jar. Provide a hand lens for those who want to make closer observations. Encourage the children to make a descriptive model and drawing of each insect.
2. After each group has made observations and drawings, begin a discussion of how the insects are the same and different.

Science Content for the Teacher   Although insects vary greatly in size, color, and the detailed shapes of their body parts, all have three main body parts: a head, a thorax, and an abdomen. Unlike spiders and other arachnids that have eight legs, insects are six-legged creatures. Insects have two antennae and wings. They are invertebrates with *exoskeletons*, relatively hard exterior body coverings that protect the softer interior parts.

Topic: The mystery of the 17-Year cicada life cycle

Phenomenon: Locusts (*Magicicada septendecim*) spend 17 years living underground in the nymph stage before emerging to become an adult.

Materials   Access to the internet
Poster paper
Markers

Sound of an adult cicada (misnamed the 17-year locust), easily found online (search for videos of cicadas)

Motivating Questions

- What does this sound remind you of?
- How old do you think this creature is?
- What do you think it is doing underground for 17 years?

Directions

1. Have the groups research the life cycle of the cicada, also known as the 17-year locust. They should find out where and when it lays its eggs, where the nymph stage of the insect lives, when the nymph becomes an adult, and the effects the adult insect has on its surroundings when it lays its eggs.

2. Have the children make drawings of the cicada at the various stages of its life cycle.

3. Bring the groups back together to discuss what they learned. In particular, why is the cicada sometimes called the 17-year locust?

Science Content for the Teacher

The species of cicada that has a 17-year life cycle is commonly known as the 17-year locust. It is a member of the grasshopper family, and is not a locust. Its life cycle includes three stages: The adult female lays eggs in slits cut in young twigs, then larvae develop. The larvae drop from the trees, burrow into the ground, and suck on juices from roots. After 13 or 17 years, depending on the species, nymphs emerge from the ground and become winged adults, which live for about a week.

Discovery Activities: Use the Following Activities to Support Discovery Experiences with Your Students.

● What Is a Seed?

Objective

- Children will describe a seed as something capable of growth.

Science Processes Emphasized

Asking questions
Predicting
Observing
Recording
Planning and carrying out investigations
Interpreting data
Contrasting variables
Arguing from evidence

Materials for Each Child or Group

Large cardboard box cut 5 to 10 centimeters (2 to 4 inches) tall and lined with plastic
Soil or starting mixture (vermiculite plus soil)
Collections of seeds and things that look like seeds but are not seeds (e.g., pebbles, flowers, parts of flowers, and buds from plants)
Lima beans or similarly large seeds for each student
Chart paper
One index card per student

Figure B.4   Young children enjoy bringing in their own seeds and observing how they grow.

Gorilla/Fotolia
Geoff Dann/Dorling Kindersley, Ltd.

Motivation   Ask the children to bring in seeds for science investigations.

Directions   1. Set out samples of the seeds that have been brought in by the children and non seeds provided by you. Ask the students to describe the seeds while you list their observations for all the class to see.

2. Ask the children to make a claim about what makes a seed a seed.

3. Have each group separate what they believe are seeds and non seeds based on their claims.

4. Have the children plant seeds and non seeds to test their claims.

5. Let the children decide how many of each item should be planted and how deep. Explain that the amount of water, light, warmth, and so on should be the same for each item. These things will be easy to control if the samples are planted in the same box.

6. Have each child label each row with the name of the item planted. Set aside a short period of time each day for maintenance and data gathering. Encourage the children to keep a daily log of what they see.

7. Some children may want to peek at the items during the experiment. If they do, they need to think about the number of each item that was planted and how they can make their inspection without disturbing the others. One way to observe germination without disturbing the seeds is to place a moist paper towel in a glass jar (a plastic sandwich bag can be used in place of the jar) and "plant" the item between the towel and the glass. Such a jar will allow students to see what is going on in the soil in the boxes, but perhaps it can be kept a secret until the students have the pleasure of digging up a few of their own seeds.

8. When the seeds have been growing for a while, have the children dig up samples of each type of seed. They can make observations, record them, and compare their new observations with the observations they made at the start of the investigation.

9. After some items have sprouted, it's useful to divide the original set of items into growers and non growers. With this set to examine, students should begin to investigate where the items come from and develop a general definition of a *true seed*.

Key Discussion Questions

1. In what ways are all these items alike? *They are all small.*

2. How many items of each type should be planted? *More than one or two, since some might die before they come up and can be seen.*

3. How deeply should they be planted? *Answers will vary based upon gardening experience, but common sense usually prevails.*

4. What should be done about the amount of water, sunlight, temperature, and so on that the items receive? *They should be kept the same so that all seeds have the same chance of living.*

5. What is the biggest difference among the items at the end of the investigation? *Some grow and some don't.*

6. What did some seeds become? *They grew into new plants.*

Science Content for the Teacher

Seeds come in all sizes, from those as small as the period at the end of a sentence to others as big as a coconut. Shape can also vary dramatically, from round and smooth to pyramid-like. Seeds have protective shells (seed coats) that keep the embryonic plant alive. Stored food will provide the energy for the seedling to reach the soil surface and begin producing food of its own.

To survive, some plants produce great numbers of seeds, and others produce seeds with structures (such as the hooks on burrs and the "wings" on maple seeds) that enable them to be dispersed. Some seeds even look like insects, which discourages seed-eating birds from consuming them.

Even with this great diversity, seeds differ significantly from all the non-seed items in this activity by being able to grow and reproduce.

Extensions

Science: Cut open some fruits and have the children find and describe the seeds. Students may then produce a poster or bulletin board with as many kinds of seeds as can be collected. The seeds can be grouped by size, shape, or color.

Math: Some students may be interested in collecting seeds to be used as "counters." These students can sort the seeds into sets and arrange them in order from smallest to largest.

● Who Goes There?

Objective	• Children will match pictures of common animals with the animals' footprints.
Science Processes Emphasized	Observing Analyzing and interpreting data Inferring
Materials for Each Child or Group	Set of photographs of the animals for which you have footprints Set of photographs showing the various environments in which the animals live Set of animal name cards Set of unlabeled animal footprints
Motivation	Suggest that children pretend they are teams of animal trackers, and explain that each team will be awarded one point for each animal they successfully track.

Directions

1. Before beginning this activity, you will need a set of unlabeled animal footprints and a set of pictures illustrating environments in which the animals are likely to be found.

2. Project pictures of an animal track and its environment. After some discussion, have the children try to think of the animal being described. The group members can discuss the possibilities among themselves before the group suggests an animal. Each group should elect a spokesperson.

3. When all the teams are ready, have one spokesperson from each team hold up the picture of the animal that his or her group selected. Encourage each spokesperson to tell why his or her group's choice is the correct one.

4. Award a point to each group that is correct. The job of spokesperson is then rotated to the next person in each group and the game continues.

Key Discussion Questions

1. Which of the tracks comes from the biggest animal? *Answers will depend on the tracks and pictures you are using.*

2. Which of the tracks comes from the smallest animal? *Answers will vary.*

3. Which of the tracks comes from an animal with claws that stick out? *Answers will vary.*

4. Which of the tracks belongs to an animal that can climb trees? *Answers will vary.*

5. Hold up pictures of various environments (e.g., a treetop for squirrels and an open plain with trees in Africa for elephants) and ask which of the animals might be found in them. Ask the students to guess which footprint might be found in most environments. (Have the teams explain why they decided on particular footprints.)

Science Content for the Teacher

Footprints hold clues about the lives and environments of the animals that made them. Each footprint reveals hints about adaptations that enable the animal to survive in its ecosystem.

Very large footprints often belong to large animals or to animals that travel over soft terrain. For example, the relatively large feet of the snowshoe rabbit support its weight on snow, thus allowing it to travel well on terrain that hinders most other animals. Most animals that live on the open range have evolved smaller feet with hooves that allow them to run fast on fairly smooth, hard land. Some footprints show evidence of claws used for defense as well as climbing. Retractable claws are an obvious benefit to animals that must be able to run quickly and silently before catching their prey.

Extensions *Science:* If you live in an area with snow in the winter, take students outside to look for animal tracks (e.g., squirrel, birds, or deer). For larger tracks, such as deer, pour plaster of paris into the prints to make molds.

Obtain or reproduce pictures of various tracks showing an action (e.g., animals walking and then running). Have the teams determine what happened.

Some students may want to research the topic of fossils, especially fossilized tracks, and what scientists have learned about the animals that made them. Other students may enjoy making answer boards on which others try to match pictures of animals with pictures of their footprints.

Art: Students may want to make pictures from a set of linoleum printing blocks of footprints or actual plaster casts from footprints found in the mud or snow.

● Male and Female Guppies: What's the Difference?

Objective Children will observe the physical characteristics of male and female guppies.

Science Processes Emphasized Observing
Classifying

Materials for Each Child or Group Male and female guppies
Two clean liter- or quart-size jars filled with aquarium water
Dry fish food
Hand lens

Motivation Ask the children if they know what a guppy is. Display the guppies you will use for the activity and tell the children they will have a chance to make careful observations of male and female guppies.

Directions
1. Distribute a jar containing aquarium water, a female guppy, and a hand lens to each child or group.

2. Ask each child or group to observe the external characteristics of the guppy and make a drawing of it, labeling the body parts. Encourage them to shade in parts of their drawings to show the guppy's markings.

3. Once the drawings are completed, distribute a jar containing aquarium water and a male guppy. Have the children observe the male guppy and have each make a labeled drawing of it.

4. Allow the children to visit with one another to see if the male guppy they drew resembles other male guppies and if their female guppy resembles other female guppies.

Key Discussion Questions How can you tell the difference between a male and a female guppy? *The female is usually larger, with a gray color and a fan-shaped fin. The male is smaller, with patches of color and a tube-like part at the base of its tail.*

Science Content for the Teacher   Guppies are tropical fish. The male is smaller than the female but has a larger tail. It is also more brightly colored. The female is usually a uniform gray. The female has a fan-shaped anal fin. The male's anal fin is pointed and tube-like.

Extensions   *Science:* The demonstration on the birth of guppies, described later in this chapter, is an effective follow-up to this activity.
Art: Some children may want to create larger drawings of the guppies they observed. Drawing paper and a supply of pastels will assist them in such a project. Encourage the children to reproduce nature's coloration faithfully by using the appropriate colors and shades of pastels. You may want to spray fixative on the children's finished drawings to preserve them.

● How Do Mealworms React to Light?

Objectives
- Children will set up and carry out an experiment to determine how a mealworm responds to light.
- Children will collect, summarize, and interpret the data they gather.

Science Processes Emphasized   Observing
Planning and carrying out investigations
Recording data
Analyzing and interpreting data
Arguing from evidence

Materials for Each Child or Group   Live mealworm (available in a pet store)
Small flashlight
20-centimeter (about 8-inch) circle of paper divided into eight pie-shaped sections

Motivation   Ask the class how they can determine if people like something. The children may suggest that they can ask people or try something and see if people smile, frown, or become angry. Some children may suggest that the number of times a person does something could be used to determine what the person likes. Tell the children they will find out how well mealworms like being in the dark and because mealworms do not talk, the children will have to design an investigation to find the answer.

Directions
1. Display the mealworms.
2. Let the students figure out how to plan and carry out their investigation. Look for controls, repeated trials, independent variables, and dependent variables. It is not expected that young children will know these terms, but you may recognize and facilitate the practices. Provide scaffolding as needed.
3. Have the children develop charts or graphs to summarize their findings.
4. Combine and make available the results from all the groups so that conclusions can be drawn.
5. Have the students make a claim about mealworms' responses to light based on the evidence.

Science Content for the Teacher   Mealworms usually avoid lighted areas. They are frequently found in bins of old grain or meal, which provide dark, dry environments. A mealworm that enters a lit area will lose touch with its food supply and possibly fall prey to birds or other predators.

Key Discussion Questions

1. Why should you do this experiment many times before concluding that a mealworm likes or dislikes light? *Mealworms don't always move in the right direction. It takes several trials to determine a pattern of behavior.*

2. What other things might make a mealworm respond by moving? *They might be afraid of us. They might not like the heat that comes from the light. They see light from other parts of the room.*

3. Why might a mealworm avoid light? *It prefers dark. The light may mean danger to the mealworm.* Ask whether they know this based on data or if it is an inference based on data.

Extensions

Science: Some children may want to design and conduct experiments to see how mealworms respond to heat, cold, moisture, dryness, loud sounds, and different kinds of food.

Language arts: Have the children pretend they are mealworms and write stories describing their adventures in a land of giants.

● How Does Light Affect the Growth of Plants?

Objectives

- Children will design and conduct an experiment to test the effect of light on the growth of grass.
- Children will observe and record the color and length of grass grown under two conditions: light and dark.

Science Processes Emphasized

Asking questions
Analyzing and interpreting data
Planning and carrying out investigations

Materials

Two paper cups
One-quarter teaspoon of grass seed
Potting soil or synthetic plant-growing material
Light source that can be placed about 25 centimeters (about 10 inches) above the cup (a fluorescent grow-light fixture works best)
Ruler
Graph paper
Easel paper for class data

Motivation

Tell the class a story about two neighbors. The grass on neighbor A's lawn grows faster than the grass on neighbor B's lawn. The two neighbors used the same grass seed and both lawns receive the same amount of water. Neighbor A does not have many trees on his south-facing lawn. Neighbor B has many trees on his north-facing lawn. The neighbors live in New England.

Directions

1. Challenge the students to propose an explanation for the difference in rate at which each lawn grows.

2. Help student groups plan an investigation using the materials provided. Show them how to plant the grass seeds. The students should decide on the length of time the grass will be in light and dark. One set of seeds representing neighbor A's grass should receive more light than the set of seeds representing neighbor B's grass. Have the students test a range of light exposure times in the class. Set up a control with seeds in the dark.

3. When the groups make their observations, they should record the appearance, color, and average length of plants. The determination of length will be challenging, because the groups will need to invent a strategy that does not require the measurement of every blade of grass. One strategy might be to measure five blades from different parts of the cup and average the measurements. Another would be to simply record the total height of the sample. The length measurements as well as other observations should be recorded on a data sheet, which should be maintained for about two to three weeks.

Key Discussion Questions

1. If we want to see if the seeds need light to grow, what must we do to the water and temperature of the plants? *We have to keep the water and temperature the same for both cups.*

2. Why did all the seeds start to grow equally well? *Seeds don't need light to sprout.*

3. Why did the plants in the dark stop growing and turn yellow after a while? *They ran out of food. They needed light to make food and grow.*

Science Content for the Teacher

Grass seeds contain a small amount of stored food in their cotyledons, which allows them to begin growing. When the food is used up, the plant must rely on sunlight for the energy required for further growth. Neighbor A's lawn receives more light; therefore, the grass grows faster.

Extension

Science/Nutrition: Some students may want to obtain seeds at a health food store that are appropriate for sprouting (e.g., mung beans, alfalfa, or lettuce). Once the seeds have sprouted, the class can have a feast while discussing the nutrients found in the sprouts.

● Is It Alive?

Objective

• Children will observe and describe the differences between living and nonliving things.

Science Processes Emphasized

Observing
Communicating
Inferring

Materials

Living animal (fish, insect, mouse)
Living plant
Candle flame (keep safe from students)
Nonliving thing (shoe, pencil, book)
A simple robot that responds in some manner to its environment, such as a toy that moves randomly until it hits an object and then moves in another direction

Motivation

Prior to class, line up the items where all the students can see them.

Directions

1. Ask the children to separate the items into two categories: living and nonliving.

2. Ask them to defend their claims based on their criteria for something to be alive.

3. Challenge the notion of the robot and the flame. Both use energy, create waste, respond to stimuli (flame responds to breezes), and move, yet they are not alive . . . or are they? (*Note:* Reproduction is not easily reconciled as a criterion for life. One can be alive and not reproduce. However, one cannot be alive without coming from another living thing.)

Key Discussion Questions

1. In what ways are living and nonliving things the same? *Answers will vary and may include such observations as living and nonliving things can be the same color or size. They can both be soft or hard.*

2. In what ways are living and nonliving things different? *Answers will vary and may include the idea that nonliving things stay the same, last a long time and don't change very much. Living things like plants have seeds; animals have baby animals.*

Science Content for the Teacher

Living things and nonliving things may share some common characteristics. They both may move, they both may make noise, and they may be the same color or weight. However, things that are alive grow, change, or develop from infant to adult, and are able to reproduce their own kind.

Extension

Health: Discuss the special responsibilities involved in caring for living things that are different from the responsibilities involved in caring for nonliving things. Some children may want to make drawings or posters that show how to care for pets or other living things.

● The Birth of Guppies

Note: This demonstration can be used as a follow-up to the Discovery Activity on male and female guppies described earlier in this chapter.

Objectives

- Children will observe the construction of an aquarium.
- Children will describe the roles of male and female guppies in the reproductive process.

Science Processes Emphasized

Observing
Inferring

Materials

Fish aquarium
Aged tap water at room temperature
Aquarium sand and gravel
Dip net
Two or three nursery traps
Thermometer
Small container with two male guppies
Small container with four female guppies
Light source (a reading lamp can be used)
Dry fish food
Assorted freshwater plants, including *Anacharis*, duckweed, and eelgrass

Motivation

Ask the children if they have ever seen the birth of guppies. After a discussion of observations they have made of guppies reproducing, tell them that within the next few weeks, they may see guppies being born. Display the aquarium and other materials.

Directions
1. Have the children observe the materials you have placed on display.
2. Begin assembling the aquarium by placing a five-centimeter (two-inch) layer of sand on its floor. Plant eelgrass in the sand. Add the aged tap water (gently so as to avoid stirring up the sand). Float the duckweed and Anacharis in the water.
3. Put the thermometer in the water and place the light source nearby. The light source will need to be moved back and forth during the demonstration to maintain the water temperature at 25°C (75°F).
4. Place the male and female guppies in the aquarium.
5. Float the nursery traps in the aquarium and sprinkle some fish food on the water's surface.
6. Maintain the aquarium over a two- or three-week period and encourage the children to make observations of changes that occur in the shape of the female guppies. A pregnant female will develop a bulging abdomen. Use the dip net to place each pregnant female in its own nursery trap. This increases the chances that the soon-to-be-born babies will survive, for the traps will protect the new guppies from hungry adult fish.

Key Discussion Questions
1. Why did we plant eelgrass and other aquarium plants in the aquarium? *Answers will vary and may include so that some living things in the aquarium would have plants to eat.*
2. What does the male guppy do in the reproductive process? *Places sperm in the female guppy*
3. What does the female guppy do in the reproductive process? *She produces the eggs that get fertilized and has a place inside her body where the new guppies begin to develop.*

Science Content for the Teacher
Guppies are classified as live bearers, meaning they give birth to live young rather than lay eggs. Therefore, guppies use internal fertilization. The eggs hatch as they are being laid, thereby classifying guppies as ovoviviparous fish. Although the eggs remain in the female's body, there is no placental connection, as is the case with viviparous species.

For this demonstration, you must know how to assemble and maintain a simple freshwater aquarium. The preceding directions provide some of the basic information. If you want to increase the likelihood of maintaining a healthy aquarium for more than one or two weeks, it would be worthwhile to talk with a knowledgeable salesperson in a pet store to learn the details of raising and caring for tropical fish in general and guppies in particular. Additional materials—such as water heaters, pumps, and filters—are necessary if you want to keep the aquarium functioning all through the year. This equipment is commonly available at pet shops.

● The Insect Aquarium

Note: This demonstration should be done in the spring.

Objectives
- Children will observe the construction of a freshwater insect aquarium.
- Children will infer the reasons for the placement of various materials in the aquarium.

Science Processes Emphasized
Observing

Inferring

Materials   Four-liter (about one-gallon) wide-mouth jar or a small plastic or glass aquarium
Source of fresh pond or stream water
Collection of live water plants and insects from a pond or stream
Small twigs from the pond or stream
Pebbles and rocks found at the water's edge
Clean aquarium sand (available from a pet shop)
Fine mesh screening to cover the top of aquarium

Motivation   Tell the children you have gathered a variety of materials to construct a freshwater aquarium. Discuss the difference between freshwater and saltwater. Tell the children that the aquarium you are going to build will not contain fish but may contain other interesting creatures. Their job will be to give you ideas as you build it.

Directions   1. In the spring prior to the demonstration, gather freshwater and a variety of plants and aquatic insects from a local pond or stream. Keep the specimens fresh and take them to class.

2. In the classroom, fill the bottom of the container with about five centimeters (about two inches) of sand and root the water plants in the sand. Place a few large twigs at the side of the jar in a way that roots their ends in the sand and put some rocks and pebbles on the surface of the sand.

3. Gently add freshwater until the water level is about 12 centimeters (about 5 inches) from the top. Float some twigs on the surface so that insects emerging from the water have a place to stay. Cover the top with the mesh and put the aquarium where it can receive sunlight and benefit from air circulation.

4. Encourage the children to create an initial descriptive model of the aquarium and its contents, make daily observations of the aquarium, and infer reasons for some of the changes they observe.

Key Discussion Questions   1. Why do you think we are doing this demonstration in the spring? *Answers will vary and may include the idea that insects hatch in the spring.*

2. Why do you think we put the aquarium in the sunlight? *Answers will vary and may include the idea that the plants need sunlight to make food.*

Science Content for the Teacher   Insects you may find in a pond are the nymphs of dragonflies, water boatmen, mosquito larvae, mayflies, and water beetles. Insects are easily found in the shallow water at the edge of a pond or stream.

Extension   *Science/Language arts:* After about a week of observation, ask the children to write a poem titled, "Changes," that includes at least three observations they have made of the aquarium.

● How Can We Help People See Us at Night?

Materials   Sheet of dark construction paper
Small mirror
Silver glitter
Glue
Transparent tape
Flashlight
Bicycle reflector (optional)

Motivating Questions

- Is it hard or easy to see people who are walking or riding bikes at night?
- What should people who are out at night do to prevent being hit by a car?

Directions

1. Darken the room and ask the children if it would be hard or easy to see a person on a bicycle at night wearing a shirt that is the color of the construction paper. (*Note:* This would be an excellent time to have a brief discussion on bicycle safety.)

2. Shine the flashlight near the paper and have the children pretend the light is an automobile headlight. Ask how visible the person would be if the children were in a car. Tape the mirror to one side of the paper and repeat the demonstration. Be sure the children notice that mirrors do not help if the light beam does not shine directly on them.

3. Draw a circle on the paper, fill the circle with glue, and sprinkle it with silver glitter. Try to produce some layers of glitter so that not all the glitter is flat on the paper. Your intent is to replicate a bicycle reflector. Have the children compare the extent to which the paper is lit without anything on it, with the mirror on it, and with the glued-on glitter. If you are able to obtain a bicycle reflector, attach that to the paper as well.

Science Content for the Teacher

How well we see something depends on how well light is reflected from the object. A bicycle reflector contains many tiny mirror-like objects that reflect light from many directions, so it is easy to see at night.

How Do Your Ears Help You Recognize Things?

Materials

Small rubber ball
Sheet of newspaper
Empty soda bottle
Empty glass
Glass of water
Movable room divider or other object to use as a visual screen

Motivating Questions

- Which sounds are easy or hard to guess?
- Why are some sounds easy to guess and some sounds hard to guess?

Directions

1. Keep all materials behind a screen for the duration of the demonstration. Ask for volunteers to sit in front of the screen facing the class. (*Alternative:* Play recordings of sounds from nature. Look for a variety of sounds from different regions: jungle sounds, city sounds, ocean sounds, etc. Ask students to imagine they are in the environment where those sounds are being produced. Have them describe the source of the sounds in writing, illustrations, or both.)

2. Use the newspaper, ball, soda bottle, and glass of water to produce various sounds—such as the crumpling of paper, the bounce of a ball, the noise of water poured from glass to glass, or the sound made blowing across the soda bottle—and have the volunteers try to identify them. Discuss what factors make it easy or difficult to recognize the sources of sounds.

Science Content for the Teacher

The human senses are important because they allow us to take in information about our surroundings. The sense we make of the sounds we hear depends on a variety of factors, including our previous experience, whether the sound is clear or muffled, how loud the sound is, and the sensitivity of our ears.

● The Mystery Bag

Objectives	• Using their sense of touch, children will name assorted objects.
	• Children will match objects that they see with ones that they feel.

Science Processes Emphasized

Observing
Inferring

Materials for Each Child or Group

Assorted objects, including pencils, erasers, paper clips, rubber bands, wooden blocks, marshmallows, and coins of various sizes
Boxes for the objects
Large paper bags with two holes (large enough for a hand to fit through) cut near the bottom of each bag
Two paper clips to close the tops of the bags

Motivation

Before class begins, place one of the objects in a bag. Explain to the children that they are going to discover how their sense of touch can help them identify things. Begin the activity by placing your hand in one of the holes in the bag to feel the object inside. Describe the object to the children. Have various children come to the front of the room to feel the object in the bag. Record what they think the object is on the chalkboard or easel pad.

Directions

1. Form two-person cooperative learning teams and give each team a box containing the objects listed for this activity. Have the teams decide who will go first in each team and have that person close his or her eyes. At the front of the room, hold up the type of object for the other team member to place in the bag.

2. Have the children who have had their eyes closed put one hand through each hole and feel the mystery object.

3. Ask the children to identify the object. If they are unable to name the object, hold up an assortment of objects and have the children vote for the one they think is correct.

Key Discussion Questions

1. What part of the body do we use most to feel things? *The hands*
2. What are some of the things the hands can feel? *How hot or cold things, whether objects are sharp, smooth, rough, soft, hard, and so on*
3. What are some things that hands can't tell? *What color an object is, how shiny or bright it is, and so on*

Science Content for the Teacher

The skin has sense receptors that are sensitive to touch, warmth, cold, pain, and pressure. These sense receptors are not evenly distributed. Pressure is felt most accurately by the tip of the nose, the tongue, and the fingers. Sense receptors in our hands give us our awareness of heat, cold, pain, and pressure.

Extension

Math: Place a set of rods of different lengths in the bags and ask the children to select the biggest rod, the smallest, the second biggest, and so on.

Art: Some children may want to build a "feely board" collage out of materials of various textures, shapes, and sizes.

● Sniff, Snuff, and Sneeze

Objectives
- Children will use their sense of smell to determine the contents of closed paper bags.
- Children will be able to identify various common odors (such as those of an onion, vinegar, an apple, and an orange).

Science Processes Emphasized
Observing
Inferring

Materials for Each Child or Group
Paper bags (lunch size)
25 centimeters (10 inches) of string for each bag
Plastic sandwich bags
Paper towels
Peppermint oil
Wintergreen oil
Camphor oil
Lemon extract
Vinegar
Onion
Apple
Orange

Motivation
Place a small amount of one of the odor-producing substances in one of the bags. Tie the bag loosely with string so that odors are able to escape but the students cannot see into the bag. Invite the students to identify the scent in the bag without looking in it or using their hands.

Directions
1. Distribute the paper bags and string and have the children write their names on the bags. Have them select one of the odor-producing foods (apple, orange, or onion), place a small piece of it on a small piece of paper towel in the bag, and loosely tie the bag.
2. Divide the children into cooperative learning groups and have the members of the groups try to identify what is in each bag without looking.
3. Have each group select one bag to share with another group. Each group should discuss their observations and reach an agreement about what is in the other group's bag.
4. Place one or two drops of each oil and the vinegar on a small piece of paper towel and seal it in a plastic bag.
5. Give each group a set of bags. Tell them to smell all of the bags and then identify and classify the scents any way they can.

Key Discussion Questions
1. How can we tell what is in the bag without opening it or touching it? *By smell*
2. What are some words that can be used to describe odors? *Good, bad, strong, sour, sweet, medicine-smelling, food-smelling*

3. How does smelling help animals survive? *By helping them track prey, by helping them sense enemies*

Science Content for the Teacher

When we smell something, we sample the air by inhaling it and having it move over receptors deep in our nasal cavity. These receptors analyze the chemicals in the air sample with great precision and transmit the findings to our brain for analysis and storage. Minute odors can trigger vivid memories.

Extension

Art: Some children may want to produce a collage of pictures of good- and bad-smelling things. The children may be able to scent portions of the collage, such as pictures of flowers.

● Using Your Senses to Classify Things

Objective

- Children will use their senses of sight and touch to classify seeds.

Science Process Emphasized

Classifying

Materials for Each Child or Group

Paper plate

Small plastic bag containing a variety of dried seeds, including sunflower seeds, kidney beans, lima beans, lentils, etc.

Hand lens

Motivation

Display a bag of seeds and tell the children they are going to see how well they can sort through such a bag. Explain to them that they are to sort the seeds into different groups on their paper plates.

Directions

1. Distribute a bag, paper plate, and hand lens to each group, and have the groups classify the seeds by placing them in like piles on a paper plate. *Safety note:* If you are doing this activity with very young children, caution them not to eat any of the seeds or put them in their noses, ears, or mouths.

2. After the groups have begun their work, display the hand lenses and ask how they could be used to help classify the seeds.

Key Discussion Questions

1. How did your sense of sight help you group the seeds? *Answers will vary, but might include references to color or shape.*

2. If you were asked to group the seeds by how smooth or rough they were, what sense would you use? *Touch* (After you ask this question, have the groups reclassify their seeds on the basis of smoothness and roughness.)

Science Content for the Teacher

Our senses provide us with detailed information about our surroundings. Even something as simple as calling a person by name requires us to first use our senses to identify the person and then decide whether we know the person or not. We can identify the person by sight or by the sound of her or his voice.

Extension

Science/Health: Bring in a variety of healthy foods and have the children group them according to taste: sweet, salty, sour, or bitter.

● Are You Part of Any Food Chains?

Objectives
- Children will trace the locations of foods they have eaten in the food chain and discover their own location in the food chain.
- Children will communicate orally or in writing information about the factors that may affect the quantity and quality of the food that reaches them.

Science Processes Emphasized
Inferring
Communicating information

Materials
Potato
Magazine photo of a hamburger

Motivation
After a brief discussion of the children's favorite meals, ask whether they have thought about how the food was produced. Hold up a potato and a picture of a hamburger and tell the children they are going to discover what these foods have in common.

Directions
1. Distribute a small potato and a photo of a hamburger to each group. Ask the groups to make food chain charts that relate the foods to them. The chart for the potato, for example, would simply show the potato and a human. The chart for the hamburger would identify grass or grain, beef cattle, and humans.
2. Challenge some of the students to create a food chain that includes a human and a great white shark. When they are done, ask them to look at their food chain to see if they have shown the complete sequence of events that leads from the Sun's energy to the energy the shark needs to survive to their own needs for energy.

Key Discussion Questions
1. How would changes in the amount of sunlight affect the food you eat? *Answers will vary but should note that limited water or sunlight can affect plant growth and thus affect animals that eat the plants and people who eat the plants and animals.*
2. If you are a vegetarian, is your food chain longer or shorter than the food chain of a person who is a meat eater? Why? *Shorter, because the energy from the Sun that is captured through photosynthesis goes directly from the fruits and vegetables to the person.*

Science Content for the Teacher
Photosynthesis, the process by which the Sun's energy is captured by plants, depends on the temperature, water, sunlight, and air. Meat eaters as well as vegetarians require access to this captured energy to carry out life processes. Photosynthesizers such as plants and several microorganisms are nature's solar panels that harness energy from the Sun and convert it into usable forms for life.

Extension
Science/Social studies: Encourage the children to identify specific geographic locales where some of their favorite foods are produced. Have them describe and illustrate the various modes of transportation used to move the food products to them.

● **Your Nose Knows**

Objectives	• Children will observe how long it takes them to notice a substance introduced into the air in the classroom.
	• Children will infer how the scent of a substance travels to their noses.

Science Processes Emphasized

Observing

Inferring

Materials

Perfume

Oil of peppermint

Oil of citronella

Four saucers

Motivation

Tell the children you will do a demonstration about smell. Ask them to think about how smells work as you give the demonstration.

Directions

1. Have the children sit around the room at various distances from the table that you will use for the demonstration. Open one of the containers and pour a few drops of one of the substances on a saucer. Tilt the saucer to spread the liquid over its surface.

2. Ask the children to raise their hands when they smell the substance.

3. After you have repeated the process for each substance, ask the children to explain how the smell got from the substance on the saucer to their noses. This is an opportunity for you to discuss the idea of particles entering the air from the substance and gradually spreading out, or *diffusing*.

Key Discussion Questions

1. Would opening a window or turning on a fan help us notice the smell more or less quickly? *Answers will vary. If the movement of air directs molecules of the substance toward the children, they will smell the substances more quickly than if the window is closed or there is no fan.*

2. Do you think dogs have a better sense of smell than humans? *Answers will vary. Some children may have seen television programs or movies that show dogs tracking crime suspects.*

Science Content for the Teacher

Sense organs gather information about our surroundings and send the information to the brain. Our sense of smell (olfactory sense) results from the stimulation of olfactory cells in the nose by molecules in the air. Nerve impulses carry information from the olfactory cells to the brain. What we know as smell is in fact the brain's response to the information it receives.

Extension

Science/Health: Engage the children in a discussion of the possible safety advantages provided by the ability to smell odors. Ask: Does your nose help keep you safe? As the children respond, comment on how the smell of food going bad gives our brains important information.

Life Sciences Sample Lesson

Title: Looking for Life in Your Own Schoolyard

Grades K–4

Suggested practices, core ideas, and crosscutting concepts related to Next Generation Science Standards:[2]

- Science practices: carrying out investigations, analyzing and interpreting data, using mathematics
- Core idea: biodiversity
- Crosscutting concept: systems[3]

Background for Teachers

In his book *Last Child in the Woods*, Richard Louv addresses the growing distance of children from direct experiences with nature. This sample lesson is a year-long activity that will provide a foundation for the exploration and discovery of many life science concepts while placing children in direct contact with the wonders of nature.

In this ongoing investigation, children will observe a one-square-meter plot in the schoolyard. It could be a woodland, a meadow, or a wetland (consider safety). If none of these are available, request that a portion of the school grounds be left unmowed throughout the year. The suggested activities in this Sample Lesson can easily be expanded and will grow throughout the year. Building on a familiar theme throughout the year will enable children to deepen their understanding by making connections in a meaningful context.

Biodiversity refers to the number and variety of living things in a particular region. Maintaining biodiversity is essential to the sustenance of *ecosystems*, which consist of all the living and nonliving elements that function together as a unit. This rather broad definition encompasses a wide spectrum of scale. A rain forest could be considered an ecosystem as well as a tide pool or puddle. When one element of an ecosystem is compromised, the other elements will also be affected. This leads to adaptations, migrations, or extinctions. Inherent in any ecosystem is the flow of energy through food chains and webs. Consider also the flow of energy through abiotic factors such as atmospheric heating, cooling, and running water.

This lesson will focus on establishing the concepts of biodiversity and ecosystem while integrating math and language arts.

Materials for Each Group:

Meterstick
Four wooden stakes
Colored tape
Permanent markers
Five meters (about five yards) of string
Magnifying glasses
Clear plastic collection jars
Sieve nets
Grid for graphing on overhead sheets

● Element 1: Content to Be Taught

Note: Specific elements and their properties and relationships will vary with the ecosystem. Therefore, the content analysis is generic.

Elements	Properties	Rules of Relationship	Emergent Properties
Plants	Green, sessile, varied	Planted in soil, eaten by animals	Changing, growing
Animals	Vertebrates, invertebrates, varied	On plants, under plants, in soil, in water, eat plants, ingest soil	
Microorganisms	Invisible to the naked eye	On plants, on animals, in soil	
Soil	Size, composition, water retention	Supports plants, used by animals, absorbs water	
Water	Stagnant, flowing, surface, subterranean	Moistens soil, used by animals and plants	

- Students will learn that biodiversity refers to the number and variety of living things in an ecosystem.

Element 2: Prior Knowledge and Misconceptions

- If students do not know how to make bar graphs, you will need to provide guidance during the lesson. They should be familiar with the meter as a unit of measurement and the properties of a square. Students may confuse biodiversity for the number of organisms rather than the number of different species of organisms.

Element 3: Performance Objectives

1. Given a one-square-meter (about one square yards) unpaved quadrant on the school grounds, each student will create a bar graph that represents the number and type of at least five species of plant, animal, or microbe found in his or her quadrant.
2. Given an incorrect description of biodiversity, each student will rewrite the description correctly, scoring a 3 on the rubric provided.

Element 4: Concept Development

Engagement Ask the children where they think they are likely to find many different forms of life. Use a think–pair–share methodology to process the children's responses. Post responses on the board. Ask children how many forms of life they think they could find in a one-square-meter area of land in their schoolyard. Record the children's predictions. Tell the children that their challenge today is to find as many different forms of life as possible in a one-square-meter plot of their schoolyard. The essential question can be posted on the board: "How many different forms of life can you find in your one-square-meter schoolyard plot?"

Exploration   *Safety note:* Reconnoiter the study site for stinging insects, potentially irritating plants such as poison ivy, oak, or sumac, thorn bushes, and anything else that may pose a hazard. Note any students with allergies to insect bites and plants and prepare an appropriate response plan for exposure or bites. Instruct the children not to handle insects. Students should wash their hands after handling soil, plants, and equipment. Encourage students to wear sunscreen and appropriate clothing (e.g., a hat, a long-sleeved shirt) to minimize the damaging effects of Sun exposure.

Assign children to research teams with the following roles:

- Group leader: Responsible for ensuring the group knows its task and follows the instructions
- Equipment manager: Ensures the group has the proper equipment and that the equipment is returned at the conclusion of the investigation
- Data collector: Ensures all data are recorded in appropriate tables
- Safety officer: Ensures safety regulations are followed

Rotate the roles each time the group visits its site.

Designate a region where the children can establish their plots. Instruct each group to measure a one-square-meter (about one square yard) plot in the designated region of the schoolyard and create a descriptive model of their quadrant in their science notebooks. Have them count the number of different life-forms in their quadrant. Don't worry about names of organisms, but have them draw or describe in writing each organism. If you can supply a digital camera, allow the children to take pictures as well. You can provide a sieve net for them to sweep the quadrants and put the organisms in collection jars to observe. Instruct the children to return the organisms to the quadrants when they finish observing them.

Explanation   Return to the essential question. Ask the children, "How many different forms of life did you find in your 1-square-meter schoolyard quadrants?" Give each team an overhead sheet with a grid on it. Instruct each team to make a bar graph on the overhead representing the number of at least five different organisms that they found. Display each group's bar graph on the overhead and tally the different types of organisms that each group found. Ask the children to compare their predictions to their actual data.

Tell them that they measured the biodiversity of the schoolyard. Ask them which data tell them about the biodiversity, the number of different organisms (the number of bars), or the number of organisms (the height of the bars). Reinforce that biodiversity refers to the number of different types of organisms, not the total number of organisms in a region.

Elaboration   There are many elaborations on this investigation that the children can explore and develop throughout the year.

- Compare the quadrant to an artificial ecosystem such as a garden, mowed lawn, or landscaped wooded area.
- Collect soil samples and test them for their composition and water retention properties.
- Collect data on the biodiversity of soil organisms.
- Identify food chains and webs within the ecosystem.
- Place squares of untreated wood on different parts of the quadrant for extended periods of time to see what effects it has on the ecosystem's plants and animals. They will find that it attracts many organisms that live under the wood, while plants will be destroyed.
- Look for signs of life such as tunnels, nests, or droppings.
- Classify the organisms into kingdoms.
- Change elements in the quadrant and predict the results.

● Element 5: Evaluation

Assessment I: Read the following letter from a child on vacation to the children. After the reading, provide a written copy as well.

"Dear Jill,

I can't wait to show you the pictures that I took at the beach. It was wonderful. We spent the entire day at the beach, where I counted 48 seagulls. Some were white, while others were gray. I guess that means there is a lot of biodiversity at the beach. Wouldn't you agree? Well, time to go fishing. On the last fishing trip, we caught 25 flounder. That proves the ocean has a lot of biodiversity, too.

See you soon,

Aaron"

Instruct the children to write a letter to Aaron and explain why they agree or disagree with Aaron's use of the term *biodiversity*.

Use the following rubric to assess the children's responses:

1	2	3
Agrees with Aaron's use of the term *biodiversity*	Disagrees with Aaron's use of the term *biodiversity* but does not explain why he or she disagrees	Disagrees with Aaron's use of the term *biodiversity* and explains that biodiversity refers to the variation in types of different organisms, not the number of organisms

● Element 6: Accommodations

English Language Learner

1. The teacher will state directions and procedures verbally as well as in writing.
2. The teacher will create a word bank with definitions to remain posted in the room.
3. The teacher will group students proficient in English language usage with ELL students.

Learning Disabilities

1. The teacher will provide extra time for writing and assessment.
2. The students will be given a checklist of activities to keep track of their progress and accomplishments.

Mobility Disabilities

1. If the child uses a wheelchair, situate him or her in a plot near a paved area that provides easy access for wheelchairs.

RESOURCES FOR DISCOVERY LEARNING

Internet Resources

Websites for Life Science Units, Lessons, Activities, and Demonstrations

- **Sea World: Science Information Content and Resources:**
  www.seaworld.org

- **The Tree of Life:**
  tolweb.org

- **Science Education Partnership Award:**
  https://nihsepa.org

- **Backyard Biology:**
  www.backyardbiology.net

- **Climate Kids:**
  http://climatekids.nasa.gov

Print Resources

Suggested Reading

Almeida, S., et al. "Involving School Children in the Establishment of an Urban Green Space: Long-Term Plant Biodiversity Study." *The American Biology Teacher* 68, no. 4 (April 2006): 213–220.

Aram, Robert J. "Habitat Sweet Habitat." *Science and Children* 38, no. 4 (January 2001): 23–27.

Bradway, Heather. "You Make the Diagnosis." *Science Scope* 24, no. 8 (May 2001): 23–25.

Coverdale, Gregory. "Science Is for the Birds: Promoting Standards-Based Learning through Backyard Birdwatching." *Science Scope* 26, no. 4 (January 2003): 32–37.

Fraser, W. J., et al. "Teaching Life Sciences to Blind and Visually Impaired Learners." *Journal of Biological Education* 42, no. 2 (Spring 2008): 84–89.

Galus, Pamela. "Snail Trails." *Science Scope* 25, no. 8 (May 2002): 14–18.

Gates, Donna M. "Pond Life Magnified." *Science Scope* 25, no. 8 (May 2002): 10–13.

Giacalone, Valerie. "How to Plan, Survive, and Even Enjoy an Overnight Field Trip with 200 Students." *Science Scope* 26, no. 4 (January 2003): 22–26.

Hammrich, Penny L., and Fadigan, Kathleen. "Investigations in the Science of Sports." *Science Scope* 26, no. 5 (February 2003): 30–35.

Houtz, Lynne E., and Quinn, Thomas H. "Give Me Some Skin: A Hands-on Science Activity Integrating Racial Sensitivity." *Science Scope* 26, no. 5 (February 2003): 18–22.

Inman, D. "Magic School Bus Explores the Human Body [review]." *Science and Children* 33, (September 1995): 52.

Keena, Kelly, and Basile, Carole G. "An Environmental Journey." *Science and Children* 39, no. 8 (May 2002): 30–33.

Keteyian, Linda. "A Garden Story." *Science and Children* 39, no. 3 (November/December 2001): 22–25.

Koschmann, Mark, and Shepardson, Dan. "A Pond Investigation." *Science and Children* 39, no. 8 (May 2002): 20–23.

Lawry, Patricia K., and Hale McCrary, Judy. "Someone's in the Kitchen with Science." *Science and Children* 39, no. 2 (October 2001): 22–27.

Lebofsky, Nancy R., and Lebofsky, Larry A. "Modeling Olympus Mons from the Earth." *Science Scope* 25, no. 7 (April 2002): 36–39.

Lener, C., et al. "Learning with Loggerheads." *Science and Children* 45, no. 1 (September 2007): 24–28.

Mannesto, Jean. "The Truth about Wolves." *Science and Children* 39, no. 8 (May 2002): 24–29.

McGinnis, Patricia. "Dissect Your Squid and Eat It Too." *Science Scope* 24, no. 7 (April 2001): 12–17.

McWilliams, Susan. "Journey into the Five Senses." *Science and Children* 40, no. 5 (February 2003): 38–43.

Mitchell, Melissa, and Mitchell, James K. "A Microbial Murder Mystery." *Science Scope* 25, no. 5 (February 2002): 24–30.

Morrison, Geraldine, and Uslick, JoAnn. "Summer Science Camp, Anyone?" *Science and Children* 39, no. 7 (April 2002): 34–37.

Moseley, C., et al. "Elementary Teachers' Progressive Understanding of Inquiry through the Process of Reflection." *School Science and Mathematics* 108, no. 2 (February 2008): 49–57.

Norrell, Mark A. "Science 101: What Is a Fossil?" *Science and Children* 40, no. 5 (February 2003): 20.

Rowlands, M. "What Do Children Think Happens to the Food They Eat?" *Journal of Biological Education* 38, no. 4 (Autumn 2004): 167–171.

Rule, Audrey, and Rust, Cynthia. "A Bat Is Like a . . . " *Science and Children* 39, no. 3 (November/December 2001): 26–31.

Science Scope 26, no. 4 (January 2003). (Entire issue emphasizes addressing science misconceptions.)

Sitzman, Daniel. "Bread Making: Classic Biotechnology and Experimental Design." *Science Scope* 26, no. 4 (January 2003): 27–31.

Stein, M., et al. "The Elementary Students' Science Beliefs Test." *Science and Children* 45, no. 8 (April/May 2008): 27–31.

Thompson, S. L. "Inquiry in the Life Sciences: The Plant-in-a-Jar as a Catalyst for Learning." *Science Activities* 43, no. 4 (Winter 2007): 27–33.

Notes

1. Using Phenomena in NGSS-Designed Lessons and Units. www.nextgenscience.org.
2. Next Generation Science Standards (NGSS) is a registered trademark of Achieve. Neither Achieve nor the lead states and partners that developed the Next Generation Science Standards was involved in the production of, and does not endorse, this product.
3. NGSS Lead States. 2013. *Next Generation Science Standards: For States, By States*. Washington, DC: The National Academies Press.

Physical Science

Putting the Content into Action

Unit Plan Ideas and Questions

● Matter and Interactions

UNIT TITLE: *Observe, Think, Sort*

QUESTION: What are some properties of matter?

UNIT OVERVIEW: Children classify the objects in collections of marbles, blocks, small tiles, and pebbles into categories based on weight, shape, color, and size.

UNIT TITLE: *Tell Me about It*

QUESTION: How can properties of matter be measured?

UNIT OVERVIEW: Children use tools such as rulers, balances, and thermometers to take, record, and describe measurements about the items in a collection of solid objects and containers of liquids.

UNIT TITLE: *Water Changes*

QUESTION: What makes water change from a solid to a liquid to a gas?

UNIT OVERVIEW: Children observe and explain why water and other substances can be changed from a solid to a liquid to a gas and from a gas to a liquid to a solid.

UNIT TITLE: *It's Dense*

QUESTION: How dense is it?

UNIT OVERVIEW: Students calculate the densities of regular and irregular objects using tools such as a ruler, a graduated cylinder, an overflow container, and a balance.

UNIT TITLE: *Matter Changes*

QUESTION: What properties identify the mystery powders?

UNIT OVERVIEW: Students gather, organize, and chart data about changes in characteristics of sugar, corn starch, baking soda, and flour as a result of testing each by heating and adding water and vinegar.

UNIT TITLE: *Physical and Chemical Changes*

QUESTIONS: Is the change physical or chemical? How can you tell?

UNIT OVERVIEW: Students observe teacher demonstrations of physical and chemical changes, make observations, and group the demonstrations into those that show physical changes and those that show chemical changes.

● Motion and Stability: Forces and Interactions

UNIT TITLE: *Spatial Relationships*

QUESTION: Where is it?

UNIT OVERVIEW: Using three objects labeled "a," "b," and "c," children describe their relative positions using the terms *in back of, in front of, above, below,* and *beside.*

UNIT TITLE: *Forces Cause Changes*

QUESTION: How did it get there?

UNIT OVERVIEW: Children demonstrate to their peers how an object's change in position is related to the strength and direction of the applied force.

UNIT TITLE: *Observe the Motion*

QUESTION: Where is it going and how does it get there?

UNIT OVERVIEW: Children gather and record data about the positions, directions of motion, and speeds of battery-powered toy cars moving across the classroom floor.

UNIT TITLE: *Graph the Motion*

QUESTION: Where is it now?

UNIT OVERVIEW: Children graph the positions, directions of motion, and speeds of battery-powered toy cars moving across the classroom floor.

UNIT TITLE: *Predicting Motion*

QUESTION: Where is it going?

UNIT OVERVIEW: Children predict the motions of objects acted upon by unbalanced forces that cause changes in speed or direction.

● Waves and Their Applications in Technologies Information Transfer

UNIT TITLE: *Vibrations Cause Changes*

QUESTION: How do sounds change?

UNIT OVERVIEW: Using a variety of objects, children demonstrate that sound is produced by vibrating objects, and that pitch can be changed by changing the object's rate of vibration.

UNIT TITLE: *Paths of Light*

QUESTION: How can light be directed?

UNIT OVERVIEW: Using mirrors, lenses, focused-beam flashlights, and pins to mark path positions, children compare the actual paths of beams of light to predicted paths of light through a maze.

UNIT TITLE: *Electrical Energy*

QUESTION: What is the path of electricity through a circuit?

UNIT OVERVIEW: Children identify the characteristics of a simple series circuit, build a circuit, and use it to produce light, heat, sound, or magnetic effects.

UNIT TITLE: *Magnets*

QUESTION: What are the properties of magnets?

UNIT OVERVIEW: Children use permanent magnets to demonstrate attraction and repulsion using the presence of poles.

● Energy

UNIT TITLE: *Generators Small and Large*

QUESTION: How are energy transfers from a hand generator and a power station the same and different?

UNIT OVERVIEW: After classroom science activities and field work at a power station, children make labeled diagrams that compare the initial energy sources and the energy transfers that occur in a classroom hand-operated generator and at the power station.

UNIT TITLE: *Energy Changes*

QUESTION: What happens to the electrical energy that comes into the school?

UNIT OVERVIEW: Children construct hands-on displays for a school science fair that demonstrate the transfer of electrical energy into heat, light, and sound.

UNIT TITLE: *Energy—The Space Traveler*

QUESTION: What happens to the energy from the Sun?

UNIT OVERVIEW: After library research work and class discussions, children explain how energy is produced by the Sun, transmitted through space, and captured by green plants.

UNIT TITLE: *Egg Saver*

QUESTION: How can energy be absorbed?

UNIT OVERVIEW: Using everyday materials, children design containers that can protect an uncooked egg dropped from the height of a stepladder to a school sidewalk.

UNIT TITLE: *Safest, Cleanest, Cheapest*

QUESTION: What are the safest, cleanest, and cheapest ways to generate energy?

UNIT OVERVIEW: After library and internet research, field work, and classroom discussions, children compare three alternate forms of energy with respect to safety, pollution, and economy.

Make the CASE *An Individual or Group Challenge*

● **The Problem**	Three-dimensional teaching often begins with a phenomenon. It can be challenging to find a suitable phenomenon that inspires students, in their quest to figure out an explanation, to dive deeply into a topic that leads them to uncover core science concepts.
● **Assess Your Prior Knowledge and Beliefs**	1. Write your interpretation of the following statement: Phenomena do not need to be phenomenal to be academically productive. 2. Discuss your interpretation with colleagues.
● **The Challenge**	Identify phenomena that you might use to anchor a unit about conservation of energy and energy transfer (PS3.B). Justify the phenomena by explaining how they could drive students to uncover core science concepts.

Classroom Enrichment Ideas

● Discovery Centers

A well-prepared in-class learning center offers children many opportunities to make their own discoveries. To be well prepared, such a center must provide a wide range of materials that encourage hands-on, discovery-based learning, ranging from print and audiovisual resources to art supplies and games. The learning center must be located where children have ready access to it yet can be somewhat removed from the larger classroom setting while doing independent activities. The following starter ideas for in-class discovery centers should get you thinking about how to create centers in your own classroom. Suggestions for connections with disciplinary core ideas are included in parentheses.

CENTER TITLE: *Energy Savers* (**PS1.A: Structure and Properties of Matter**)

IDEA: Challenge the children to build ice cube "keepers." Provide foam packing peanuts, ice cream buckets, cardboard, tape, and small cardboard boxes. Have the children use baby food jars to hold ice cubes that are allowed to melt at room temperature to get data for a control.

CENTER TITLE: *Matter Can Change* (**PS1.A: Structure and Properties of Matter**)

IDEA: Carry out activities that reveal changing phases of matter, such as melting, freezing, and evaporating.

CENTER TITLE: *Pushes and Pulls* (**PS2.A: Forces and Motion**)

IDEA: Use a toy car to show how pushes and pulls can affect the positions and motions of objects, such as starting, stopping, moving with constant speed, speeding up, and slowing down.

CENTER TITLE: *Magnet Time* (**PS2.B: Types of Interactions**)

IDEA: Using bar and horseshoe magnets, conduct activities to identify the poles and show attraction and repulsion.

CENTER TITLE: *Simple Circuits* (**PS3.B: Conservation of Energy and Energy Transfer**)

IDEA: Build a working simple series circuit with batteries, wire, a bulb, and a switch, then test a variety of materials to determine how much each is an electrical insulator or conductor.

● Bulletin Boards

BULLETIN BOARD TITLE: *Sound and Light* (**PS3.A: Definitions of Energy**)

IDEA: Divide the bulletin board into three sections and label them *Light*, *Heat*, and *Sound*. Subdivide each section into three subsections, allowing space for children to attach pictures, and add the following subtitles: *Where does it come from? How does it move? How do we use it?* Provide photographs, internet and printer access, drawing paper, and markers so children can locate or create pictures to place in each subsection.

BULLETIN BOARD TITLE: *Find the Forces* (**PS2.B: Types of Interactions**)

IDEA: Place the title *Find the Forces* across the top of the bulletin board. Provide or have children locate photographs of people actively participating in gymnastics, dancing, or sports. Each week, place one of the pictures on the bulletin board. Have children attach index cards with the words *push* and *pull* near the pictures to identify where forces are acting.

BULLETIN BOARD TITLE: *The Simple Circuit* (**PS3.A: Definitions of Energy**)

IDEA: Create a three-dimensional bulletin board that is a working circuit. Temporarily mount and hook up a battery, wires, a switch, and a bulb holder with a bulb. Have children create a label for each item. (*Safety note:* You must use insulated wire and ensure that neither the bulb nor any bare ends of wire touch any surface. Also, be sure that the circuit is switched off after each use.)

● Field Trips

Field trips provide amazing opportunities for discovery learning, as they take children out of the classroom and immerse them in the real world. Whether you teach in a city, suburban, or small-town school, you can find ideas for field trips all around you. Here are ideas for field trips for all schools.

FIELD TRIP TITLE: *Force, Motion, and Machines* (**PS2.A: Forces and Motion**)

IDEA: Contact the showroom of a car, boat, airplane, or snowmobile dealership or the repair facility at a bus station, garage, or airport to arrange the excursion. Alert the individual who will serve as your tour guide that the children will be interested in how the design of the vehicle minimizes air and surface friction, how it's propelled, and what type of energy it uses. As a follow-up to the trip, have children draw diagrams and build models of what they saw. They can also invent modifications to the vehicle that would further reduce friction.

FIELD TRIP TITLE: *Energy-Conserving Home* (PS3.B: Conservation of Energy and Energy Transfer)

IDEA: Look around the community for a building or home that was built or retrofitted to save energy. One with an active or passive solar system, windmill, off-peak power storage system, or underground design would be especially interesting. Installers of alternative energy systems and building contractors are good sources of information on energy-efficient building techniques and places to visit. After the visit, children can study the school and their homes for energy-efficient features as well as needed improvements.

FIELD TRIP TITLE: *Forces on the Playground* (PS3.C: Relationship Between Energy and Forces)

IDEA: Children locate and classify playground forces and identify relationships between the forces.

FIELD TRIP TITLE: *Building Going Up* (PS1.A: Structure and Properties of Matter)

IDEA: From a safe distance, children observe the materials used at a building construction site to identify their properties and how the properties contribute to building construction.

Examples of Topics and Phenomena for the Physical Sciences

PHENOMENA ARE "observable events that occur in the universe and that we can use our science knowledge to explain or predict."[1] They don't need to be flashy or sensational, but they should generate compelling questions that create real opportunities for students to develop an explanation or solve a problem. Some examples of phenomena and associated activities arranged by topic are listed below.

Topic: Forces and Interactions

Phenomenon: Loose objects continue to move when vehicles stop quickly.

Materials
Small toy wagon or truck
Doll that can ride in or on top of the toy wagon or truck
Two large rubber bands

Motivating Questions
- Why do we need to wear safety belts?
- What direction will the doll move when the wagon suddenly stops?
- If the doll were wearing a safety belt, would it still move?

Directions
1. Display the wagon or truck without the doll. Gently roll it into the wall.
2. Put the doll in the wagon, gently push the wagon, and have the children predict in what direction the doll will move when the wagon strikes the wall.

3. After they observe the wagon striking the wall, relate the wagon and doll to a car and passenger. Discuss the likelihood of the passenger striking or going through the windshield if the car hits something or stops suddenly.

4. Use the rubber band to restrain the doll and repeat the demonstration. Ask the children for observations.

Science Content for the Teacher   A fundamental law of motion is that an object at rest or in uniform motion tends to continue in that condition. An unrestrained passenger in a forward-moving automobile continues to move forward if the car stops, since he or she is not connected to the car.

● Topic: Forces and Interactions

Phenomenon: Wheels make objects easier to push or pull.

Materials   Easel paper and markers
Pack of index cards

Motivating Questions
- Is it easier to pull something with wheels or something without wheels?
- How do the shapes or sizes of wheels affect the force needed to move the vehicle?

Directions
1. Take the children for a walk around the school, both inside and outside the building. Challenge them to find as many wheeled vehicles as they can. Record properties such as size, width, and number. (Observe safety when near vehicles.) As they search, model how a scientist keeps track of information by writing notes on an index card about each wheeled vehicle observed. Use a different index card for each vehicle. Look for such things as automobiles, bicycles, cafeteria and custodial carts, wagons, and trucks. Don't miss the wheels under audiovisual carts and movable chalkboards or room dividers.

2. When you return to the room, prepare a three-column chart that includes a drawing of each vehicle and the properties of wheels on it. Have the children discuss how wheels help move objects.

Science Content for the Teacher   Friction is a force that acts against the forward-moving wagon. If the force is large enough, it can slow down or stop the wagon. Wheels reduce the friction between objects and the ground. As a wheel turns, only a small amount of it touches the ground, which reduces the friction between the object and the ground, and makes the object easier to move.

● Topic: Matter and Interactions

Phenomenon: Raisins rise and fall in carbonated soda.

Materials   Unopened 2-liter bottle of club soda
About 25 raisins

Motivating Questions
- Where do the bubbles in soda come from?
- What is in the bubbles?
- Why do the raisins go up and down?

Directions	1. Have the children make some observations of the club soda before you open the cap.
	2. Open the cap, have the children observe the bubbles that form throughout the soda, and then display the raisins.
	3. Drop the raisins into the club soda and have the children make observations about the motion of the raisins.

Science Content for the Teacher   Club soda is water to which carbon dioxide has been added under pressure. Raisins have a density that is close to the density of water. Thus, they will almost but not quite float. The carbon dioxide bubbles coat the surface of the raisins, increasing the volume of the raisins but only minimally increasing their mass. The raisins and attached bubbles move toward the surface of the soda. When they reach the surface, the bubbles burst and the raisins sink. This process continues as long as carbon dioxide gas is released in the soda.

Topic: Mixtures

Phenomenon: Sugar disappears when mixed with water.

Materials   Empty, clear two-liter soda bottle
One-quarter cup of sand
One-quarter cup of sugar
Saucer

Motivating Questions
- When you mix sugar and sand, where did the sugar go?
- How could you separate the sugar and sand?

Directions
1. Fill the bottle half full of water and keep it out of sight. Display the sand and sugar, then mix them on the saucer, and challenge the children to invent a way to separate them.
2. After a discussion of alternative strategies, show the bottle containing water. Ask the children if they have ideas about how the bottle could be used to separate the mixture.
3. Add the mixture to the bottle and shake it vigorously. The sand will settle to the bottom, and the water will dissolve the sugar. Challenge the children to think of a way to get the sugar back.

Science Content for the Teacher   Sugar, sand, and water do not chemically react to produce a new substance. The dissolving of sugar in water is a physical change because the sugar can be recovered by evaporating the water.

Topic: Types of Interactions

Phenomenon: Magnets attract some materials but not others.

Materials   Magnet
Assortment of objects such as a rubber band, a metal tack, a piece of chalk, and paper clips

Motivating Questions
- Which of these objects do you think will be pulled toward the magnet?
- How are the objects that are pulled to the magnet different from objects that are not pulled?

Directions	1. Write the names of the objects on the board.
	2. Display the magnet and have the children predict which objects will be pulled toward it. Note their predictions under the names of the objects you wrote on the board.
	3. Have the children touch each object with the magnet. Record the results in another row on the chart and explain that the objects that are attracted are those that contain iron (steel).

Science Content for the Teacher A magnet has the ability to attract objects that contain iron, nickel, cobalt, and their alloys. Most common objects that are attracted to a magnet contain iron in the form of steel.

Discovery Activities: Use the Following Activities to Support Discovery Experiences with Your Students.

● States of Matter Scavenger Hunt

Objective • Children will identify properties of solids, liquids, and gases.

Science Processes Emphasized Observing
Communicating

Materials for Each Child or Group In addition to solids normally found in a room, have a selection of liquids such as water (in a variety of colors) and inflated balloons in different shapes and sizes.

Motivation Tell the children they will go on a scavenger hunt. They need to find three of each item with the following properties:
Item 1: Maintains its own shape and always takes up the same amount of space (definite volume)
Item 2: Takes the shape of its container and always takes up the same amount of space
Item 3: Takes on the shape of its container and can take up different amounts of space

Directions
1. Let the children search the room for three examples of each item.
2. When they are done, have the students list the names of the items they found under each category posted in the front of the room.
3. Choose a few items from each list and discuss whether they meet the criteria for the categories in which they were placed.
4. Define the categories as solids, liquids, or gases.

Key Discussion Questions
1. How do the items differ? *By their ability to keep their shapes and occupy a definite or indefinite volume*
2. Could any of the items be found in all three forms? *Yes, most commonly water, but many other forms of matter can be solids, liquids, or gases, depending on the temperature (motion of the molecules).*

Science Content for the Teacher
Matter is commonly found in one of three forms or states: solid, liquid, or gas. Solids have a definite shape and volume. Liquids take on the shape of their containers and have a definite volume. Gases have neither a definite shape nor volume. The difference in states is a function of heat energy. As heat increases, the motion of molecules increases. Molecules that are more tightly bonded require more energy to be moved and separated.

Extensions
Science/Art: Have children make drawings of various changes, such as an icicle melting, water in a pond freezing, and a pond drying up during the summer.

Science/Physical education: Some children may want to make drawings of various sports that utilize water or ice. The children can discuss their drawings with the class and consider what would happen if the water depicted in them changed to ice or if the ice changed to water.

● From Gas to Liquid

Objectives
- Children will observe the result of water changing from gas to liquid.
- Children will infer the source of the water that condenses on the outside of a can.

Science Processes Emphasized
Observing
Inferring
Arguing from evidence

Materials for Each Child or Group
Shiny metal can or container
Paper towels
Crushed ice

Motivation
Ask students where they think they could find water. Post their ideas for all to see. Tell them you will guide them in finding water from an unlikely source. Challenge them to figure out where the water comes from and to give reasons for their answers.

Directions
1. Distribute a can and a paper towel to each group and ask the children to polish the outside of the can with the towel. Have the children describe what they observe when they examine the outside of the can.
2. Have each group add crushed ice to the can.
3. Have the children again observe the outside of the can. In a short time, a thin film of water will appear on the can.

Key Discussion Questions
1. Where do you think the water that formed on the outside of the can came from? *The air*
2. How could we get the water that formed on the outside of the can to go back into the air? *Answers will vary. Some children may suggest that they remove the ice from the can and add hot water.*

Science Content for the Teacher
Air contains water vapor, which is water in a gaseous state. The amount of water vapor that air can hold depends on various factors, including its temperature. If the temperature of air is lowered sufficiently, the water vapor in it will condense on any available surface. The temperature at which this occurs is called the *dew point*. The cold can cause air near its surface to condense and form a film of liquid water.

Extension *Science/Health:* Ask the children to breathe on a mirror or windowpane and observe the surface. The film of water they see on the surface results from the condensation of the water vapor that is contained in the breath they exhale. The water is a by-product of the process by which food is converted to energy in the body.

● What Is Your Squeezing Force?

Objective • Children will measure the amount of squeezing force they can apply.

Science Processes Emphasized Measuring
Interpreting data
Using mathematics

Materials for Each Child or Group Bathroom scale thin enough for children to grip

Motivation Display the bathroom scale and explain that it provides a measurement of the amount of pull Earth exerts on our bodies. Tell the children they will use the scale to see how much pushing force they can exert with their hands.

Directions 1. Divide the class into groups and have each group member squeeze the top and bottom of a bathroom scale together. The children should use both hands. As each child concentrates on squeezing the scale, another member of the group should write down the reading on the scale's weight display.

2. Have each group make a graph that shows the name of the person and the squeezing force he or she applied.

Key Discussion Questions 1. Is the force you used to squeeze the scale a push or a pull? *The children should realize they are exerting two pushes with each hand. They are pushing the top of the scale down and the bottom of the scale up.*

2. When we weigh ourselves, what is pulling us down on the scale? *Earth is pulling on us.*

Science Content for the Teacher A bathroom scale has a spring system that reacts in response to the pull of gravity on any mass placed on the scale. Some scales include electrical devices that convert the movement of the springs to electrical information that is displayed in the form of a digital display.

Extension *Science/Health:* Since young children experience rather steady growth in their skeletal/muscular systems, they may find it interesting to measure their squeezing force at the beginning, middle, and end of the school year, and prepare a simple graph of the results.

● Secret Messages and Chemical Changes

Objectives • Children will observe physical and chemical changes.
• Children will describe the characteristics of physical and chemical changes.

Science Processes Emphasized Observing
Communicating
Making a hypothesis

Materials for Each Child or Group

Cotton swab
Sheet of white paper
Iron nail
Roll of masking tape
Plastic container of water
Paper towels
Desk lamp with incandescent 100-watt light bulbs
Small container of freshly squeezed lemon juice
Small, clear plastic containers (such as disposable cups) containing copper-sulfate solution (*Safety note:* The containers of copper sulfate should remain under your supervision in a central location. The groups will place their iron nails in the container and simply observe the changes. At the end of the activity, you are responsible for disposing of the solutions. *At no time should the children handle copper sulfate.*)

Motivation

This activity should be done following activities or discussion on physical changes. Ask the children to review the characteristics of a physical change and discuss the possibility that some changes may result in the production of new substances. Tell the children they will do some activities that may help them think about such changes.

Directions

1. Distribute the lemon juice, cotton swabs, and paper. Have the children write secret messages on their papers using the swabs and lemon juice.

2. Allow the papers to dry. While they are drying, have the children record their observations of the lemon juice patterns on the papers.

3. Under your supervision, have the children exchange messages and take turns heating them over the desk lamps.

Key Discussion Questions

1. When the secret writing became visible, how do you think the lemon juice changed? *The lemon juice changed to something else. It got darker.*

2. Do you think you could make the writing turn back into lemon juice? *No, we probably couldn't make it turn back into lemon juice.*

3. Do you think you saw a physical change? *No, some new things formed. The color of the lemon juice changed and the brown stuff wasn't there when we started.*

Science Content for the Teacher

When matter undergoes a physical change, it changes in form but remains the same substance. Physical changes are usually easy to reverse. In contrast, this activity shows two chemical changes. In the first case, heat added to the lemon juice caused the formation of molecules that absorb light, giving the juice a dark color.

Extensions

Science: Have some children observe an additional chemical change. Have them wedge some steel wool into a small glass, moisten it, and invert it in a pan of water. There should be an air space between the steel wool in the inverted glass and the water. Within a few days, the children will be able to observe the formation of rust on the steel wool—a chemical change.

Science/Language arts: Activities such as this one can make children more sensitive to the concept of change. Recognizing changes in the environment can serve as an important first step in writing experiences that focus on change. You may want to have the children write poetry about the changes they observe in the world around them.

● Pendulums

Objectives	• Children will predict how changing the string length and mass of a pendulum bob affect the motion of the pendulum.
	• Children will measure the effect of changing the string length and mass of the bob on the motion of the pendulum.

Science Processes Emphasized

Observing
Predicting
Using mathematics
Using models
Measuring
Collecting and analyzing data

Materials for Each Child or Group

Horizontal wooden support at least 1 meter (about 40 inches) long
Four screw eyes fastened along the length of the support
Spool of heavy-duty twine
Four sticks of modeling clay
Stopwatch
Metric ruler

Motivation

Display a picture of children on a swing set. Ask the children if they have used a swing set. Wonder out loud whether the length of the swing makes a difference. Ask them to make predictions and to give reasons for their predictions. Challenge them about how to test their predictions. Suggest that they can model a swing set and person with string and clay.

Directions

1. Have one member of each group be responsible for making the bob from the clay and attaching it to string.

2. Have the children predict how changing the length of the string will affect the swing.

3. Let the children change the length of the string and describe the outcome on the swing. They should notice that the swing goes faster or slower depending on the length of the string.

4. Suggest that the children measure the amount of time it takes for the swing to make one complete arc. Give them a stopwatch to measure time. Have the children start with a 1-meter length of string and shorten it by 10 centimeters (about 4 inches) during each of the five trials. In starting the pendulum movement, always move the bob 10 centimeters (4 inches) to the left of its stationary position before releasing it.

5. The children should find the time of one back-and-forth movement by completing five such movements and then dividing by five. Once they find the time, have them check it against their predictions.

Key Discussion Questions

1. Did you predict that the length of the string would affect the period of the pendulum? *Answers will vary.*

2. What did you observe when just the length of the string was changed? *The length of the string affects the period. The longer the string, the longer the period.*

3. Did you predict that the mass of the bob would affect the period of the pendulum? *Answers will vary.*

4. What did you observe when just the mass of the bob was changed? *Changing the mass of the bob does not change the period of the pendulum.*

Science Content for the Teacher A pendulum is a weight, or bob, suspended from a fixed point that is able to swing back and forth freely. The period of a pendulum is the time it takes for the bob to make one complete back-and-forth swing. Galileo discovered that the period of a pendulum is independent of the mass of the bob and depends only on the pendulum's length.

Extensions *Science:* 1. Have the children repeat this procedure, using three different bobs made of one-quarter, one-half, and three-quarters of a stick of clay. Maintain the string lengths at 1 meter (about 40 inches). Each time the bob is changed, the children should predict the period and then check their predictions against their observations. 2. Ask the children if they think the period of a pendulum depends on how far the bob is released from the point at which it is hanging straight down. They can then conduct an activity to check their ideas. (The period remains the same, regardless of the position from which the bob is released.)

Science/Social studies: This activity provides an excellent opportunity for the children to become aware of Galileo. Read a brief biography of Galileo in a reference book and have the children do some social studies activities that focus on him. For example, they can make a timeline and mark the time of Galileo's life as well as such events as the discovery of America, the American Revolution, the launching of the first space satellite, and the first Moon walk. The children could also locate Italy on a world map and find the town of Pisa, where Galileo made his observations of the swinging pendulum.

● Heat and the Fizzer

Objective • Children will experiment to discover the relationship between temperature and the speed of a chemical reaction.

Science Processes Emphasized Experimenting

Materials for Each Child or Group Three Alka-Seltzer tablets
Three clear plastic cups
Ice cube
Cool and hot water

Motivation Review the difference between physical and chemical changes with the children. Tell the children that in this activity, they will observe the results of a chemical change and discover how heat affects chemical changes.

Directions 1. Distribute three cups and three tablets to each group. Provide access to ice cubes as well as to hot and cold water.
2. Tell the children they are going to use their senses of sight and hearing to gauge the speed of the reaction of the tablet with water.
3. Have the children prepare the three cups of water and arrange them from cold (tap water plus an ice cube) to cool to hot. Tell the children to write their observations of bubble production and fizzing after they have dropped one tablet in each cup.

Key Discussion Questions

1. Make a claim about the effect of temperature on the speed of each reaction. *The hotter water made the reaction faster.*

2. What evidence to you have to support your claim? *The reaction with hot water produced more bubbles in a shorter time.*

Science Content for the Teacher

One of the products of the reaction of Alka-Seltzer with water is carbon dioxide gas. The rate of production of carbon dioxide bubbles is one indicator of the rate at which this reaction takes place.

Extension

Science/Health: Have the students compare the ingredients in a variety of over-the-counter upset stomach remedies. Then have them research the common causes of an upset stomach and the preventive steps people can take to reduce their dependence on over-the-counter remedies.

● Toy Car in the Wagon: Pushes and Pulls

Objectives

- Children will identify one type of force as a push and another as a pull.
- Children will observe the tendency of an object to remain in one place or remain in uniform motion.

Science Processes Emphasized

Observing
Making hypotheses

Materials

Child's wagon
Large toy car with functioning wheels

Motivation

Display the wagon, but keep the car out of sight. Tell the children you are going to use the wagon to help them learn some interesting things about how objects move. Ask for a volunteer to assist you.

Directions

Note: Because this demonstration requires ongoing discussion, key discussion questions are included in each step.

1. Ask the children why the wagon is not floating in the air. Use their responses to help them understand that Earth is pulling the wagon downward. Explain that this pull is called a *force*. Then pick up the wagon and ask the children if you used a force. Put the wagon down and ask your volunteer to use a force to pull the wagon. Have the volunteer demonstrate a push. Summarize by explaining that forces can be pushes or pulls.

2. Ask the children how the direction and force are related. *The movement is in the same direction as the force.*

3. Place the toy car in the back of the wagon so the back of the car is touching the back of the wagon. Have the children make predictions about what will happen to the wagon and car if the volunteer pulls the wagon forward at a steady but high speed. Before the volunteer demonstrates this, ask how the toy car in the wagon will move during the journey and at the stop. Have the children watch the demonstration closely. They will observe that the toy car continues to move forward after an abrupt stop. Repeat this with the toy car at the front of the wagon.

Key Discussion Questions

See Directions.

Science Content for the Teacher

When the wagon is stationary, all forces acting on it balance each other. Earth's pulling force is balanced by a reacting force: Earth pushing on the cart in the opposite direction. The wagon displays forward motion if an unbalanced force acts on it. Although the term is not used, the toy car placed at the back of the wagon is used to demonstrate *inertia*. In other words, an object set in motion tends to keep moving.

Extension

Science/Physical education: Bring a variety of athletic equipment to class, such as a baseball, a baseball bat, a football, a field hockey stick, a field hockey ball, a jump rope, and so forth. Have various children demonstrate how forces are involved in using these objects.

● Teacher on Wheels: Action and Reaction Forces

Objectives

- Children will observe that an action force applied in one direction produces a reaction force in the opposite direction.
- Children will predict the direction and magnitude of reaction forces.

Science Processes Emphasized

Observing
Predicting

Materials

A pair of inline skates or a skateboard
Length of board measuring 25 by 3 by 50 centimeters (about 10 by 1 by 20 inches)
12 large marbles
Old textbooks of assorted sizes (or large bean bags)

Motivation

Tell the children that you intend to get on inline skates or a skateboard to demonstrate action and reaction forces. That should be sufficient motivation!

Directions

1. Put on the rollerblades or stand on a skateboard. Have a volunteer hand you some old textbooks or bean bags. Ask the children to predict what will happen if you throw a textbook or bean bag from your perch on wheels. Execute a rapid underhand throw of the textbook or bean bag to an awaiting container.

2. Vary the number of books or bean bags and the direction and speed with which they are thrown. Have children make predictions prior to each demonstration of action and reaction.

Key Discussion Questions

1. When I threw the book while I was standing on the skateboard (rollerblades), what was the reaction and what was the action? *The action was the book being thrown. The reaction was your movement in the other direction.*

2. What happened when I threw the book faster? *You moved in the other direction faster.*

3. Jet and rocket engines work because of action and reaction. What is the action and what is the reaction when these engines operate? *The hot gases going out the back of the engine is the action. The plane or rocket moving forward is the reaction.*

Science Content for the Teacher

This demonstration illustrates Newton's third law of motion, although it is unnecessary to refer to it as such. This law states that for every action, there is an equal and opposite reaction. For example, when we apply a force to Earth as we try to take a step, a reaction force pushes our body forward. Similarly, any time we apply a force to an object, a reaction force is produced. This law of nature can be taken advantage of to produce motion in any direction. A jet engine causes an airplane to move forward as a reaction to the action force produced when hot gases are expelled from the rear of the engine.

Extensions *Science:* Have a group of children attempt to build a device that will launch small objects in one direction and display a reaction force in the other direction.

Many toy stores sell plastic rockets that are launched as a result of the rearward movement of water out the back end. A small pump is used to fill the rocket with water. A small group of children may wish to demonstrate (under your close supervision) the launching of such a rocket on the playground.

Science/Physical education: Some children may want to extend their knowledge of action and reaction forces by identifying athletic events that depend on these forces. For example, the downward jump on the diving board by a diver is the action force; the reactive force is the upward propelling of the diver.

How Do Instruments Make Sounds?

Materials Ruler
Assortment of musical instruments: cymbals, bells, small drum, triangle, guitar, clarinet, etc.

Motivating Questions Point to each instrument and ask:
- How does this instrument make sound?
- What do these instruments have in common?

Directions
1. Let children examine the instruments and try to make a sound with them. Have them work in teams.
2. Tell them to find out which part of the instrument seems to be most responsible for making the sound.
3. While one child makes sounds with the instrument, the other child must touch the instrument and report what they feel. They should compare the feeling while the instrument is playing to the feeling when the instrument is not playing.
4. Indicate that they are feeling vibrations, the rapid movement of the instrument.
5. Inform the children that sounds are made by vibrations.

Science Content for the Teacher All sounds are the result of vibrating objects. High-pitched sounds come from objects that vibrate very fast. Each musical instrument produces a sound because the musician causes some part of it to vibrate.

Can Sound Travel through a Solid Object?

Materials for Each Group Meterstick

Motivating Questions
- Have you ever heard sounds while you were swimming underwater?
- Have you ever heard sounds through a wall?
- Do you think sound can travel through a meterstick?

Directions

1. Have the children work in pairs. One child will stand and the other child, the listener, will be seated. The child standing will hold one end of the meterstick and the listener will hold the other. The meterstick should be parallel to the floor and 50 centimeters (about 20 inches) away from the listener's ear.

2. Have the child who is standing gently scratch his or her end of the meterstick. The listener should say whether he or she heard the scratches.

3. Repeat the procedure with the meterstick 25 centimeters (about 10 inches) away from the listener's ear.

4. Finally, have the listener position the meterstick so that it is gently touching the jawbone joint in front of his or her ear and have the standing student gently scratch the meterstick. The listener should hear the sounds clearly.

Science Content for the Teacher

Sound waves are disturbances that move through a medium. The medium may be a solid, a liquid, or a gas. A dense solid, such as the hardwood in a meterstick, carries sound waves very well. When the standing child scratches the meterstick, the sound waves travel through the meterstick and into the tissues and bones near the listener's ear, eventually reaching his or her eardrum.

● What Type of Cup Loses Heat the Fastest?

Materials

Plastic cup
Styrofoam cup
Metal cup or empty soup can with label removed
Ceramic cup
Source of hot water
Thermometer

Motivating Questions

- If you were going to have a cup of hot chocolate on a cold day, which of these cups do you think would keep it hot for the longest time?

- If you were going to have a cup of cold chocolate milk on a hot day, which of these cups would keep it cold for the longest time?

Directions

1. Display the cups and have the children make predictions about their heat-retaining abilities. You may want to have the children arrange the cups in order of their ability to retain heat.

2. Fill each cup half full of hot water. (*Safety note:* Alert the children to the dangers of working with hot water.)

3. Have the children put a thermometer in each cup as soon as the water is added and record the temperature at time zero and again after one minute, two minutes, three minutes, four minutes, and five minutes.

4. Have the children graph their data as temperature versus time.

Science Content for the Teacher

All solids conduct heat; however, some conduct heat better than others. Metals tend to be good conductors of heat. Thus, a cup made of metal will permit heat to pass through it easily, resulting in the cooling down of the liquid within the cup. Ceramic materials, on the other hand, are good insulators, so most china cups will retain heat. The Styrofoam cup is an excellent insulator because bubbles of air are part of the materials that make up the cup.

● Can You Build a No-Frills Telephone?

Objectives
- The children will construct a telephone-like device that allows them to communicate with one another.
- From their experimentation, the children will infer that a vibration moving through a thread is the basis for how their devices work.

Science Processes Emphasized
Communicating
Inferring
Designing solutions
Arguing from evidence

Materials for Each Child or Group
Two paper cups
Two toothpicks or buttons
Two-meters (about seven-foot) or longer length of strong sewing thread or dental floss
Additional thread, buttons, and cups for children who want to invent more complicated phone circuits

Motivation
Display the materials. Ask the children if they can guess what they will make with them. After they have made some guesses, tell them they will make telephones that will actually work.

Directions
1. Provide a model telephone that you made from strings and cups. Deliberately make it subpar. For example, have the strings loosely attached to the cups so the vibrations are not transmitted efficiently to the cup.
2. Demo the model phone and let the children try it.
3. Challenge them to make a better phone.
4. Have them explain why they think their designs should be better.
5. Let them test their designs and explain why their designs are better or worse than the one you made. Some groups may want to construct more complicated telephone circuits.

Key Discussion Questions
1. Which cup is used like the bottom part of a telephone? *The speaker's cup*
2. Which cup is used like the top part of a telephone? *The listener's cup*
3. How could you make a telephone that will let one person speak and two people listen? *Answers will vary. Have children try an experiment to test their ideas. Some will find that tying a second cup somewhere along the string will permit the second listener to hear the sounds made by the speaker.*

Science Content for the Teacher
When we speak, our vocal cords vibrate and produce sound waves that travel through the air. When the children use their string telephones, sound waves vibrate the bottom of the speaker's cup. These vibrations move through the string and cause the bottom of the listener's cup to vibrate and reproduce the sound waves in the air inside the listener's cup. These sound waves strike the listener's eardrum and cause it to vibrate. In a real telephone, the vibrations produced by the speaker are converted to variations in electrical impulses that travel through wires.

Extension
Science/Art: Have the children design and then draw various arrangements of thread and cups for more complex telephone systems prior to further experimentation.

● Simple Circuits

Objectives
- Children will assemble a simple series circuit and a simple parallel circuit.
- Children will describe the similarities and differences between a series circuit and a parallel circuit.

Science Processes Emphasized
Observing
Defining problems
Communicating
Designing solutions

Materials for Each Child or Group
Three bulbs
Three bulb sockets
Eight pieces of insulated bell wire, each 2.5 centimeters (about 1 inch) long and stripped at the ends
Two D-cell batteries
Switch

Motivation
This activity should follow a class discussion about the nature of simple circuits and the functions of various circuit components. Challenge students to create a circuit with at least two bulbs, one of which will stay on if the other is removed.

Directions
1. Provide students with the materials listed.
2. Have the children design a circuit to meet the requirements.
3. Allow the children time to test, record results, redesign, and retest their circuits.

Key Discussion Questions
1. What are the reasons you chose the first design?
2. Describe how you tested the design and what you learned from the test.
3. Did your design satisfy the design challenge? Explain why you think the design did or did not succeed.

Science Content for the Teacher
Circuits can be represented by diagrams and symbols. In a series circuit, all the electrons go through all the bulbs (or other resistances) in the circuit. A gap, or break, at any place in the circuit will stop the flow of current through the entire circuit. A defective bulb, a loose connection, or a break in the wire will stop the flow of current. If the voltage is large enough, electrons may jump across gaps in the circuit, a phenomenon evidenced as a spark. In a parallel circuit, the current divides. Some of it flows through each resistance. If a resistance is removed from a parallel circuit, the current continues to flow through the remaining resistances.

Extensions
Science: If you have access to a small electric motor, have a group substitute it for a bulb in the series circuit and in the parallel circuit to determine the effect of a running motor on the brightness of the bulbs.

Challenge one or two groups to combine their resources and make a circuit that is partly parallel and partly series.

Science/Social studies: Some children may enjoy studying one of the bulbs more closely to see if they can find the path that the electrons take. This could be the beginning of some library research on the scientist who invented the incandescent bulb: Thomas Edison. Have the children focus their attention on how everyday life has been affected by Edison's many inventions.

● Electrical Conductors and Nonconductors

Objectives
- Children will distinguish between materials that conduct electricity and materials that do not.
- Children will describe properties of conductors.

Science Processes Emphasized

Experimenting
Describing

Materials for Each Child or Group

D-cell battery
Dry-cell holder
Flashlight bulb
Flashlight bulb holder
Strips of aluminum foil
Box of paper clips
Sharpened pencils
Box of toothpicks
Box of crayons
Box of steel nails
Three pieces of insulated bell wire, each about 25 centimeters (10 inches) long and stripped at the ends
Assortment of 2.5-centimeter (1-inch) lengths of bell wire of various thicknesses

Motivation

This activity should follow activities or class discussions about the characteristics of simple circuits. Ask the children to describe the function of the wire used in circuits. They will indicate that the wire serves as the path for electrons. Then display the materials and indicate that the children will find out whether the electrons can pass through them.

Directions

1. Have each child or group assemble a simple circuit using two of the pieces of wire, a battery, and a bulb. After the bulb lights, detach the wire attached to the negative end of the battery and attach the third wire in its place. The exposed ends of the two wires (one from the battery and one from the bulb holder) will serve as probes to be touched to the materials tested.

2. Ask the children to check that their testers work by briefly touching the exposed ends together. If the battery is fresh, the bulb is in working condition, and all the connections have been properly made, the bulb will light.

3. When all the circuits are working, have the children test the various materials by touching both exposed wires to the materials at the same time. If the material is a conductor, the circuit will be completed and the bulb will light. Have the children note which materials are good conductors of electricity. They should manipulate each material to see if those that are conductors share similar characteristics.

4. Have the children describe properties that distinguish electrical conductors from nonconductors.

Key Discussion Questions

1. Which of the materials were good conductors of electricity? *Aluminum foil, paper clips,* and *wire pieces*

2. Which of the materials did not conduct electricity? *Toothpicks* and *crayons*

3. Was there anything that conducted electricity but conducted it poorly? *The lead (graphite) in the pencil.*

4. What are some hypotheses that you made? *Metals conduct electricity.*

5. What other activities could you do to test your hypotheses? *Answers will vary.*

Science Content for the Teacher

Substances that allow the movement of electrons with relatively little resistance are known as *conductors*. Materials that do not allow electrons to pass through them are *insulators*. Conductors have free electrons that can transfer energy. There are no perfect conductors, since all materials offer some resistance to the flow of charges. Metals are better conductors than nonmetals, but differ in conductivity. The following metals are arranged from highest to lowest conductivity:

Silver
Copper
Aluminum
Tungsten
Platinum
Tin
Steel
Lead

Extensions

Science: Some children may want to invent activities that will reveal whether good electrical conductors are also good conductors of heat. Others may want to modify their tester circuits so that the entire apparatuses can each be packaged in a small cardboard box. The tester should have two probes extending from the side and the light bulb extending from the top.

Science/Social studies: Some children may be interested in discovering what areas of the world are sources of the various metals used in this activity. To identify these regions, the children can use an encyclopedia or search the internet and look under terms such as "copper" and "aluminum."

● Measuring Forces

Objectives
- Children will construct a simple device that can be used to measure forces (see Figure C.1).
- Children will use their force measurers to find how an inclined plane makes work easier.

Science Processes Emphasized
Using models
Measuring
Carrying out investigations
Using mathematics

Materials for Each Child or Group
Large box
Piece of cardboard measuring 25 by 12 centimeters (about 10 by 5 inches)
Three paper clips
Rubber band
1-meter (40-inch) length of board

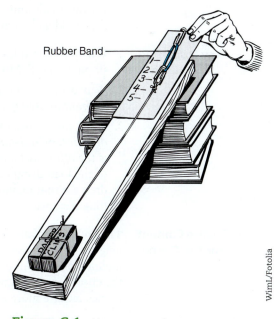
Rubber Band

Figure C.1 How to use a force measurer

WimL/Fotolia

String
Small box of paper clips, crayons, or chalk
Five books
Wood wax and cloth for polishing the board

Motivation   Write *100 lb.* on the large box. (The box does not have to weigh 100 lb.; it is for engagement purposes only.) Tell the children it is too heavy to lift up to the table. You can only exert enough force (push or pull) to lift about 50 lb. Ask the children for suggestions about how you can get the box to the top of the table. Wait for them to suggest using a ramp. Wonder out loud how a ramp would help. After all, the box still weighs 100 lb. and you can only exert a force of 50 lb. Suggest that the children make a model to seek a solution.

Directions   1. Have each child or group of children make a force measurer by clipping one paper clip to the piece of cardboard, attaching a rubber band to the paper clip, and clipping another paper clip to the end of the rubber band. (Alternatively, you can use spring scales.) Now have the children make their own scale divisions on the cardboard. The scale divisions can be arbitrary but consistent. The first division should begin at the bottom of the rubber band.

2. Tell the children to assemble the inclined plane by elevating one end of the board and placing three books under it. The children should wax the board until its surface is smooth.

3. Have the children determine how much force is needed to lift the box of paper clips from the tabletop straight up to the high end of the board using their force measurers. To do this, they will need to tie a string around the paper-clip box and attach the string to the paper clip hanging from the bottom of the rubber band on the force measurer. Have them note the amount of force required.

4. Now have them measure the force needed to move the paper-clip box to the same height by means of the inclined plane. They should pull the paper-clip box up the length of the board, parallel to the surface of the board.

5. Have the children compare the amounts of force required and experiment with various loads and inclined-plane heights. Have them record the forces used, then hold a class discussion of the results.

Key Discussion Questions   1. Which required less force: pulling the load straight up or moving it along the sloping board? *Moving it along the board.*

2. Why do you think people use inclined planes? *You can move heavy objects up without applying a lot of force.*

3. Show the children that the distance the load moves vertically is the *load distance*, or *resistance distance*, and that the distance along the sloping board is the *effort distance*. Now ask the children how the effort distance compares to the load distance. *The effort distance is longer.* (This question helps the children see that inclined planes require that the small-effort force moves over a long distance.)

Science Content for the Teacher   The inclined plane is a simple machine used to move heavy objects to various heights. Ramps used to load boxes on a truck and roads that slope upward are inclined planes. An inclined plane multiplies force at the expense of distance, since the effort force must move farther than the distance the load is raised. Steep inclined planes require more effort force than less steep planes.

Extensions   *Science:* Have two or three groups of children assemble inclined planes of various slopes and move the same load up all of them to observe the increased force needed on the steeper inclined planes. If possible, secure a toy truck with wheels that roll easily and have the groups compare the effort forces required to move it up the various slopes.

Science/Math: Have some children measure the effort distance and load distance of an inclined plane. Then have the children make the inclined plane steeper and repeat their measurements of effort and load distance. They can then repeat their measurements with the inclined plane in steeper and less steep positions.

How Do Heating and Cooling Change a Balloon?

Objective   • Children will predict and observe how balloons are affected by heating and cooling.

Science Processes Emphasized   Observing
Predicting
Communicating

Materials   Two or three round balloons
Hot plate
Saucepan one-quarter full of water
Access to a refrigerator

Motivation   Display the balloons, then inflate each one to about one-half its capacity and tie a knot in the neck. If the balloons are new, stretch them a few times before inflating to make them more elastic. Ask the children to predict what will happen to the sizes of the balloons as they are heated and cooled.

Directions   1. Have a volunteer draw the balloons at their exact sizes on the chalkboard.

2. Place one balloon on the saucepan so it is held above the surface of the water by the sides of the pan. Have another volunteer take the other balloon to the school kitchen to be stored in a refrigerator. Turn on the hot plate and set the heat indicator to low or warm.

3. Have the children note changes in each balloon every half hour for the next two hours. After they make their observations, have them try to explain what caused the changes.

Key Discussion Questions   1. Why do you think the heated balloon became larger? *The molecules of the gases in the air in the heated balloon started to move faster. They started to bounce into each other and the sides of the balloon more.*

2. Why do you think the cooled balloon became smaller? *It lost energy. The molecules of the gas slowed down and didn't bounce into each other or the sides as much. They moved closer together.*

Science Content for the Teacher   The heat energy of an object is the total energy of motion of all atoms that the object possesses. An object gains energy if it is placed in an environment that has more heat energy than itself and loses heat energy if it is placed in an environment that has less heat energy than itself.

Extension   *Science/Health:* Discuss how the loss of heat from an object can be diminished. This will give the children an opportunity to talk about the need to wear particular types of clothing to decrease or increase heat loss.

● Heat Conduction

Objectives
- Children will observe the ability of various materials to conduct heat.
- Children will make a claim concerning the nature of objects that conduct heat.
- Children will predict which of three objects will conduct heat the fastest.

Science
Processes
Emphasized
Observing
Making hypotheses
Predicting
Arguing from evidence

Materials
Candle
Ring stand and burette clamp
Safety matches
Timer
Container of water to extinguish matches
Glass, steel, and aluminum rods of equal thickness

Motivation   This demonstration should follow a class discussion about heat as a form of energy. (*Safety note:* The demonstration requires the lighting of a candle by you and manipulation of the candle flame by you. Appropriate safety measures should be observed.)

Ask the students which material would be best for making a cooking fire pan: glass, steel, or aluminum. Ask them to provide the reasons for their claims.

Directions
1. Set up the following demonstration:
   Clamp each of the three rods horizontally on the ring stand. Place equal size drops of wax at regular intervals about two centimeters (about one inch) along each of the rods. Position the rods so that the drops of wax are facing down.

2. Begin with one rod and lower it so that one end of the rod is about one centimeter (about half an inch) from the tip of the flame. Assign each drop of wax a number, starting with "No. 1" for the drop closet to the flame.

3. Ask the students to predict what will happen to the drops of wax as heat is applied to one end of the rod.

4. Distribute timers among the students or have one class timer. Begin heating the rod and record the time it takes for each drop of wax to melt and drip at least once on the table. You may provide a chart to record the time of melting and the wax number. Repeat this step for the other two rods.

5. Ask the class to revisit their claims and use the data collected to support, modify, or refute their claims.

Key Discussion
Questions
1. Which rod was the poorest conductor? *Glass*
2. What conclusion can you make about heat conducting? *Metals are good conductors of heat.*

3. What are some objects that are good conductors of heat? *Pots and pans*

4. Why do you think most pots are made from metals? *They conduct heat well.*

Science Content for the Teacher

The carrying of heat by a solid is called *conduction*. Heat energy is transferred through a conductor as a result of the increased movement of molecules at the point on the object where heat is applied. The increased motion of these molecules causes adjacent molecules to increase their energy. In this activity, the glass rod will be the poorest conductor. The best heat conductor among the metal rods will be the aluminum one, followed by the brass, and then the steel.

Extensions

Science: Have some children find out how the transfer of heat takes place in air. They should focus their investigation on the term *convection*. Have some children bring in samples of kitchen utensils that are both conductors and insulators (e.g., a stirring spoon with a metal end and a wooden handle).

Science/Math: Have students graph their data using "Time for Wax to Melt" on the vertical axis and "Distance from Heat Source" on the horizontal axis. Ask them how the slopes (steepness of the lines) compare. *The steeper the slope, the faster the rate of heating and the better conductivity.*

Physical Sciences Sample Lesson

Title: The Path of Light

Suggested practices, core ideas, and crosscutting concepts related to Next Generation Science Standards:[2]

- Science practices: carrying out investigations, analyzing and interpreting data, using mathematics, constructing explanations
- Core idea: electromagnetic radiation—mirrors can be used to redirect a light beam
- Crosscutting concept: cause and effect[3]

Background for Teachers

Light is energy that can be described as behaving as a wave or particle. Light seems to travel in waves similar to the way water travels in waves. It also seems to travel in energy packets called *photons*, which have no mass. Unlike sound waves, light does not need a medium through which to travel. Light can be reflected, refracted, diffracted, or transmitted. When light is reflected, the angle at which it is reflected is equal to the angle at which it hits the mirror. That is, the *angle of reflection* is equal to the *angle of incidence*. The angles referred to are the angles formed between the light ray and an imaginary normal line (the line perpendicular to the mirror; see diagram). Light also travels in a straight line. This lesson addresses these two properties of light: (1) reflection and (2) light travels in a straight line.

An image is formed in a mirror because the light reflected from the object hits the mirror and is reflected according to the law of reflection. If the reflected rays enter the eye, the individual can see the image. The image appears to be located where the lines of reflection would meet if they were extended beyond the mirror.

Materials   Two to four mirrors
Light source capable of producing a beam (*Safety note:* Use LED flashlights that can produce a light beam or a light box capable of creating a beam of light.)
Newsprint paper
Ruler
Pencil
Wooden or plastic children's play blocks

Element 1: Content to Be Taught

- Children will learn that light travels in a straight line and that mirrors can be used to redirect a light beam (**PS4.B: Electromagnetic Radiation**). They will learn that the angle of incidence equals the angle of reflection.

Element 2: Prior Knowledge and Misconceptions

Students should know that they can see their reflection in a mirror. They also should understand that the image we see is created by light that reflects off an object and enters our eyes. Our eyes do not generate light. The students will need to know how to use a protractor to measure angles, or you can use this lesson as an opportunity to teach them how to use a protractor. (Alternatively, students can carefully color in the angles, label each one, and cut them out to compare sizes.)
Some possible misconceptions students may have about light are as follows:

- Light can bend around corners.
- Objects generate their own images that bounce off mirrors.

Element 3: Performance Objectives

- Given a target, light source and two mirrors, each student will arrange the mirrors so the light from the source hits the target. They will each support their answers by drawing a ray diagram that illustrates the law of reflection. Acceptable responses will score at least a 2 on the accompanying rubric.

Element 4: Concept Development

Engagement   Introduce the phenomenon of reflection by setting up a remote control to turn on a device (a monitor, a projector, or a similar remote control device) by pointing it so the infrared beam reflects off a wall or mirror to turn on the device. (You will need to play with this a little to get it right. The easiest way is to set up a mirror so you can see the reflection of the device.) Aim the remote at the image in the mirror. The signal strength of the remote and the distance the signal travels will have an effect. The phenomenon is more mysterious if you reflect the beam off a wall. Put a reference point on the wall so you know where to aim the remote.

Ask the students to explain how they think the signal reached the device. Use a think–pair–share or talk–and–turn strategy. Let the students report out loud to express their ideas. Introduce the essential question, "How do infrared rays travel?"

Exploration Tell students that the remote emits infrared rays to communicate with the device. Infrared rays are forms of electromagnetic radiation, as is visible light. Therefore, we will use visible light to explore how infrared rays travel.
Assign children to teams of three with the following roles:

- Measurer: Responsible for tracing the light beam and location of the mirrors
- Manager: Ensures that the procedure is being followed correctly
- Lab technician: Sets up the mirrors and holds the flashlight
- Recorder: Ensures that all data are recorded in appropriate tables

Rotate the roles for each trial.
Instruct the students as follows:

1. Provide a piece of newsprint on for each group.
   a. Use the blocks to model walls. You might use the layout of the rooms in the immediate vicinity of the classroom.
2. Choose a location for the light source. Place the light source so that it projects a beam of light that can be seen on the tabletop.
3. Demonstrate how to place the mirror upright (perpendicular) on the paper to reflect the light beam.
4. Position a target for the beam of light that requires the students to use the mirrors to redirect the light.
5. Challenge the students to position the mirrors to direct the beam to the target.
6. Have the students use a ruler to trace the path of the light rays to and from each mirror.
7. Have the students label the angles formed by the paths of light formed by the reflection of light off the mirrors. Then have them measure the angle between the light rays and the mirror.
8. Have the students record the measurements of the projected and reflected angles in their science notebooks by using a table like the one below to record their angle measurements. Have them repeat the process two more times, using different angles.

Trial	Measurement of Light Beam Angle, in Degrees
	Projected
	Reflected
	Projected
	Reflected
	Projected
	Reflected

Explanation Ask the children what they discovered about the way light behaves—specifically, "How do light rays reflect off a mirror?" Clarify that light travels in a straight line and that the angle at which it hits the mirror is the same as the angle at which it reflects off the mirror. This property of light is called the *law of reflection*. The angle at which light hits the mirror is called the *angle of incidence*. The angle at which the light reflects off the mirror is called the *angle of reflection*.

Elaboration   Challenge the children to use their models to set up mirrors in the actual school rooms that will direct the beam to a desired location.

● Element 5: Evaluation

Give students a light source and a diagram of mirrors located at different angles. Ask them to locate the spot at which the light beam will fall after it reflects off the mirrors and to justify their answers using diagrams and written explanations.
Use the following rubric to assess the children's responses:

3	2	1
The location is accurately depicted and the diagram illustrates angles of incidence equal to angles of reflection. The written explanation supports the understanding that mirrors redirect light beams in predictable ways.	Either the location is accurately depicted and the diagram illustrates angles of incidence equal to angles of reflection or the written explanation supports the understanding that mirrors redirect light beams in predictable ways.	Neither the diagram nor the written explanation supports an understanding that mirrors can reflect light beams in a predictable manner.

● Element 6: Accommodations

Learning Disabilities
The use of diagrams, simulations with light beams, written instructions, and verbal instructions will provide multiple modes of presentation.

Visual Disabilities
Create diagrams using glue to raise the lines of the ray diagrams. If the child has some visual ability. Using strings to represent the rays that the child can feel may also provide additional assistance.

RESOURCES FOR DISCOVERY LEARNING

Internet Resources

Websites for Physical Science Units, Lessons, Activities, and Demonstrations

- **Bill Nye Demo of the Day:**
  www.nyelabs.com

- **The Atoms Family:**
  www.miamisci.org/af/sln

- **The Science Explorer:**
  www.exploratorium.edu

- **PhET Interactive Simulations, University of Colorado at Boulder:**
  phet.colorado.edu

Print Resources

Suggested Reading

Burns, John, et al. "Solving Solutions." *Science Scope* 24, no. 2 (October 2000): 30–33.

Cavallo, Ann M. L. "Convection Connections." *Science and Children* 38, no. 8 (May 2001): 20–25.

Chessin, Debby. "Simple Machine Science Centers." *Science and Children* (February 2007): 36–41.

Cox, Carole. "Isaac Newton Olympics." *Science Scope* 24, no. 8 (May 2001): 18–22.

Frazier, Richard. "Rethinking Models." *Science Scope* 26, no. 4 (January 2003): 29–33.

Galus, Pamela. "Reactions to Atomic Structure." *Science Scope* 26, no. 4 (January 2003): 38–41.

Hammrich, Penny L., and Fadigan, Kathleen. "Investigations in the Science of Sports." *Science Scope* 26, no. 5 (February 2003): 30–35.

Harris, Mary E. "Slurper Balls." *Science Scope* 25, no. 4 (January 2002): 22–27.

Hechtman, Judith. "The Science of Invention." *Science and Children* 40, no. 5 (February 2003): 16–18.

Lucking, Robert A., and Christmann, Edwin P. "Tech Trek: Technology in the Classroom." *Science Scope* 26, no. 4 (January 2003): 54–57.

Proto, Christopher, and Marek, Edmund A. "Dissecting Light." *Science Scope* 23, no. 7 (April 2000): 14–16.

Radhe, Sue Ellen, and Cole, Lynn. "Star Trek Physics." *Science Scope* 25, no. 6 (March 2002): 52–57.

Roy, Ken. "Safety Is for Everyone." *Science Scope* 26, no. 5 (February 2003): 16–17.

Sarow, Gina A. "Miniature Sleds, Go, Go, Go." *Science and Children* 39, no. 3 (November/December 2001): 16–21.

Shaw, Mike. "A Dastardly Density Deed." *Science Scope* 26, no. 4 (January 2003): 18–21.

Stroup, Diana. "Balloons and Newton's Third Law." *Science Scope* 26, no. 5 (February 2003): 54–55.

Villano, Diane D. "Classroom Catapults." *Science Scope* 24, no. 5 (February 2001): 24–29.

Weimann, Kimberly. "Blue Solids, Red Liquids, and Yellow Gases." *Science Scope* 23, no. 5 (February 2000): 17–19.

Wetzel, David R. "Fan Car Physics." *Science Scope* 23, no. 4 (January 2000): 29–31.

Notes

1. Using Phenomena in NGSS-Designed Lessons and Units. www.nextgenscience.org.
2. Next Generation Science Standards (NGSS) is a registered trademark of Achieve. Neither Achieve nor the lead states and partners that developed the Next Generation Science Standards was involved in the production of, and does not endorse, this product.
3. NGSS Lead States. (2013). *Next Generation Science Standards: For States, By States.* Washington, DC: The National Academies Press.

Index